D0938736

THE LAST
POPULAR REBELLION

'Whether we fall by ambition, blood, or lust,
Like diamonds, we are cut with our own dust.'

John Webster, *The Duchess of Malfi*

THE LAST POPULAR REBELLION

Robin Clifton

The Western Rising of 1685

Maurice Temple Smith   London
St. Martin's Press   New York

First published in Great Britain in 1984
by Maurice Temple Smith Ltd
Jubilee House, Chapel Road
Hounslow, Middlesex, TW3 1TX

Clifton, Robin
    The last popular rebellion.
    1. Monmouth's Rebellion
    I. Title
    942.06'7   DA448.9

ISBN 0 85117 247 4
Typeset in 11 point Plantin 1½ point leaded by
Tellgate Limited, London WC2
Printed in Great Britain by
Billing and Sons Ltd, Worcester

First published in the United States of America in 1984
All rights reserved. For information, write:
St. Martin's Press, Inc., 175 Fifth Avenue, New York, NY 10010

Library of Congress Catalog Card Number 84-40230

ISBN 0-312-47123-8

Contents

Maps

For
Russell and Julian

List of Abbreviations

This list is not intended as a Bibliography. Full references are given in the footnotes on the first occasion a work is cited.

Bodl.Lib.		Bodleian Library.
Brit.Lib.		British Library.
	Add.MSS.	Additional Manuscripts.
	4162	The Reverend Andrew Paschall's 'Narrative of the rebellion'.
	30077	Lists of presumed rebels.
	31956	Edward Dummer's Journal of the rebellion.
	Egerton MS.1527	The Duke of Monmouth's Pocket Book.
	Harl.MSS.	Harleian Manuscripts.
	6845 ff.262-282	Nathaniel Wade's confession.
	6845 ff.284-288	The Axe Papers, events in Somerset just before, and at the beginning of, the rebellion.
	6845 ff.289-296	King James II's 'Account of the battle of Sedgemoor'.
Lansd.MSS.1152		Lansdowne Manuscripts, various examinations of the rebels.
CJ		Journals of the House of Commons.
CSPD		Calendar of State Papers Domestic.
CSPV		Calendar of State Papers Venetian.
LJ		Journals of the House of Lords.
PC Register		Registers of the Privy Council.
PRO		Public Record Office.
Q/S R		Quarter Sessions Rolls.
Q/S MB		Quarter Sessions Minute Book.
SAS		Somerset Archaeological Society.
SP Charles II		State Papers Domestic of the Reign of Charles II.
SRO		Somerset Record Office.
	DD/PH	Phelips Manuscripts.
	DD/PM	Portman Manuscripts.
	DD/SF	Sanford Manuscripts.

Preface and Acknowledgements

The rebellion of 1685 is one of the most written-over insurrections in English history. Since the first serious work by George Roberts in 1844 a dozen books have appeared on the subject, half of them in the past fifteen years. A further book on the subject clearly requires explanation.

In this work I have attempted to cover several aspects of the rebellion which previous authors have left untreated, or have considered only briefly. Most books on 1685 have focused upon one or other of two principal themes. A minority have essentially been biographies of the man who led the rebellion, with only a chapter or two on the uprising itself. The best of these is still Elizabeth D'Oyley's *James, Duke of Monmouth* which was published in 1937. The majority of authors have preferred to write narratives of the rebellion itself, prefaced by introductions of varying length on the political circumstances of England in 1685, together with a brief résumé of the Duke of Monmouth's life up to that date.

Both of these topics must of course be considered, and in this work the Duke receives two chapters, and the rising four. My treatment of both is, however, selective. In discussing the rebellion I have concentrated upon two aspects: what its chances of success were at different points; and how well Monmouth led it. In considering the life of the Duke, detailed narrative has again been sacrificed to concentrate upon two central issues: to identify the main influences which shaped his character; and to explain the personal and political circumstances which led to his becoming a rebel. Biography, and narrative of the rebellion, are treated selectively and are linked, and not left as separate episodes.

It was my intention to make this work different from most of its predecessors in three further ways. No previous work has examined the region where the rebellion took place; and so two lengthy chapters have been devoted to the social and economic structure of Somerset, and to the county's political and religious history, in the belief that much of the ready response to Monmouth in 1685 is to be explained locally.

Secondly, considerable attention is given to the motives and social composition of the rank and file rebels, and here I hope to have taken discussion somewhat further than usual by asking some different questions. Finally, the title I have chosen indicates my wish to set 1685 more firmly in its immediate and longer-term context than has been done so far. Considerable selectivity has been needed to attempt these five separate purposes within a reasonable compass, and I make no pretence to full coverage of the known details of Monmouth's life, or of day-to-day events during the rising. These are well treated in existing studies.

In the years spent writing this book I have profited from the assistance of a number of people, which it is now my pleasure to acknowledge. I have been most fortunate, first of all, in receiving criticisms and suggestions from three outstanding historians. My former supervisor Dr Christopher Hill put his formidable knowledge of the seventeenth century at my disposal, and gently prompted progress in writing the work. Mr Edward Thompson, my former colleague at the University of Warwick, first suggested the topic to me and provided lengthy, encouraging, and sharp comments on the drafts he saw. Mr Keith Thomas' observations on topics to be considered, and questions to be asked, were of great assistance in clarifying my ideas. I am grateful too to Professor William Lamont and the graduate seminar at the University of Sussex for a most penetrating discussion of my conclusions. At the University of Warwick my colleague Dr Joan Lane was most generous in supplying references culled from her work on diaries, while Dr Henry Cohn and Dr Bernard Capp were always willing to discuss popular revolts in this period.

It is with very real gratitude that I thank Mr D.M. Shorrocks and his staff at the Somerset Record Office, for their patience with a researcher who wanted to spread his net as widely as possible within the county archives. Mr R.W. Dunning, editor of the *Victoria County History of Somerset*, very willingly discussed the locality and the period with me, as did Mr MacDonald Wigfield. The staff of the Devon and Dorset County Record Offices were very helpful, as were those of the Lyme Regis Borough Record Office. The Marquis of Bath kindly gave me permission to read the Coventry and Thynne manuscripts at Longleat House. At the Bodleian Library, Oxford, the Cambridge University Library and the Public Record Office, I received the staffs' prompt and professional attention. It is not usual for an author to thank his publisher – at least in print – but Maurice Temple Smith's forbearance over several years must be gratefully recorded.

Several people have assisted me very directly in preparing this work. Rachel Countryman was endlessly patient and helpful in translating my probate inventory material into computer print-out. I owe particular thanks too to Ann Stanyon for the time and labour she spent in preparing the maps. Christine Henderson helped with the time-consuming task of preparing parish lists of the rebels; and Rosalind Coates read the drafts with great care, to save me from many mistakes and infelicities. Caroline Johnson typed early versions of the work, and Yvonne Slater the final copy; and to both I owe the particular gratitude of semi-legible writers to their typists.

Finally, I was kept at writing this book over many years by the advice, humour and threats of several friends and relatives. If they have not yet been mentioned by name, they will know who they are, and how they have helped. To them all, my grateful thanks are due.

Coventry, 1983

CHAPTER ONE
'That Poor Populous Place'

Somerset in the seventeenth century was one of the largest, wealthiest and most heavily populated areas of England. Extending sixty miles from east to west and between thirty and fifty from north to south, comprising just over a million acres, it was the seventh largest county of the realm. The indicators of population and wealth set it in the top quarter of counties in Stuart England, although this eminence was of comparatively recent growth: the 1334 lay subsidy had placed Somerset twenty-second of twenty-nine counties in wealth per square mile; and the poll tax of 1377 revealed a population density barely more than the average for southern England. By 1558, however, it was considered the third most populous county of the kingdom, and its Ship Money assessment of £9,000 in 1636 shows that it was reputed to be one of the wealthiest counties of England, ranking third equal with neighbouring Devon in fact. Like other Ship Money assessments, however, Somerset's was probably too optimistic, for in 1672 and 1693 the county ranked lower, eleventh and then thirteenth in taxable value. But its population increase is indisputable. Hearth tax records, and the Bishop Compton census of 1676, point to a population of around 210,000 in the later seventeenth century, making it the seventh most populated county of England. More people meant more poverty: in the 1670s only five counties paid more than Somerset in poor rates.[1] The county was, as will be shown, rich in its agriculture and trades; but it harboured also a growing problem of poverty.

Just as striking as its size, population and prosperity, was Somerset's physical diversity. A line drawn across it from west to east would move down from bleak and windswept Exmoor, into the fertile lowlands of Taunton Deane, up again over the short but steep ridge of the Quantocks, before descending once more to the wide marshes and partially drained pasturelands of the Somerset levels, to rise slightly once more over the belt of mixed grassland, arable and woods which merged in the east with Wiltshire and Dorset. Soils, sub-climates and human activities all reflected this varying topography, dividing the county into five major areas. In shape Somerset resembles a great saucer sloping gently from a broad rim into the centre, with its upper left quartile bitten out by the Bristol Channel. The first region is bounded in the north by the rim of the saucer, the Mendip Hills. The second region is the corn-pasture woodland zone constituting the eastern and southern rim of the saucer, from Bath and Frome down to Yeovil, and across to Chard in the south of the county. A third area is the pocket about Taunton and the Vale of Taunton Deane, distinguished from the preceding region more by the extra fertility of its soil and density of population than by any obvious change in physical features. Fourthly, the hills of Exmoor make up the saucer's western rim; and the county's last region lies in the centre of the saucer and extends to the Bristol Channel, the marshlands drained and undrained which are bounded abruptly by the Mendips and the Quantocks to the north and west, and by the belt of more gently rising land between Frome and Chard to the east and south.

The first region, the Mendips, is very distinctive: a range of limestone hills, sometimes quite steep, running thirty miles across the county from their rise near Frome to the maritime headlands about Weston-super-Mare. Stone walls on hill-sides mark out the small sheepfarms, and stones litter the short grass growing on thin soils. Teasels were produced for the county's cloth industry on the northern slopes of the hills, and in sheltered valleys considerable quantities of barley and oats. Few villages existed in the heart of the Mendips, most settlement taking place by the sea coast and along the River Ax on the southern face of the hills, where extensive common rights in the marshlands enabled villagers to maintain large numbers of cattle. The famous cheeses from Cheddar indicate the richness of these pastures which account for the string of settlements running from Shepton Mallett to Wells and Axbridge, along the southern face of the Mendips. Apart from sheep farming, the major activity of the hills proper was mining for lead, coal, or quarrystone. Worked by individual miners or by small partnerships, and controlled by an elaborate legal structure administered by special courts, the lead mines had reached the peak of their production by 1670 and were thereafter in decline. The miners' technology and capital were insufficient to reach the deeper lodes, and the landlords who leased out mining rights were disinclined to reinvest their profits. Coal too was worked by small groups of independent miners, and though production rose during the seventeenth century – reaching 100,000 tons per annum in the 1680s – landowners once again made most of the profit.[2] The mines were concentrated close together, most coal coming from a five mile area about Radstock and Farrington

Gurney on the eastern edge of the hills. By contrast, the lead workings were highly dispersed and this was true too of the extensive limestone quarries of the region. Not only the local villages, but such major undertakings as Wells Cathedral and Glastonbury Abbey were built from this stone, and its varieties in colour kept the quarrymen in work: creamy white from Doulting, pinkish stone from Holcombe, white from Stratton-on-the-Fosse, grey from Litton. But whether their branch of the industry was prospering or declining the miners and quarrymen of Mendip shared the reputation of being men set apart, a violent and hard-drinking race who kept to themselves. Though the moorland parishes and towns at the foot of the Mendips contributed a number of volunteers to the rebellion in 1685, it is significant that almost none came from the hills themselves.

Travellers sometimes commended the bracing air and the long clear views of the Mendips but most complained, like Celia Fiennes, of the tiresome 'roads full of hills', and hurried on to more pleasing parts. Of these none was more popular than the county's second major region, the belt of rising land forming the eastern and southern rim of Somerset's saucer. Here seekers of wild scenery (in limited quantities), or fruitful landscapes, or an industrious population could all find something to admire. The central area of this tract had formerly been covered by the once extensive Forest of Selwood, and considerable areas of woodland still remained. Farms here were small and principally given over to dairying, with only a limited amount of corn grown and that mainly in the south. Even in Domesday times this had been the most densely settled area of Somerset and by-occupations had soon become necessary to support the growing population. Glove-making and lace-making were established about Yeovil by the Tudor period, and stocking knitting followed, but over the area as a whole cloth weaving and its associated trades were the earliest and the primary supplements to farm incomes.

Though clearly defined, this region of Somerset was by no means homogeneous. About Bath in the north travellers found low but steep hills and deep narrow valleys, small dark patches of woodland breaking up the pastures, and stony infertile strips of land. Near Frome the hills were less abrupt and some corn grew in the fertile valleys, but 'these Towns and . . . innumerable Villages, Hamlets and scattered Houses' were supported mainly by dairying, and by spinning and weaving. A Privy Council report of 1623 spoke of the area as 'a great part of it forest and woodland, bordering upon the county of Wiltshire from whence it hath continual supply of corn, and also out of western parts of this

county, the people of the county (for the most part) being engaged
about the trade of cloth-making'. Further south again about Yeovil and
Chard the hills become mere undulations, and the traveller entered a
'low and flat . . . rich enclosed County, full of Rivers and Towns'.
Leland was impressed by the 'very fair and fruitful champain' he found
near Bruton, and more corn grown about Crewkerne fed the large
market at Chard. Thomas Gerard in 1633 described Martock, where the
land rises gently from the central moors, as 'seated in the fattest part of
this Countie, especially for errable which makes ye inhabitants soe fatt
in their purses'. Local opinion held that the peas and beans grown here
were equal to the best of Leicestershire's, and hamlets such as
Peasmarsh and Mudford illustrate both the principal crop and the
variable soil.[3] The great cheese market at Yeovil, however, one of the
largest in the south-west and supplying all the nearby counties, shows
that dairying was still the major farming activity. Thickly populated
and intensively farmed, the south-eastern corner of Somerset was
essentially a corn-dairying area, and contained fewer spinners and
weavers than Frome to the north, or Taunton to the west.

Travellers like Daniel Defoe, who looked for evidence of
manufactures, found it in plenty in Somerset's third region, the Vale of
Taunton Deane about and to the north-west of Taunton. The town and
the cluster of villages nearby contained some eleven hundred looms, the
traveller would be told, providing so much employment that even five-
year old children could support themselves. But the rich succession of
meadow, orchard and arable was what caught the eye of most visitors.
John Norden in 1607 called Taunton Deane the 'Paradise of England',
and in *Polyalbion* the poet Drayton wrote:

> What eare is so empty that it hath not heard the sound
> Of Taunton's fruitfull Deane? Not match'd by any ground.

Here dairying gave place to the fattening of cattle and sheep, and fields
of barley and wheat were broken by apple orchards, hop vines, and
market gardens. In some parishes here – and nowhere else in Somerset –
the acreage of arable land equalled that under grass, and much of this
region's corn went to feed the inhabitants of the cloth-dairying area in
the east of the county.[4] The only drawback to this demi-paradise was
that its labour-intensive industries – cloth, market gardening, orchards,
corn-growing – attracted a large labour force which could not be
permanently employed because of the seasonal or intermittent nature of
their work. Over-population was hidden behind the Vale's pleasant
face.

Besides its pleasing aspect, the region about Taunton was popular with visitors because it was so comfortable to travel through. The reverse was true for the next major area of Somerset, the moors in the low centre of the county. As she struggled 'through lanes full of stones and, by the great raines just before, full of wet and dirt . . . over a large common or bottom of deep black land', Celia Fiennes reflected bitterly upon the truth of the proverb: 'bad for the rider, but good for the abider'. But some inhabitants would not have agreed even thus far; justifying his request to be removed to a more upland parish in the county the vicar of Chedzoy in 1683 spoke with feeling of the effects upon his and his family's health of many years passed 'in this low and watery country'. Bounded to the north by the Mendips and to the west by the Quantocks, the Somerset Levels were 230 square miles of low flat land draining some eight hundred square miles of upland. The rivers crossing the levels – the Axe, Brue, Parrett, Yeo and Tone – had scarcely any fall, and at the sea their outfalls could be blocked by high tides. Still worse, storms in the Bristol Channel could drive sea water and rivers deeply back into the lowlands, to produce catastrophic flooding. Even normal conditions appalled travellers: in 1633 Thomas Gerard found the river at Aller so broad that it resembled an arm of the ocean, at Borough the flooded moors were 'so covered in water as to resemble a sea', and at Somerton he described a land 'for the most part drowned in winter'.[5] Villages were built on the isolated low hills that rose from the levels, or on the slight ridges such as the Polden Hills which divided off the different moors.

But travellers and disgruntled clergy did not see the land with the eye of a peasant farmer. At least from medieval times large open drainage ditches had been dug and maintained – in 1685 one of these played a significant part in the battle of Sedgemoor – and with some embanking these ditches or rhines permanently drained nearly one-third of the marshes by 1600. Most of the area still liable to flooding dried out in summer, and the layers of water-borne silt produced fertile meadow and pasture for herds of dairy and beef cattle. Some soils, about North Petherton and Moorlinch for example, drained so well that the plough could be used in alternation with pasture, and corn from here was sent to the markets of east Somerset. Farms in the drained areas were quite large, averaging eighteen acres at Wedmore, compared with five to ten acres in the Lincolnshire fens. Unstinted grazing in the moors increased the number of animals each family could keep, and fishing and fowling, and cutting reeds and alders further supplemented incomes.[6] The absence of stints upon livestock run in the moors indicates that there was no severe pressure of population upon resources, so that despite floods and much wet misery villagers in the moors were generally better off than their fellows in the east or south of the county. Set apart by a modest prosperity and a distinctive economic regime, the population of the levels was different too in that it was aggressively capable of defending its way of life. The regulation necessary to control use of the commons – for example the election of port reeves to drive the moors, and to supervise the times when different items could be taken from them – created the organization to see off would-be enclosers and plundering armies alike, as was shown several times during the seventeenth century.

Like the Mendips, the levels was a region set apart. Isolation made this true too of the fifth and last major area of Somerset, the uplands of Exmoor. Leland found the far west of Somerset unrewarding 'al by forest, baren, and morisch ground, wher is stone and breeding of young cattle, but little or no corn or habitation'; and nearly two hundred years later Defoe wrote of 'a filthy, barren Ground'. But more rye and oats was grown than travellers noticed, and freeholders with large farms claimed from the moor, supplemented by unstinted moorland grazing, could be prosperous men.[7] On the other hand their undertenants, with few animals and little land, were desperately poor and needed some by-occupation to survive. Nor did the region entirely comprise desolate sheep walks, for rich grass grew on the fertile soils in well-watered valleys about Monksilver, Nettlecombe, Dulverton and Dunster. Besides Exmoor there were two other upland areas in western Somerset. The Quantock Hills run northwards from Taunton to the sea, dividing the Vale of Taunton Deane from the central marshlands. Their thin variable soil, covering a loose shaley rock, afforded only grazing for sheep and cattle. The same was true of the other range of hills, the Blackdowns south-west of Taunton. An extension of the Devonshire uplands, the Blackdowns are not high but their steepness, and thin soils mixed with gravel, account for the one thousand acres of the Neroche forest surviving here only a few miles from heavily populated Taunton and Chard. Exmoor, the Quantocks, and the Blackdowns supplied very few rebel volunteers in 1685.

Though very diversified geographically, socially the county was more homogeneous. It contained no resident nobility able to control local affairs; indeed, under Charles II, Somerset boasted only one noble family, the Pauletts, and their influence was no more than that of any greater gentleman. Peers such as the Earls of Pembroke and Rochester, and the Marquis of Hertford owned land in the county but they interfered little in its affairs. The Bishop of Winchester was lord of the manor of Taunton Deane, but his role in the town's affairs had been negligible well before Taunton received its charter in 1628. Similarly the Bishops of Bath and Wells were not major land-owners locally, and possession of the manor of Chard gave them little influence in the well-populated south. Some thirty families of greater gentry were the county's most influential group, running the magistracy, and monopolizing the Lieutenancy and seats in Parliament. A few like the Luttrells of Dunster could trace their lineage for centuries, but the majority had achieved prominence during the reign of Elizabeth or later. Most could claim control of a nearby town – the Pophams Wellington, the Phelipses Ilchester, the Spekes Ilminster, the Luttrells Minehead – but their social leadership was precarious, and rested upon tradition and some level of connection at court. The county 'magnates' were no wealthier than another hundred or so leading gentry families who divided up the remaining seats on the magistracy, and who in general followed the lead of the magnates in county politics. Beneath them were perhaps nine hundred families of lesser gentry, often substantial men with several manors but clearly lacking the income to be placed on the commission of the peace, and almost all of them destined to remain minor gentry. Although they were generally deferential to the greater gentry, the latter had no automatic grip upon their obedience. No clear line separated the bottom of this group from Somerset's large and self-confident population of prosperous yeomen. The independent attitude of the farmers about Martock in south-eastern Somerset was well described by Thomas Gerard in 1633: 'wealthy and substantial men though none of the best breed; which is the cause their neighbours about them are apt enough to slander them with the title of clownes, but they care not much for that, knowing they have money in their purses to make them gentlemen when they are fitt for the degree'.[8]

More information on these different social groupings can be obtained from the inventories of their goods, made by neighbours after their death, for probate purposes. Several thousand inventories survive for seventeenth-century Somerset, almost all of them from the Archdeaconry of Taunton which covered the western third of the county. Of Somerset's five major regions therefore, the Mendips and a large part of the eastern and south-eastern rim are not included, but Taunton Deane and the western hill moors are well covered, and the central levels and southern rim afford a good proportion of inventories. The five years 1681-1685 inclusive returned 490 inventories, and the following material is based upon this pre-rebellion sample.[9]

For such a rural county the number of farmer or landowner inventories found was surprisingly small. Just 240 or 49 per cent of all inventories were those of men engaged in farming directly or as landlords. With a further 10 per cent of inventories impossible to classify as to occupation even broadly, we are left with 41 per cent of inventories in a sample of nearly five hundred where the deceased followed a non-agricultural calling. Within the 240 agricultural inventories the range of wealth was not particularly wide. There were six very wealthy men with total moveable estates worth between £461 and £740, which when the value of the leases they held is added rises to between £1,000 and £2,000. Below these six (the gentry proper in economic terms), were twenty men with moveable property valued at £201 to £400 who may be considered lesser gentry or wealthier yeomen. Together these two groups of prosperous men comprised just 10·8 per cent of the inventories, but their moveable estate accounted for 42 per cent of the total wealth of the 240 agriculturalists. The six gentlemen owned 15·4 per cent of the agriculturalists' total estate, emphasizing the importance of the twenty wealthier yeomen or lesser gentry below them who accounted for one quarter (25·1 per cent) of the total.

Below the two wealthiest categories was that of men owning goods valued at £100 to £200, frequently described as 'yeomen' by the inventory-takers. They comprised nearly one-fifth (19·1 per cent) of the 240 agriculturalists' inventories, but held one-third of the sample's moveable estate (32 per cent). Underneath them was the largest single category, farmers with between £21 and £100 in moveable goods. These were the husbandmen, men barely on or just over the margin of economic independence, many of whom would be obliged to take wage labour at some time in the year. Comprising 45 per cent of the total number of agricultural inventories, they held only 23 per cent of the total goods owned by farmers and landowners. The last grouping is the agricultural labourers, men with up to only £20 in total moveable goods. For such poor men they are surprisingly well represented in the sample, with sixty inventories or one-quarter of the total number for agriculturalists. Very few of the labourers (11 per cent) owned neither animals nor grain, but only one-third possessed any crops, either harvested or in the fields, and their land holdings were almost invariably only one to three acres in size. Considerably more, however, owned a few animals, one half possessing three or four beasts, generally a horse, two or three cattle, and a pig. Very few (only 10 per cent) owned any sheep, and these were generally held in tiny flocks of less than half a dozen. The number of labourers with a few animals is surprisingly high and emphasizes that this lowest class did not all exist in misery; but the group's median figure for total possessions is low – at only £11 – and points to chronic poverty at the lowest levels.

Even including the sixty labourers' inventories, the 240 farmers in the sample were reasonably well-to-do. A few rich men help produce an inflated average figure for total agriculturalists' goods of £88; but the median figure which gives less prominence to the rich is a respectable £45, markedly higher than the £35 median for the entire sample of 490. By combining means and median figures and dividing by two, we obtain a mid-point average figure for farmers of £67. Only one quarter (24·2 per cent) of the 240 farmers owned more than twice as much as the mid-point average, emphasizing the relatively narrow spread of wealth in the Somerset countryside. The prospering men who owned goods of between the MPA and twice the MPA in value were 14 per cent of the sample; while just over a quarter (28 per cent) owned from half the MPA to the MPA in goods; and one third (34 per cent) owned less than half the MPA. Poverty existed in the Somerset countryside, but the social pyramid was a rather flattened one.

Mixed farming predominated in the central and western area of the county covered by the inventories. Just under four-fifths of all 240 farmers in the sample owned both corn and animals. Cattle and horses were the beasts most frequently found, appearing in 66 per cent and 64 per cent of inventories respectively, but in markedly different quantities. Most farmers owned only one or two horses, but the median value for cattle ownership was £17, representing a small herd of five or six beasts including calves. The size of herds could vary greatly, however, 58 per cent of inventories containing cattle listing herds twice as valuable (or more) as the mid-point average of £20.9. Four men owned herds worth more than £100, all of them members of the select group of six gentlemen leading the county's wealth. Just over one half of the inventories refer to pigs, usually in ones and twos, and sheep, appearing in 43 per cent of inventories, were found mostly in the western moorland parishes.

Grain appears in about as many inventories as animals (80 per cent compared to 82 per cent respectively), but crop values were considerably less than those of livestock. The median value for all animals was £20, whereas that for corn was just £13. Because so many inventories refer unspecifically to 'corn' the balance between the different grains is difficult to establish, but in seventy-seven inventories precise acreages of wheat, barley etc. are given, and on the basis of these some conclusions can be reached. In this sub-sample wheat was markedly more popular than barley, 97 per cent of the seventy-seven inventories referring to the former, but only 40 per cent to the latter. The richness of the soil in this area of Somerset is further indicated by the low percentage (only 16 per cent) of farmers obliged to raise rye or oats. Peas and beans, however, were of considerable importance, appearing in 29 per cent of inventories. Where barley was grown its median acreage was almost identical to that for wheat, 8·9 acres compared to 8·2 acres respectively. The figure for rye or oats was rather less, at 6·75 acres; while peas and beans were commonly grown in considerable quantities, the median holding for them being 4·5 acres. Reverting to the larger sample of inventories containing 'corn' without differentiation, the relatively uniform size of arable holdings is shown by the fact that only 18 per cent of the 192 farms referred to grew grain to the value of twice (or more) the size of the mid-point average of £18.6.

Using the sub-sample of seventy-seven inventories containing precise crop acreages, it is possible to establish a median size for Somerset farms. Eight acres was normally under the plough, which with another four for fallow produces a twelve acre arable farm (average, i.e. mean, figures are 13·8 acres plus 4·6 for fallow, resulting in a 18·4 acre holding; but two very large farms distort these mean figures). Given the near-universality of mixed farming some land must also be added for pasture, of around 6 to 8 acres, for 6 to 8 beasts. This results in a median farm of around 20 acres in size, and rather larger – almost 26 acres – if averages are used. In an area of such good soils and intensive mixed farming, these figures indicate a degree of independence, even modest prosperity, for the family farmer – given good harvests. They also suggest that most farmers in the sample had no need for wage-labourers, working the land by their own and their family's labour.

For most farmers their limited prosperity was achieved by hard work and sober living. Gentry apart, the contents of their houses reveal very few luxuries; and if the inventories of the wealthiest twenty-six agriculturalists are excluded as representing gentry or lesser gentry, the median figure for household goods in the 214 remaining inventories is just £9. Lists of the farmers' tools and equipment are profuse: chains, rakes and ladders, sheep hurdles, pails and barrels, plough-gear, and wains. But the equipment for most peasant farmers came cheaply, 72 owning 'tools' valued at £1, and a further 23 at £2 (the latter the median figure); and although a few had implements valued at £30 to £40 – usually ploughs and wains – the capital of most farmers was largely tied up in livestock, grain, and buildings, rather than in equipment.

Very few of the inventories contain clear evidence that farmers practised any supplementary occupation, although 'tools' is a general term and may in some cases have included a craftsman's equipment. Only two spinning turns are specifically mentioned, although the low value set on them – barely a shilling or two – might well leave some unnamed in the miscellaneous category 'other lumber £1' so often encountered. Five farmers, however, owned one weaver's loom apiece, and because they were all substantial men with moveable estates ranging from £63 to £211, they are properly considered agriculturalists rather than weavers: at £1 to £2 apiece their looms were paltry compared with the £25 to £92 their corn and animals were valued at. (Four much smaller farmers owning looms are classified with weavers, since their cloth work would have formed a proportionately larger part of their income). None of the five larger farmers with looms was credited with any woven cloth in his inventory, and they possibly kept their single loom apiece as potential employment for a younger son, since its earnings could have made little difference to their incomes.

A striking feature of all agriculturalists' inventories is the small quantity of cash they kept in the house, the median value being just £4. No less than one third of the sample, however, had loaned money to their neighbours, and though the sums could be very large indeed – one man had £540 owing to him – only four out of the total of eighty-one were owed over £100. The median figure was only £10, and the debts were typically owed by several persons rather than by one. The better-off farmers in this area of Somerset were supplying much of the working credit needed to lubricate trade, agriculture, and manufacturing locally. One-third of the farmers in this sample held some land on lease, and probably in quite large quantities since the median figure for leases is £55. But no indication is given of how many years remained in the lease, and so its true annual value – let alone the amount of land held on lease – can not be established, although the top twelve leases worth £300 to over £1,000 must have represented considerable acreages. Leases have not been included in the totals of farmers' goods (or those of any social category) because inventories do not also record land held freehold, and serious errors would result if leasehold, but not freehold, land was included in the figures.

Lastly, books are listed in the possessions of thirty agriculturalists, mostly among the wealthier sort, although a few men worth around £20 owned them. Those with most books were two booksellers who lived in Pitminster and Taunton, with £10 and £16 in stock out of total estates of only £56 and £36 respectively. The nine clergy present in the full sample of 490 inventories also possessed substantial collections; valued at £5 to £30, books represented from one-tenth to one-fifth of their owner's moveable estate. A handful of other men also had obvious professional reasons for owning books – the barber, surgeon, apothecaries, 'mariners', grocers, and mercers – but book-owning cordwainers with total estates of only £20 to £30 show that literacy extended well down the social scale. Of particular significance are the twelve weavers (out of a total of only sixty-three) who owned books. With another nine bookowners in other branches of the cloth industry, they constituted one-quarter of book-ownership, proportionately far more than any other social group; and one explanation for the clothworkers' notorious propensity to join in the religious and political disputes of their superiors can possibly be found here.

In only a few localities was the tenor of Somerset rural life disturbed by disputes or riots over enclosure. The county contained very little common land overall, more than three-quarters of its area being enclosed by the end of the seventeenth century. Much of Somerset had been farmed in severalty ever since its first clearance, and medieval population growth had reduced what common field existed. In the seventeenth century, travellers remarked upon the county's long-enclosed aspect. From the Blackdown Hills south of Taunton they saw a 'vast prospect on each side full of enclosure . . . large tracts of grounds full of enclosures, good grass and corn beset with quicksetts and hedgerows'. Further east orchards were mingled with grass and corn, and the visitors found a land 'much for enclosures, that makes the ways very narrow'. This aspect of the countryside would be of considerable importance during the 1685 rebellion. At the end of the Civil War John Lilburne, once an officer of horse, had commented on the difficulty of employing cavalry in Somerset, for the county's hedged fields and narrow lanes severely restricted the ability of horsemen to deploy and charge, while affording small groups of infantry endless opportunities to ambush them.[10] The Duke of Monmouth's raw cavalry in 1685 never matched the quality of the professionals opposing them, but so long as the rebels remained in Somerset it was difficult for the royalists to exploit their advantage in horse to the full.

By the later seventeenth century common land survived in three principal areas in Somerset. Much lay in Exmoor, where areas were enclosed for a year or two and then released as common grazing again. No disturbances arose over this practice; but attempts to enclose in some of the county's second major common land area led to intermittent trouble. Medieval Somerset had contained six woodland areas, three of which had been largely cleared and enclosed by Stuart times. North Petherton and Mendip contained very little woodland, as did Kingswood near Bristol, although the latter still afforded sufficient cover for highwaymen for a promoter to argue in 1668 that complete disafforestation here would be to the public good. A fourth forest area on Exmoor was little disturbed by enclosure during the seventeenth century, and it was in the remaining two regions that attempts to clear the land and extinguish common rights produced resistance. Straddling the Somerset-Wiltshire border, Selwood Forest had been under attack since Domesday times, but was still impressive when Leland visited it and estimated it to be thirty miles in circumference. Selwood was one of the western forest areas which fought attempts at enclosure in the years 1628-31, when 'divers lewd and desperate persons' expelled surveyors and the militia escorting them, and intermittent resistance continued here for years afterwards. Bands of armed neutralists, 'Clubmen', were created in this borderland between Somerset and Wiltshire during the Civil War; and it is significant that in the north of the woodland area, about Frome, the Duke of Monmouth in 1685 recruited over 150 men when his forces paused here for less than a day. The last forest area was Neroche, 6,000 acres of the Blackdown Hills just south of Taunton. Clearances were opposed here too, for the forest sprawled through fourteen parishes most of which enjoyed common rights to the woodland. Early in the Civil War here 'the Rable broke up all the Hedges and Fences and layd all in common again'. Like Kingswood Forest, Neroche was again threatened in the later part of Charles II's reign, when arrangements were made in 1685 to end common rights in it.[11]

The major enclosure battle in Stuart Somerset was fought, however, not in the woodlands, but in the county's third principal area, where common rights were vital, the marshes of the central levels. Of some 66,000 acres liable to winter flooding here, only one-third had been drained and enclosed before the Civil War. Under the early Stuarts three thousand acres had been drained by a major reclamation scheme of the period; but a further proposal to improve five thousand acres of King's Sedgemoor had been frustrated by villagers who commoned upon the marsh. Preliminary moves in 1618 and 1623 had been blocked, and though Charles I issued nine commissions, his agents could achieve nothing. Sir Cornelius Vermuyden had no better success in 1655; and an Act passed in 1669 to drain the moor resulted in 'a great outcry among the commoners and consultations how to defend their right'. Renewed efforts in 1683-84 to drain and enclose two thousand acres about Weston Zoyland were frustrated by the refusal of local juries to cooperate, leaving a local supporter of the plan to lament how 'a clownish humour in a few ill-natured men should defeat so useful an undertaking'.[12]

These last drainage attempts were undoubtedly important in 1685, for opposition to them revived the 'Clubmen' tradition in the area which dated from the 1640s. Although Clubmen became active elsewhere in Civil War Somerset, the men of the central levels created the largest and best organized neutralist force in the county, and produced in Humphrey Willis, a local yeoman, 'the one outstanding leader of the Somerset Clubmen'.[13] Kept alive by repeated attempts to drain the moors and thus deprive villagers of part of their livelihood, the Clubmen tradition was still active in 1685. Within days of the rebel army's arrival in Taunton the marshlanders were holding meetings to decide on their reaction should another plundering army traverse the moors. Though the Duke of Monmouth recruited strongly in the larger towns in and about the moors – Bridgewater, Glastonbury, Wells, and Shepton Mallett – his hopes of raising a Club Army were only partially realized, most of the moorlanders keeping to their customary neutrality. Although Somerset was an early-enclosed county, it thus contained some localities where enclosure was a live issue, and where this combined with a Civil War experience of plundering armies, communities with a remarkable capacity for organized self-defence had resulted. But they were a mixed blessing to the rebels in 1685, for with a heightened political consciousness came a strong distrust of outsiders.

For most of the county enclosure was an exceptional problem, and the impression made on most travellers of a prosperous countryside is supported by the number of fairs found in late-Stuart Somerset. About 120 localities regularly held fairs, and though most were local affairs, those at Bridgewater and Wells attracted traders from outside the county (and Somerset men regularly attended Bristol's two great fairs); while those held at Taunton, Frome, and Glastonbury were of county-wide importance. Larger centres such as Bridgewater, Bath, and Wells had three to four fairs per year in addition to the normal weekly market, and some such as Taunton's July fair, lasted for three days. They were sufficiently numerous for regional specialization to be evident. Fairs at seaport towns in a belt stretching from Porlock, Minehead, and Dunster to Bridgewater and Burnham dealt with a variety of goods – coal and iron, wool and dyestuffs, fish and timber. The majority of the fairs were further inland, nearly one half of them in the southern and south-eastern quarter of the county, where great quantities of cheese were sold together with beef-cattle, oxen and sheep. Horses were sold at fairs in the central levels, alongside a range of goods made from flax, willow, and alder. Marshland towns (such as Langport) had winter fairs specializing in fish and water fowl. The fairs and the weekly markets were served by a host of small traders, their activities reflected in the numerous licenses issued at Quarter Sessions to buy, transport and sell corn, butter and cheese. Mercers and other shopkeepers from towns also attended fairs, even those held in larger villages, while the permanent residences of grocers and even mercers in such rural parishes as Curry Rivell, Stogumber, Curland, Dulverton, and Bishop's Hull reveal a measure of solid prosperity in the countryside.[14]

Sharing in this to some extent were the county's large and highly specialized force of craftsmen. Eighty-seven of the 490 inventories for 1681-85 were supplied by such men (cloth-workers are excluded from this sample and will be considered later). The inventories demonstrate how rural craft-work was, only nineteen coming from Taunton and Bridgewater, the two large towns in the sample area; and even when 'town' is stretched to include such doubtful cases as Minehead and Dunster, North Petherton and Crewkerne, the urban proportion of craftsmen rises only to 36 per cent. Most of the artisans in the sample lived in villages and hamlets. They followed a wide variety of trades, 32 separate occupations being listed in the inventories, with carpenters (11) and tanners (10) the most numerous, followed by smiths (8) and cordwainers (7). The latter included two surprisingly wealthy men with personal estates of £150 and £136; but there is no clear pattern of wealthier trades, with ten other craftsmen following nine different occupations owning goods of £100 or more. As a group craftsmen were somewhat less prosperous than the agriculturalists, although their median figure of £35 for total goods indicates some degree of comfort. Proportionately more craftsmen, however, are found in the lower bands of wealth than the farmers – 28 per cent as opposed to 25 per cent in the £1-£20 band, and 35 per cent compared to 28 per cent in the £21-£50. Their numbers in the upper categories were correspondingly lower, with only 14 per cent of craftsmen owning more than £100 in moveable property, compared to 30 per cent among farmers.

Cash transactions played a greater role in the lives of craftsmen than among agriculturalists. The former kept slightly more cash in their houses than farmers (a median of £5 as opposed to £4), and the debts owing to them were, given their lesser income, rather more significant, the median being £9. They spent a little more on domestic comforts, with a median of 28 per cent of their estate invested in household goods compared to 25 per cent among farmers. Most significantly, one half of the sample owned raw materials or finished products – 'shop goods' – indicating that they were independent manufacturers. The value of these goods was considerable (a median figure of £10) which, when the £2 for 'the tools of his trade' is included, means that the typical craftsman held one-third of his estate in goods dictated by his livelihood.

Just over one half of the craftsmen owned some livestock (52 per cent), though horses (found in thirty-three inventories) considerably outnumbered food animals such as cattle (18 cases), sheep (12 cases), and even pigs (27 cases). Only one-third grew any grain, and quantities were small, the median valuation of £3 being scarcely equivalent to two acres of wheat or barley. Grain and food animals might supplement the income of a minority, but most craftsmen and particularly the poorest lived entirely off their trade, even in the most rural areas.

The largest single occupation in Somerset, however, apart from agriculture, was cloth-making. The county was one of England's major cloth centres in the seventeenth century, with the industry concentrated in two distinct and contrasted regions. In eastern Somerset a long narrow band stretched from Bath down to Frome and on to Yeovil, extending back from the Wiltshire border as far as Shepton Mallet. This zone was an extension of the 'western' cloth region of Gloucestershire and Wiltshire, which had been famous for its traditional undyed broadcloth since medieval times. Somerset's other cloth area lay in the south of the county, centred upon Taunton and extending back through Wellington and Chard into eastern Devon. This was an extension of the Devonshire textile industry, known as the 'south-western' region. Significant concentrations of spinning were also found about Minehead and Bridgewater where much of the industry's wool was imported. Separated by the marshes of central Somerset, the county's two cloth areas differed in several important respects. Until the seventeenth century the 'western' (Wiltshire-Gloucestershire-eastern Somerset) region had been by far the more important of the two. Its broad cloths, up to 63 inches wide and 28 to 32 yards long, formed most of the 'Old Draperies' exported to the Low Countries and Germany in 1600, making up a large part of England's total cloth exports. The cloth was sold undyed, 'in the white', to be finished abroad. It was expensive, hand-woven and heavy, weighing up to 24 ounces per square yard (the heaviest cloth made today for men's overcoats weighs 17 ounces per yard). In the 'south-western' area, Devon and south

Somerset had made less cloth, and made it for the poorer end of the home market. The kersies, Devonshire dozens, and other local variations woven here were cheaper, coarser, and shorter in length than the higher class 'western' cloths, using poorer wool and setting fewer lengthwise or warp thread. The woven cloth was usually not fulled, the process which shrank cloth and made it more dense, and so the pattern of the weave remained visible. Only 12 to 13 yards long (hence the term 'dozens') south-western cloths were cheap and durable, but coarse to sight and touch.[15] Finally, the south-western cloth was marketed through Exeter and by Exeter clothiers, whereas that from the west was packed to London to be sold in Blackwell Hall by London middlemen.

Both areas profited from a generally expanding market during the Tudor period, but in the seventeenth century government interference (the Cockayne Project), war in central Europe, and a fundamental change in consumer demand destroyed the old industry. By 1700 barely a thousand of the old western broadcloths were exported, and though there was still some domestic demand, as there was for south-western kersies and dozens, the 'Old Draperies' were effectively gone, replaced by new products during a long and painful transition period. At the end the relative positions of the two regions had been reversed. By 1700 the western area, Gloucestershire and Wiltshire, was producing just 54,000 cloths for export each year; whereas expansion in the south-west had made Exeter a major port, exporting over 100,000 cloths annually, and contributing £850,000 in serges alone, out of a national total of under three million pounds for all textile exports. Aulnage figures reveal the extent of the change and show the importance of Somerset. Taxes of £1500 were taken from Devonshire between 1683 and 1686, but only £600 from Gloucestershire and £300 for Wiltshire, with Somerset paying £800.[16] Cloth-making in the western region continued, though on a lower base, while in the south-west it greatly expanded. Drastic changes in the type of textile accounted for both developments.

In the west the change was two-fold. As early as the 1580s 'Spanish Cloths' had been made in Taunton and by the 1620s this new variety of cloth was being woven in Shepton Mallett, subsequently spreading eastwards to Frome and Wiltshire. It used very soft and short-staple Spanish wool for both warp and weft, resulting in a much lighter and softer cloth, but one difficult to weave because the finer threads broke easily. Varying amounts of high quality English wool were mixed with that from Spain (so that 'Spanish cloth' is a slightly misleading term), but used in proper balance the two produced a cloth which, though expensive, was, at 17 ounces per square yard, much lighter than the old broadcloth. At the same time the demand for pleasingly coloured cloth was met by dyeing wools before they were spun. By mixing coloured yarns with the undyed white, cloths of subtle shadings could be woven, and though these too were expensive there was a good market for them. Cheaper coloureds or 'medleys' were made by using undyed yarn, and then dyeing the cloth 'in the piece' after weaving.[17] Neither dyeing, nor the use of fine wool, was new to the industry; the change lay in the extent of their use; and this was true too of the change which saved the south-western or Devonshire-south Somerset textile industry.

Before the advent of man-made fibres textiles were of two basic types, woollens and worsteds. The west of England's 'Old Draperies', and its new medleys and Spanish cloths were all woollen cloths. They were made, that is to say, from lengths of short wool, which was carded before spinning to produce a mass of short fibres lying at different angles. Spinners were thus able to produce a soft thread, and the resulting cloth was not only soft to the touch, but had the characteristic 'fluffy' appearance of woollen cloth because of the presence of short cross-wise fibres in the yarn. The second basic form of textile was the worsted. Here the wool was combed before spinning to remove all the short lengths, and lay the remaining longer fibres parallel and lengthwise in the thread. Combing was a heavy and dirty operation reserved for men, whereas women often carded the short wools. Yarn spun from the longer combed wool was used in both warp and weft to produce the worsted, a textile hard in touch and wear, with a flat shiny surface. Fulling was unnecessary since it was already a strong material, and the pattern of the weave was left visible. Worsteds had long been made in Yorkshire and parts of East Anglia mostly for the domestic market but what was produced in seventeenth-century Devon was a new hybrid, the serge, combining worsted yarn for the long warp threads with short woollen yarn for the crosswise weft. Usually fulled to make it somewhat denser, the new fabric was lighter than the old broadcloths but thicker than most of the other 'new draperies', and as hard-wearing as its common name 'perpetuano' suggests. Made in short lengths from cheaper wools it was also less expensive, and was a favourite among customers, and with small clothiers and weavers lacking the capital to make full-length cloths. By the Civil War serge had replaced kersies as the south-west's basic textile and production rose tenfold over the century. Exported directly from Exeter to the principal foreign markets of the Netherlands and France, it was also very popular at home, nearly half the production reaching English customers. Its only disadvantage was that serge-making required nearly three times the man-hours that cloth did, and if it was to remain a cheap material the wages of combers, spinners, and weavers, had to be squeezed.[18]

By 1700, differences between the western and south-western cloth areas – and, therefore, between eastern and southern Somerset – had increased. Making different kinds of textiles, sending them to different ports for different markets, the south-west expanded far more quickly than the west and needed to cut wages more severely than the west; consequently the two cloth regions began to diverge in economic and social structures. In the western region (including eastern Somerset) smaller clothiers and independent weavers survived, partly because they could more easily obtain land to widen the basis of their income than they could in the Devonshire area. Clothiers were evenly spread across the countryside in the west, but in the south-west they were concentrated in Exeter and a few major towns. Medleys and Spanish cloth also produced dyers, fullers, and shearmen spread among the clothiers in the west, whereas such finishing as existed in the south-west was concentrated largely in a few centres such as Exeter, Tiverton and Taunton. Generalizations are perilous, but the south-west appears to have been more economically differentiated and capitalist than the west, where smaller clothiers still survived.[19]

Some fundamental problems were common to both areas however. The change to new draperies was not made easily. Sheer hardship was needed to drive workers to the new textiles. New products meant new techniques, and experienced weavers, spinners, and carders had to give up old skills and learn new ones, their wages suffering until their expertise grew. Serges and Spanish cloths both depended heavily upon foreign markets, and these were volatile in the later seventeenth century. France doubled the duties on English serge in 1677 and imposed extraordinary fees on English shipping, while at Morlaix (important to both Exeter and Lyme Regis) the sale of English woollens was for a time banned. In Portugal and Flanders tariffs or prohibitions protected local workmen against English cloths. The manufacture of Spanish cloth in eastern Somerset was badly hit by the collapse of the Levant market, exports falling by nearly one-third between 1684 and 1688. Ten years of political uncertainty, from the Popish Plot onwards, magnified what the historian of the western cloth industry has called 'the general recession of 1683-86'. As indicated by the hallage receipts of the London cloth market, English textile production in the early 1680s fell back to the 'depressed trading conditions' of 1676-78.[20] And although merchants always grumble over trade conditions, the volume of complaint in the later seventeenth century reveals a strong feeling of malaise in the industry.

Clothiers were alarmed over competition from French linens and exotic Indian fabrics, weavers over Huguenot refugees who could put them out of work; and both argued that competition from Somerset and Devon cloth workers who had migrated to Ireland in the 1670s would cut into their living. The quantity of cloths sent from Ireland was actually trifling, but the clothiers' agitation was sufficiently intense for an Act to be passed in 1698 banning such exports. The long controversy over the Blackwell Hall factors further illustrates the industry's fears. Because few county clothiers could afford to stay in London long enough to sell their cloths, the Blackwell Hall factors – in origin simply market clerks – took on the role of middlemen. When times were hard clothiers then accused them of driving small men out of business, by delaying the sale of cloth and forcing their suppliers to accept long credit. The factors were also charged with engrossing wool and yarn to force up the prices charged to clothiers. Complaint about them became general among west country clothiers after 1677, and at the Bruton Quarter Sessions in January 1685 the Somerset Grand Jury formally presented their activities as a grievance.[21]

No conspiracy existed among the factors: they simply passed on to clothiers the harsh facts of competition. A basic cause of trouble was the number of small clothiers making less than a score of cloths per year, with no reserves and little credit. A Gloucestershire muster roll of 1608 reveals seven weavers to every clothier in the county, suggesting that many clothiers were little different from the two or three weavers they employed. The clothiers caught poaching in eastern Somerset during the 1680s and 1690s in the company of glaziers, bakers, and cordwainers were scarcely wealthy capitalists: like the company they kept, they were small tradesmen. Little more than £300 was needed to set up in business, cloth could be sold at local fairs, and with a little land they could survive off a very small turnover.[22] But small men were also tempted to reduce costs by producing inferior cloths and forcing down weavers' wages, creating so much trouble that wealthier clothiers were disinclined to lament their passing in the harsh economic climate of the seventeenth century.

Poverty among clothworkers, however, was not simply created by the greed or necessities of clothiers small or large; it sprang from the very nature of the industry. Independent weavers did exist – as late as 1698 Celia Fiennes saw men selling cloth at the Exeter market who 'must have their money, which they employ to provide their yarn to give more againe'; and in eastern Somerset not a few combined their trade with farming three or four acres, and thus enjoyed some independence. Independent spinners – often the wives of farmers or craftsmen – sold yarns at the nearest market, and master spinners and master-weavers could sometimes bargain at equality with clothiers. But most combers and carders, spinners and weavers were dependent wage workers on low wages, because their trades were easily learnt by the unemployed and the unskilled. The cloth industry was highly labour intensive. Two weavers, with a boy about the loom, needed two to three weeks to complete a length of cloth, and supplying them occupied nine or ten more people opening the wool, carding or combing it, and spinning the yarn. Finishing involved fulling, shearing, burling, dyeing, and packing the cloth, so that all told one loom employed about fourteen workers. Responding to the demand for labour, the surplus population of town and village flocked to cloth-producing areas. Apprenticeship regulations were ignored in the belief that they did not apply to new textiles appearing after the 1563 Act, and Parliament was so flooded with complaints over this that in 1693 a Bill was introduced to enforce the relevant clause of the Elizabethan Act. Parish authorities saw the industry as a dumping ground for their poor with the result, as an M.P. was told in 1693, that weaving which had formerly been 'esteemed a good Trade, [was] now one of the poorest, it being commonly practiced by Parishes to bind out their poor Boyes to weavers'. With premiums of up to £5 for each child, poorer weavers took on too many boys for apprenticeship or 'training', whose competition later depressed their own wages.[23]

Abundant labour thus kept wages low. Moreover, contemporary wisdom was that labour would only work when forced to it by low wages, and observing the celebrations of Saints Monday and Tuesday when weavers had money in their pockets, clothiers were inclined to agree. They also believed that French weavers received only two-thirds of an Englishman's income, an exaggeration but another good reason for low wages. In the mid-seventeenth century south-western weavers were awarded rates of 8d. per day, compared to 11d. for labourers in other trades, and up to 2/- for skilled men such as carpenters, masons and bricklayers; while spinners received only 3d. to 4d. In eastern Somerset and Wiltshire around 1700, a weaver in constant employment could receive £20 per year gross placing him, as Miss Mann observes, 'not among the artisans and handicraftsmen, but among the 364,000 "labouring people and outservants" at £15 per year net in Gregory King's estimate of 1696'. The work of wife and children would increase a family's income, but against this no weaver was in constant employment. Truck was also a major abuse: 'paying in commodities above the market price is a great mischief', noted a writer in the 1690s. But the greatest hardship was probably irregular employment.[24] After working for a fortnight to complete a cloth, weavers had to wait for clothiers to deliver them more yarn and another commission, and delays arising from business inefficiency and slow transport could lengthen to spells of prolonged unemployment during a recession. Many small clothiers could not afford to begin new cloths until they had disposed of the last one, and weavers who had accepted commissions from two or three clothiers simultaneously during good times could expect little consideration from the latter when times were bad.

Their probate inventories help to set the weavers in perspective. To obtain a reasonably large sample the search for cloth-workers' inventories in general was extended back to 1671, i.e. for this category alone a fifteen-year period before the rebellion was examined. This yielded seventy-five inventories containing reference to looms; but twelve of these had to be eliminated, seven because the men involved were essentially clothiers, and five because they were primarily yeoman farmers. The size of the sample, therefore, was sixty-three inventories. Three essential points emerged from their study. Weavers were usually quite poor; most in the sample owned more than one loom, i.e. they were employers of labour as well as workers themselves; and the majority owned no land or animals, and had to live entirely off their earnings from weaving.

Most weavers in the sample lived at no better standard than agricultural labourers, even though they were frequently employers of labour. The wealthiest weaver owned £102 in total moveable estate, and his was the only case to reach £100. Only seven owned more than £50 in goods. The median value was much less, just £21 or equal to the property of a 'well-off' agricultural labourer. But the thirty weavers with £20 or less in wordly goods were not simply wage-workers: one half of them owned 2 or more looms (three owned 5 and one owned 7!), and they, therefore, employed other weavers at wages. The dire poverty of the latter – too poor to own a weaving loom valued usually at only £1 – may be inferred from the low standard of living of their employers. Over the entire sample of sixty-three, the majority of weavers (57 per cent) owned two or more looms, although the number owned did not rise evenly as income levels increased – thus the man owning most looms, eight, possessed only £44 in total estate. Not all looms of course may have been in use, and some of the five, six, seven or eight owned by individual weavers were possibly old, broken, or cannibalized items.

For most weavers in the sample there was no supplement to their income from the land. Over one half (56 per cent) had neither grain nor livestock in their inventories. Only twenty-eight possessed land and/or livestock, and their holdings of both were typically very small, the medians being two acres of arable land (value £4), and two or three beasts (value £6). For twenty-one of the twenty-five with animals and/or land, the total value of their land and animals did not exceed £11. The six weavers who possessed crops and livestock valued at between £23 and £33 were most probably husbandmen whose family also practised weaving as a supplement; but they are included in the sample to ensure that it is not skewed to emphasize the landless weaver. These wealthier weaver-husbandmen also account for half of the twelve leases of land held by weavers (median value £15).

Few weavers owned the wool they worked on, or the cloth they produced – only four inventories list cloth (median £11), and just eight refer to wool (median £7). Of these eight independent weavers four owned wool or cloth in quantity, up to £30 worth of cloth, and wool rising to £41 in value; but the other four held it in quantities worth only a few pounds. These eight weavers also account for most of the references to horses found in the weavers' inventories, arguing that they were indeed putting work out to other weavers. Fifteen weavers' inventories refer to spinning turns, often in two's, three's or four's, revealing an obvious supplement to a weaving family's income; and given the low value set on turns the real number was probably larger. The same may be true for book-ownership: twelve weavers are recorded as owning books, their value arbitrarily set at £1 in most inventories, suggesting that these men owned several books and that others with only one or two, worth a shilling or two, perhaps had them listed as 'other lumber'. One-fifth of the sample is nevertheless a high proportion for these generally poor men, most of the weaver book-owners being valued at less than £20 in total goods. The majority of them lived in Taunton, or in the villages of Trull and Bishops' Hull nearby, suggesting the influence of the Taunton market upon literacy, although nonconformity may be involved too.

Spinners were traditionally even poorer than weavers, and to prove this by labouring over their inventories is probably unnecessary; and may also be unwise, because spinning turns were noted in a very haphazard fashion by inventory takers, and were so common that all manner of people might own one. Thus, of the fifty-four inventories found which referred to turns, twenty-two were for men working in other branches of the cloth industry (chiefly weavers); but husbandmen and yeomen also owned turns, as did tradesmen as unlikely as a carpenter and a sweep. The fifty-four men owning turns were not particularly prosperous, with a median for total moveable estate of £18; and when the 26 turn-owners who clearly had another principal occupation are removed, the median for the twenty-eight remaining spinners without qualification is even lower, at just £12 for total estate.

Other cloth-makers found in the inventories include 14 clothiers, 6 serge-makers, 8 fullers, 6 shearmen, 3 wool merchants, 2 apiece of burlers and feltmakers, 1 dyer, and 1 comb-maker (the latter very poor with just £6 estate). Both burlers were affluent men with £148 and £374 in goods; the dyer (£14) was as impecunious as the feltmakers (£53 and £11); one shearman had an estate valued at £389, but the remaining five owned between £7 and £87; and the three woolmerchants' goods were all valued at between £100 and £200. Worth more attention are the twenty clothiers and serge-makers. Six were wealthy men with estates ranging from £237 to £540, four owning goods valued at over £400. Seven had estates equivalent to yeomen, with valuations of between £108 and £162; and seven more were no more prosperous than labourers or husbandmen, with less than £100 in goods. Only three of the group, and those the most prosperous, owned grain or livestock in any quantity; the remainder had as little interest in agriculture as the weavers they employed. Only one had a large sum of cash in his house (£52), and just 4 had debts owing them of £50 or more, but the proportion of their estate locked up in business capital – 'shop goods' – varied from a fifth, to as much as three-quarters for the wealthier men. Finally, a high proportion of them (8 out of the 20) lived in one town, Taunton. The remainder were scattered about Somerset's rural parishes, as were most of the fullers, shearmen, feltmakers, and wool merchants. Nearly a quarter of the sample of sixty-three weavers, however, came from Taunton, and when the weaving parishes about that town are included, the proportion rises to one half. No less than the rural parishes, many of Somerset's towns lived in large part by cloth.

Towns in seventeenth-century Somerset were numerous, but not particularly large. In this respect indeed the county was unusual: ranking in the top half dozen for size, population, and perhaps wealth, Somerset nevertheless contained no large towns such as Exeter, Norwich, or York, Coventry, Leicester, or Northampton. It was a county without a respectably sized urban centre, for Taunton the largest town had a population of barely 4,000 in 1700, and the next largest towns, Bridgewater and Shepton Mallet, a little less.[25] The cathedral city of Wells, and the cloth towns of Frome and Chard, all had barely three thousand inhabitants and were the largest of the county's miscellany of market towns, cloth centres, ports, and (in the case of Bath) a social resort for the upper classes. The number of these smaller towns – at least a dozen of them with two thousand to three thousand population – partly explains the absence of any larger county centre; but the large ports and commercial centres of Exeter and Bristol at either end of Somerset also restricted local urban growth.

The county was, however, also served by smaller ports of its own. Along the Bristol Channel were Watchet and Dunster, decaying centres with a little traffic to and from Ireland, overtaken by the better harbour at Minehead, which had grown partly by engrossing their commerce. Described by Gerard in 1632 as 'a little Market Towne' Minehead had eighteen hundred inhabitants by the end of the century; and with a new quay built by the town's rulers, the Luttrell family, in 1682, its ships traded as far afield as Virginia and the West Indies. Commerce with Ireland, however, was its mainstay, importing cattle to be fattened on the Somerset grasslands, until the trade was banned by Parliament in 1668, prospering thereafter on Irish wool and yarn for the county's cloth industry. Closely tied to Somerset's economy (though not within its boundary) was Lyme Regis, the county's other outlet to the south. Like its greater neighbour Exeter, Lyme Regis was chiefly important to Somerset as an export centre for cloth. One of the more important outports in the early seventeenth century, Lyme's share of the cloth trade had declined as that of Exeter expanded, and its imports of salt, wine and linen cloth from the French Channel ports were too small to redress the balance. An attempt to revive its interest in the Newfoundland fisheries came to nothing, and by the later seventeenth century the livelihood of Lyme's 1,400 inhabitants was precarious. With no domestic industry (the town exported cloth but made none), and a very restricted hinterland for its weekly market, its prosperity depended upon its role as a port. In turn this depended upon maintaining in good repair the Cob, a 50 yards' length of stone breakwater, which gave the town an artificial harbour. Repeatedly damaged by storms and high tides, the Cob's upkeep was more than the town's slender finances could bear and occasional grants of up to £100 had to be wheedled from the Crown. The town's manifest parliamentary sympathies under Charles I, and its prominent crop of Dissenters under his son, made this a difficult task and all the energies of its rulers during the later seventeenth century merely prevented stagnation from collapsing into outright decline. By 1674 the poor exempt from the Hearth Tax nearly outnumbered those still able to pay: 173 compared to 186.[26]

No such problems faced the county's major port, Bridgewater. Like Minehead it traded extensively in livestock, with so many beasts coming from Ireland that the passage of the Irish Cattle Act of 1668 brought fears here of a sharp drop in land values. Bridgewater was a major source of wool, yarn, dyes, and oil for the cloth industry; a county-wide distribution centre for coal brought from Bristol or South Wales; and a market for luxuries such as wine, tobacco, and grocery goods. The office of Controller of Customs was valued at £60 p.a., worth the attentions of a knight of the shire to obtain its reversion. With a large trade in imports as well as an extensive local market in the prospering Somerset levels, the foremost of Bridgewater's three companies of tradesmen was naturally that of the distributors – merchants, grocers, mercers and apothecaries; but the other two companies also reflected its market function, the one composed of butchers, skinners, tanners, glovers and shoemakers, the other comprising innkeepers, chandlers, bakers, tailors, smiths, and braziers. Trade brought wealth: with nearly the same total population Bridgewater had only one-third the number of exemptions from the 1674 Hearth Tax as Taunton; and in 1642 its 146 citizens liable to the subsidy collected that year paid a total of £93, compared to the £50 paid by 202 men in Taunton, an average of 12/4d each in Bridgewater compared to just 5/- in Taunton. But it was not a healthy town, for winters brought such flooding that cattle could not graze in the fields, roads were blocked, and its inhabitants shook with the ague.[27]

More attractive to travellers were the cities of Bath and Wells, paired in more ways than the title they gave to the diocese. Both possessed natural springs (though only Bath's were credited with medicinal properties); each depended upon patronage, lay or ecclesiastical; neither had a large market, nor a very significant cloth industry. As Celia Fiennes noted of Wells, it 'must be considered halfe a Citty, this and the Bath making up but one'. Each half was small enough for the grant of Quarter Sessions or Assize to be worth months of campaigning to acquire, and each was so small that when the Assizes were held they 'filled it like a faire'. Wells was the larger of the two, but Bath's connection with the fashionable world made it much the wealthier paying in 1669 £121 in Hearth Taxes, compared to £25 from Wells.[28]

Smaller towns were scattered across the county, such as Ilminster and Crewkerne, Langport and Yeovil, owing their considerable markets to fortunate location on road or river, but they often practised secondary trades as well – flax-growing and glove-making at Yeovil, cloth at Ilminster and Crewkerne. Other towns had been struck by decay: the ancient county town Somerton had long been of no consequence; Ilchester had once flourished with ten parishes but by 1633 'there remaines only the carkass of it'; and Glastonbury, still making considerable quantities of cloth in the 1650s, was described half a century later as 'that ragged poor place'. In the west, small towns such as Dulverton and Wiveliscombe survived on a combination of marketing and cloth-making. But while combing, spinning, or weaving was found in most small towns and villages of Somerset, these trades flourished particularly in Frome and Chard, and to a lesser extent in Shepton Mallett. In the south of the county Chard had a large market, was the centre for the collection of Excise and had been granted a Charter in 1641. The cheap coarse cloths made here attracted a large force of unskilled labour, and though poor rates rose to their maximum the town still needed help from its neighbours by the late 1670s to relieve unemployment. In 1670, 234 persons were excused payment of Hearth Tax, after Taunton and Shepton Mallett the largest for any Somerset town. Poverty had become a major problem in Shepton Mallett despite its early adoption of the New Draperies, and the growth of stocking-knitting. A house of correction was built in 1622, and though the town does not appear in Poor Law orders passed in the Quarter Sessions of the 1670s and 1680s, the poor were very numerous, with over four hundred excused the 1674 Hearth Tax, more even than Taunton. Cloth-making at Frome attracted Defoe's enthusiastic notice, the industry's 'increasing and flourishing Circumstances' producing a town where wealthy clothiers built whole new streets, and employed so many new arrivals that the town was said to outpeople the venerable city of York. Once again, however, cloth gave but also took away: over-populated outparishes such as Beckington were 'extremely burthened with poor people' and begged support from their neighbours, and in Frome nearly two hundred heads of households were excused taxation in 1674.[29]

Notwithstanding the importance of these three centres, to contemporaries Taunton was the Somerset cloth town par excellence: 'a large, wealthy, and exceedingly populous Town' providing constant work for 1,100 looms, was a typical claim. In 1683 the town's able-bodied men were described by their Mayor as 'most of them journeymen combers and weavers'.[30] This was only a slight exaggeration: of eighty-one inventories for Taunton men between 1681 and 1685, 40 per cent worked in the cloth industry. A few were wealthy men – of the eight described as clothiers or sergemakers only one had a personal estate of less than £100, and the average was £281. The two burlers represented were also prosperous with moveable goods valued at £148 to £274, but the tucker (£50), and two fullers (£11 and £23) were unexpectedly poor. The dozen Taunton weavers whose inventories survive show a median value of £14, little more than the average labourer, but they varied widely between £9 and £64. Between them they owned forty-six looms, nearly four each on average, and were, therefore, master-weavers living by the work of employees as well as by their own labour. Their unimpressive totals for all goods and the sparse median of £10 for their household items imply bleak poverty for their employees, since these master-weavers were the most prosperous of their craft. The two 'simple' weavers with just one loom apiece had only £12 and £13 in total worldly goods.

Taunton, however, was more than merely a cloth town, as observant visitors realized from the size of its weekly market. Thomas Gerard in 1633 found it quite plausible that 140 butchers alone attended each week, given the size and population of Taunton's hinterland; and in 1698 Celia Fiennes was impressed by the size of the corn market, although she noted that most houses were still made of timber and plaster, instead of the more fashionable brick and stone. More specialized trades among the inventories suggest the variety of Taunton's commerce – pewterers, apothecaries, locksmiths, and a book-seller, drapers, four quite prosperous mercers, and a grocer worth £647. And the presence of three alehouse-keepers and three innkeepers in only five years of inventories implies a town with considerable resources of hospitality – of all kinds. Visitors were impressed by the town's appearance – 'a neate place', 'a faire and pleasant place' – but its landed neighbours never thought Taunton worth a gentleman's residence and they knew it as 'that populous poor place'. Poor it was, but 'populous' is more doubtful. Its size was consistently and considerably exaggerated by locals and by visitors. Defoe accepted a figure of 1,100 looms at work in the town, suggesting a population of nearly ten thousand, while the Tory Lord FitzHarding tried in 1683 to rally loyalists by declaring that the town was 'not so considerable as they warrant. There cannot be above ten thousand souls in it'. At this time even the mayor thought it contained three thousand able-bodied men, implying a total of ten thousand inhabitants. In fact the 1641 Protestation returns, Hearth Tax figures, and birth-rates all point to a figure of not over four thousand, and an estimate of 1703 set the total at 3,880. This exaggerated view of Taunton's size was to be important politically during the Exclusion Crisis, and in 1685; and the misconception may have been prompted by quite recent growth caused by heavy immigration, for in 1535 Taunton had been so small that Leland spared it less than two lines, and it ranked very low in fourteenth century tax figures.[31]

But the town was poor. Taunton paid only one-fifth as much as Bath in the Hearth Tax of 1669, and in the 1642 poll tax its citizens paid at only half the rate, on average, of those of Bridgewater. In 1664, 225 households paid the Hearth Tax, but a return of 1674 listed 393 as exempt. Over half of those paying did so for one or two hearths, and in the pauperized 'second parish' of St. James the proportion rose to 80 per cent. With only one-third of the town's population, St. James provided two-thirds of those too poor to pay, and most people here were tenants living in houses owned by non-resident landlords. By the late 1670s property-owners in St. James were paying £350 p.a. in poor relief and, near the end of their resources, won orders between 1677 and 1684 that the adjacent parishes of West Bagborough, West Monckton, Withiel, Rushton and Stoke St. Mary should give assistance. But these too had their poor, and West Bagborough for example contributed nothing, claiming that the poor rate there was already at its legal maximum. Amenities within Taunton were allowed to decay. In 1684 the town appealed at the Quarter Sessions for help to re-establish its house of correction now 'very much in decay', and a year earlier it had persuaded the county to repair the 'ruinous' bridge of the River Tone which connected the town's two parishes. At the same time an earlier proposal was revived to make navigable the River Tone between Bridgewater and Taunton. This would markedly reduce carriage costs on food and bulky goods, for the price of coal rose from 1/6d for a 2 bushell horse load to 2/- over the 12-mile journey. A few years later Taunton's mayor was advocating the scheme once more, as a solution to the town's 'very miserable condition, in relation to trade and the increase of the poore, for the Towne cannot subsist them'; and hoping that the work provided would cure a rising crime rate caused by poverty.[32]

As a major centre of the cloth industry, Taunton experienced further strains. Among the many regional cloths which disappeared during the seventeenth century, besides the 'Dunsters' and 'Bridgewaters' was the 'Taunton cotton', a cloth despite its name. Early in the century between one thousand and two thousand had been despatched each year from Exeter. Assuming 20 cloths p.a. from each loom, and 10 persons serving each loom, the 'Tauntons' had employed some 1,000 workers at their peak. In 1647, however, only 860 pieces were produced, and this fell to 190 in 1666. Demand briefly revived and 828 lengths were made in 1680. But irreversible decline then set in, and the 'cottons' were extinct at only 23 lengths by 1686. Six years had seen the numbers employed in this branch of cloth-making drop from over four hundred to less than a score. Even if only half the production came from Taunton itself, nearly two hundred of approximately one thousand able-bodied men of the town had been forced out of their trade. Most would eventually join the sergemakers, for Taunton and the surrounding area were thought at this time to be completing seven hundred serges or worsteds per week, but the 'redeployment' of almost one man in five in the space of a few years, and during a recession, was a crisis for the town.[33]

Political factors worsened economic recession in Taunton. After news of the Popish plot and proroguing of Parliament early in 1679, a local gentleman wrote that 'so many Clothiers and Serge men have lessened or gave offe their Trade' because of this 'Pannicke Fear', that 'ill Times' had struck rents, wool prices, and the local economy generally. Two years later Exclusion alarms and parliamentary elections had so depressed trade that five hundred serge makers in Taunton were unemployed, and more were thought likely to join them. In their desperate condition they became 'mutinous, flocking up and down the adjacent parts with insolent and peremptory resolves that they are ready to break their neighbours' rights, before they would starve'. Threatened by a visit from them, gentlemen living nearby wrote urging the mayor to 'take some order'. Despite Tory suspicions there was no apparent political motive behind these demonstrations, but cloth workers and clothiers gave a big welcome to the well-known London Whig Alderman Cornish when he visited Wiltshire and eastern Somerset in June 1683.[34]

Politics and Taunton's cloth industry were linked in another way. As punishment for its anti-royalism during the Civil War and at the Restoration, the town lost its Charter in 1661 and with it the right to be governed by a corporation of mayor and aldermen. The charter was not restored until 1677, and during the sixteen year interval Taunton had no formal government at all. Petitioning unsuccessfully in 1669 for the charter to be restored, a group of influential local gentry pointed out that although constables were still appointed, there was effectively no authority to maintain public order, enforce market regulations, or sustain public welfare. No assistance or protection could be given to the town's cloth industry, nor were there any magistrates to restrict the influx of poor seeking work as spinners and weavers, or to provide relief when they were thrown out of work. During the Charter negotiations of 1669 townspeople argued forcefully that something must be done to protect 'the great number of workmen . . . that came to be employed in Serge making [and] are not continued in work'. But it was eight years more before a new charter was granted, and in that time Taunton remained a large 'open parish', its cloth industry attracting the county's workless poor.[35]

When a corporation was finally re-established, like other authorities in the area, it could find no other way of dealing with the poor than by depositing them in the cloth trade. Pauper children went almost automatically into the industry: of 122 poor boys apprenticed in Taunton between 1672 and 1690 93 per cent became clothworkers, mostly weavers. So poor were Taunton's weavers, a report claimed in 1700, that 'for luere of a little money [they] take 3, 4 or 5 Apprentices', to be thrown out and increase the competition for work a little later. Other weavers would ignore formal apprenticeship altogether, and 'for a little money will undertake to instruct persons in Three or Six months in that Trade' – with the same result. Single women preferred cloth working to domestic service because, although the wages were low in both, the former offered more personal freedom; and craftsmen's wives could increase the family budget by casual work in the industry. So many of Somerset's unskilled workers worked in cloth that the House of Commons was told, in 1701, that less than a half of the weavers in and about Taunton had served apprenticeships, and only a perfunctory training was given to those who had. In 1691 Taunton was clamouring for protection from (non-existent) Irish competitors undercutting the town's cloth wage rates, and by 1700 Taunton's weavers were begging their MPs to save the industry by making them a statutory company with power to control entry to the trade. Contemporary warnings of doom require cautious handling, but it seems clear that over much of Somerset – and in Taunton in particular – the cloth industry was over-populated, under-paid, and justifiably nervous about its markets. The Somerset Grand Jury warned bluntly in 1687 that cloth making in the county was in a condition of deep decay.[36]

These conditions led to an increasing pre-occupation with the problems of the poor, especially in the crowded centre-south of the county. When Daniel Defoe rode into the county from Devonshire, early in the next century, he was shocked when at Wellington, the first Somerset town he entered, he found himself 'immediately surrounded with Beggars, to such a Degree, that one had some difficulty to keep them from under our Horse Heels . . . such a Crowd of them as if the town was come out into the Street'. The problem here was not new. A considerable town in a large open parish, situated in the heart of Somerset's serge-making area and just eight miles from Taunton, Wellington had barely coped in the early seventeenth century when 273 inhabitants were supporting nearly one hundred poor. By 1691, however, 235 rate-payers (only sixty-six of them in the town, the majority living in the rural tithings) were burdened with nearly four hundred poor. In 1684 the Quarter Sessions were informed that the poor of Wellington were 'very numerous and want Imployment', and a stock was ordered to be raised for their relief. But nothing was done, and in 1693 renewed alarm that the poor 'doe vastly increase' led to a proposal for raising £500 to provide work. The urgency of the situation was underlined by a corn riot in the late 1680s, when a Taunton baker taking corn out of Wellington had his cargo seized; but Defoe's reception some time later shows that intentions still out-paced deeds.[37]

Other towns in this well-populated area were experiencing difficulty with their poor in the 1670s and 1680s. Milverton was another large, open, and cloth-making parish, adjoining Wellington and just ten miles from Taunton. It too was over-burdened by the cloth industry. So costly were the Milverton poor to support that in 1678 rate-payers refused to accept any increase, and were supported by local JPs. The overseers had to appeal to the Lord Chief Justice to end the deadlock, and felt pleasantly justified when townsfolk rioted a few months later, destroying hedges and seizing corn stocks. At West Monckton, 4 miles from Taunton, there were disputes over the cost of a new poor house; 3 miles from Taunton, Thorne St. Margaret appealed to adjacent parishes for help; and 10 miles from Taunton at Bridgewater, there were charges that the poor rate had risen above its legal maximum. The same complaint was heard south of Taunton at Ilminster, where the poor were so numerous that the assistance of other parishes was sought, while at neighbouring West Dawlish fines on dissenters were pressed into service, and the parishes about over-populated Chard fiercely resisted involvement in that town's problems. Throughout the region in the late 1670s and early 1680s there was a drive to suppress alehouses (at Bishop's Lydiard just outside Taunton they were 'restricted' to five!); in 1678 the number of vagrant beggars caused alarm at Quarter Sessions, and prompted discussion of a better law to suppress them; and pamphleteers in the 1680s and 1690s regularly asserted that in Somerset's cloth areas poor rates had increased from three to six times since the Restoration. Complaints made at Quarter Sessions broadly confirm this assertion, for the problem parishes were mostly about

Taunton and Chard (in the 'Devonshire' cloth region); or in the eastern fringe of the county, such as Beckington and Henstridge (near Frome), and Pensford and Kilmersdon (further north toward Bath).[38]

But the problems of poverty and over-population, and the difficulties facing the Somerset cloth industry, while very real, must be kept in proportion. Somerset's agriculture supported a large class of middling and lesser gentry, and the county's yeomen and husbandmen were, according to travellers and the evidence of inventories, comfortably placed and sometimes thriving. The number of fairs, and the presence of mercers and sometimes grocers in many towns and even villages, reveals a vigorous commerce living off the agricultural sector. Poverty was concentrated in particular areas, which often passed unnoticed by contemporaries. And even where it was worst, inhabitants were capable of initiative and enterprise in dealing with it. In 1680 the residents of North Petherton, a large and commercially progressive agricultural parish between Taunton and Bridgewater, were stung into action by rising poor rates, spreading alehouses, and a growing shanty-town area. They appointed a twenty-four man committee of Assistants to aid the overseers of the poor, and charged them with a thirteen point programme to expel strangers, prevent cottage-building, and eradicate poverty.[39] It possibly worked, for nothing more is heard of North Petherton's poor in Quarter Sessions records. The action was initiated and carried out by local men and not by the JPs, who simply approved the plan; and the signatories to the programme contained only two gentlemen, the other twenty-seven being lesser men of the parish. The episode is revealing of Somerset's economy and society in the later Stuart period: severe strains existed, but the county included independent and capable men among its middle and lower classes, who could respond to economic and social challenges. Politics and religion could stimulate them too: such men played an important part in Somerset's history during the Civil War and, a generation later, in the long crisis over the Popish plot and Exclusion, which led on to the uprising of 1685.

Footnotes to Chapter One

1. H.C.Darby, ed., *A New Historical Geography of England*, Cambridge 1973, pp.141, 191; J.Thirsk, ed., *The Agrarian History of England and Wales Vol. IV*, Cambridge 1967, p.72; T.Rogers, *A History of Agriculture and Prices in England*, Oxford 1866-1902 7 vols., I, 104, 114-17, 122-3.

2. R.Athill, ed., *Mendip, A New Study*, Newton Abbot 1976, pp. 146-8, 150-5; J.U.Nef, *The Rise of the British Coal Industry*, London 1966, 2 vols., i, 19-20.

3. C.Fiennes, *The Journey of Celia Fiennes*, London 1947, pp.17, 236-7; D.Defoe, *A Tour Through the Whole Island of Great Britain*, London 1968, 2 vols., i, 280; J.Thirsk, *Agrarian History IV*, p.80; L.T.Smith, ed., *The Itinerary of John Leland 1535-43*, London 1964, 5 vols., i, 150; T.Gerard, 'The Particular Description of the County of Somerset 1633', *Somerset Record Society*, 15 1900, p.123; Bodleian Library, Aubrey MSS.13, f.16.

4. D.Defoe, *Tour*, i, 266; J.Thirsk, *Agrarian History IV*, p.75.

5. C.Fiennes, *Journey*, p.243; Aubrey MSS.13, f.62; T.Gerard, 'Description', pp.214, 219, 231, 132.

6. J.Thirsk, *Agrarian History IV*, pp.78, 79.

7. J.Leland, *Itinerary*, i, 168; D.Defoe, *Tour*, i, 263; J.Thirsk, *Agrarian History IV*, p.76.

8. T.Gerard, 'Description', p.125; T.G.Barnes, *Somerset 1625-1640*, London 1961, ch.1; D.Underdown, *Somerset in the Civil War and Interregnum*, Newton Abbot 1973, ch.1; R.G.H. Whitty, *The Court of Taunton in the 16th and 17th Centuries*, Taunton 1934, *passim*.

9. Somerset Record Office, Probate Inventories, DD/SP, 443, 1681-85.

10. C.Fiennes, *Journey*, pp.244, 14; J.Lilburne, *England's Birthright Justified*, 1645, p.17, in W.Haller, ed., *Tracts on Liberty in the Puritan Revolution*, Vol.3, pp.257, 307.

11. H.C.Darby, *Domesday Geography*, pp.164-5; Bristol University Library DM 412 pp.179-81; E.Kerridge, 'Revolts in Wiltshire against Charles I', *Wiltshire Natural History Magazine*, 68 1948, pp.66-7; Somerset Record Office (henceforth SRO), Portman MSS., DD/PM, Box 7; J. Collinson, *The History and Antiquities of the County of Somerset*, Bath 1791 3 Vols., i, 16, 20, 24, 43-4.

12. J.Billingsley, *A General View of the Agriculture of the County of Somerset*, London, 1795, p.11; M.Williams, *The Draining of Somerset Levels*, Cambridge 1970, pp.85, 96-9, 101, 112; Bodl. Lib. Aubrey MSS.13, f.51.

13. D.Underdown, *Somerset in the Civil War*, p.107.

14. N.F.Gilbert, 'A Survey of Somerset Fairs', *Somerset Archaeological and Natural History Society*, 82 1936, pp.83-159; *VCH Somerset*, ii, 308; SRO, Q/S Rolls 151/7.

15. J. de L.Mann, *The Cloth Industry in the West of England from 1640 to 1880*, Oxford 1971, pp.xv, 25.

16. G.D.Ramsay, *The Wiltshire Woollen Industry in the Sixteenth and*

Seventeenth Centuries, Oxford 1943, p.117; J.Mann, *West of England Cloth*, pp.25-6; W.G.Hoskins, *Industry, Trade and People in Exeter 1688-1800*, Exeter 1968, p.39.

17. J.Mann, *West of England Cloth*, pp.xiv-xvii, 8-14.

18. K.G.Ponting, *A History of the West of England Cloth Industry*, London 1957, pp.12-13; W.B.Stephens, *Seventeenth Century Exeter*, Exeter 1958, pp.4, 50; W.G.Hoskins, *Exeter*, p.4; J. Mann, *West of England Cloth*, p.7.

19. J.Mann, *West of England Cloth*, pp.89, 92, 95, 97; W.G.Hoskins, *Exeter*, pp.13-14, 36-7; W.B.Stephens, *Exeter*, pp.131, 135.

20. W.B.Stephens, *Exeter*, pp.92, 99; J.Mann, *West of England Cloth*, pp.15, 21; D.W.Jones, 'The "Hallage" Receipts of the London Cloth Markets, 1562-c.1720', *Economic History Review*, 25 1972, p.13.

21. W.B.Stephens, *Exeter*, pp.94, 95; E.Lipson, *The History of the Woollen and Worsted Industries*, London 1965, p.26n; W.G.Hoskins, *Exeter*, pp.33-4; J.Mann, *West of England Cloth*, pp.68, 72, 81; SRO, Q/S Rolls 164/11.

22. J.Mann, *West of England Cloth*, p.89; SRO, Q/S Rolls 190/3.

23. C.Fiennes, *Journey*, p.246; J.Mann, *West of England Cloth*, pp.96-7, 99-100, 105.

24. J.Mann, *West of England Cloth*, pp.104-7, 324.

25. See below, Chapter One. fn.31.

26. T.Gerard, '*Description*', p.12; J.Collinson, *Somerset*, ii, 26-8; W.B.Stephens, 'Cloth Exports of the English Ports 1600-1642', *Economic History Review*, 22 1969, pp.228-43; *Calendar of State Papers Domestic 1677-78 Addendum*, pp.243, 502, 631; *CSPD 1670*, p.272; C.A.F.Meekings, *Dorset Hearth Tax Assessments 1662-64*, Dorchester 1951, pp.318-19, 566-8.

27. D.Defoe, *Tour*, i, 268-9; C.Fiennes, *Journey*, p.243; *CSPD 1683-84*, p.362; *CSPD 1670*, p.49; *CSPD 1667-68*, p.255; *CSPD 1666-67*, p.312; E.Dwelly, *Somerset Hearth Taxes 1674*, Vol.2, Hampshire 1929-32, completed by T.L.Stoate, Bristol, 1976, pp.310-14, 294-5; T.L.Stoate, *The Somerset Protestation Returns and Lay Subsidy Rolls 1641-42*, Bristol 1975, pp.258-64, 246-8.

28. C.Fiennes, *Journey*, pp.241, 242; *CSPD January-July 1683*, pp.40, 45, 305; *CSPD 1683-84*, p.131; *CSPD 1668-69*, pp.113-114.

29. T.Gerard, '*Description*', pp.203-4, 72; C.Fiennes, *Journey*, p.242; *VCH Somerset*, ii, 312, 322, 415, 424-7; *CSPD 1683-84*, pp.435-6; SRO Quarter Sessions Minute Book 1676-87, ff.116, 118v, 467v; E.Dwelly, *Somerset Hearth Taxes Vol.2*, pp.282-4, 12-15, 255-56; D.Defoe, *Tour*, i, 287.

30. D.Defoe, *Tour*, i, 266; *CSPD July-September 1683*, p.251.

31. T.Gerard, '*Description*', p.55; C.Fiennes, *Journey*, pp.243-4; *CSPD 1675-*

76, p.39; *CSPD July-September 1683*, p.9; T.Stoate, *Somerset Protestation Returns*, pp.114-18; E.Dwelly, *Hearth Tax for Somerset 1664-65 Vol.1*, Hants. 1916, pp.1-16; C.M.Law, 'Some Notes on the Urban Population of England and Wales in the Eighteenth Century', *Local History*, 10 1972-3, p.25; J.Leland, *Itinerary*, i, 161; H.Darby, *New Historical Geography of England*, p.178.

32. *CSPD 1668-69*, pp.113-14; T.Stoate, *Somerset Protestation Returns*, pp.258-64, 246-8; E.Dwelly, *Somerset Hearth Tax 1664-65 Vol.1*, pp.1-16; E.Dwelly, *Somerset Hearth Tax 1674, Vol.2*, pp.310-14; SRO, Q/S MB 1676-87, ff. 9v, 20v, 62, 63, 207, 330, 387v, 455; *CSPD 1684-85*, p.214; C.Fiennes, *Journey*, p.243; SRO, Sanford MSS.55/1088, 2, 4.

33. W.B.Stephens, *Exeter*, pp.10, 29, 67, 104, 134.

34. SRO, DD/SF 149/3109; *CSPD 1681*, p.515, 15 October 1681; *CSPD January-June 1683*, p.313.

35. Public Record Office, SP 29/263/55 I-VII. See also below, pp.42-3.

36. SRO, DD/SF 250/3924; 55/1102; *Commons Journal*, xiv, p.67; PRO, PC 2/72, p.464.

37. D.Defoe, *Tour*, i, 265; SRO, Q/S MB f.402; SRO DD/SF 54/1166, 250/3924, 242/3874.

38. SRO, DD/SF 146/3074, 146/3086, 65/1336 no's. 17, 18, 65/1678 no's. 60, 63; Q/S MB, ff.401, 169, 340, 302, 387, 116, 358, 118, 476v, 27iv, 423, 192.

39. SRO, Q/S MB ff.232v-234.

CHAPTER TWO

'The Nursery of Rebellion'

Somerset enjoyed a dubious reputation among the rulers of Restoration England. 'The sink of all rebellion in the west', and 'the nursery of rebellion in these parts', were descriptions applied to the county – and to Taunton its leading town – by local royalist gentry.[1] This opinion was formed largely during the Civil War and Interregnum. Before 1640 the county's leading gentry had indeed grown disaffected toward the royal government because of the burdens imposed upon them during the decade of personal rule, but in this they were typical of the rulers of most counties in England, and there was little that was exceptional in their reluctance to assist the central government in 1640. Similarly, Puritanism in pre-Civil War Somerset was neither extreme nor of long standing. Over most of the Tudor and early Stuart period in Somerset 'what we call Puritanism was simply the established faith in the established church', observed Professor Barnes. Polarization in religion only began after 1632 with the appointment of William Pierce to the see of Bath and Wells, which covered most of the county. A strong Laudian, Pierce tried to suppress lectureships even where they were held by parish priests; he supported the church wakes and ales abominated by the stricter sort; and he began a campaign to move altars to the east end and to rail them off. These changes were distasteful to majority opinion and there was some open opposition – silenced lecturers were founding conventicles after 1635, and a parish such as Bickington steadily defied all orders to move its altar – but a separate 'puritan' opposition was only beginning to form when the situation was transformed by the crisis of 1640.[2]

For a time the county remained united, its M.P.s supporting the attack upon Strafford, proposals to reform episcopacy, and the attack upon government policies of the 1630s; but divisions appeared during 1641, and were sharpened by first-hand accounts of the November uprising in Ireland, spread by refugees arriving in Minehead. By 1642 activists were trying to force their neighbours to support King or Parliament, and when the war started Somerset was a county where the lower classes made a clear and conscious choice for Parliament.

Royalists here mostly comprised the wealthier gentry and their tenants, whereas their opponents were, to quote a contemporary observer, 'yeomen, farmers, petty freeholders, and such as use manufactures that enrich the county', led by a sprinkling of gentry and people of inferior degree, who by 'good husbandry, clothing, and other thriving arts, had gotten very great fortunes'. In the opinion of Professor Underdown, the Civil War in Somerset was 'in some respects . . . a conflict between two different kinds of society'. Parliament's supporters fought because they were convinced that the 'Commission of Array implied the resumption of the arbitrary taxation of the 1630s by a corrupt, popishly inclined Court, bent on reducing them to slavery'.[3] In their capacity to act without or even against their gentry superiors, and in their devotion to the true religion and 'Liberty and Property' as reasons for fighting, the county's lower classes in 1642 anticipated two of the more remarkable features of the 1685 rebellion.

When the war began they displayed a third parallel with the later rebellion, in the tenacity with which they supported their cause. In August 1642 a great crowd of farmers, clothmakers and other craftsmen, up to twelve thousand strong it was said, frightened off the Marquis of Hertford and his royalist cavalry from their base at Wells, and delivered Somerset to Parliament. The King's forces subsequently won control and Roundheads in the county had to keep a low profile, but in a number of sieges they showed their zeal for the cause. The tiny port of Lyme Regis, just across the county boundary of Somerset, held out against Prince Maurice and six thousand men for two months in 1644 before the royalists gave up; and Taunton endured two major sieges, with the parliamentary defenders winning on both occasions. The town first came under attack from September to December 1644, and though fortified only by 'pales and hedges and no line about the town', its defenders swore a covenant never to surrender. When hunger began to do its work, the town's commander Robert Blake (a Bridgewater man, and later an Admiral of the Commonwealth) offered to surrender all except the castle. His proposal was rejected by the royalists, led by a prominent Somerset gentleman Sir Francis Wyndham, who continued trying to starve out his neighbours until driven off by Sir William Waller's relieving army in December 1644.

For a siege of near-epic quality, however, few English towns can rival Taunton's second siege in April and May 1645, when the royalists once more attempted to take it. This time the King's forces made sustained attacks under heavy artillery fire, and succeeded in breaking into the defences. Blake and his garrison fought on, and the siege became a series of hand-to-hand fights as the attackers struggled from house to house and up the barricaded streets. When they sent spies (including a woman) into the town to set fire to it, Blake caught and hanged them. Two-thirds of Taunton was destroyed, and eventually the parliamentarians held only the centre of the town. Down to the last of their ammunition they had suffered three hundred killed and wounded, when a parliamentary army drove off the besiegers. A member of the relieving force was shocked by what he found as they rode in, 'heaps of rubbish . . . consumed houses . . . here a poor forsaken chimney, and there a little fragment of a wall'.[4] Taunton was devastated by war in a way that recalls twentieth-century experience; and it is not surprising that 11 May, the anniversary of the relief of the second siege, became a local holiday celebrated with food, drink, and sermons during the Commonwealth and well into the Restoration. And lest it be thought that any town would resist as Lyme Regis and Taunton did, simply to keep out a looting army, it should be noted that three thousand royalist troops could only hold Bridgewater for a few days in July 1645 against Parliament's army: a preliminary bombardment was sufficient to make the inhabitants clamour irresistibly for surrender.

The loyalty of Parliament's supporters in Somerset was particularly tested because the county was, for most of the war, a no-man's land, a disputed buffer zone between the King's secure base in Cornwall and Devon, and Parliament's less-than-safe grip on southern England. Control of Somerset changed hands four times in three years, each occasion dragging a new, large, and hungry army through the county. Parliament held what the clothworkers and farmers had won for it in August 1642 until summer of the following year, when its troops were swept aside by Hopton's Cornishmen at Lansdowne and Roundway Down. Royalist control lasted until July 1644 when the Earl of Essex's western offensive briefly retook the county, and resumed when the Earl surrendered his army at Lostwithiel. The royalists then flooded back, to be partially checked by the sieges of Taunton and Lyme Regis. Most of the county was held for the King, however, until 1645, when the New Model Army broke Charles' forces at Langport and relieved Taunton from its second siege. Not until 1646 were the last royalist garrisons reduced at Dunster and Farleigh.

With control swaying to and fro, the fighting in Somerset was often very bitter. Lansdowne is one of the Civil War's lesser-known battles, but it was a prolonged, bloody and indecisive affair, with so much musket-fire at close range that, as a survivor recalled, 'the air was so darkened by the smoke of the powder, that . . . there was no light to be seen but what the fire of the vollies of shot gave'. Brutalized by such engagements, the troops of both sides looted the countryside and committed atrocities against its population, as they crossed and recrossed the county in armies several thousand strong. They left in their wake 'a trail of ruined villages and gutted mansions', observes the historian of the War here. Some of the royalist forces were particularly bad: the troops of Lord Goring by 'continual butcheries, rapes, and robberies' cut their reputation deeply into the county's memory, and those of Sir Edward Dodington murdered prisoners and civilians with a brisk impartiality. Parliament's troops were normally better-paid and disciplined but they too looted on occasion, although their three visits to Wells Cathedral may have been – like that of the rebels in 1685 – partly to get lead from the roof to make bullets. Parliamentary taxes, however, fully compensated for what its troops did not loot. In February 1643 Somerset was rated to pay £1,050 per week, when the county had already found most of the three regiments of foot and one of dragoons, which Parliament had ordered the three southwestern counties to prepare on the outbreak of war.[5]

Exposed thus to the losses and costs of war, Somerset became one of the strongest centres of the neutralists, the Clubmen. They became active in 1645, particularly in central and eastern Somerset, raising forces of up to five thousand strong and making both sides treat them with care. The Somerset royalist Sir John Stawell urged the King to make concessions to win them over, and their self-confidence was so strong that Fairfax found one of their leaders 'most peremptory and insolent in his carriage'. The Clubmen of mid-Somerset generally favoured Parliament, but the attitude of the easterners, in the cloth-making county about and to the south of Frome, is less clear, although they were certainly less plainly royalist than their neighbours in western Wiltshire. What is evident is their degree of independence, political sophistication and organizing ability. Humphrey Willis of Woolavington in the mid-Somerset levels, the Clubmen's 'general' in his locality, proposed that they should elect their own officers, choose men to present their petitions to King and Parliament, and follow rules he laid down for raising men and taxing parishes to support them.[6] To some extent the strength of the Somerset Clubmen helps to explain why the Duke of Monmouth was able so quickly to raise a strong, loyal and competent army in this county a generation later.

Somerset Puritanism was no less deeply affected by the war. Probably growing in numbers, certainly gaining in self-confidence and aggressiveness, the county's Dissenters in the 1640s and 1650s created

Somerset's later reputation as one of the most factious areas of England. The Laudians were quickly dealt with, in 1641, Bishop Pierce being sent to the Tower and his son William, Archdeacon of Bath, together with several other clergy, spending varying periods of time in prison. The majority of the county supported petitions to reform but not abolish episcopacy, although occasional outbreaks of iconoclasm displayed the rising temper of the radicals. Following the war, royalist or 'deficient' clergy were purged, over a hundred losing their livings – one in five of the county's parishes – creating many scores to be settled in 1660 when the King came into his own again. With the bishops abolished and Anglicanism in the doldrums, an active minority tried to set up a full Presbyterian system in the county. By 1648 Somerset was one of only eight counties in England displaying at least in outline the reformed discipline, and not till 1653 did any other of the south-western counties follow its lead.[7]

The structure was, admittedly, incomplete. Only four of the nine proposed classes (Presbyterian regional administrations) were set up, and all were short of ministers and elders. Centred upon Taunton, Ilchester, Bath, and Wells, they were very large, comprising over a hundred villages and towns apiece, but each was served only by one or two dozen ministers. In 1650 the organizers could still lament 'the want of Church Government' in the county but with a total of over 70 ministers, and a solid core of 20 to 30 elders in each classis, they had established Presbyterianism permanently in Somerset.

They achieved this in time to be blamed for Pride's Purge, the Regicide, and the proclamation of the republic, and although the Presbyterians generally deplored these events as vigorously as the royalist clergy they were yet another score to be set against them. As 'Puritans' their reputation suffered still further when, after the war, sectarianism began to spread. A handful of Independents quickly established themselves in the county, but more numerous were the Baptists, led by the fiery army preacher Thomas Collier, a Somerset man from Westbury-sub-Mendip. As early as 1646 a Baptist was preaching in Middlezoy church, and the sect's other early congregation in Taunton was soon joined by more in Bridgewater, Chard, Wells, Stoke St. Mary, Wedmore, Hatch Beauchamp, and Somerton. Other Baptists met just across the county boundary in Luppit and Dalwood (Devon), and in Lyme Regis. By 1653 Somerset Baptists had formed an association and were publishing pamphlets. The spread of independent churches strengthened opposition to tithes, both at parish level and in Parliament, where two of Somerset's four MPs in the Barebones assembly supported plans to abolish tithes and reform the universities.[8]

By then even more shocking ideas were being spread. Late in the 1640s the county heard discussions of the mortality of the soul, and the attractive antinomian suggestion that adultery and drunkenness were not sins but aids to true religion. A mason in Somerset strengthened the improper proposal he put to a lady friend by arguing that it entailed no sin, for there existed no heaven and no hell; and another man of the county referred to the Lord's Supper merely as an invitation to consume 'three pints of wine and a peny loaf'. The first Quakers appeared in Somerset in 1655, although they had earlier been active in Bristol; and the following year James Nayler's procession through Glastonbury and Wells *en route* for Bristol, where he made his notorious Christ-like entry, provided ample fare for scandalized debate. In that same year, 1656, a Friends' Meeting was established at Street, and by 1661 there were 209 Quakers in Somerset prisons.[9] With church doctrine, ritual, and organization so comprehensively under attack from such a variety of sects and congregations, Somerset's natural rulers were well instructed during the 1650s in the dangers of tolerating Puritanism. When opportunity offered after 1660 they would attempt, brutally if spasmodically, to eliminate this threat to good order.

Before then, however, they had to digest further affronts. The end of the Civil War brought only an uneasy peace. The wealthier gentry were mostly excluded from government of the county, many because of their royalism, others because they lacked the ruthlessness to implement the financial and religious policies of England's new rulers. They were replaced by men below them in social rank, men sometimes of a 'striking obscurity' whose activities before 1640 would have been limited to their parish. Possessing few or no links with the county families these new rulers did not hesitate to tax, fine, or confiscate. When the county militia was reorganized in 1650 few men of the substantial families were even invited to join. Excluded from power and heavily taxed, fines and sequestrations increased the county families' alienation from the new regime, and the toleration afforded to puritans and sectaries completed it.

The fines and sequestrations imposed on many Somerset royalists were heavy, and were politically important because the victims looked for revenge after 1660 and so perpetuated Civil War divisions into the next generation. Sir Edward Wyndham, commanding the first royalist army to besiege Taunton, claimed to have lost £50,000 by the plunder of his estate. Sir William Portman died a prisoner, having paid £5,000 in fines and owing a further £30,000. Lord Paulet paid £16,000, while lesser royalists such as the Spekes, the Bassets and the Helyers paid around £2,000 each. Humphrey Walrond's fines were so great that he emigrated to Bermuda, while Sir John Stawell paid an even heavier price for his loyalty. Four years' imprisonment and the eventual sale of his estate, worth £64,000, followed his stubborn refusal to cooperate with the authorities. A large part of these fines and sequestrations was paid to local parliamentarian victims, and long-lived county feuds resulted. Richard Bovett of Taunton and another Roundhead, John Barker, both benefited from Stawell's disaster; and Taunton was partially rebuilt with £7,000 taken from impositions on Stawell and Portman. Already unpopular because the town had humiliated them in two sieges, detested when its inhabitants greeted the regicide by meeting to offer 'lives and fortunes' in the cause of Parliament, Taunton had become the object of a very personal animosity among the royalist gentry by the Restoration.[10]

Charles II returned to England in 1660 fully aware that to forgive and forget the events of the previous twenty years was the only statesmanlike policy. Unhappily, this was asking too much of his followers, who found that the Restoration restored little of what they had sacrificed over two decades, and in Parliament and in the provinces they looked for revenge. Any individual or group rebellious in the past, and who now stepped far enough out of line to be recognized, might receive severe treatment. Somerset was no different from anywhere else, save that parliamentarians and Puritans here had been distinguished by an extra edge of zeal during their days of power, and there remained some zealous enough to speak up after the Restoration. Not surprisingly, those in Taunton were the first to suffer.

For a time it seemed that the town might escape severe punishment. Initially, with other factious centres such as Northampton and Coventry, Leicester and Gloucester, it suffered only the ceremonial destruction of its scant remaining sections of town wall. But some inhabitants lacked discretion, and in May 1661 they openly celebrated the anniversary of their relief from the royalist army. The High Sheriff complained to the government and Quo Warranto proceedings were begun to call in the town's Charter, but the Corporation Act offered a simpler procedure because a majority of the aldermen would not take the sacrament, and were thus disqualified for office under the Act. No replacements were sworn, and deprived of a quorum the corporation's powers lapsed. For the following sixteen years Taunton had no governing body. In 1669 some of the gentry felt the punishment had lasted long enough, and petitioned for a new charter. They were unsuccessful, but the resulting correspondence shows how the town was suffering.[11] Its cloth trade was unregulated and unprotected, its poor unchecked and unrelieved. One constable had to maintain law and order among the four thousand population; but to charge anyone he had to take the offender at least 2 miles to the nearest Justice, and any offender to be held in custody had to be transported a further 15 to 20 miles. In 1669 the petitioners believed that four resident JPs with a commensurate number of constables, was needed to preserve the peace. With the largest weekly market in the west outside Exeter and Bristol the town had no authority to settle disputes, regulate weights and measures, and attend to the many needs of buyers and sellers.

Some of the opposition to a charter in 1669 came from those with vested interests to protect, like the Bishop of Winchester who collected market tolls; but most came from the neighbouring gentry who, as the Secretary of State observed, simply wished to keep the town charterless. So considerable were the problems which built up after the failure of 1669 that the next initiative for a charter, in 1675, came from Peter Mews, the recently-appointed Bishop of Bath and Wells. An uncompromising royalist, wounded at Naseby and still possessed of a martial air, Mews saw the need for a charter simply to keep law and order: unless one were granted 'I know of no way to reduce that place to order', he wrote. With his backing progress was made this time, but opponents delayed by taking issue with every clause. The (normal) proposal to make the Recorder and Town Clerk dismissable by the Crown impugned, it was said, the loyalty of the gentlemen who would hold these offices. The town needed many new creations of freemen to stimulate its economy, and the cheapest and quickest technical method to create them was by the Sign Manual: the opposition fought to make them created by the Privy Seal, so expensive that the petitioners' intention was lost. Not until July 1677 was the Charter passed, and Taunton was ruled by a mayor, corporation, and three (usually absentee) JPs.[12] By then it was rather too late: the townsfolks' parliamentary traditions had been revived by their experience of freedom, economic hardship, and cavalier spite. Nowhere is this seen more clearly than in the history of the 11 May celebration.

Institutionalized during the 1650s and celebrated by sermons and feasting, the anniversary had by the Restoration become the town's unofficial holiday. The passage of time added details, until festivities in some years extended over two or three days. By 1670 celebrations began at dawn with a drum beating the reveille. Shops stayed closed, and in Nonconformist meeting houses such veteran local preachers as George

Newton lectured from first-hand knowledge on the heroics of the siege, and the barbarities of the King's troops. Solemnity was then cast aside as the population assembled about bonfires in the market place to eat and drink. As the day progressed and the beer was drunk they painted their faces, threw hats in the air, and fired off pistols. Whooping and shouting men and women danced around the flames, to the doggerel chant:

> Rejoice you dogs, tis the eleventh of May,
> The day the cavaliers ran away.

Proceedings continued into the night, and sometimes reached riot proportions. Even when the authorities tried to suppress it – as the Bishop and the Deputy-Lieutenants did in 1676 when the town's Charter was at a critical point – the festival was simply driven indoors. Its popularity spread, and there is evidence of its celebration in rural Somerset as well as in Taunton.[13]

Remarkable as this local anniversary was, it should not be accepted at face value as evidence of Taunton's unquenched parliamentarianism or even republicanism. Ceremonies begun for one set of reasons often continue for quite different ones; and the closeness of the date to Mayday (the celebration of which had probably ceased in this Puritan town) suggests that an alternative holiday in early summer was generally welcomed. Most of those who celebrated in the 1670s were too young to remember the siege, and undoubtedly enjoyed the day as an opportunity for some charivari. But the festival cannot wholly be explained away. So far, no other royalist defeat is known to have been celebrated locally after the Restoration; and few in Taunton could have been unaware of what was being commemorated, particularly when nonconformist ministers catechized their audience on it every year. Inhabitants commonly referred to the date as 'their rebellion'; and an informant in 1671 hit on the celebration's real significance when he wrote that 'this solemnity and rejoicing being kept by men, women and children throughout the whole town . . . does also entail [it] to their posterity'.[14] Commemoration of the heroic siege contributed significantly to Taunton's general anti-cavalier stance; efforts at suppression only advertised it the more; and the town's ill-treatment over its charter gave even substantial citizens a grievance to be aired in this manner.

Confronted by disobedience on this scale, Somerset Deputy-Lieutenants and JPs watched town and county closely for signs that any had stepped from defiance to disloyalty and conspiracy. 'Evidence' was inevitably found, and in 1662, 1664, 1665, 1666, and 1672 frantic letters were sent to the Privy Council about supposed republican plots, hatched usually in Taunton, although Bristol, Ilchester, Glastonbury and Westbury also received mention. The alarms could be prompted by as little as a refusal to pay 'all rates and taxes' in Taunton, but they usually followed reports of ex-Cromwellian officers meeting together. Particularly notorious was one Richard Bovett who had risen high and fast as the regime's man of all work in the county during the 1650s. Sometime JP, Colonel in the militia, speculator in episcopal lands, and beneficiary from fines on royalists, Bovett figured in almost every 'conspiracy'; though he was too old in 1685 to ride out with the Duke, seven Bovetts took part in the rising, including three from Taunton.[15]

Although it is most unlikely that anything serious lay at the bottom of these alarms, their frequency indicates nervousness among the ruling gentry, and resentment among 'ex-Cromwellians' now relegated to obscurity by the turn of fortune's wheel. The same observation can be made on the flow of disgruntled, quasi-seditious, talk preserved in Quarter Sessions informations. Never sufficiently organized or serious to merit the term conspiracy, sometimes vengeful and sometimes boastful, now expressing a startling contempt for the King's government, now simply hoping for stirring times once more, these depositions suggest how attitudes formed during the Civil War and Interregnum lived on after 1660. The man who sang 'Essex's March' in a Taunton alehouse and then 'fell on a vindication of Oliver Cromwell', made as little secret of his sympathies as the fellow townsman who described his vicar's surplice as 'the smock of Babylon', or the draper who posted up 'seditious papers' in public. The confidence of these men in their cause sometimes grew into boastfulness, like the Castle Cary man who (again in drink) described at some length how he had broken the King's laws and would do so again, or the republican who told a royal official that he could still raise three hundred armed men whenever he wished. While Charles II's coronation was being celebrated, a Glastonbury man predicted that the King would lose his head if he took the Crown and silenced sceptics by claiming private knowledge: 'I do know more than you.' Even a relatively harmless nostalgia for the old days and hopes that 'the times would turn', could be laced by specific and threatening allusions to horsemen and swords, or by hopes that national defeat by the Dutch would restore the old cause.[16]

More common than plain-speaking and boasting, however, were expressions of hatred and revenge. A Wincanton man said in November

1661 that 'it had been no matter if all the cavaliers had been hanged', in Langport a man displayed the brace of pistols he was saving for the local royalist Sir John Stawell, and a dyer from Wrington tartly observed that although 'the Cavaliers did vapor now' their rule would come to a sudden end. John Wood of Barnwell regularly predicted that the country would never do well until it had beheaded another King, and when his neighbours caused trouble over this he swore to revenge himself by destroying their wheat. Most remarkable among these men for whom the Civil War was still being fought was John Diches a labourer from Hatch Beauchamp. He attacked a drinker in a tavern because the other 'was in the King's army and spoke against ye Anabaptists, but he was in ye Parliament Army, and upon yt Account he strooke this Informant'. Somerset JPs were threatened and mocked, particularly when they attacked conventicles, and a trooper of the militia unwise enough to bandy words with a Taunton crowd on an 11 May celebration was disarmed and beaten up when he tried to shoot his way out.[17]

Vilification of the government extended as far as the person of the King himself. An old Cromwellian soldier in Stogumber discussed the royal family in terms of 'the old rogue and the young rogue', and at Batcombe Christopher Swallow called the King a liar because he had broken the promises made at Breda. More primitive notions of a king's duties appeared at Clevedon when a servant reported his master for saying that the King was appointed 'to keep the land honest, but was dishonest himself, for he had three score [sic] bastards'. Others refused to drink the King's health, ridiculed royal warrants, and called Charles a rogue. Most of the chorus of complaint dwelt on political and religious issues, but in some cases an economic element can be seen. When hearth tax officials distrained her neighbour's goods a woman of Hinton St. George upbraided them sharply: the King's officers would never give up levying taxes until the King's head was cut off as his father's had been, 'for it was . . . levieing hard taxes on ye People which made him lose his head'. Equally plain words were heard by the Bishop of Bath and Wells in 1677, who was told by William Vowles that he did not care if the French conquered England for he could not be worse off than he was now, and he would give the remaining years of his life to see the country invaded.[18]

The significance of these depositions requires some consideration. It is not my argument that Restoration Somerset was the most discontented county of England, nor Taunton the most rebellious town. The Privy Council encountered persistent 'faction' in centres as diverse as Chichester, Newbury, and Sudbury in Suffolk; and while Somerset figured prominently in every 'republican conspiracy' uncovered in the south-west in the 1660s and 1670s, at least as many other 'plots' were discovered in London, and in the North.[19] But if they were not necessarily the most dangerous, Somerset and Taunton were most certainly among the select group of counties and towns from which the government could expect trouble.

A similar disclaimer is necessary concerning the meaning of the complaints recorded in Quarter Sessions depositions. Individual statements made by individual men they scarcely prove the mass unpopularity of the restored monarchy, and for every critic of the government there was plainly a loyal man ready to inform on him. But the talk should not be underestimated, for all that it was sometimes lubricated by ale. It was more specific, and more sharp, than the mere grumbles about the government found at all times and places. Two decades of experiment in government had left the speakers with little respect for authority, and scant reverence for the King. Such men carried a sceptical and iconoclastic attitude over from the Interregnum into the England of Charles II. Always a small minority their opinions were not normally important, except in time of crisis when the majority began to feel that the government was not fulfilling its duty. Then the dissidents would have a more attentive audience. The small farmers and clothworkers of Somerset had made a deliberate choice for Parliament in 1642, and when the government of Charles II in turn became unpopular they would not lack advice on how to think and act.

More than factious towns, republican conspiracies, and anti-monarchical talk, however, the government was concerned with the problem of the Dissenters. Unable to believe that such a powerful group, which had convulsed England for two decades, would quietly accept total defeat the King's advisers persistently believed Nonconformity to be both stronger and more aggressive than was the case. And as one of the more puritan counties, Somerset once more came under hostile scrutiny. Three major sources confirm the strength of dissent here: the episcopal enquiry into nonconformity in 1669; the applications for licenses to meet and preach following the King's Declaration of Indulgence in 1672; and Bishop Compton's census of 1676. The last is the least informative for Somerset, recording a total of 5,856 Nonconformists (and 176 Catholics) for the county, but affording no parish-by-parish details as do the other two sources. In the 1669 enquiry Somerset emerged as the county with the largest number of conventicles – 155 spread over ninety-nine parishes – but this eminence is misleading because several important areas, such as London, are missing from the returns. This 1669 enquiry is, however, useful for the numbers attending conventicles. The figures given range from the reasonably precise 18 listed for Nether Stowey and 20 for Stoke St. Gregory; to approximations of 50, 60 and 80; and on to rounded guesses of 100, 300, and the '500 at least' for Beckington. But even when the numbers are reduced by two-thirds or three-quarters to take account of exaggeration, there remain many parishes where over a hundred Dissenters gathered: Bathford and Dunkerton in the north-eastern corner about Bath; Beckington, Whatley, Batcombe and Yeovil on the eastern margin; Glastonbury on the edge of the moors; several towns and villages about Taunton such as North Curry, Wellington, West Monckton, Kingsbury Episcopi, and Taunton itself; and finally Chard where the number was 'uncertaine, but alwaies very great, sometimes 200, 300, 400, 500, 600, oftentimes 700'. Though the clergy making these returns often exaggerated, their estimates were sometimes based on close observation, like the 300 in Whatley who met 'Att the house of Richard Agerton on Sundays, and att Andrew Shore's on Thursdays'.[20]

The overall total of attenders given for Somerset conventicles in 1669 was some 11,000, double the number listed in 1676. The discrepancy is possibly explained by the more severe criteria of the later survey, Compton asking for those who 'either obstinately refuse or wholly absent themselves', from the Anglican communion; in other words, the hard core of dissent. Two further points emerge from the 1669 figures. Many Somerset parishes contained a multiplicity of meeting places – 11 in West Monckton for 400 conventiclers, 9 in Bridgewater for 260, 6 each in Pitminster, Dulverton and Stogumber for between 100 and 200, 5 for North Petherton's 90 dissenters. Secondly, most of the 30 ministers named served a number of parishes. John Galpin of Ashpriors preached in no less than 15, John Baker of Curry Mallett in 9, three ministers visited 7 apiece, and six served 5 apiece.[21] The dedicated itinerant life of nonconformist clergy is clearly evident in these figures.

The fullest picture of Somerset Nonconformity is to be derived from the 1672-73 license applications for preachers and meeting places. These confirm the county's importance as a centre of Puritanism. With 82 licences issued to individual preachers Somerset ranks third after London and Devon (105 each); and with 169 licenses issued for meeting places it is in this respect second only to Devon with 189. The overwhelming strength of Presbyterianism compared to other dissenting groups is also evident, 120 of the 169 meeting-place licenses being accounted for by this one group. Presbyterians met in exactly one

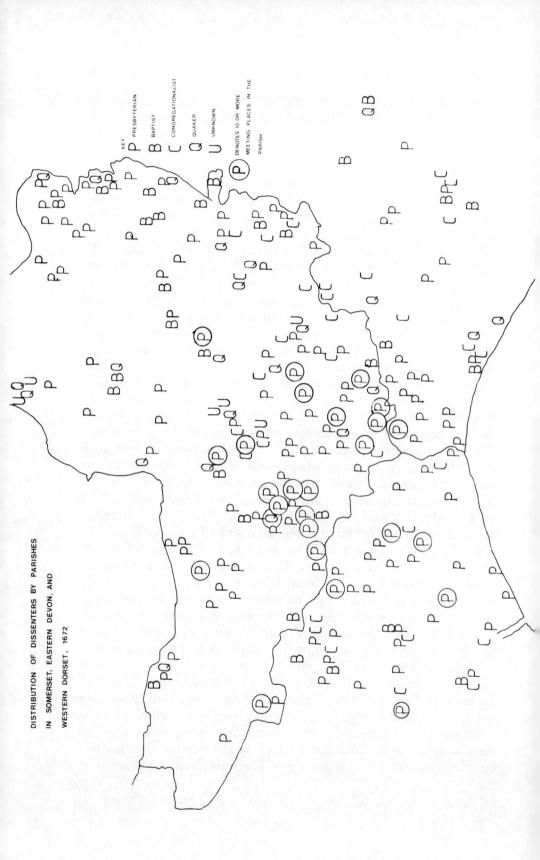

DISTRIBUTION OF DISSENTERS BY PARISHES
IN SOMERSET, EASTERN DEVON, AND
WESTERN DORSET, 1672

KEY

P   PRESBYTERIAN

B   BAPTIST

C   CONGREGATIONALIST

Q   QUAKER

U   UNKNOWN

Ⓟ   DENOTES 10 OR MORE
      MEETING PLACES IN THE
      PARISH

quarter of the county's 480 parishes. The other denominations were all much smaller, and of approximately equal size: Baptists 19 meeting-place licenses; Congregationalists 12; with 19 unspecified. (G. Lyon Turner in his monumental examination of the *Original Records of Nonconformity* concluded incorrectly that the latter represented Quakers: in the accompanying map, a recently-published list of Friends' meetings in Somerset in 1668-1672 has been used instead, and the six licence applications which do not tally with Quaker records have been listed as unspecified.)[22]

Nonconformity as a whole was not evenly spread over the county, as the map shows. There existed a marked concentration of dissenting parishes in the north-east about Bath, with another in eastern Somerset about Frome and Brewham, but the major focus was within a quadrilateral in the south of the county extending from Wellington to Bridgewater over to Yeovil and across to Chard, with a tongue extending into the Vale of Taunton Deane and toward the Bristol Channel. There were few Nonconformist parishes in the west, and the central and northern areas of Somerset were also relatively empty. This geography of dissent is very similar to that described by Calamy for the 1662 evictions, his ejected ministers coming mostly from the north-east, the east, and the south of the county. Presbyterianism, however, was not dominant in every area of the county. Strong in the north-east with only a few Quakers to dispute their sway, they were replaced about Frome by Baptists, and in the south-east about Yeovil by Congregationalists and Quakers. In terms of numbers, however, the core of Somerset dissent lay between Bridgewater, Taunton and Chard, and here Presbyterianism was dominant with virtually no Baptist or Congregational meetings and very few Quakers. In some towns Presbyterians were remarkably active – there were 25 applications for minister and meeting-place licenses in Taunton, 21 at Bridgewater, 15 at Chard and 12 in or near by Ilminster; but rural parishes also had several ministers and meeting places – 18 at West Monckton, 14 at Winsham, and seven more parishes made applications for at least 11. (To distinguish the important parishes in the map, those with nine or more applications are ringed).

It is also evident that two different denominations very rarely coexisted in the same parish. Either a region was wholly dominated by one faith (as the Presbyterians monopolized the southern and north-eastern areas); or where several denominations are found in one region their members occupy separate parishes, as in the east and south-east. Only in the larger towns are they found together. This pattern probably reflects the later arrival of Baptists, Congregationalists, and Quakers compared to Presbyterians, who settled in areas unoccupied by their stronger cousins. Finally, the geography of dissent in Somerset broadly reflects population density, with few nonconformist congregations in the thinly-settled west and north, but ministers and meeting-places thriving in the heavily-populated arc from Taunton south-eastwards to Martock and Wincanton and then northwards to Frome and Bath. Preachers went where they could achieve most, to the larger market towns and more thickly populated rural parishes. In so doing they also brought the Word to the county's cloth-workers, who accounted for much of the population of the south and east. Indeed population, puritanism, and cloth-making were intimately mixed in these two regions of Somerset, helping to create that lower-class independence of mind noted by Professor Underdown during the Civil War, and which would provide the Protestant Duke with many of his volunteers a generation later.

Nonconformity was, therefore, well established in Restoration Somerset. It was not, however, as hostile to monarchy and the social order as was commonly assumed. Presbyterians made up three-quarters of its strength, and after the Civil War their political and social attitudes were virtually undistinguishable from those of the Anglican clergy. Somerset Presbyterian ministers deplored the regicide, and two of their most distinguished members were imprisoned by the Commonwealth; Clement Walker in the Tower, and William Prynne nearer home, in Dunster Castle. Presbyterians were still further estranged from the Cromwellian regime in the 1650s, when the Protector took no action to check the spread of sectarianism and even encouraged the heretics. As Calamy shows, many Somerset Presbyterians and other Dissenters considered very seriously the arguments for conforming in 1662, and most would willingly have been comprehended had Parliament and the Anglican church not been determined to drive them out. Even when persecution began the nonconformist position was clear: they might take reasonable precautions to safeguard liberty and property, but there was to be no resistance. Fines and imprisonment were a cross sent by God to try His people.[23] In the circumstances it was something of a perverse triumph for the government to arouse opposition in such material: by treating all dissenters as rebels, some were eventually made into such.

The process began with the 1662 ejections, Calamy recording eighty-three Somerset clergy who suffered eviction rather than conform. Nearly one in every six of the county's parishes was affected, and every town of consequence saw a minister purged. In Taunton three were dispossessed. One was the local pillar of Dissent, George Newton, presented to the living of St. Mary Magdalen by Sir William Portman thirty years before. He had delivered the first 'anniversary sermon' in the town in 1646, denouncing the royalists as those 'implacable and desperate enemies of God and of His people', and he continued preaching in the town after 1662. His assistant Joseph Allen died in 1668 at the early age of thirty-five, worn out perhaps by preaching – he regularly delivered from seven to fourteen sermons a week in and about Taunton. Another vigorous preacher was James Stevenson of Martock. Born in Scotland, he had held an Irish living before removing to Somerset after the uprising of November 1641, and in Martock 'he would often pray to be delivered from the blood-thirsty Papists, of whose cruelties he had seen so many affecting examples'. A veteran too was Timothy Batt, a native of Somerset who had accompanied the Earl of Essex on his disastrous expedition to the west in 1643. Presented to Ilminster and then to Creech St. Michael, like his fellows he remained an active minister after deprivation. At least two of the ministers ejected in Somerset had lived in New England for several years before returning, and almost all of them were men of character and learning who took the course of separation only after much debate; but perhaps the most formidable was Dr. Cornelius Burgess. Appointed a chaplain to Charles I in 1627, Burgess had joined the opposition to become one of the Long Parliament's favourite fast-day preachers, and a leading member of the Westminster Assembly of Divines. In 1662 he lost not only his well-paid living in Wells but also his heavy investment in episcopal lands, and he spent his last years 'reduced to straits'.[24]

In some ways the ejection and subsequent persecution strengthened dissent. Once the tie between a minister and his particular parish was cut, once ministers were driven to settle in new areas where they were less well known, a new type of itinerant missionary preacher appeared, serving dissenters in a number of parishes often some distance apart. The spread of nonconformity throughout the county was thus sustained and strengthened. The loss of income from tithes also forced preachers to adopt a second profession, and teaching was an obvious choice. Nonconformist schools sprang up in Langport, Milborne Port, North Cadbury, Ilminster, and Glastonbury; and in the last town Samuel Winney's reputation as a grammarian was such that a Justice asked those wishing to prosecute him if they wanted their children to 'grow up dunces'. In Downhead Matthew Warren undertook an even more essential task, training youths to supply the next generation of preachers. Above all, persecution re-kindled the nonconformist belief that they were the Lord's chosen people and fired the preaching that held dissenters together, so that sermons delivered in cellars and barns, in forests, or through prison bars to a crowd outside, became part of the Puritan tradition in Somerset.[25]

It soon became clear that a heightened morale would be needed for survival as the Restoration government, after first striking at puritan ministers, went on to attack dissenting magistrates, school-teachers, and rank and file in Corporation, Five Mile and Conventicle Acts. The legislation, severe in itself, was enforced by Justices who in many cases had no intention of proceeding fairly: the laws existed to destroy Nonconformity, and that spirit should govern their implementation. Conventiclers could be arrested with needless brutality, and their meeting houses pillaged; they could be held for months in overcrowded prisons before trial; they could face charges of riot or sedition which were patently nonsensical; in court they could be deprived of the right to speak, or to point out technical flaws in proceedings; the Bench could stoop to intimidation; and fines could be enforced by such reckless distraint of goods that whole families were ruined. Unjust laws, brutally implemented, created a bitterness in some Dissenters which over-rode the counsels of caution they received from pulpit and pamphlets. Quarter Sessions indictments show that Somerset JPs launched drives against Nonconformists in their area in 1662-63, 1670, 1673-74, and after the Exclusion Crisis. On each occasion they provoked abuse, threats, and occasionally violence.

Sometimes the reaction was startling. Anglican clergy were openly called villains, their vestments ridiculed, their liturgy 'more fitt to read to pigges than to Christians', their congregations composed of 'whores and rogues'. When disturbed some conventiclers simply thrust the intruders out of doors, saying that their warrants were illegal; but others followed more violent courses, threatening to tear their persecutors in pieces or dash out their brains, consigning them to hellfire, and offering to speed their journey with knife, pistol, or club. An officer of the Bishop of Bath and Wells rash enough to approach a Wells meeting with only one attendant was seized, disarmed, and beaten up. When the militia were brought in to provide escorts the conventiclers quickly took on a quasi-military air, employing sentries and passwords, and posting horsemen on roads leading to the meeting. When all else failed they packed 'foreigners' armed with stones about the local members of the congregation, so that the latter could not be recognized and arrested.[26]

The centre of resistance was, predictably, Taunton. Referring to

Dissenters here, Peter Mews the Bishop of Bath and Wells, a man not given to panic, wrote in 1677 that 'The Peace not only of this Country [County] but all ye West of England depends upon ye dissolving of ye seditious Conventicle'. The secular arm agreed: in 1665 two Somerset Deputy-Lieutenants had been deeply alarmed at the activities of ejected ministers – numbering no fewer than eleven – in and about Taunton. By 1672 the town's Presbyterians were sufficiently bold to request licences for meeting places not only in private houses, but also in the Town Hall and the Church House (the latter both denied). In the same year they built St. Paul's, a large brick meeting house fitted out with pews and galleries, nominating seven Taunton merchants as its trustees. Among them was John Hucker, a substantial serge-maker, builder, and general merchant, who acquired some local notoriety by purchasing the ruins of Athelny Abbey in 1674 for quarry stone. He was to be an important follower of Monmouth in 1685. Backed by men such as Hucker, Taunton nonconformity was too strong for the local clergy to tackle, led as they were by William Pierce, eldest son of Bishop Pierce. William had been Archdeacon of Taunton since 1643, and he held the position until his death in 1682. During the Interregnum he had been reduced to a day-labourer, threshing corn and carrying cheese to market, living off bread and salt, and lacking money even to buy ale. After the Restoration he had neither the nerve nor the authority to assert himself against parishioners; he quarrelled with his bishop and was suspended by him between 1670 and 1672; and by the time of Peter Mews' elevation to the see Pierce was an aging man in his sixties.[27] With no local check upon them the boldness of Taunton Puritans had increased, and Bishop Mews undertook a personal campaign against them.

It proved a long business. When he sent officers to make arrests, a cordon of sentries invariably gave the alarm and doors were barred. In May 1676 Mews was able to drive the anniversary celebrations indoors by drafting constables from Bridgewater, but the Presbyterians retaliated by throwing libels into the houses of the newly-formed town corporation. Late in 1677 the mayor tried without success over three successive Sundays to enter St. Pauls. On the fourth attempt Mews took a hand, and with two Deputy Lieutenants and some militia broke into the building to find the congregation singing Psalms which, they said, was not against the law. As the officers tried to make arrests the conventiclers surged in a body out of a side door, brushing aside the militia and knocking down Colonel Berkeley who stood in their way. Members of the corporation were then threatened with violence in the street and George Newton, the senior minister, defiantly printed and distributed one of his 11th of May sermons, 'a most barbarous and infamous Libel upon ye King's army'.[28] Skirmishing continued, but the Taunton conventiclers were not subdued until 1683.

Somerset was thus a county where nonconformity was particularly strong in the Restoration period, stronger numerically than almost anywhere else in England. It appeared the more threatening, too, because on one side of the county lay Devon, with another very large concentration of Dissenters; and on the other flank was Bristol, England's second port and city, again with more than its quota of prominent and active Nonconformists. Somerset (and Devon and neighbouring Wiltshire) was also a centre of turbulent semi-employed cloth workers; and when one includes the county's independent-minded husbandmen, yeomen and lesser gentry, and its frankly parliamentarian sympathies during and to some extent after the Civil War, it becomes clear why magistrates here were alert for republican conspiracies, pounced on loose talk in taverns and alehouses, and took Dissenters for their inveterate enemies. Yet to a considerable extent they created the opposition they encountered, by their treatment of ex-parliamentarians in centres such as Taunton, and Dissenters throughout the county. To a considerable extent they also misconceived the strength of this opposition, failing to appreciate how isolated it normally was from majority opinion. Only during crises did the two tend to coincide; and it was at these times that secular and religious dissent became politically important, because then the minority provided the arguments, sometimes the leadership, and above all the outspoken example of opposition, which could seriously question government policy. One such crisis was the Popish Plot.

Although Somerset contained very few Catholics – less than two hundred according to the 1676 census – this in no way limited the depth of anti-Catholic feeling in the county, which here as elsewhere in Tudor and Stuart England depended only to a small extent upon the presence of local recusant families to stimulate it. The uncertain drift of national policy in relation to Louis XIV's France, and the more certain growth of Popery in court circles about the Duke of York, led to uneasiness in Somerset as elsewhere; and Bishop Mews' campaign against Protestant dissenters in the 1670s enjoyed less magistrate support than might have been expected partly because of this uneasiness. As early as 1667 it was reported from eastern Somerset that 'the gentry, as well as the ignorant and ill-affected, help to beget the jealousy [here] of Popery'; and following the Duke of York's public adherence to Catholicism in 1673 more and more Protestants recalled the original point of the recusancy laws – to suppress Catholic rather than Protestant dissent. In 1677 Mews found that the King's policies were being represented in his diocese 'as ill . . . as can possibly be', and referring to the supposed growth in the influence of Popery he wished that measures could be taken to rid his flock of 'those causeless fears that govern them concerning religion'. A wave of alarms during the dry summer of the previous year, that arsonists were setting fire to towns throughout the county, illustrates the unsettled mood of the area just before the Popish Plot.[29]

Though the horror and fear felt by seventeenth century Englishmen for Catholicism is a cliché of historical writing, its brutal strength is seldom fully communicated to readers of the present day. But without a feeling for the depth of these emotions the Popish Plot cannot be understood; and without a grasp of how widely they were felt it is easy to assume that no-Popery meant more to Puritans than to Anglicans, and so misread the seriousness of the crisis. Sir Edward Phelips was a prominent Somerset gentleman living at Montacute House near Ilminster. He was an impeccable royalist of impeccable lineage. His father had fought for Charles I, and assisted Charles II to escape in 1652. The son was a firm Anglican and renowned as a hammer of Dissenters, a staunchly royalist MP who in 1681 organized loyalist addresses to the Crown. This pillar of Church and King was also rabidly anti-Catholic. Among his documents on the Popish Plot is a twenty-five-point list, copied out in his own hand, of 'The variety of Papist torments that have been practised upon the bodies of protestants'. Beginning with children cast out for dogs to devour, pregnant women hung up with their bellies slit open and foetuses protruding and babies put to suckle their dead mothers, it proceeds through boiling to death, burial alive, disembowelling, hanging on tenter-hooks and a variety of other revolting homicides, meticulously recorded, to a list of the vile deeds of Popes and God's judgement upon them, eventually arriving at 1679 and an up-to-the-minute account of the Popish Plot. Phelips was one of the most respected and substantial royalist and Anglican gentlemen of Somerset. But his horror of Popery was such that as an MP he would not vote for the Duke of York, and abstained when the first Exclusion Bill was moved in 1679.[30] He is a salutary reminder not only of the remarkable depth of anti-Catholic feeling, but also of its very widespread character – the Popish Plot, Exclusion, and the rebellion against James II in 1685 were not simply or primarily motivated by 'Puritan' feeling, any more than the revolution of 1688 was.

The Popish Plot initiated a long political crisis which had barely reached a conclusion by the death of Charles II. Successive stages of this crisis drew substantial numbers of the Somerset population into national politics for the first time since the Civil War, so that when Monmouth landed in 1685 he could appeal to a people more than usually receptive to the old cry of religion and liberty. Initial reaction in the county to news of the Popish Plot was one of fear bordering on panic. One letter-writer lamented the lack of precautions taken locally: no searches of Catholics' houses, no county-wide watch set, no checks made on suspicious persons such as the 'man in woman's apparel' seen near Milverton. Another wrote fervently that they were 'hoping and praying for a full discovery of the accursed plot', and for effective measures against Papists and especially church Papists, that hidden fifth column of treason. In December 1678 the county was swept by a report that forty thousand French troops had landed at Weymouth, and those who reached for arms to defend themselves found that the militia did not have weapons available for one man in twenty. April 1679 saw further alarms, coming this time from Lyme Regis, and prompted by French military preparations at the port of Morlaix across the Channel.[31]

As investigation of the Popish Plot developed, during 1679, into the Exclusion Crisis Somerset achieved notoriety as a Whig bastion. Obvious causes were its past history, and the continuing independence of mind of much of its population, but the lead given by a number of local landowners was important too. Foremost among them was the Earl of Shaftesbury, with his country residence at Wimborne St Giles across the county boundary in Dorset. Though he owned no land in Somerset his influence here was considerable. During elections to the first Exclusion Parliament in February 1679 the Earl wrote to support the candidate he favoured at Bridgewater, urged his friends here to work against Stawell, the court candidate, and 'in obedience to Lord Shaftesbury's will' a would-be Whig candidate stood down to prevent vote-splitting. He encouraged an unsuccessful Whig to petition against the result at Milborne Port in south-eastern Somerset, and in Taunton John Hucker, prosperous serge-maker and a rebel in 1685, made interest at the Earl's behest.[32]

Other influential Whigs included Thomas Thynne of Longleat, just over the Wiltshire boundary and close to the restless area about Frome. An active Whig, close friend of Monmouth, and one of the richest commoners in England, 'Tom of Ten Thousand', promoted and in 1680 presented to Charles II the massive Wiltshire petition calling for Parliament to meet. Another notable who lived just outside Somerset was Edmund Prideaux of Ford Abbey Thorncombe, close by Lyme Regis. Son of Oliver Cromwell's Attorney-General, Prideaux was an active Exclusionist, a Dissenter, and MP for Taunton in the second and third Exclusion Parliaments. In 1685 he was accused (falsely) of joining the rebellion, though he may have given it support, and escaped only by giving Jeffreys a large bribe. Two important Devon Whigs active in Somerset were Sir William Courtenay and Sir Walter Yonge, both Dissenters and Exclusionists. In Somerset itself half of the county's gentry families had supported Parliament during the Civil War, and although all had made their peace in 1660, by 1670 several had once more returned to opposition. Sir Francis Rolle was a Nonconformist who entered Parliament in 1669 after a by-election at Bridgewater, supported by many Dissenters whose votes should have been disallowed. Near Ilchester lived William Strode, Whig, Dissenter, and Member for the town, son of one of Somerset's parliamentary leaders during the Civil War, and one who spent money lavishly during Exclusionist elections.

The doyen, however, if not the recognized leader, of opposition to the court in Somerset was George Speke of Whitelackington, near Ilminster. An old cavalier, fined £3,000 and imprisoned for his part in the Civil War, suspected of royalist conspiracy in 1655, Speke became a JP at the Restoration, and was sheriff of Somerset in 1661-62. He owed his downfall to his wife, a strong-minded Dissenter, whom Bishop Mews picturesquely described as the most dangerous woman in the west. She was arrested at a conventicle in 1663, and when Speke tried to protect her he found to his fury that his past record counted for nothing. Speke's violent temper did the rest, and by 1678, he was on very bad terms with the Anglican gentry, and had joined the Green Ribbon club. Returned to the second Exclusion Parliament he distinguished himself by his violent talk against the Duke of York, just as in the elections he had acquired notoriety by his loose tongue. In July 1679 he attacked an Anglican minister as a Jesuit, ordering his followers to strike the man down and then, warming to the support he received from 'the Fanatiques', went on to call the King and York Papists, and Monmouth right heir to the throne. When he told some former soldiers that if they would fight for the Protestant Duke, he and other gentlemen would supply them with arms, he was arrested and charged at the Assizes.[33] Released when he wisely submitted, Speke, nonetheless, never learnt caution and in 1685 gave considerable assistance to the rebels.

Speke was also the centre of a considerable Whig clan in Somerset. One daughter married Thomas Jennings, an active Somerset Puritan;

another John Trenchard who, as an outspoken Exclusionist, sat for Taunton in all three Parliaments between 1679 and 1681. An habitué of the King's Head tavern in Fleet Street, the London Whigs' informal headquarters, Trenchard regularly attended Monmouth at the Duke's house in Soho, and served on the Commons' committee for the first Exclusion Bill. Suspected of complicity in the Rye House Plot but released for lack of evidence, Trenchard assessed Monmouth's chances accurately in 1685 and fled abroad, to return with William III and become a Secretary of State in 1692.[34]

Of Speke's sons, his youngest Charles joined the rebels in 1685 and was executed. His second son John was a more circumspect Whig who represented Ilchester in the Exclusion Parliaments, and married a daughter of Edmund Prideaux. Hugh, the third son, was a London lawyer who acquired notoriety as a political agitator, dabbled in the Rye House Plot, was still in prison in 1685 (thus escaping participation in the rebellion), and claimed responsibility for inciting the violent anti-Catholic riots of 1689. John and Hugh had both attended the Inns of Court and were members of the Green Ribbon Club, and when Shaftesbury effectively took over investigation of the Popish Plot they became his legal assistants, collating evidence and helping to prepare the charges brought by the informers. In June 1679 John received and sent on to his brother papers from Bedloe and Prance, and in the same month he attended Oates in the mornings to go over material for the trial of the five Catholic priests. Trenchard, the Taunton MP, was another of Oates's visitors, but like Speke he abandoned the Plot when public attention began to wane. Hugh, however, was too fascinated to drop out. He received a warning in November 1679 that his prominence was putting his life in danger, and so associated was he with the Plot informers that he became known as 'Bedloe Speke'. He worked with all the informers who followed Oates: Bedloe, Prance, Stephen Dugdale, and John Arnold, preparing their evidence, journeying into the countryside to assist them, and in August 1679 arranging a meeting at Whitelackington for his father to meet Bedloe and Prance and two lesser figures. His prominence was such that he received begging letters from those trying to climb on the Plot bandwagon.[34]

Opposition feeling in Somerset during the Plot and Exclusion was, therefore, greatly strengthened by a number of closely-linked gentry families, possessing in some cases close contacts with the London Whigs. Taunton, however, was the most notable centre of opinion against the Duke of York. Exclusionist beliefs were spread by such influential men as the serge-maker John Hucker, the members of the parliamentarian Bovet clan, and William Baker the town's aulnager (tax collector) whose work, as an informer noted, took him into 'constant concourse and correspondence with all substantial traders in the West'. But the town's most notorious Whig was a goldsmith named Thomas Dare, who in his rashness and reasons for joining the opposition camp, curiously parallels the great 'county' Exclusionist George Speke. Dare's father had been a cavalier during the War, but this carried no weight when his son challenged a church rate imposed in Taunton soon after the Restoration. In the carefully chosen words of a Somerset vicar who sympathized with Dare's position, the Bishop 'abetted them who contended for what might pass as fitt'. Like Speke, Dare's bad temper then worsened the dispute, and having been cast as a rebel he behaved like one. He swore that the King was directed not by his Privy Council but by a foreign cabal of the French ambassador, the Duchess of Portsmouth, and Louis Duras, Earl of Feversham, a soldier friend of the Duke of York who would command the royalist forces in 1685. He was active in promoting a Somerset petition in favour of the King calling Parliament, and gave lengthy and specious answers defending the practice of petitioning, despite the King's declarations against it. His most remarkable feat was to thrust a Whig petition, drawn up by himself, into the King's hands as Charles was leaving the House of Lords. When asked by his sovereign how he dared do such a thing, the Taunton goldsmith answered that he dared because his name was Dare. For once unimpressed by a witty sally, the merry monarch saw to it that the humorist suffered. Dare was turned out of Taunton's corporation, fined £500, and imprisoned until he paid it. Released after nearly a year in prison he was soon in trouble again for seditious words, and fled to the Netherlands where he attended Shaftesbury on the latter's death-bed in 1683.[35] He became Monmouth's treasurer in 1685.

Dare was too rash to be much trusted by his colleagues, and the Whig organization at Taunton was run by John Trenchard, the MP. He was secretary of the town's Green Ribbon Club which met at the 'Red Lion' public house. This was run by one William Savage, who reputedly harboured dubious characters as lodgers, presumably to act as Whig bully-boys: among them 'a fellow with one eye and a fur cap' was one of the more striking. Savage accepted direction from Trenchard, lending money to a Trull gunsmith to set up in Taunton, after Trenchard had said that such men would be wanted soon. During Trenchard's many absences in London his place was taken by his deputy, a Dissenter named John Friend. Friend was a man of some substance who owned a house and shop in Taunton, though he lived in rooms conveniently placed above the town's coffee-shop. He had some local influence, enough to recommend a fellow-Nonconformist for a position in the Excise at Chard. To his rooms were sent letters from the London Whigs, and from them local supporters arranged distribution of broadsides and fly sheets which, as Bishop Mews sourly observed in 1679, were more trusted than the government *Gazette* and dignified with the title of 'Publike Letters'. Hucker, the Spekes, and the Taunton aulnager, were frequent visitors to Friend's rooms.[36]

Here local Whigs also discussed arming themselves. In 1683 Friend admitted to having bought half a dozen muskets, but claimed this was at the time of the alarm over a French invasion. Baker, the aulnager, was said to have taken some of the guns and four barrels of gunpowder, but this was never proven, as happened with persistent reports that a wagon-load of arms had been delivered to a house in Wellington, near to Taunton. In 1683 Hucker's house was searched after JPs heard he had three hundred muskets, but only one old gun was turned up and there was talk among the searchers of 'a false brother among us'. Rumours that Trenchard too had guns were never confirmed, but after diligent search the JPs eventually found three men, all ex-Cromwellian soldiers, prepared to swear that Trenchard had enlisted them and others in 1681 'for the Duke of Monmouth'; but their depositions collapsed into hearsay. There was plainly no lack of boldness among Trenchard's circle. A group of his friends was found in Ilminster, who refused to take the oath of allegiance if it contained the phrase 'heirs and successors'. An informant swore that Trenchard had said that Monmouth would be their general when the King died, and other witnesses spoke of his ironic habit of joking that the Trenchard family had as good a claim to the throne as York. His associates in Taunton said that 'Monmouth shall not lack men for money', and Dissenters with whom he was connected in Ilminster swore to fight for their religion. A Taunton man visiting London was heard to say that he and his friends were for Monmouth and against the King, though he may have been a republican for his support for the Duke was only 'pro temp'.[37]

A well-organized informal news service from the capital nourished opposition groups in the west. Besides the letters sent by London Whigs to the provinces, and personal accounts by such as Trenchard, London Dissenters regularly sent news to their provincial brethren in Taunton, Lyme Regis, and Dorchester, as well as to Devon centres such as Axminster, Tiverton, Honiton, and Cullompton. Travellers spread rumours, which could be surprisingly detailed, such as the account heard in Lyme Regis of French money paid to the King to dissolve Parliament. Friends and relatives in the capital also sent news to many Somerset gentlemen. Sir Edward Phelips received full accounts of 'Plot' developments, and Edward Clarke a young Whig lawyer wrote regularly to his family and friends about Parliament, Popery, and the Duke of York. Even in the marshes of central Somerset a clergyman could write in 1679 that 'we are full of the great alteration at Court'. Best informed were those connected with the Spekes, for John and Hugh wrote often and at length, so much so that one recipient, Sir William Portman, upbraided Hugh for sending possibly dangerous material through the mail.[38]

Just as important as news from London were events in Somerset itself, in stirring up what a local cleric aptly termed 'the torrent of these talking times'. Not the least significant were three general elections between 1679 and 1681, contested in the county with remarkable vigour. Somerset returned a total of sixteen MPs, the two Knights of the Shire, and a pair of members each for Taunton, Bridgewater, Bath, Wells, Minehead, Ilchester, and Milborne Port. Even in the first General Election of February 1679 most of the seats were disputed. In the county election Lord FitzHarding, the candidate most loyal to the court, was persuaded to stand down and the seats were taken by Sir John Sydenham, described as one of the leaders of the disaffected party in the west, and the colourless Sir Hugh Smith. At Taunton, where voting was open to some seven hundred inhabitants who paid church and poor rates, John Trenchard swept in, and the 'moderately' anti-court Sir William Portman, who had held the seat since 1661, just defeated a challenge from Edmund Prideaux, who, however, took the seat from him in the subsequent Exclusion Parliaments. Bridgewater too saw a disputed election in February 1679, in which a few high church aldermen tried to control a popular vote of some 350 townsmen. They failed: Sir Halswell Tynt was elected safely, and the other opposition candidate, Sir Francis Rolle, won enough commoner votes to defeat the court candidate and chief local landowner, Colonel John Stawell. At Ilchester an angry two-way contest occurred between avowedly court and openly opposition pairs, in which the latter represented by William Strode and John Speke were victorious. Eight candidates fought an acrimonious election at Milborne Port amid charges of vote-rigging.[39]

The results in 1679 delighted the Somerset Whigs, one of whom wrote jubilantly that Coleman, the Duke of York's notorious secretary, 'was mistaken when he thought the Dissolution of P. would advance

France and Rome'. Shaftesbury concluded that only two Somerset MPs would oppose Exclusion, with four doubtful and ten for him. The estimate was a shade optimistic, for although only two did vote against the Bill on 21 May 1679, six were absent, leaving eight to vote for exclusion. In subsequent elections this broad support for exclusion among Somerset MPs did not alter greatly: and though some Members such as Trenchard and Speke were hotly for the measure, most endorsed it with rather less enthusiasm and would have agreed with the soundly cavalier Sir William Portman, who in 1679 described himself as 'against Popery and the Duke of York yet . . . firm to Church and King'.[40] For the county's substantial gentry the problem was to reconcile the divided loyalties expressed in Portman's statement.

Two other developments in Somerset intensified local political interest during 1679 and 1680. The first was the petitioning campaign during the winter of 1679-80 for the King to summon the recently-elected Parliament. The earliest of the monster petitions was delivered on 13 January 1680, and nine days later Thomas Thynne presented Wiltshire's petition containing, it was claimed, thirty thousand signatures. The Whigs in Somerset were active in promoting theirs and Hugh Speke was deeply involved. He sent fifty copies of the Middlesex petition to his Somerset friends to start them off on their canvassing and promised to send more, printed as for Somerset, when these were ready.[41] The second event to stir Somerset was Monmouth's tour of the county in August 1680. His impact there will be discussed in Chapter Four; here it is sufficient to emphasize the personal triumph he enjoyed. In Dryden's words:

> Th'admiring crowd are dazzled with surprise
> And on his goodly person feed their eyes.
> His joy conceal'd, he sets himself to show
> On each side bowing popularly low
> His looks, his gestures, and his words he frames ·
> And with familiar ease repeats their names.
> Thus form'd by nature, furnish'd out with arts,
> He glides unfelt into their secret hearts.

Stimulated in a variety of ways, there is ample evidence of anti-York, anti-government, pro-Monmouth feeling in Somerset during the plot and Exclusion years. Bishop Mews was startled by the anti-clerical feeling he observed following elections to the first Exclusion Parliament, and by the common local assumption that none who served under the Crown were fit to be trusted as MPs. Even in towns thought to be under the control of the better sort much disaffected talk was heard. At Bath in December 1680 there was agitated discussion of the King's 'obligation' to call frequent Parliaments, and a local attorney spoke up for 'the liberty of the people against the prerogative'. After the second Exclusion election a Bath alderman comprehensively abused York as 'a rogue, a rascal, a traitor, a rebel, and the son of a whore', and the corporation covered up for him; while another leading citizen here told townsmen that the King was letting in Popery by simply allowing his brother to sit beside him. In the Bishop's own city of Wells matters were no better: the mayor suppressing an address criticizing Shaftesbury, and blandly pleading that if he tolerated it he would have to answer to the next Parliament. A little later it was announced here that on 17 November the Pope would be either hanged or drowned in effigy, pope-burning having been forbidden. The constitutional rights demanded in an address sent to Taunton's MPs in the name of the town's burgesses so alarmed some of the latter, that they wrote to Bishop Mews disassociating themselves from the document. Mews probably received their claim with some reserve, for the same burgesses had recently appointed a mayor without requiring from him the statutory oath, nor evidence that he had taken the Anglican sacrament. In Lyme Regis there was open discussion of Monmouth's legitimacy, and nearby at Ford Abbey Edmund Prideaux spoke publicly of the country's descent into the pit of Popery. An acting sheriff of Somerset in 1682 brazenly protected Dissenters from prosecution, while Nonconformists near Bristol were being armed and organized for self-defence by a local lawyer, Nathaniel Wade, to be prominent in the 1685 rebellion.[42]

Opposition was sometimes displayed in unlikely settings. On the Taunton to London stage-coach a passenger lectured his captive audience on the limits to the Crown's authority, and perhaps in revenge for their boredom the other passengers informed on him when they reached their destination. Satirical ballads on the Duke of York were sold openly at Bridgewater fair, and when complaint was made to a town alderman he simply laughed. No amusement was shown, however, when a clergyman nearby at Ham, in the heart of Colonel Stawell's own loyalist domain, warned parishioners that if the King died 'we should be in danger of Popery'. He was made to recant, but the authorities were left worrying over the effect of such a statement made by an Anglican cleric. Political interest in Somerset had not abated by the time of elections to the third Exclusion Parliament, and Whigs found their meetings well attended. At Ilminster the appetite for news was such that the Whigs' London correspondent, Hugh Speke, was begged to write at least once per week.[43]

For all their talk and defiance, however, the Whigs in Somerset, as elsewhere, were driven on to the defensive after Charles II summoned and dissolved his last Parliament, early in 1682. Moderate gentry in Somerset and members of corporations saw the Whigs stir up those whom they ruled and foresaw, as one gentleman put it, their 'liberties turned into a plebeian tyranny'. The arch-moderate Sir William Portman left his Exclusionist friends in 1681 and began to drink the health of the Duke of York. Encouraged by the change in 'respectable' opinion, and emboldened by letters from the government, Tory JPs began to put pressure on Whigs and Dissenters. George Speke, Thomas Dare, and Alderman Hickes of Bath were all tried and fined for seditious words. Minor figures who had promoted petitions were also put on trial and their friends browbeaten by the Bench, while more or less indiscriminate house searches, and the posting of militia to watch certain houses, intimidated isolated Whigs. Corporations then came under attack. Bridgewater, Wells, and Chard found their charters in question; although as Stawell conceded in the case of Bridgewater re-chartering could only have a moral effect because 'the loyal party are so few and poor', (and he might have reflected that Taunton's new Charter of 1677 had done little to contain that town). New charters, however, might well buy loyalty: thus Chard was given a new fair and a more convenient time for its market, and Lyme Regis received an annual grant of £100 for the maintenance of the Cob. The threat of royal displeasure (and the implied loss of its fashionable visitors) brought the Bath corporation to heel – though not the town's general population. Grand Juries comprising 'men of considerable estate' were persuaded to vote loyal addresses to the Crown at Taunton and Bridgewater; and at the Bruton Quarter Sessions in 1682 the discovery of Shaftesbury's 'Bill of Association' inspired the jury to express their 'sense of duty to the King and the succession'. An indication that the tide was turning can be seen in the offer to inform against the Spekes made by two men of Chard. Their dubious local reputations told against them, but the Secretary of State took much more seriously assertions made in Somerset during August 1681 that Stephen College the 'Protestant joiner' then being tried for treason at Oxford, was in fact a Catholic.[44] Nothing came of the matter, partly because the evidence concerned events several years past, but also, no doubt, because the King and his brother wished to hang College as an ultra-Protestant traitor, and not as another Catholic one.

But while individual Whigs, Grand Juries, and some corporations, were amenable to different forms of pressure there were two organized knots of opposition in the county more difficult to subdue. These were the dissenting conventiclers, and the town of Taunton. Nonconformists in and out of Parliament had identified themselves with the Whigs and Exclusion, thus reinforcing their Civil War reputation for disloyalty to the Crown, and when the time came Tories took their revenge upon them. The time was signalled in Somerset at the Bruton Quarter Sessions of January 1682, when the royalist Edward Phelips passed an emphatically-worded resolution to enforce the penal laws, with sanctions against slack officials. The conventicles at Taunton and Frome were noted as the biggest in the county, with those at Bridgewater, Chard and Ilminster listed as secondary targets. Almost at once 6 people were taken at a West Dawlish meeting, but 35 others escaped. The old difficulties of enforcing the laws recurred when attempts were made to deal with the Whitelackington conventicle near Ilminster, attended by the Speke womenfolk, though possibly not by George Speke himself. Although the services here lasted for nearly three hours, they commenced at two a.m. to frustrate the attentions of Captain Walrond and his troop of militia. Little was actually achieved against Dissenters until mid-1683 when news of the Rye House Plot spurred JPs into another surge of activity. Meetings at North Curry, Curry Rivell, and Chard were broken up, and twenty-two Dissenters (half of them women) were arrested at Ilminster. In July 1683 Colonel Stawell with Sir Francis Warr, Sir Edward Phelips and a strong force of militia descended on Bridgewater. After searching the houses of the 'grand Fanatics', they stripped the Dissenters' meeting house and made a bonfire of its contents. The connivance of a local JP at first frustrated similar resolute action at Lyme Regis, although 110 people were arrested at one point (eighty of them women), but with the encouragement of the Bishop of Bath and Wells another attempt was made, and the seats and pulpit of the Lyme Regis and Bridport meeting houses were torn out and destroyed.[45]

Pleasant as such triumphs were they would count for nothing unless the other centre of resistance was subdued, the town of Taunton, the 'nursery of rebellion in the west' as Tory clergy and gentry now termed it. The task would not be easy. In the 1670s Bishop Mews had tried and failed, and the town's 'factious spirits' had now been invigorated by the Popish Plot, Exclusion, and the early stages of the Tory reaction. After the first Exclusion Parliament Sir William Portman had been replaced as MP by Edmund Prideaux, the son of a famous rebel, even though Portman was a major local landowner, had sat for the town since 1661, and had worked hard for its new charter. In defiance of this same charter, Nonconformists regularly became aldermen and even mayors of the town, and in 1681 its burgesses had printed an address supporting their two exclusionist MPs. The town's parliamentary franchise was very wide, and three elections under the schooling of Trenchard's Whigs and Shaftesbury's 'agent' John Hucker had settled a large part of the inhabitants into a habit of opposition to the court. In 1681 they showed their mettle after the King's Declaration concerning the recent dissolution of the Oxford Parliament had been read from the pulpit, as ordered by the government. A copy of the most sensational pamphlet of 1681 was delivered anonymously to a local clergyman James Douche, with the recommendation that he now read this from the pulpit 'for it is of much more concernment than the King's proclamation'. The pamphlet was *The True Englishman speaking Plain English*, written by the confused Whig informer Edward Fitzharris. It sought to implicate the Queen and the Duke of York in the Popish Plot, as well as arguing that Charles was as guilty of treason to the nation as James, and should be deposed. Fitzharris was tried for treason and executed on 1 July 1681; the pamphlet was delivered to Douche nine days later. Local Tories swore that Trenchard and 'the rebellious town of Taunton' were responsible, but could prove nothing. They secured the appointment of a loyal man as the next mayor however, and with the Bishop began harrying the town's conventicles. This raised the Dissenters' fighting spirit and by 1682 they were 'very high', and swearing that they would not abandon their public meetings. The unhappy Reverend Douche was told to expect bloody noses soon, and at that year's 11 May celebration – now 'kept higher than Christmas' – there was much violent talk, and a murder was committed as the crowds dispersed for home.[46] An explosion was not far off.

Not unexpectedly it came at the 11 May anniversary in 1683. In the late afternoon the mayor Stephen Timewell attempted to disperse a large crowd in High Street. He was attacked, and a hearth tax collector who went to his aid was beaten up. The watch then made some arrests, but the crowd set upon them again releasing most of the prisoners and forcing Timewell and his men to beat 'an honourable retreat'. The crowd possessed the streets and bonfires burned late into the night. A few days later the mayor was publicly insulted at Wellington fair, and the hearth tax collector once more beaten up. A full report was sent to London and the militia was ordered to protect Timewell, and to arrest as many rioters as possible, for the King 'cannot have but a just resentment of this method used not only to continue the memory of a horrid rebellion, but to transmit it as a thing of imitation to posterity'.

Timewell's enquiries quickly revealed that with the exception of William Baker the town aulnager (and prominent Whig) the rioters were 'every one . . . very poor', and that prosecutions resulting in fines would achieve little. He therefore tried to impress obedience upon the town by requiring all males over eighteen to swear the oath of allegiance. Having made his gesture Timewell was at a loss for further action, but opportunely for him news was received of the Rye House Plot, and an intensive series of house searches by the militia followed in Taunton. These uncovered very few guns and no incriminating documents but they had a considerable intimidatory effect, and capitalizing on this at the end of July 1683 Timewell attacked the heart of Presbyterianism in Taunton, the great brick meeting house of St Pauls. From here, and from the Baptists' meeting too, gates and doors were removed, and seats, galleries, and pulpit torn out, to leave an empty shell. Ten cart-loads of fittings were burnt in the market place, with church bells ringing and the drink flowing until three in the morning.[47]

The magnitude of the blow at first stunned Taunton's opposition. Its members remained 'linked and close' while informers suddenly appeared in the town with tales that local men had been bribed with strong beer to be ready at an hour's notice 'to fight for Monmouth and Trenchard'. Trenchard himself and his wife were arrested and placed in the Tower, John Friend disappeared into a London prison, and Hucker, Bovett, and the rest were closely watched. In September 1683 the government's account of 'the late horrid plot' was received by the loyal party in Taunton, and drums, bonfires, and more heavy drinking followed. Parallel with the Justices' drive against rural nonconformity Timewell attacked Taunton conventicles, and made arrests in nine in all by the beginning of 1684. But by then his days of success were coming to an end. Dissenters were meeting once more, just outside the town where his writ did not run, and the remarkable number of thirty preachers, he was told, had rallied from the rest of the county to help their brethren. At the town's coffee house a 'public newsletter' was read giving details of Monmouth's eventual refusal to confirm the official version of the Rye House Plot, causing the opposition to become 'strangely impudent'. Timewell himself found his shop trade so reduced (from £40 to 40/- per week he claimed) that he was forced to retire to a small estate he owned two miles from the town. Trenchard, having been released from the Tower, reappeared in town, declaring that he would again stand as its Member when a parliament was summoned once more, and his associates (including Friend) became

'very industrious, already making votes' for him. In an attempt to hold
the line Sir William Portman was appointed Recorder of the town, but
there were never sufficient influential loyalists resident in Taunton to
keep it in order.[48] The Charter contained provision for three JPs to be
appointed from the local gentry to help keep order, but none of the
places was filled because nobody outside the town wanted to be held
responsible for it.

The royalist offensive had been revived, for a while, by the Rye
House Plot of 1683. This involved two separate circles of conspirators,
the first consisting of London republicans who talked of regicide and
one of whom owned the 'Rye House' in Hertfordshire; and the other a
group of 'aristocratic' Whigs, headed for a while by Shaftesbury and
then after his death in January 1683 by Monmouth. There is little clear
evidence that conspiratorial talk extended very far into practical details,
particularly among the circle led by Shaftesbury and Monmouth, but
they did, however loosely, talk of raising resistance to the King and his
brother in several areas of the realm – London, Scotland, the north-west
about Cheshire, and the south-west. In the last area, Bristol, Somerset,
and Taunton were prominent. John Trenchard, the Taunton MP, was
alleged by one witness to have said that he could raise 1500 armed men
in the town, and several Whig gentry in Somerset and Devon were
discreetly sounded out, including Sir Francis Rolle former MP for
Bridgewater, Sir William Courtenay, Sir Walter Yonge and Sir Francis
Drake. Government investigations in the west, and a wave of house
searches of prominent Somerset Whigs, uncovered some indications of
arms-buying by the latter in 1682 and early 1683, and a hint or two that
they may have been 'enlisting men' for the Duke's future service, but
nothing was found that would stand up in court. One by one the Whigs
arrested on suspicion, many of them Somerset men or with Somerset
connections, were released. Trenchard had spent six months in the
Tower, having been given pen and paper and bluntly ordered to
confess: he had kept his head and nothing was proven against him.
Similarly Nathaniel Wade and John Tyley, two of the links between
London and Bristol, emerged from prison, as did Trenchard's deputy
John Friend, and Christopher Bettiscombe, son of a Dorset gentry
family who had been travelling in the west on behalf of the Whigs.
Wade, Tyley and Bettiscombe would join Monmouth in the 1685
rebellion; but for the moment they prudently disappeared abroad.
Trenchard however returned to Somerset in January 1684, and was
given a hero's reception.[49]

The Rye House investigations, and the public's response to them, epitomized the government's problem in trying finally to crush the Whigs. Corporations could be frightened, and particular individuals intimidated – thus some Whigs began putting their land into trusts to avoid confiscation; George Speke, William Strode, and Edward Clarke were all presented at the 1684 Assizes as 'Persons dangerous and disaffected'; and Hugh Speke was finally convicted and imprisoned for intemperate speeches about the Earl of Essex's suicide. House searches conducted by the militia for hidden arms frightened many gentlemen: the prominent Warwickshire Whig and (somewhat distant) acquaintance of Monmouth, Sir Richard Newdigate, recorded in his diary several days of depression and illness after such a search. But among the mass of the population old attitudes persisted, and official accounts of the Rye House Plot were received with scepticism. In Bridgewater it was dismissed as 'butt a story of a parcell of desperate swearing fellows'. Support remained strong for Monmouth, with a Taunton serge-weaver found spreading a tale in Devon that the Duke had been declared a traitor 'only because he was a Protestant prince', and swearing that twenty thousand would fight for him; and a Taunton carpenter and blacksmith in October 1683 – after all the government's declarations – singing 'a song of ye Duke of Monmouth', and declaring they would fight for him. Constitutional ideas spread during Exclusion remained so strong that in 1684 the King issued a denial that he was bound to call Parliaments triennially, and of six laymen and bishops to whom copies were sent four lived in Somerset. Early in 1685 the mayor of Bridgewater wearily reported preparations for a Parliament made by the 'Grindallizing self-willed humourists' whom he governed.[50]

The Church too received its quota of disrespect. Sneers about Bishop Mews ('Peter Patch and the Patchers' – Mews had lost an eye at Naseby), changed to talk that the Devil would soon complete his work after lightning had damaged a church tower at Chewton-on-Mendip. Much-troubled Bridgewater was disturbed by a scandal early in 1685 when it was alleged that a beneficed minister here was reviving old Civil War heresies by denying the Creed, and claiming that there were no eternal torments for the damned. Words spoken casually suggest that key phrases used during the political crisis had become etched deeply on the popular mind. When four tenants living in a North Curry house attacked their landlord during a dispute, they were encouraged by spectators who shouted 'fight on brave soldiers and gaine the Cavalier's Estate'. In the same year, 1684, a plague of caterpillars devastated the bean crop of central Somerset, and the vicar of Chedzoy recorded that 'they were in 10 days' time damnified £4 or £5,000 by these Toryes as our country farmers call them'.[51] Somerset's trade with Ireland was considerable and so the farmers may have used 'Tory' in its original sense of an Irish plunderer, but after several years of Whig and Tory politics their ambiguity may not have been wholly innocent.

The Exclusion Crisis had two principal results. It revived in Somerset a strong tradition of political activity among the county's clothworkers and farmers, an activity which persisted (as we have seen) after the Tory reaction in 1682-83 had driven most upper-class Whigs to take cover. And it established the point that England's best hope, if liberty and Protestantism were to survive, lay with the Protestant Duke. The argument was simple and symmetrical. York was disqualified for the throne, as an attorney told a public-house audience in Cirencester, because of his Catholicism; and a group as unsophisticated as some fifteen-year-old boys, drinking in a Chichester tavern, could appreciate that point, as they toasted confusion to the 'Popish Duke'. On the other hand, as some more drinkers in Wiltshire predicted, while toasting Monmouth, the other 'Duke would make a very good King'.[52]

To these two basic arguments, the Tory reaction and the apparent destruction of the Whigs in 1683 added a rider: Monmouth was not now just the best hope, he was the only one. After Shaftesbury's death a wealthy Dissenter in Wiltshire prophesied that 'if God did not strengthen the lords in the rest of the party, England would be reviled, and all hope lay in the Duke of Monmouth'. This providential note was sounded even more strongly by some London Dissenters after the Duke had fled into exile in 1684. They observed 'how miraculously God has preserved him hitherto, which sure was for some great work'. And they could surmise what God's purpose was for the Duke: 'he was the person they must expect deliverance from'.[53] Though Monmouth was not to know it, even at the nadir of his fortunes following his disgrace over the Rye House Plot, he was for some Englishmen the hero who would return to lead them out of bondage.

Footnotes: Chapter Two

1. *CSPD 1682*, p.98; *CSPD Jan.-June 1683*, p.323.

2. T.G.Barnes, *Somerset 1625-1640*, Oxford 1961, p.15; D.Underdown, *Somerset in the Civil War and Interregnum*, Newton Abbot 1973, pp.21-3.

3. D.Underdown, *Somerset in the Civil War*, pp.38-40, 99, 106, 115-117.

4. D.Underdown, *Somerset in the Civil War*, pp.94-5, 108-110; C.Wanklin, *Lyme Regis*, London 1927, pp.19-35.

5. D.Underdown, *Somerset in the Civil War*, pp.46-7, 75, 81, 87.

6. D.Underdown, *Somerset in the Civil War*, pp.91, 99, 105-8; see also D.Underdown 'The Chalk and the Cheese: Contrasts among the English Clubmen', *Past and Present*, 85 1979, pp.25-48.

7. D.Underdown, *Somerset in the Civil War*, p.25; P.M.Hembry, *The Bishops of Bath and Wells 1540-1640*, London 1967, pp.230, 245, 248-9; *The County of Somerset divided into severall Classes*, London 4 March 1647/48; *The Attestation of the Ministers of the County of Somerset*, London 9 August 1648.

8. G.R.Nuttall, 'The Baptist Western Association', *Journal of Ecclesiastical History*, 11 1960, pp.213-18.

9. Somerset Record Office, Q/S R, 90/28, 29; S.C.Morland, 'The Somerset Quarterly Meeting of Friends', *Somerset Record Society*, 75 1978, pp.2-3, D.Underdown, *Somerset in the Civil War*, p.146.

10. SRO, DD/PM, H/512 Box 7; *CSPD 1661-62*, p.63; *CSPD 1667-68*, p.199; D.Underdown, *Somerset in the Civil War*, pp.126-8, 159-63.

11. S.Tomlinson, *History of Taunton*, Taunton 1882, p.127; *CSPD 1661-62*, pp.423-4; SP 29/263/55, I-VII (the 1669 petition).

12. *CSPD 1675-76*, p.39; Longleat House, Coventry MSS, Vol.92 ff.2-3, Vol.7 ff.66, 204.

13. SRO, Q/S R, 111/49, 50, 103/5, 148/44; Coventry MSS, Vol.7 f.150; *CSPD 1671*, pp.309-10.

14. Privy Council Register, 60/312 (1668); *CSPD 1671*, pp.309-10.

15. *CSPD 1661-62*, pp.434, 444, 595; *CSPD 1663-64*, pp.636, 666-7, 590; *CSPD 1664-65*, pp.35, 544; *CSPD 1665-66*, pp.25, 272-4; *CSPD 1666-67*, p.273; *CSPD 1667*, p.428; *CSPD 1670*, p.313; *CSPD 1672*, pp.161-2.

16. SRO, Q/S R, 105/35, 106/50, 100/23, 99/23, 24, 40, 13, 14, 102/68.

17. SRO, Q/S R, 101/23, 103/7, 108/6, 21-24, 39.

18. SRO, Q/S R, 108/23, 153/16, 19, 129/9, 132/6, 155/4, 136/18.

19. See W.G.Johnson, 'Post-Restoration Nonconformity and Plotting', Manchester M.A.Thesis 1967, pp.12-13 and *passim*; *CSPD 1663-64*, p.553; Bodleian Library Tanner MSS., 38 f.126.

20. G.Lyon Turner, *Original Records of Early Nonconformity*, London 1911, 3 vols., i, 5-13; iii, 112, 142.

21. G.L.Turner, *Original Records*, iii, 142, 78.

22. *CSPD 1672-73*, p.xiv; G.L.Turner, *Original Records*, ii, 1079-1126; S.C.Morland, 'The Somerset Quarterly Meeting of Friends', *Somerset Record Society*, 75 1978, pp.2-3.

74 *The Last Popular Rebellion*

23. D.Underdown, *Somerset in the Civil War*, pp.162, 167, 170-3; G.R.Cragg, *Puritanism in the Period of the Great Persecution*, Cambridge 1957, ch.2.

24. E.Calamy, *The Nonconformists' Memorial*, revised S.Palmer, London 1775 2 vols., ii, 377, 367-9, 376, 147-8, 378, 384.

25. E.Calamy, *Nonconformists' Memorial*, ii, 355, 353, 365, 366, 374, 357, 358; J.Murch, *A History of the Presbyterian and General Baptist Churches*, London 1835, p.230.

26. SRO, Q/S R, 106/50, 103/22, 120/3, 114/32, 79, 103/19; *CSPD 1670*, p.370; Coventry MSS., 7 ff.30, 83.

27. Coventry MSS., 7 f.130; *CSPD 1664-65*, p.476; G.L.Turner, *Original Records*, ii, 1099; Bodleian Library Aubrey MSS., 13 f.84; P.H.Hembry, *Bishops of Bath and Wells*, pp.228-9.

28. Coventry MSS., 17 ff.66, 128v, 130v, 132; 11 f.185.

29. *CSPD 1667*, p.428; Coventry MSS., 7 ff.72, 90. On the causes of anti-catholic alarms see R.Clifton, 'The Fear of Popery' in *The Origins of the English Civil War*, ed. C.Russell, London 1973, esp.pp.146-57, 164-5.

30. SRO, DD/PH, 211/85; Dr. Williams' Library, William Morrice's Entering Book, ff.238-40.

31. Coventry MSS., 7 ff.72; SRO, DD/SF, 146/3074.

32. SRO, DD/SF, 146/3067, 149/3109; *Dictionary of National Biography*, vol.16 p.351, 18 pp.730-1, 19 pp.1123-25; D.R.Lacy, *Dissent and Parliamentary Politics in England, 1661-1689*, New Brunswick 1969, pp.387-8, 450, 439, 442-3.

33. *CSPD 1663-64*, pp.116, 138; *DNB*, 18 pp.730-1; Coventry MSS.,7 f.164; *CSPD 1679-80*, pp.471, 691.

34. *DNB*, 19 pp.1123-5; *CSPD 1679-80*, pp.178-9, 185, 214, 281-2, 483; *CSPD 1680-81*, pp.79, 85-6, 232; *CSPD 1683-84*, p.20.

35. *CSPD 1679-80*, pp.428-9; *CSPD 1680-81*, p.152; *CSPD July-Sept. 1683*, p.247; Bodleian Library, Aubrey MSS., 13 f.42; Bristol University Library, Bull MSS., DM 155, f.129.

36. *CSPD July-September 1683*, pp.77, 82, 61, 192, 355, 358; *CSPD 1683-84*, pp.7-8, 229; Coventry MSS., 7 f.158.

37. *CSPD July-Sept. 1683*, pp.367, 77-8, 82, 358, 278, 321, 355, 431, 313, 425-6, 367-9; *CSPD 1683-84*, pp.7-8, 84-5; *CSPD 1682*, p.158.

38. *CSPD 1679-80*, p.505; *CSPD 1680-81*, p.236; *CSPD 1682*, pp.493-4; SRO, DD/PH, 211; SF 149/3109, 150/3109; Aubrey MSS., 13 f.36.

39. Aubrey MSS., 13 f.42; Coventry MSS., 7 ff.148, 150; SRO, DD/SF, 149/3109, 146/3074; Bull MSS., DM 155, f.135; S.W.Bates-Harbin, *Members of*

Parliament for the County of Somerset, Taunton 1939, pp.172, 175-6; D.Lacey, *Dissent and Parliamentary Politics*, p.411.

40. SRO, DD/SF, 149/3109; J.R.Jones, 'Shaftesbury's "worthy men": a Whig view of the Parliament of 1679', *Bulletin of the Institute of Historical Research*, 30 1957, pp.232-41; Dr. Williams' Library, Roger Morrice's Entering Book, ff.238-40; *CSPD 1679-80*, p.207.

41. SP 29/442/54.

42. Coventry MSS., 7 ff.148, 154, 164; *CSPD 1679-80*, pp.402-3, 428-9, 597; *CSPD 1680-81*, pp.646, 211, 688; *CSPD 1682*, pp.587-8, 168, 543-4, 97.

43. *CSPD 1680-81*, pp.492, 210, 150, 60; *CSPD January-June 1683*, p.94; Aubrey MSS., 13 f.61.

44. *CSPD 1679-80*, pp.535, 475, 447, 451, 459, 688-9; *CSPD 1680-81*, pp.257, 360, 409, 415-16, 420, 515, 573; *CSPD 1682*, pp.26, 158, 244-5; *CSPD January-June 1683*, pp.322-3.

45. D.Lacey, *Dissent and Parliamentary Politics*, ch.VII; SRO, Q/S R 150/1, 155/3, 157/16, 156/21, 2; *CSPD 1682*, pp.36, 46, 60, 72-3, 84; *CSPD July-Sept. 1683*, p.60.

46. SRO, DD/SF, 146/3078; *CSPD 1682*, pp.97-8, 113, 145, 208-9.

47. *CSPD January-June 1683*, pp.250, 266, 291; *CSPD July-Sept. 1683*, pp.9, 279, 350.

48. *CSPD July-Sept. 1683*, pp.213, 289, 358, 398; *CSPD 1683-84*, pp.23, 229-30.

49. D.J.Milne, 'The Rye House Plot', London Ph.D.Thesis 1949, is the most detailed study. The material in this paragraph is from Ford Lord Grey, *The Secret History of the Rye House Plot*, London 1754, pp.16-18; *CSPD January-June 1683*, pp.321, 362-3, 368, 385; *CSPD July-Sept. 1683*, pp.9, 61, 64, 77, 82-3, 130, 416; *CSPD 1683-84*, pp.285-6.

50. SRO, DD/SF, 146/3078; DD/SF, 79/1697; SRO, Q/S R, 153/4, 156/35; *CSPD January-June 1683*, pp.338, 430; Warwickshire Record Office, Newdigate MSS., CR 136, B 1/5, 1/6, B 15/1307; *CSPD 1684-85*, pp.22-3; *CSPD 1685*, p.54.

51. SRO, Q/S R, 148/25, 153/22, 158/13; *CSPD 1683-84*, pp.45-6; Aubrey MSS., 13 f.66.

52. *CSPD 1682*, pp.492-3; *CSPD January-June 1683*, p.181; *CSPD 1683-84*, p.269.

53. *CSPD July-September 1683*, p.13; *CSPD 1683-84*, p.270.

CHAPTER THREE

To Be a Royal Favourite

'Handsome, weak, and empty-headed' is the conventional judgement upon James, Duke of Monmouth, the oldest but illegitimate son of Charles II. Outrageously indulged in youth by his father, a licensed, violent, rake in early manhood, Monmouth's vanity and stupidity supposedly made him first Shaftesbury's puppet during the Exclusion Crisis; and then the victim of James II in one of England's most hopeless rebellions, once the Earl's guidance had been removed. Such comments tend to be judgements rather than explanations, however, and the Duke's life needs more careful treatment to explain why he launched a rebellion, and why several thousand men followed him into it. It will not be argued that the conventional judgement is completely wrong; rather that it under-estimates some of his talents, and fails to explain his character. What historians see as shallowness, foolish pride, and stupidity, appeared to Monmouth as conduct dictated by honour and self-respect. The son of Charles II, he resembled more in his obstinate loyalty to principle and honour James Duke of York, his uncle and enemy, the man with whom he is more often contrasted than compared. Both failed ultimately because they were trapped in courses of action from which a man cleverer and less scrupulous — such as Charles II — would have escaped.

Sufficient is known of his childhood to show that certain early influences were strong in moulding the man. Even by the standards of the time Monmouth's boyhood was harsh. Pride in his birth and rank confronted deep poverty and considerable neglect; he was raised by a beautiful, violent and incompetent mother who had openly to earn her living as a court whore; his father entirely deserted the boy until his early teens, and was described to the child by his mother alternately in tears and tirades; at the age of nine he underwent two brutal kidnappings, the second of which cut him off forever from his mother; and four years later he abruptly exchanged the poverty and neglect of exile for the luxury and license of Charles II's court. Wilfullness, violence, and a deeply ambivalent attitude towards his father, might naturally have been expected from such experiences.

Born at Rotterdam on 9 April 1649 he was the child of very young parents. His mother Lucy Walters was then just eighteen, his father the new King of England, one year older. He was christened James, perhaps after his paternal grandfather, and pride in his royal line of descent made him sensitive all his life to slurs upon his mother's rank, and that of her family. John Evelyn described his mother's parents as 'some very mean creatures', while Clarendon and James II dismissed them simply as 'Welch'. In adulthood Monmouth would assert over the dinner table that his mother had been descended from Edward IV, and that he, therefore, had Plantaganet blood from her side. This claim was as wild as the slurs which prompted it: Lucy's parents were middling Welsh gentry. Her father, William Walters, owned an estate near Haverfordwest; her mother, Elizabeth Vaughan, was a sister of the first Earl of Carberry and had brought the respectable portion of £600 to her wedding. The marriage was a failure, and Lucy's parents separated in 1640 when their daughter was nine. She went with her mother to London, her father staying in Wales. Lucy grew up in the London of the Civil War, living near Covent Garden, and entering the fringes of the capital's social life. Near the war's end the handsome parliamentarian officer Algernon Sidney became her lover and, in a story which James II claimed to have heard from Lucy herself, 'trafficked for her first; and was to have had her for forty broad pieces', but had to leave his bargain when his regiment was sent to Ireland in 1648. With her lover gone, and custody of the seventeen-year-old girl awarded to her father living in the depths of Pembrokeshire, England lost its charms for Lucy and so, displaying the talent for sudden and rash decisions which never left her, she resolved to seek out young aristocrats where they were thickest to be found, in the royalist camp abroad with Prince Charles. In March 1648 she crossed for the Netherlands in the suite of Lord Glamorgan, adopting the surname of Barlow after a distant relative who had worked as an agent for Glamorgan in Ireland.[1]

An aunt in The Hague, named Margaret Gosfright, provided her with lodgings, and the girl proceeded to make herself known to Robert Sidney, the younger and royalist brother of Algernon. But his time with Lucy ran out as quickly as his brother's had, for within months chance put the greatest prize within the girl's grasp. In May 1648 part of the parliamentary fleet mutinied and sailed to the royalists in Holland. With an opportunity now to intervene decisively in the Second Civil War, Prince Charles left Paris and hurried to Helvoetsluys where the ships were anchored. He arrived on 9 July, and left eight days later with the ships under his command. In the week's hectic interval between arrival and departure Lucy used Robert Sidney and a groom of the bedchamber to meet, charm, and seduce, the heir to the throne. Her son was born nine months later almost exactly to the day. Indeed Lucy's time with the prince was so brief, the timing of the pregnancy so close, that there were assertions that the child's father was not Charles at all but an earlier lover, probably Robert Sidney. Charles never believed the sceptics, but his brother the Duke of York did, averring that his nephew resembled the courtier more than the King, 'even to a little wart on his face'.[2]

At the time, however, York and others found it politic to remain silent. Charles returned to The Hague in September 1648, tired and dispirited from a cruise which dissension had turned into a fiasco. While the Second Civil War was lost, the King tried and executed, and the monarchy abolished, royalists could only wait for their fortune to change and Charles abandoned politics for a round of sensuality with his young mistress. Pregnancy made her bloom, John Evelyn remembering 'a browne, beautiful bold but inspid creature'; and even the King's brother described a woman 'very handsome, of little wit and some cunning'.[3] When the baby was three months old Lucy was taken to St. Germain to present Henrietta Maria with her first grandchild. The couple's idyll lasted until September 1649 when Charles moved to Jersey, the better to watch developments in Ireland and Scotland. Next year he left for Scotland, to lead an army southward to the shipwreck of royalist hopes at Worcester. He never again resumed relations with Lucy.

In his absence she supported herself and her child in the only way she could, becoming mistress of Theodore, second Viscount Taafe. By him she had a daughter, christened Mary, in 1651. When Charles returned to exile in October 1652 she 'used in vain all her little arts' on him, the King amiably making it clear that the episode was finished. But Lucy refused to give up, and when Charles retired from France to Cologne in 1654 she pursued him with letters, and enlisted the support of his sister, Mary Princess of Orange. In her correspondence the delicate Mary referred to Charles and Lucy as 'husband' and 'wife', euphemisms which caused trouble twenty-five years later. Finding the King adamant, Lucy's temper and her circumstances both deteriorated. In October 1654 her stormy relationship with Taafe was giving rise to 'scurrilous stuff' among English exiles in Paris, and the following year she left him taking her two children with her to The Hague.[4]

Here she became the mistress of Thomas Howard, brother of the Earl of Suffolk and Master of Horse to Princess Mary of Orange. But her poverty deepened for Howard had his own family to support, was suspected by royalists of being a parliamentary spy, and was soon to be 'discarded' by the Prince of Orange. She began to demand money from the King, backing up the claims by increasingly frequent displays of bad temper. Charles's agent at The Hague, a groom of the bedchamber named O'Neill, tried to keep her quiet with promises of a pension, but by 1655 the King was writing that 'both for her sake and mine' she should be persuaded to leave The Hague, where she was too much in public view for his good. Lucy would not be moved, however, and in January 1656 Charles granted her an annuity of £1,500 backdated to 1654. The Treasury contained nothing to honour this promise and Lucy's rage exploded. She tried to kill a maid whom she suspected of informing on her, behaved 'infamously' with Howard, and caused O'Neill to write in despair to the King that 'everie idle action of hirs brings your majestie upon the stage'. Her present behaviour, coupled with two abortions procured in the past, threatened a major scandal and the King must 'necessitate' her and take control over the boy.[5]

A strange compromise was found. Lucy was given money and a pearl necklace, and together with Howard, her children, and her brother, was sent to England. She was to await the Restoration living quietly in London where, it was hoped, she would not embarrass the King. But Lucy could not live quietly. The group spent money freely, eating and drinking well, hiring a coach, and ordering another built and decorated to their own specifications; but the end came when Lucy once again grew suspicious of a maid and had her imprisoned. Not surprisingly the woman then informed on her employers, and by the end of June 1656 all were lodged in the Tower while the authorities tried to decide whether they were spies, imposters, or fools. Settling for the last the government shipped them all back to Flanders, and in London *Mercurius Politicus* made propaganda out of the Protector's generous treatment of the woman 'who passed for Charles Stuart's wife', and the boy said to be his son.[6]

The fiasco silenced Lucy for a while, but when she emerged again in Brussels in August 1657 she was penniless and desperate, having been deserted by Howard. At Bruges, Hyde noted 'many shrewd discourses which will quickly get into England; pray, let her go to another place'; Ormonde in Brussels heard of disturbances involving mother and son; and at Skenvoorde the Earl of Bristol expressed his fears too. This wave of alarm was justified: Lucy had decided to settle with both men who had abandoned her. She employed a bravo to attack Howard in the street, and he received a 'very dangerous wound' in the arm. As for Charles, unless her pension was paid she would post up in public all his old letters to her.[7]

Desperate measures were now called for. Mother and son were staying with Sir Arthur Slingsby in Brussels, and Charles ordered him to kidnap the boy. Slingsby bungled the task, attempting to recover some money Lucy owed him as well. The consequence was an appalling scene in the public street, with Slingsby trying to remove the boy and drag Lucy away to a debtor's prison, while Lucy resisted fiercely 'with great outcries embracing her son'. Neighbours flocked out, Slingsby had to give up, and mother and son took refuge nearby. The Spanish authorities sharply reproved the English for this 'most barbarous, abominable, and unnatural action', and the Governor wrote severely to Charles concerning this 'occurrence which everyone condemns'. Then Slingsby blurted out that he had been acting on the King's orders and threatened to sue the Spanish if Lucy was not released to him to pay her debts, while the Spanish Governor was reproved by the Council of Brabant for interfering in a civil action at law. When the confusion died down Charles persisted that the boy must be delivered to him, for Lucy was 'ruining an innocent child by making a property of him to support herself in [her] wild and disgraceful courses'.[8]

Schooled by adversity, Lucy seemed to bow before the storm and in January 1658 appeared ready to surrender the boy. Delays and qualifications then began, and in March 1658 Charles turned to direct action once more, employing 'little Tom Ross' one of his spymasters. This time there was no hitch, and at the age of nine James was removed from his mother for ever. It was at first intended to make Ross, a bookish man despite his talent for plotting, the boy's tutor but more sensible councils prevailed, and he did not take up his responsibilities for another two or three years. In the meantime, James was lodged with a crony of the King, Lord William Crofts, and took the latter's surname passing for a distant relative. Crofts's passions were dancing, hunting, and duelling, and the sober Edward Hyde had been 'mad and weary of life' when this rake was appointed Gentleman of the Bedchamber. Possibly through the influence of Henrietta Maria, however, 'James Crofts' was enrolled for a time in a *petite école*, and then at the academy of Familly; and an Oratorian, Father Goffe, gave him some instruction in Catholicism, although the boy was never converted. The influence of Crofts was stronger, however, than that of teacher or priest, and four years after his abduction the Venetian ambassador to England could only observe tactfully that the boy had been educated 'in accordance with the quality which belongs to him . . . in the manner of a prince'.[9]

Lucy did not long survive their separation. For a short time her old spirit reasserted itself — a royal chaplain tried and failed dismally to reform her, and she seized some of Howard's papers and tried to blackmail him — but then it flickered out. She became ill (venereal disease claimed James II), and at last sought the consolation of religion making a general confession of her life to John Cosin, later Bishop of Durham. She died toward the end of 1658 at the age of twenty-eight.[10] At her deathbed Cosin promised to keep her confession secret while the King still lived. This was an understandable precaution, given the political situation in 1658 and Lucy's relationship with Charles, but in later years it gave rise to rumours that she had spoken of a marriage to the King, and given her confessor a 'Black Box' containing documentary proofs of the ceremony. When Cosins died in 1672 nobody was left to refute such talk, and the existence of this 'Black Box' became an article of faith among some of the opposition after 1679.

There is no evidence that his mother ever directly informed James that she and the King had been married, although so little is known about her that silence is inconclusive, and considering her desperate condition and violent temper it seems most probable that her son was told he was a prince. What is clear is that she always insisted that James was the son of the King. She even boasted of his paternity while in the Tower in 1656, and when she could afford servants they were instructed to treat the child with particular deference, and to refer to him as 'master'. In her last years he was her only hope of maintenance, and the self-importance this bred in the boy could only have been increased by the desperate measures undertaken by Charles II to secure him.

At another level too James would have wanted to believe his mother had been married. Deserted by his father, only briefly in contact with Lucy's passing lovers, and cut off by exile from his maternal relatives, his mother provided the boy's only continuous relationship with an adult during his formative years. And though often neglectful, Lucy was also young, beautiful, and energetic. We may infer what James though of her from such episodes as his swearing, upon arriving at the English court at the age of fifteen, that he would be the death of any man denying that she had been married to the King. And yet, not quite outside his hearing, the court not only scoffed at the marriage but asserted that Lucy had been a common whore. The boy's uncle wrote that she 'lived so loosely . . . [and] abandoned herself and grew so common that she died in Paris . . . of a disease incident to her profession'. When Robert Sidney lost her in 1648 he shrugged off the matter: 'let who will have her for she is sped'. To John Evelyn she was 'a most beautiful strumpet'; to the judicious Clarendon 'a private Welchwoman of no good fame'; to royal servants an accomplished harlot, who had lost her honour well before she met Charles.[11] At the Restoration court this teen-age boy heard vicious disparagement of female virtue, and witnessed the treatment of women made into harlots: the woman of easy virtue was an all-too-real presence for him, and insistence upon his mother's marriage to the King was a means of denying that she was such a creature. When he swore that his mother and the King had been married James was not merely or principally asserting his own legitimacy; he was trying to cleanse the memory of a mother who had provided him with the only affection he had known during an insecure childhood. His need to believe in the marriage was an emotional reaction and not a political calculation, and unfortunately for him it was also too strong to be controlled.

The boy's harsh childhood also affected his attitude to his father. Mother and son had experienced dire poverty, and Lucy's repeated and fruitless applications to Charles for money appeared to show where the blame lay. The King was also directly responsible for two attempts to kidnap James, the first a terrifying experience for a nine year old, the second quickly followed by his mother's death. By the time he came to England the boy probably felt that his father fully owed him the wealth and honours showered on him, and his stubborn refusal to ask the King's pardon after 1679 may have owed much to the experience of childhood. But Lucy too was responsible for some scars: she was violent, impetuous, and improvident; and quite apart from their family's poverty, their frequent removes to another home and the scarcely less frequent changes of lover probably induced a strong feeling of insecurity in both her children.

In two other ways the Duke was marked by his early years. His education was almost totally neglected — in 1658 at the age of nine he could neither read nor count. Instruction only began when he was taken to Paris after the abduction, and lasted full time only three years because he underwent no formal education after coming to England. As an adult he could read and write, though his orthography was child-like and his spelling bizarre even by the standards of the day. Worse than that, however, he formed no early habit of reading and later found himself very ill-equipped intellectually to enter the world of Restoration politics. If responsibility for this deficiency lay with his mother, she partly compensated by instilling in her son a genuine if not very deep religious piety. The undenominational prayers for morning, evening and other occasions found in the pocket book taken off him after Sedgemoor, are unlikely to have been learned from anyone else.[12] Father Goffe's efforts did not attract James toward Catholicism (although the Duke was to remember him affectionately twenty years later, in 1679) and throughout his life Monmouth remained a firm, if not particularly moral, Protestant.

Between the abduction in 1658 and the Restoration Charles saw very little of his son, even though Crofts lived conveniently close to Paris, and he was in no hurry to summon him to England after the Restoration. Not until August 1662 did James arrive at court, in the distinguished company of the Queen Mother, Lord Jermyn, and Prince Edward of the Palatinate. Thereafter the boy's conquest of his father was swift. By 1668 Charles, writing to one of the few people with whom he was completely frank, his sister 'Minette', Duchess of Orleans, could 'confess I do love him very well'. This may have begun as a feeling of guilt but it soon deepened. A pretty child grew into an attractive youth. At his first view of him in 1662 Samuel Pepys saw 'a most pretty sparke'; and James II remembered a teenager 'very handsome . . . tall, well-shaped, a good air, civil behaviour . . . a favourite with the ladies' — a remarkable commendation, given James's hostility toward his nephew when he wrote it. A portrait from this period shows a confident-looking dark-haired boy, handsome indeed but with a slightly plump face and pouting mouth, conveying the impression of an irritable cherub.[13]

But the boy's charm rested on more than a pretty face. His energy and spontaneity captivated the King. He was constantly active, 'the most skittish leaping gallant that I ever saw, always in action, vaulting, leaping or clambering', wrote Pepys. The Venetian ambassadors in both London and Paris agreed in describing him as 'high-spirited' and 'very spirited'. Sometimes this energy erupted into farcical horse-play as in 1667 when, after a Garter ceremony, Monmouth chased some other Knights, still wearing their flowing robes, all around Hyde Park and then conducted races in commandeered hackney cabs. On another occasion, at a production of Shadwell's *The Sullen Lovers* Monmouth topped off the costume of an over-dressed French fop by leaping on stage and presenting the actor with his own sword. And in a nice finish to the gesture he bade the man keep it. Such impulsive and clowning behaviour appealed to the sardonic side of Charles II, who once ridiculed the King of Spain's love of ceremony with the comment that the latter 'would not piss but another must hold the pot'.[14]

Monmouth's skill at dancing also appealed to the King, whose early cronies such as Lord Taafe and Crofts were often accomplished in the ballroom. Lucy Walter's son soon showed his ability: confident and graceful, handsome and growing tall, the youth shone at the balls and dances which formed the staple of court entertainment. Even the sober Clarendon, who had little use for such diversions, pronounced that James 'performed these exercises gracefully which youths of that Age used to learn in France'.[15] He soon acquired his father's love of racing, accompanying him to Newmarket each year in the spring and autumn, and was an early convert to the Duke of York's newly-introduced sport of fox-hunting.

His son's naiveté also amused the King. In his innocence the boy was so taken with a French visitor to court that he swore her complexion was not painted but natural — and 'was quickly laughed out of it'. At Newmarket races James followed the advice of a French astrologer the Abbé Pregnani, and lost heavily on all his bets. And Charles tried — without success — to persuade James that his own hair became him far better than a wig, when the boy prepared to visit the French court. Though a youthful innocent — for a while — the boy was sufficiently quick-witted to talk agreeably with his father. Writing to his sister 'Minette' Charles observed of his son 'you will not find him to want wit'.[16] Amusing and reasonably sharp, the boy also appealed to the strong domestic streak in his father's nature (displayed for example in his affection for his infants by the Countess of Castlemaine), an adolescent boy nicely balancing Charles's informal 'family'. The relatively small age difference between father and son also made for an easier relationship, Charles being only in his thirties when his son was a teenager.

Charles's affection — indeed love — was openly manifested. Courtiers noted repeatedly that 'the King do still doat', or 'do doat infinitely upon his son', or that he was 'so fond of him that everyone admires it'. An Italian visitor was startled by the physical expression of Charles's 'tender affection' for the youth, which led him to 'kiss and embrace him in public'. Gifts of honours and titles were an equally clear measure of affection. In November 1662 the boy was created Duke of Monmouth, Earl of Doncaster, and Baron of Fotheringay. The Scottish title was included because the following year James was married to Anne Scott, only daughter of Lady Wemys widow of the Earl of Buccleuch — and heiress to one of the largest fortunes in the land, estimated at £10,000 p.a. 'Discovered' in the 1650s by General Monck during his command of the army in Scotland, the girl had been at first intended for his own son Christopher; but John Maitland, Duke of Lauderdale, perceived in the marriage of the King's favourite son to a

Scottish heiress a means to strengthen his grip upon Charles's Scottish affairs, and concluded negotiations with Anne's mother. James received titles commensurate with his royal birth, and took the surname of Scott (though none of his wife's money, prudently entailed out of his grasp by Lady Wemys). Christopher Monck, at fourteen the same age as the new Duke of Monmouth, was — not for the last time in his life — cut off from his expectations by his peer and rival.

The royal bastard was next invested with the Order of the Garter, and directed to take precedence over all other Dukes of England except York. On public occasions he now followed third, after the heir apparent, and the ageing Prince Rupert. He was given part of the new building constructed at the Cockpit for a town residence, and in 1664 Charles paid £7,000 to buy him John Ashburnham's house in Chiswick. Plate for the house and jewellery for his person were also included. Next year he received a pension of £6,000 p.a., and various cash sums were added from time to time — £18,000 in 1667, £4,000 in 1668, £13,000 in 1670. Given command of a troop of horse in 1666, the youth enjoyed it so much that two years later Charles paid Lord Gerard of Brandon £8,000 to resign his Captaincy of the Life Guards in favour of Monmouth. This gave the young man command of the army's élite formation, seniority over all other regular officers, and personal responsibility for the King's safety and more broadly, that of the court. Advancement indeed for a nineteen year old. By now Charles was so proud of his son that Monmouth was sent to France in 1668 to sweeten Louis XIV, before Sir John Trevor's embassy arrived to explain away England's sudden alliance with the Dutch. The Duke succeeded so well that Louis offered him a commission in the French army, then moving off to the battle-front, an embarrassment to Charles II who was trying to appear as a peace-maker. Monmouth was withdrawn a little hastily, but was sent abroad again in 1672 to charm the French once more.[18]

The King's favours to his son quickly encouraged others to follow suit. Oxford and Cambridge entertained him lavishly and awarded honorary degrees in 1663. A book of French verse was published with such a fulsome dedication to Monmouth that his uncle allegedly took offence. Justus Walters, brother to Lucy and her companion in the 'Tower' fiasco of 1656, visited court and was well received. Edward Montague suffered the opposite fate, banished from court for rudeness to the young Duke as well as excessive attention to the Queen. Newly-arrived ambassadors found it advisable to visit the Duke as soon as possible, the Venetian ambassador commenting that Charles was very pleased by 'any act of regard shown his son'. Ruvigny, the French ambassador, went one step further, offering Monmouth a share in 'a certain engine' intended to reduce friction in coaches and wagons (and make a lot of money for its patentees). Calculation was mixed with affection in the treatment Monmouth received from the King's women. Barbara Villiers, Countess of Castlemaine, the King's stormy mistress, quickly decided to see in the boy no rival to her own infant children by Charles, and it was soon observed that the lad 'do much hang upon my Lady Castlemaine and is always with her'. At New Year's Eve balls he regularly led the royal mistress out, and they remained on friendly terms throughout her ascendancy. Castlemaine's repeated and violent scenes with Charles may have strengthened James's belief that, if pushed hard enough, the King would always surrender to a favourite. The Queen too found the Duke attractive: young, unhappy, and defensive, she enjoyed the company of this teenage extrovert, like her a newcomer to the court. Monmouth held balls in honour of Catherine and her ladies, and in return was invited to the small and select gatherings she preferred.[19]

Royal favour on such a scale inevitably had political consequences. Courtiers and others began to wonder whether the King had any long-term plans for his bastard, particularly since the King's marriage to Catherine of Braganza was barren of issue (as the disappointed Spanish court had warned it would be, in 1662, when Charles chose the Portuguese princess). The King was still young, but when the Queen's only two pregnancies miscarried in 1665 and 1668, the possibility of James Duke of York inheriting the Crown grew stronger. York was unpopular to many before he converted to Catholicism in 1668 — a severe, humourless, and unforgiving man, he was also married to the Earl of Clarendon's daughter, and was thus tied to the fading fortunes of this elder statesman. There was good reason for Charles's attitude to his son to be regarded with deep interest, and following his policy of keeping everybody uncertain over his intentions the King gave courtiers ample food for thought. When the boy was invested with the Order of the Garter in 1663 Charles was so pleased with his bearing that at the subsequent feast, when Monmouth was dancing with the Queen, his hat held correctly in his hand, he came up to the couple and, kissing his son, ordered him to wear his hat while with the Queen. Nobody could miss this implication of equal status; and the same was true when Monmouth joined the King, York, and Prince Rupert in wearing deep purple in mourning for the deceased Duchess of Suffolk — the youth mourned 'as a Prince of the Blood'. Promotion to Captaincy of the Life Guards in 1668 stimulated rumours of still more advancement.[20]

In a court such as this, however, extravagant gestures were not needed to start rumours of legitimization. In 1663 the boy had just arrived, and was captivating a King reputed to be 'sullen' toward his new Queen. Three times in May alone of that year Pepys recorded new rumours concerning legitimization. Then in July 1663 George Digby made his premature attempt to unseat Clarendon, including among his charges one of 'venting scandal against the King, as though the Duke of Monmouth were to be legitimized'. Though the accusation against Clarendon was absurd, it shows that the Duke's position was already a subject for speculation. The rumours continued in coffee houses later in the year, and early in 1664 they were still heard. Disaster in the Second Dutch War and the fall of Clarendon revived them in 1667. As Lord Admiral, the Duke of York carried much responsibility for the naval failure, and with the heir's reputation declining further consequent on his father-in-law's flight into exile, some courtiers inevitably saw 'more at the bottom than the removal of the Chancellor . . . the King do resolve to declare the Duke of Monmouth legitimate'. Those who feared York's revenge once he had recovered found comfort in talk of removing him from the succession, to which his conversion in 1668 gave renewed impetus. Important men found the legitimization project plausible in and after 1668. Lord Conway wrote that 'either a bill of divorce is to follow, or a bill to affirm that the King was married to the Duke of Monmouth's mother, as Clarendon told me'. The Earl of Carlisle, and Anthony Cooper, later Earl of Shaftesbury, urged Charles to 'own Monmouth'; and when Buckingham switched from 'legitimization' to divorce and re-marriage for the King, Lauderdale took his place, whispering of Monmouth in the King's ear.[21]

By 1668 memories of Lucy Walters' character and behaviour were becoming sufficiently vague for talk of the King legitimizing his son even to have given place, in some circles, to assertions that father and mother had been married, and the Duke, therefore, born in wedlock. In January 1668 rumours spread in the countryside that St.Asaph and three other bishops could testify to the marriage, and a month later Viscount Conway considered that Charles 'would offer himself to have been married to the Duke of Monmouth's mother, but is afraid of the Duke of York'. In the summer of 1669 as a new session of Parliament approached, the Venetian ambassador was trying to discover where renewed talk of the Duke's legitimacy emanated from.[22]

Even before Monmouth had reached manhood, therefore, powerful interests were talking openly of his possible legitimacy. A teenager still, he could do little to forward the talk, though he made plain his belief in it. In 1664 he had openly spoken of his mother's marriage to the King; and at about the same time the arms of England, Scotland, and France were painted on his coach, but as an observer commented 'What it speaks of him being a bastard I know not'. Charles permitted a remarkable vagueness about the style to which his son was entitled. The arms granted to the Duke in April 1665 contained no indication of illegitimacy, and a bar sinister was only added two years later. Reference to James as 'the King's natural son' was deleted from the marriage contract, and in grants made to the Duke — such as the Captaincy of the Life Guards — he was styled Charles's 'beloved son', with no reference to illegitimacy. Such complacency on the part of the King could only have encouraged Monmouth's fantasies about his mother, but the boy had already received what seemed final confirmation from his tutor (and abductor) Thomas Ross. As a royalist spy-master during the 1650s the latter was undoubtedly privy to strange secrets from those times; and as a man with his way to make in the 1660s he soon saw advantage in promoting the marriage story. According to the Duke of York, Ross first confirmed the story to the boy, and then tried to persuade John Cosin not only to add his testimony, but to swear that he had conducted the ceremony. Cosin refused and informed the King. Ross was temporarily disgraced, but later reinstated as James's tutor. York gave no date for the story but some time around the Restoration seems implied.[23]

The flattery of courtiers, the indulgence of a King, talk of legitimacy and all it entailed — Monmouth's adolescent years at court were in some ways worse for his development than the hardships of childhood. In Clarendon's choice phrase, the King 'took not that care for the strict breeding of him as his Age required'. Nor did the boy's tutor make up the deficiency. Ross was too busy hunting for preferment to undertake the thankless task of disciplining his charge, and his dedication to James of a translation he prepared of the Fall of Carthage tells simply of an uneasy conscience. The youth remained at best semi-educated — at the age of fifteen a letter to his father 'made the poor young Duke sigh and sweat, not being used to write'. This admission came from the boy's tutor himself, and Ross's complacency is indicated by his explanation when he allowed Monmouth to gamble away some travelling money the King had given him: 'I cannot wish my little lord to be so singular and sit by while others lose five pounds with cheerful satisfaction'. Gambling filled much of the boy's time — Pepys's early glimpse of him playing cards with the Queen's maids of honour was characteristic.

Dancing, hunting and racing occupied the rest of the day, supplemented as he grew into adolescence by drinking and whoring. By the end of 1666 Pepys's references to the Duke are wholly condemnatory: Monmouth was spending his time 'the most viciously and idly of any man'; galloping around Harwich during the invasion scare of 1667, the Duke and his fellow courtier-soldiers did nothing but 'debauch the country women thereabouts'; and the proposed visit to France in the following year would 'be becoming him much more than his whoreing and roguing as he now do'. During the winter of 1667-68 Charles had the disturbing experience of paying court to an actress 'not of extraordinary beauty, but a very graceful dancer', only to find that his eighteen-year old son had preceded him in her bed.[24]

With promiscuity went expensive living. A commission appointed in 1664 to manage the Duke's income and allow him 'a competent maintenance' proved totally unable to control him. Monmouth could run through £9,000 in nine months on 'Private Expenses and Cloaths' alone. His accounts show £50 paid for one wig, and individual purchases of £100 to £200 from his tailor. His wife was no better, spending up to £1,200 on a pair of diamond earrings, and Monmouth's pension of £6,000 p.a. from his father was understandably inadequate to meet their combined outgoings. With Anne's income entailed out of the Duke's reach the couple had to rely upon occasional gifts from the King of several thousand pounds at a time to pay their debts.[25]

Birth, personality, and heavy spending made Monmouth the natural leader of his peer group, the 'great many blades' who frequented the capital's coffee houses, setting standards of fashion and behaviour for young men about town. Samuel Pepys was incensed by the appearance of a young naval clerk wearing 'his hat like a fool behind', a style known as the 'Monmouth cock', and still prevalent among west-country gentry in the following century. In violence too Monmouth was the leader, his conduct reaching a peak over Christmas and New Year 1670-71, when in the space of a few weeks he gave orders for a savage mutilation and took part in a murder. Sir John Coventry, an M.P. and brother of a Secretary of State, made a poor joke in the House of Commons, enquiring whether the King's interest in the theatre ran to male or to female actors. When Coventry returned home that night four men attacked him and slit his nose. Two were from Monmouth's troop of Guards, and it was plain who had directed the attack. Andrew Marvell's lines from 'The King's Vows' show how far Monmouth was from popular favour at this point:

> I will have a fine Son in makeing tho marred,
> If not o're a Kingdome, to reign ore my Guard;
> And Successor be, if not to me, to Gerrard.
> ⋯⋯⋯⋯⋯⋯⋯⋯⋯⋯⋯⋯⋯⋯⋯⋯⋯⋯⋯⋯⋯
> Which if any bold commoner dare to oppose
> I'll order my Bravo's to cut off his Nose,
> Tho' for't I a branch of prerogative lose.

Incensed by the attack, Parliament passed the 'Coventry Act', making it a capital offence to cut, maim, or disfigure any person. A few weeks later the King, Prince Rupert, and the Dukes of York and Monmouth attended a revel at Lincoln's Inn Hall. At its conclusion Monmouth left the others and sought out his courtier friends, including the late General Monck's son Christopher newly created Duke of Albemarle, the Duke of Somerset, the Earl of Rochester, and Viscount Dunbar. They went to a brothel near Lincoln's Inn Fields, began a drunken brawl, and when a beadle named Peter Visnell tried to suppress it, he was run through. Some said Albemarle held the sword, others Monmouth.[26] Both Dukes received royal pardons. In 1685 Albemarle was to command the Devonshire militia, and Somerset that of Somersetshire — neither of them with any credit — against their former roistering leader.

These actions confirmed opinions at Westminster, and among those of the political nation who considered the matter, that the young Duke was simply a wastrel, a typical unpleasant product of the court. The gulf between Monmouth, and the politicians who were increasingly suspicious of Charles's policies, was demonstrated in 1677 when the Earl of Shaftesbury, sent to the Tower for his activities in Parliament, used his spare time to characterize the members of the House of Lords. Monmouth received three V's in his list, the fullest degree of 'vileness'. The opinion was reciprocated: when Shaftesbury and the two other Lords held in the Tower petitioned for release Monmouth joined York and Danby in urging the King to refuse, otherwise royal authority would be trampled on.[27] For their part, the opposition had strong political and moral reasons to dislike the Duke.

Though he participated in no more homicides, Monmouth throughout the 1670s seemed to epitomize the immoral, extravagant, courtier. He could spend £300 on one set of masking clothes alone, and hired the largest houses in London so that his masquerade balls — attended by 'lewd women and debauched men' — would always have a different setting. He took as a close companion the ageing soldier Sir Thomas Armstrong. A devoted royalist during the Civil War, Armstrong had married a niece of the Earl of Clarendon and acquired a

Lieutenancy in the Guards but then fell from grace, his life becoming 'very vitious', and 'debauched Athiestical', according to Burnett and Sprat respectively. He killed a gentleman over an actress shortly after he had attached himself to Monmouth and remained in semi-disgrace at court, but the Duke could not bring himself to cast off this violent Falstaff whose ill behaviour reflected constantly upon his patron. The Duke also gained notoriety from his succession of mistresses, having a child by Elizabeth Waller (daughter of the old parliamentarian) in 1669; sharing the resourceful Moll Kirke with his uncle and Lord Musgrave in 1673; and being 'catch'd abroad' in 1675 with Eleanor Needham — who bore him four children. Between these affairs he alarmed a number of husbands including his crony Christopher the young Duke of Albemarle, who in 1671 hurriedly removed his wife from court when Monmouth 'cast his eye that way'. Not surprisingly Monmouth's relations with his own wife were formal and distant, although she bore him four children two of whom died in childhood. A lively but inexperienced girl at her marriage Anne saw little of her husband during the 1670s, going off to Bath or visiting the Queen, while Monmouth attended the King at Windsor or travelled abroad. Life at court made her watchful and sharp, so that by 1673 Evelyn wrote after observing her at a dinner party that she 'is certainly one of the wisest and craftiest of her sex; she has much witt'. In her youth she spent money as freely as her husband, but when the Duke was disgraced in 1679 she dismissed forty servants, and carefully distanced herself from him, retaining in some degree the friendship of both Charles II and James II. She remarried in 1687 and lived on until 1732, dying at eighty-two.[28]

Such caution was impossible for her husband, whose personality and behaviour kept him court favourite for most of the 1670s, in good favour with both King and heir apparent. He hunted regularly with his uncle, stood god-father to the daughter born to Mary of Modena in 1676, and when an aggressive M.P. told York to leave his idolatry it was Monmouth who hustled the man from the room. The two Dukes dined together regularly and it was noted 'by those that are nere unto his Royall Highness that he has a particular kindness and affection for his Grace upon whom, indeed, all the world now looks as a rising sun'. As King's mistress, the Duchess of Portsmouth was careful to attend banquets given by Monmouth; and the King dined with him so regularly that one of Danby's correspondents in 1674 could be surprised that he 'seems still to gain ground with the King'. His physical poise and co-ordination remained with him, so that when *Calisto* was performed at court in 1675 he was one of the male dancers who drew praise, and when a new design of sledge appeared at Christmas 1676 he was among the few able to master it.[29]

Honours continued to shower upon him, identifying the Duke even more closely with the court — membership of the Privy Council and of the House of Lords in 1670, a Chief Justiceship in Eyre in 1672, High Chamberlain the next year, as well as Lord Lieutenant of the East Riding of Yorkshire, and Governor of Kingston-on-Hull. In 1674 he became Master of Horse, Chancellor of Cambridge University, and a Privy Councillor of Scotland. He was so obviously the King's favourite that a group of courtiers tried to groom another royal bastard, Charles FitzCharles known as 'Don Carlo' (born to Catherine Pegge in the early 1650's) to supplant him, but wholly without success. Immoral and extravagant in his life, the creature and favourite of an increasingly isolated court, Monmouth's open liking for France also distanced him from opposition opinion during the 1670s. Although he fought against the French in 1673 and 1678, he did so strictly as a professional soldier. He made it plain where his heart was by going to fight for France as a volunteer in 1677, when Louis's conquests in Flanders were alarming Parliament, and just after the Commons had voted that any who supported France were enemies of the Kingdom.

By parentage, interest, and upbringing, Monmouth was thus part of the court, but it was not for these reasons alone that Shaftesbury considered him so 'vile' in 1677. The Duke had by then also alarmed the opposition because he effectively commanded England's small professional army. As a boy he had accompanied his uncle, the Lord Admiral, when the fleet fought the Dutch all day in the battle off Lowestoft in June 1665. His enthusiasm and courage stirred the King's pride — James 'did behave in all the Dutch war as well as anybody', he wrote — and minor commissions preceded command of the Guards in 1668. Besides presiding impressively over this élite's annual parades — attended by his father and uncle — the Duke took an inventory of his troops' equipment, uncovering some startling deficiencies. Encouraged by this application to duty the King put him on a commission with York, Rupert and others to regulate army matters left unattended, following the death of the Captain-General the Duke of Albemarle, in 1670.[30] By 1672 Charles was ready to appoint his son to command of the English troops being sent to fight with the French against the Dutch, spiting the Duke of Buckingham who had expected this honour himself.

Monmouth thus arrived in France with 'the most magnificent equipage', was presented to Louis, and received for his force precedence on the march and in camp over all French regiments, the King's Guards only expected. But this was his only satisfaction from the 1672 campaign. Dogged by delays, shortage of equipment, and indiscipline, the English troops did nothing while Turenne drove deep into the United Provinces. Monmouth returned to England in August 1672 to attend the birth of his son, and again in April 1673 to take the sacrament imposed by the Test Act, but his interest in the war was quickened when, upon his second return to France, he was given command of one of the four bodies of French troops besieging Maastricht. Assured of being to an 'extraordinary degree in the [French] King's particular favour' the Duke proceeded to seek glory.[31]

His chance came on the 25 June 1673, when he was ordered to clear some entrenchments in front of Maastricht's Brussels gate. He led two battalions into a counter scarp and a half moon, against heavy fire and a rain of several thousand grenades. Over four hundred troops were lost, but he took the position and left men to hold it. Next day the Dutch exploded a mine under the entrenchments and re-took them, sweeping the French survivors aside. Monmouth counter-attacked at once, gathering up some French musketeers under the celebrated D'Artagnan, and a handful of English nobles, servants, and soldiers. Running over the tops of trenches swept by fire, he was first into the ruins of the half moon and the Dutch were once again thrown out, this time permanently. His French musketeers suffered heavily, with D'Artagnan killed by a shot in the head, while among the English party several were killed, and Captain John Churchill was wounded. Sir Thomas Armstrong, at the Duke's side, was untouched.[32]

This episode created the Duke of Monmouth's military reputation, and it was endlessly told and re-told during the Exclusion Crisis. In reality, of course, it proved nothing of his qualities of generalship, simply that he was a very good junior officer. The first attack demonstrated that he could carry out a frontal assault against a prepared position, attacking with such speed that the defence was surprised and overwhelmed — a captured officer believed that his force had been betrayed, so swift was the assault. The counter-attack further showed Monmouth's capacity to improvise, and revealed a valuable instinct for vigorous action in an emergency. The engagement was only an episode in a long siege, and Maastricht did not surrender for another month. But Monmouth returned to England a war hero. Louis XIV had been present at the episode, and wrote a flattering commendation. Charles was delighted with his son, the government needed a victory, the nation was thirsty for glory; and a legend was thus created which a few years later was seriously to embarrass the regime.

Five frigates were waiting for the Duke at Calais, the harbour guns saluted him, and he was welcomed extravagantly in England. Courtiers delivered him mock reproofs for his rashness, a gentleman wrote flatly that Monmouth's action alone had caused the town's surrender, and an English chronicle modestly asserted that 'among all the actions performed at this Siege, there was none more signal than the Achievement of the Duke of Monmouth'. On a summer night in 1674 the hero and the Duke of York re-enacted the battle outside Windsor Castle, with a cast of hundreds of soldiers and an elaborate reconstruction of the trenches and defences. The audience showed 'great satisfaction' at the climax when Monmouth and a handful of Guards valiantly re-took the half moon. There was talk of giving him command of the Fleet now that York was driven out by the Test Act and Rupert ageing fast, but nothing came of it.[33] Monmouth considered rejoining his regiment in Flanders, but in 1674 the war was running down, and he settled back to enjoy being a soldier-courtier.

His position in the army after 1673 was anomalous. Following the death of Albemarle in 1670 the army had no commander-in-chief, and Charles agreed with York in appointing none thus guaranteeing royal control of the armed forces. But if the King's son showed himself loyal and effective, why not train him for the position? Accordingly, in January 1674 Charles ordered Monmouth to conduct an inspection of the army, after which he was effectively to share command with the Secretary of State Arlington. Any orders given by Monmouth were to be presented to the King who would pass them on to Arlington for counter-signature. This position of supervised command had, as an observer noted, 'no name. . . . However it is initiating him into business'; and as the initiation proceeded Charles gave his son more and more specific responsibilities. Colonels of regiments were instructed to obey the Duke's commands, and his powers were then extended to cover the quartering and general duties of troops in billets, the relief of garrisons, the suppression of riots, and the movement of troops about the country.[34] Besides these general duties, Monmouth took action in the daily life of the army over a remarkably wide range of issues. Although his uncle York usually made appointments above the rank of captain Monmouth intervened where he could, and sent letters of encouragement to those who had been disappointed. He enquired into the case of a captain accused of irregularities in officers' and soldiers' pay, and replaced a colonel whose ill-health had led to indiscipline within his regiment. He ordered the officers of the garrison at Hull not to enlist married men, as they caused trouble when the garrison was moved. When an ensign was provoked into attacking and killing his captain, Monmouth heard the case and found for the ensign. He sent instructions to a major concerning the men he was recruiting, and to a colonel on equalizing the strength of the companies in his regiment. Officers temporarily without troops to command were found interim positions. Soldiers injured on active service were placed in garrisons, and the Duke took an interest in plans to construct a hospital for the wounded. In 1679 he was instructed by the Privy Council to build barracks for soldiers in London to end the problems caused by quartering them on civilians, but lost his position before anything could be done. As titular commander of the brigade left in France after 1674 he interceded repeatedly, though not very effectively, with the French authorities to improve their conditions of service, and he fought hard to re-engage an officer whom Louvois had dismissed unjustly.[35]

Apart from these detailed activities the Duke was involved in three broader attempts to reform and improve the army. In 1675 he drafted ten articles to serve as the basis of a code of discipline in his own regiment. Blaspheming, swearing, and drunkenness were banned, as were disrespectful words to superiors. Absence without leave was to be severely punished in camp as well as on the march. The importance of proper quartering for troops was recognized in a provision to deal with those who cheated landlords, and death was prescribed both for sentries sleeping at their post and for troops who sold arms or equipment to civilians. Officers were specifically warned of their responsibilities — to see that pay was correct and regular, to supervise the making and breaking of camp, and to avoid quarrelling with one another. Like most military codes its intentions were impeccable, but implementation was more difficult than drafting. The same could be said for an attempt made by the Duke, with some help from Buckingham, to reform the system of military drill. In May 1674 commanders of regiments were informed that a new manual was to be published incorporating lessons learnt during the recent war, and in the following year Monmouth placed an order with the royal printer for one hundred copies of this *Abridgement of English Military Discipline*. The system was based upon the then very successful French model, and having experimented with his own regiment the Duke in 1676 ordered a further 1,500 copies printed, so that the entire army could be initiated into the secrets of Louis XIV's victories. Three years later in 1679 the King ordered the *Abridgement* to be used in Scotland and Ireland as well, so that all his forces would be standardized upon the same system of training. When

Monmouth attempted in 1685 to turn raw volunteers into soldiers in less than one month, he was working from a training manual he had been familiar with for ten years, and had tried to apply for five. At the time of its introduction, however, the *Abridgement* ran into a good deal of conservative opposition within the army, and whether it was extensively used is uncertain. This was not the case with the third measure of reform Monmouth was involved in, a revision of the methods used to pay the army. The extensive disbandments of 1679 put such pressure on the existing system that it broke down, and Monmouth and the Paymaster-General of the army Sir Stephen Fox concluded a new agreement which maintained a higher standard of honesty and efficiency.[36]

Although he lacked a formal title denoting command of the army (such as Captain-General), and although he did not run it with the close control to be expected from a truly professional soldier, Monmouth was too active to be dismissed simply as a paper commander. Charles awarded him specific responsibilities, and in the years 1673 to 1679 the Duke, still only in his twenties, was gradually initiated into military business, and possibly groomed for command: as the examples of York and Prince Rupert show, Charles had a tendency to keep military responsibilities within the family. Monmouth could quite reasonably have had high expectations, and he inevitably acquired the habits and attitudes of a full commander. He became accustomed to exercising authority within the army and, knowing that the King would support his son on most issues, sensible officers did his bidding. The army was small, little more than 6,000 strong, and within such a restricted establishment the Duke soon became familiar with a good proportion of the officers. He shared his father's easy and informal manner and could easily suppose that many, perhaps most, of the commissioned ranks had become attached to him through friendship or favour. During the Exclusion Crisis several officers did join him in opposition to the court, even though he was at that time stripped of army rank and could not protect them.[37] It is easy to see, therefore, why in the 1680s Monmouth believed that the army — 'his army' — would never fight against him. He chose not to remember that, although the Duke of York had fought at sea and not on land after the Restoration, he had spent the 1650s learning to be a soldier under Turenne; and that, although York lacked his nephew's intimate acquaintance with the army, he had after 1670 controlled most of the senior appointments, including all to regimental command.

Three other consequences followed from Monmouth's association with the army in the 1670s. In the first place, he quickly came to regard himself as its effective Captain-General and in 1675 petitioned Charles for the rank, arguing that he needed it if his orders were to be obeyed in time of emergency. After the riots in London that summer his father saw force in this argument, but was dissuaded by York who argued that Monmouth already outranked other officers as the senior colonel, and that civilian control of the army was still as necessary as ever. With this Monmouth had to be content, although piece-meal additions to his authority gave him many of the powers of a Captain-General. When the issue came up again three years later however, he would not be so easily pacified. Also of importance for the future was the role Monmouth came to play as army commander in support of the civil government. In 1676 he was instructed to provide regular escorts for traders' wagons travelling between London and the north. The previous summer he had been ordered to suppress cloth-makers' riots in London, and each year thereafter when the King left London for Newmarket he was careful to make his son responsible for suppressing any disturbances in the capital during his absence. This background made it inevitable that Monmouth would quickly be involved in the Popish Plot investigations, for he commanded the best force available to make searches, arrest suspects, and guard prominent places and people, and he had grown accustomed to using his troops in an emergency. And finally, effective command of the army brought Monmouth in the 1670s to the verge of participation in politics.

Hitherto, he had been important politically only because of the possibility that the King might legitimise him. This essentially passive role continued — there was renewed speculation in 1673 when York publicly demonstrated his Catholicism by refusing the Test Act — but in the 1670s Monmouth began to be politically important in another sense. Because of his Scottish marriage, the opposition to Lauderdale's severe regime in Scotland looked to him for assistance on several occasions, in 1673, 1676, and 1678. On the last occasion Charles sent his son to speak to a party of Scottish nobles who had come to London to denounce Lauderdale; and while they were 'all much charmed with softness of [Monmouth's] temper and behaviour', they recognized that the King was simply putting them off. According to Gilbert Burnet, however, in April 1678 Charles was seriously considering the replacement of Lauderdale by Monmouth, because the former's brutal regime was stirring up rebellion. Events overtook this possibility.[39]

Ireland was another contentious area considered for Monmouth, albeit here more in a figure-head role. In 1670, just after the Earl of

Essex had replaced Ormonde as Lord Lieutenant, there was talk of replacing Essex in turn by Monmouth as titular head, with real power to be exercised by the Earl of Anglesey as Deputy. The plan came to nothing, but a more serious effort was made in 1676. Danby was then trying to restore Ormonde, and was opposed by Vice-Treasurer Ranelagh who proposed to secure Monmouth's appointment as Lord Lieutenant, with Viscount Conway as Deputy to perform the functions of office. The title and the salary for a time tempted Monmouth, and Sir Thomas Armstrong his agent was 'almost daily' in Ranelagh's London house. Danby gave the scheme consideration and the Duchess of Portsmouth fully supported it, but after a year Monmouth, it was noted, 'does not yet persist in the plan' and the position went to Ormonde. Monmouth had some satisfaction from Essex's discomfiture, for the latter had obstructed his claim to £4,000 from the Earl of Northumberland's estate, and blocked his pursuit of concealed Crown lands in Ireland.[40] Before the Popish Plot Monmouth's relations with his future Whig associate, Essex, were just as bad as they were with his other future ally, Shaftesbury.

By the late 1670s, therefore, Monmouth was beginning to see himself, and be seen by others, as a political figure of some weight. The country's leading soldier, indisputedly the favourite of the King, considered for high office in Scotland and Ireland, he was careful to remain on good terms with the King's mistress (it was Portsmouth who told him he would be Master of Horse), and he cultivated the friendship of Henry Bennet, Earl of Arlington, one of the Secretaries of State. It was undoubtedly Bennet who took the initiative, for as early as 1665 he was reporting to the King on the young Duke's Christmas with Lord Crofts in Suffolk; but as Monmouth grew older the two dined together regularly. Arlington had a hand in most of the Duke's successive promotions and honours, from the troop of horse in 1666, to the visit to France in 1668, arranging supplies for the Duke in Flanders in 1672, and counter-signing his orders in the army after 1674.[41]

During this time Monmouth also began to dispense the range of patronage which accrued from his titles and honours — elections and appointments within Cambridge University, letters to bishops recommending suitors for livings, support to candidates for royal charity. But the Duke's patronage only amounted to assistance for unimportant men, and simply emphasized his lack of a power base independent of royal favour. Monmouth's positions and titles were mostly honour, not power or profit; and when his friendship with Arlington came to an end in 1676, and Arlington lost his influence with

Charles, Monmouth became intimate with no other royal advisor. Similarly, his finances depended entirely upon the King: in 1678 almost all his income of £8,000 p.a. came from a royal pension, other sources amounting to only £455.[42] As he approached his thirtieth year the Duke found himself on the brink of national politics, courted by the powerful as a semi-independent actor, but totally dependent upon the King's good favour, and probably quite unaware how dependent he was upon that favour. He might have remained safely on the brink but for two events which propelled him forward. One was his sudden quarrel with the Duke of York; the other was the Popish Plot.

War between France and the United Provinces was resumed in 1677, and young men at court enlisted as gentlemen adventurers. When Albemarle and the Earl of Ossory went to fight for the Dutch, Monmouth and the Huguenot Louis Duras Earl of Feversham were sent to fight for Louis. Recalled after some scuffles about Charleroi, Monmouth was given command of the land force which Charles II had been obliged to raise against France. Feversham became his deputy. The Duke of York was disappointed, having hoped for the command himself, and at the beginning of 1678 the heir's appetite for war against France surprised and alarmed the parliamentary opposition. In Flanders Monmouth found the morale of his Spanish allies so low, and the French threat to Bruges and Nieuport so developed, that he had to ignore his orders and concentrate simply upon the defence of Ostend. His letter to the King explaining the position was clear and convincing, and Charles replied giving his son complete freedom of action.[43] The French danger eased, and Monmouth and Feversham returned to England in March 1678, leaving their troops in position.

The Duke now revived his petition to be appointed Captain-General of the army. Since he had just led troops on active service (and done so competently), and was likely to see more hostilities in the future, the request was too reasonable to refuse. Moreover, he had behaved well after the request had been denied in 1675. A warrant was drawn up. The Duke of York then warned Secretary of State Williamson to be sure that the style 'natural son' was included in it. Monmouth heard of this, ordered his secretary to erase the term 'natural', and watched while this was done. Charles then signed the warrant unread in a pile of other papers, but York was suspicious and, retrieving it, found the erasure. He expostulated to the King about Monmouth's supposed dishonesty; and the King, deeply angered, personally destroyed the document and ordered a new one drawn up, incorporating the illegitimacy point. York was appeased by receiving the meaningless title of 'Generalissimo', and Monmouth received his Captaincy.[44]

But he received it with an apparently gratuitous slur, for most of his previous warrants had made no reference to bastardy, a fact which York knew perfectly well. Monmouth had fulfilled his military duties with credit, remained loyal to the Court, been dignified with honours and titles, and considered for important offices. His self-esteem was high, he believed he was entitled to a normally-worded commission such as he had received for other positions in the past, and he could only see personal jealousy in his uncle's action — an ageing former commander, disappointed in his hopes of seeing action again, trying to cheapen his nephew's new honour by smearing it with the taint of bastardy. So angry was Monmouth that in May 1678, he broke ranks for the first time and voted in the Lords with the opposition, on a motion that the army's new levies should be speedily disbanded as dangerous to the country's liberties.[45]

Renewed fighting in Flanders saved him from further indiscretions. Charles gave his son a pension of £1,600 p.a. for three years, and sent him back to the English forces with virtually a free hand to act. He took his troops from the coast to Mons where the Prince of Orange attacked the French, seeking a last-minute advantage before a peace was signed. Monmouth performed energetically in the fighting, being seen 'in person wherever any action or danger was', and was complimented on his demeanour by his opponent the Duke of Luxembourg. He believed that he had outmanoeuvred the French, and that only the incompetence of his Spanish allies had prevented a considerable success. He plainly disliked his allies and would have preferred fighting with the more efficient French, but the 'Journal' of his campaign reveals a very professional commander taking considerable pains, and making the troops' welfare his prime consideration. In particular, he tried to ensure that the English received good food and adequate billets, and that pay and equipment were as good as could be managed.[46]

It was a popular and successful commander who returned home in mid-August 1678. Monmouth had found his métier in the army, and this in turn gave him the standing to be taken seriously in politics, and for him to believe that he could play a part in politics. Though poorly educated, some observations on history and politics made in his pocket book show an attempt at self-improvement. No longer the King's wild young favourite, he was a man nearly thirty years old who had spent a decade and a half exhausting the pleasures of the ballroom, table, and bed, and was now ready for a new role. He had commanded the army in peace and led troops in war, been considered for high office, and been employed in minor diplomatic roles. By late 1678 the Duke of Monmouth was ready to enter national politics. It was doubly unfortunate for him that the major crisis of the Restored monarchy was about to break, and that the quarrel with his uncle was still fresh and sharp. In mid-August 1678 Monmouth returned to a court which was beginning to talk about a Popish Plot to kill the King.

Footnotes: Chapter Three

1. *The Diary of John Evelyn*, ed. E.de Beer, Oxford 1955, 6 vols., iv, 457; E.Hyde, *The Continuation of the Life of Edward Earl of Clarendon*, Oxford 1759, 3 vols., i, 391; J.MacPherson ed., *Original Papers . . . and Life of James II*, London 1749, 3 vols., i, 76-7, (hereafter James II, *Life*); H.Fornéron, *Louise de Kéroualle*, London 1887, p.174; G.Scott, *Lucy Walters, Wife or Mistress*, London 1947, pp.32-40, 54.

2. James II, *Life*, i, 76.

3. J.Evelyn, *Diary*, ii, 561-2; James II, *Life*, i, 76.

4. James II, *Life*, i, 76; W.Macray and H.Coxe eds., *Calendar of the Clarendon Papers*, Oxford 1869, 4 vols., ii, 419; J.Thurloe, *A Collection of State Papers*, London 1742, 7 vols., i, 665; 'The Nicholas Papers, Vol.II', ed. G.Warner, *Camden Society*, 50 1891, p.110.

5. 'Nicholas Papers, Vol.II', p.217; J.Thurloe, *State Papers*, i, 683, 684; 'Charles II's Letters to Lord Taafe', *Times Literary Supplement*, 30 April 1971, pp.507-8.

6. J.Thurloe, *State Papers*, v, 160, 169, 178; *Mercurius Politicus*, No.318, 10-17 July 1656.

7. *Cal.Clarendon S.P.*, iii, 341, 343, 352, 354, 400.

8. *Cal.Clarendon S.P.*, iv, 392-3, 396.

9. *CSPD 1655-56*, pp.123, 179; *CSPD 1657-58*, p.342; *Cal.Clarendon S.P.*, ii, 130; *CSPV 1661-64*, p.168.

10. J.Thurloe, *State Papers*, vii, 347, 428, 457; James II, *Life*, i, 76-7.

11. J.Thurloe, *State Papers*, v, 178; *The Diary of Samuel Pepys*, ed. H.Wheatley, London 1935, 10 vols., iv, 50; James II, *Life*, i, 76-7; J.Evelyn, *Diary*, iii, 561-2.

12. *CSPD 1657-58*, p.342; F.Poynter ed., *The Journal of James Yonge*, London 1963, p.21; Brit.Lib., Egerton MSS. 1527.

13. H.Bryant ed., *The Letters . . . of Charles II*, London 1935, p.232; S.Pepys, *Diary*, ii, 331; James II, *Life*, i, 75-6. The portrait is a miniature by Samuel Cooper, in the Royal Collection at Windsor Castle.

14. S.Pepys, *Diary*, v, 27; vi, 289; *CSPD 1661-64*, pp.168, 171; J.Downes, *Roscius Angelicanus*, London 1708, p.29; M.Ashley, *Charles II*, London 1973, p.156.

15. Clarendon, *Life*, i, 392.

16. M.Bryant, *Letters of Charles II*, pp.212, 220, 221.

17. W.Knowles, ed., *Lorenzo Magalotti at the Court of Charles II*, Laurier Press 1980, p.41; Clarendon, *Life*, i, 392-5.

18. *CSPD 1663-64*, pp.103, 128, 180, 185, 365, 539; *CSPD 1667-68*, pp.227, 336, 586; *CSPD 1664-65*, p.582; *CSPD 1667*, p.55; *CSPD 1670*, p.198; H.Bryant, *Letters of Charles II*, pp.211-14, 220-1; *CSPV 1666-68*, pp.213-14.

19. *CSPV 1666-68*, p.282; *CSPD 1667-68*, pp.397-8; S.Pepys, *Diary*, ii, 331, 396, 428; *HMC* 14th Report, Portland MSS III, p.294; 12th Report Rutland MSS., p.22.

20. S.Pepys, *Diary*, iii, 87, 101; iv, 18, 50.

21. S.Pepys, *Diary*, iii, 111, 120, 124, 339; iv, 36; vii, 110, 185; *CSPD 1663-64*, p.199; Bodl.Lib.Carte MSS., 36 f.25, 38 ff.635-6; James II, *Life*, i, 44; O.Airy ed., *Burnet's History of My Own Time*, Oxford 1847, 2 vols. i, 469-70; Andrew Marvell, *Works*, ed. H.Margiliouth, Oxford 1971 2 vols., ii, 315.

22. *CSPD 1667-68*, p.165; *CSPD 1668*, pp.258-9; *CSPV 1669-70*, p.180.

23. S.Pepys, *Diary*, iii, 95 and n.2; James II, *Life*, i, 76.

24. Clarendon, *Life*, i, 392; Brit.Lib.Royal MSS.17A, xx; *CSPD 1664-65*, p.76; S.Pepys, *Diary*, vi, 105, 263, 346, 349, 354; W.Knowles, *Magalotti*, pp.76-7.

25. Brit.Lib.Add.MSS. 5544; *CSPD 1663-64*, p.574; *CSPD 1664-65*, p.230; *CSPD 1667-68*, pp.277, 336; *CSPD 1670*, p.198; *CSPD 1667*, p.55.

26. E.D'Oyley, *James, Duke of Monmouth*, London 1937, pp.76, 77; *CSPD 1671*, pp.106, 142, 183; *CSPV 1671-72*, pp.40, 640; Brit.Lib.Add.MSS. 27962 T, ff.130, 135; A.Marvell, *Works*, i, 174; ii, 321-2.

27. K.D.H.Haley, *The First Earl of Shaftesbury*, Oxford 1968, p.466; *HMC* Portland MSS. Part III, p.355.

28. Bodl.Lib.Rawlinson MSS. C421 f.155; *HMC* 12th Report App.V. Rutland MSS., p.36; Longleat House, Coventry MSS.104, f.43; *Memoirs of Thomas Earl of Ailesbury*, ed. W.Buckley, London 1890 2 vols., i, 76; J.Evelyn, *Diary*, iv, 6, 500; G.Burnet, *History*, i, 577; T.Sprat, *True Account*

of the Horrid Conspiracy, London 1685, p.29.

29. 'Letters addressed to Sir Joseph Williamson . . . 1673-74, vol. I', ed. W.Christie, *Camden Society*, 8 1874, p.119; M.Haile, *Queen Mary of Modena*, London 1905, p.57; *HMC* 12th Report, App.V, Rutland MSS., p.33; *HMC* 7th Report Verney MSS., p.467; J.Evelyn, *Diary*, iii, 49; *HMC* 11th Report Part VII, Hamilton MSS., p.9.

30. H.Bryant, *Letters of Charles II*, p.232; *CSPD 1679*, pp.282, 321, 441.

31. 'The Despatches of William Perwich, English agent in Paris, 1669-77', *Camden Society*, 5 1903, pp.216, 250-1; *CSPV 1671-72*, p.249.

32. Longleat House, Coventry MSS.101, f.66; 'Perwich Despatches', *Camden Soc.*, pp. 252-3; PRO, State Papers Domestic, 78/137, f.142.

33. J.Heath, *England's Chronicle, to King William and Queen Mary*, London 1689, p.596; *HMC* Bath MSS. Vol.1, p.44; J.Evelyn, *Diary*, iv, 42; *CSPD 1673*, pp.524, 531; *CSPV 1673-75*, pp.75, 86-7, 106, 120-1.

34. *CSPD 1673-75*, pp.119, 200, 327-8, 476; *CSPD 1676-77*, p.316.

35. *CSPD 1673-75*, pp.76, 164, 479-80, 542, 547, 566, 575, 587, 596; *CSPD 1676-77*, pp.59, 132; *CSPD 1675-76*, pp.62, 441; J.Childs, *The Army of Charles II*, London 1976, p.89.

36. *CSPD 1673-75*, pp.91-2, 438; *CSPD 1676-77*, p.132; J.Childs, *Army of Charles II*, pp.51, 64-5.

37. J.Childs, *Army of Charles II*, pp.38-9.

38. James II, *Life*, i, 73-4; *CSPD 1676-77*, pp.316, 346; *CSPD 1673-75*, pp.257, 476; *CSPD 1676-77*, p.479.

39. James II, *Life*, i, 74; K.Haley, *Shaftesbury*, pp.327, 337, 340-1; G.Burnet, *History*, i, 435; ii, 146-8; *HMC* 11th Report Part VI, Hamilton MSS., p.154; *HMC* Ormonde MSS, Vol.V., n.s., p.48; *CSPD 1678*, p.193.

40. *HMC* 12th Report, Rutland MSS., p.19; O.Airy, 'The Essex Papers', *Camden Society*, 24 1913, pp.59, 88-9, 103, 120, 122, 127; C.Pyke 'The Intrigue to Deprive the Earl of Essex of the Lord Lieutenancy of Ireland', *Transactions Royal Historical Society*, 5 1911, pp.89, 103; *CSPD 1673-75*, p.171; *CSPD 1673*, pp.364, 543; *CSPD 1673-75*, pp.497-8, 506; *CSPD 1676-77*, pp.36, 489.

41. *CSPD 1665-66*, pp.121, 593; *CSPD 1671-72*, pp.290, 325, 334; *CSPD 1673-75*, p.119; J.Evelyn, *Diary*, iii, 558; iv, 6, 94, 97.

42. *CSPD 1671*, pp.228, 353; *CSPD 1673-75*, pp.250, 375, 412, 595; *CSPD 1675-76*, pp.124, 397; *CSPD 1676-77*, pp.250-1, 309, 381-2, 407, 413, 478, 529; *CSPD 1678*, pp.148, 580.

43. *CSPD 1677-78*, p.682; Coventry MSS.83, ff.132, 175; Brit.Lib. Add.MSS. 32095, ff.81-2.

44. *CSPD 1678*, pp.133, 137; James II, *Life*, i, 496-8.

45. K.Haley, *Shaftesbury*, p.485; James II, *Life*, i, 496; for the wording of grants to Monmouth see Bodl.Lib.Ashmole MSS.1112, f.125; Brit. Lib.Add.MSS.17018, ff.57-8, 59-60.

46. *CSPD 1678*, p.210; Coventry MSS.3, f.185; *HMC* Ormonde IV, p.178; The 'Journal' is in *CSPD 1678*, pp.322-8; see also *HMC* 7th Report, p.494, and *CSPD 1678*, pp.352, 358.

CHAPTER FOUR

Power and Honour

No man in England was more sceptical of the Popish Plot than its supposed victim, Charles II. In private he dismissed it as 'a case so improbable', a 'contrivance'; and in a well-turned phrase he wondered who could be so obtuse as to wish him replaced by his brother. For some time Monmouth shared his father's scepticism. When an increasingly alarmed Privy Council finally prevailed upon Charles, at the end of September 1678, to hear what it had unearthed after six weeks' investigation, the King stayed only for the morning session before hurrying off, with his son, to the Newmarket races. Both missed Titus Oates's masterly performance that afternoon which convinced doubters on the Council, and led to renewed questioning of Oates two days later, by the King. Following this second interrogation Monmouth, too, became convinced that Oates had uncovered something, particularly when two soldiers of his own regiment came forward to swear that the Catholic Lord Petre was collecting arms and attempting to buy converts.[1] As Captain of the Guards and Master of the Horse Monmouth had good professional reasons for taking the conspiracy seriously, besides his natural concern for his father, and when Parliament resumed in October and both Houses began investigating the Plot he was naturally and inevitably drawn in.

Appointed to the Lords' committee on the Plot, he was chosen to report its recommendations to the Upper House — restricted personal access to the King, closer supervision of the royal cooks, changing the locks on palace doors and — the Duke's own suggestion — three trusted officers as the King's close bodyguard 'to accompany him wherever he goes'. Monmouth placed sentries about the rambling Palace of Westminster, and paid special attention to the Tower. He inspected it and strengthened its garrison, and was then requested to 'bring in a project for [its] regulation in future'. Following the discovery of Sir Edmund Berry Godfrey's body in October 1678 there were mass alarms all over England concerning parties of night riders, hidden Papist arms, and bright lights and strange noises observed near Catholic houses. Monmouth at first gave the army individual orders to intercept the nocturnal horsemen, but by the end of November the reports had become so numerous that he simply issued a blanket instruction to capture any night riders wherever they appeared.[2]

All these measures were simply extensions of the two roles Monmouth's position in the army had led him to undertake during the 1670s: responsibility for the King's safety, and cooperation with the civil power over law and order. Thus, a year before Oates's revelations the Duke had noted, as he left for the continent, that some officers of 'ability and experience should be left near the King'; in February 1679 he had opposed the King's riding unprotected to Parliament; and he was anxious over Charles's safety during his own absence in Scotland three months later. He had suppressed riots in London, and mounted convoys for merchants in 1675-76; sent troops to the Border to maintain law and order two years later; and instructed Yorkshire Deputy Lieutenants on the need for security. Given this background, and with professional troops at his disposal, Monmouth soon received more requests to help Parliament investigate the Plot. He was made responsible for the safety of informers, first Oates and Richard Needham, and then Stephen Dugdale, whose evidence so impressed even the sceptical King that he told Monmouth to keep the witness safely in his own house. After Miles Prance the Catholic silversmith claimed to have witnessed the murder of Godfrey at Somerset House, Monmouth and the Earl of Ossory were asked to take Prance to the scene and examine him on his story. Ready access to troops also made the Duke a logical person to carry out the house searches ordered by Parliament's investigating committee. In January 1679 he sent troops to the house of a Captain Kelly accused of 'dangerous correspondence with priests and others'; and at the same time received an account from soldiers sent to remove 'wallet, papers and books' from the home of the Catholic Lord Tixall, accused by Stephen Dugdale. More importantly it was Monmouth who conducted the search of Edward Coleman's house — formerly secretary to the Duke of York — and found the letters written to Père le Chaise and others, which appeared to confirm the existence of a Plot and first cast suspicion upon the Duke of York.[3]

The King's son was, therefore, a natural instrument for the parliamentary committee which, under Shaftesbury, took over investigation of the Plot from the Privy Council. But he was a non-fanatical instrument. When Coleman's wife insisted that she owned some of the letters discovered, and that they were of a very private nature, Monmouth returned the packet to her unopened. As Professor Kenyon observes, Mrs. Coleman was 'obviously a woman of considerable charm and address', but even people lacking in her charms were treated by the Duke with moderation. He retained a Catholic servant in his household for a year after the Plot began before sending him off to Paris with a letter of recommendation addressed to Father Goffe, his old Oratorian teacher. When the Privy Council passed a general order for Papists to be disarmed, Monmouth delayed a week before sending this inflammatory order to his Deputy-Lieutenants in the East Riding. On the other hand Parliament was extremely nervous concerning the army, strengthened in dubious circumstances during the past year, and its commander took strong action to quieten the Houses' fears, dismissing ninety-one known or suspected Catholics from his own regiment. Sir Richard Verney found this action 'very circumspect'.[4]

Such moderation was of a piece with the Duke's broader position at the time. A diligent servant of those investigating the Plot, he nevertheless remained a member of the court. In December 1678 he voted against impeaching Danby, though he had little personal sympathy for the man who had married a daughter to another royal bastard, the Earl of Plymouth, and then sought to advance Plymouth over Monmouth. A month earlier the Duke had voted against obliging Catholics to take an oath denying transubstantiation before they were allowed to sit in Parliament: here too he had voted with the court and against the opposition gathering under Shaftesbury. When new elections were held in January 1679 following the dissolution of the Cavalier Parliament, the two dependents of the Duke returned for the Commons were both listed by Shaftesbury as part of the court interest. When Gilbert Burnet spoke to the King in early December 1678 about reports that Monmouth would soon be legitimized, Charles appeared unconcerned and confident of his son's loyalty; indeed other reports at the same time spoke of the Duke's 'great favour' with his father. Even as the crisis deepened during 1679 Monmouth kept his distance from the opposition. He did not join Shaftesbury in opposing the King's proposal of limitations upon a Popish successor, when this was debated in the Privy Council in April 1679; and when the first Exclusion Bill was introduced in Parliament on 10 May 1679 Monmouth was not even present, attending instead the races on Banstead Downs. Sir William Temple concluded that Shaftesbury at this point was claiming greater intimacy with the Duke (in order to influence the King) that he in fact possessed.[5]

This distance between the King's bastard and Shaftesbury's parliamentary opposition is not surprising. Little more than a year earlier Shaftesbury had dismissed the Duke as 'very very vile', and Monmouth had urged his father to keep the Earl in the Tower. Monmouth had feuded intermittently with another Whig peer, the Earl of Essex, over Irish lands and the Duke of Northumberland's inheritance for much of the 1670s. As a riotous courtier who had injured a Member still sitting in the Commons, as the King's son commanding a large and very suspect army, the Duke was still too closely identified with the court for the solid 'Country' M.P.s to trust or like him. These men believed that the recent 'War with France was pretended for the sake of [raising] an army'; and not only argued that the army should be disbanded, but that 'precautions must be taken to ensure that another should never be raised, and the royal Guards were to be replaced by militia detachments'. The Captain-General could never stomach such talk.

The only common ground between Monmouth and the opposition was hostility to the Duke of York, and even this arose to a considerable extent from different causes: fear of a Popish successor on the one hand, and a personal quarrel on the other. Monmouth's feud with his uncle grew, if anything, more intense in 1678 and 1679. Following the affair of the Captain-General's warrant York stopped another patent for Monmouth (granting the latter a pension of £1,666 p.a. on the Irish establishment) to insert the correct but now highly offensive style 'natural son'. The Lord Lieutenant of Ireland was further instructed not to pass any warrant for the Duke which omitted reference to his illegitimacy. Not surprisingly the only time Monmouth stepped out of line with the court during the Popish Plot's early stages was when he left the Lords early, on 15 November 1678, to avoid voting on a proviso which would have exempted York from a new Test Act. Monmouth observed with pleasure his opponent's increasing difficulties, as York ceased to attend the Privy Council in November 1678, struggled to keep his position in the Lords, became implicated (though not yet accused) in the Popish Plot via Coleman's letters, and was finally invited by the King to go into temporary exile in March 1679. But even this last success was soured for Monmouth, because to placate his brother Charles publicly repeated a declaration made earlier, in January 1679, that he had not been married to Monmouth's mother; and the enmity continued. In exile during 1679 York wrote of his nephew as 'the only dangerous man' who could lead the opposition, that the King's kindness to his son was so great that it would harm both brothers, and that 'there is one thinge that troubles me much and puts thoughts into my head . . . his Majesty has never gone about to make a good understanding between me and the Duke of Monmouth . . . thinke of this and I am sure you may draw consequences from it'.[6]

York was not entirely suffering from the paranoia of exile, for well before he left England in March 1679 there had been disturbing signs of Monmouth's popularity with the masses, if not yet with the respectable classes, and consequent fears that he might try to build on this politically. As the country's disquiet deepened a year or two before the Popish Plot, an unease expressed by Andrew Marvell's *Growth of Popery and Arbitrary Government in England*, several prophecies and visions had warned of violent times to come, when the nation would be saved by Charles's son. In June 1677 a London fortune-teller had spoken of poisoning and the spread of Catholicism, with England redeemed by the odd trio of the Dukes of Monmouth and Buckingham, and the Earl of Sarum. Later that year a 'maiden gentlewoman' prophesied tolling bells and open graves, gangs of murderers and a 'pale King lying as if dead', and 'in the midst of these tumults she heard the Duke of Monmouth called on very earnestly'. Other visions spoke simply of a handsome youth or 'an adorable mortal', who would put an end to bloodshed. Once the Plot was revealed, and Monmouth was seen using his troops to counter it, his popularity grew rapidly and he quickly joined the King as a second supposed victim of the Plotters. After Oates had set out the framework of the conspiracy a flood of secondary informers tried to join in. Faced with the problem of inventing new revelations which were credible and alarming, William Bedloe, Edward Everard, Richard Needham and Stephen Dugdale all cast the King's son as a victim, second only to the monarch himself. The most convincing of these secondary informers, Stephen Dugdale, provided a simple and obvious explanation for this extra target: 'it would not availe to take off the King, unless the Duke of Monmouth were alsoe disposed of'.[7]

Equally remarkable as testimony to the Duke's new-found importance was a curious episode which took place on 9 November 1678. The Commons was then debating whether York should be exempted from a proposed new Test Act, and the King sent them a message intended to be conciliatory and calming. The tension was considerable: midway between celebrations of the Gunpowder Treason's anniversary and Elizabeth I's accession, with nothing yet revealed concerning the Popish Plot though all knew the government had been investigating it for weeks, there was sufficient public anxiety for a man as eminent as the Governor of the East India Company to ask a government clerk whether he should send his family out of the capital, for he found in London just the same mixture of doubt and fear as had preceded the great massacres in France in 1572 and Ireland in 1641. In his statement to the Lower House Charles accordingly promised agreement to any bills:

> to make you safe in the reign of any successor so as they tend not to impeach the right of succession, nor the descent of the Crown in the true line.

This was quite clear, but when he went on to accept:

> anything that may give comfort and satisfaction to such dutiful and loyal subjects

his meaning was lost on a nervous audience, and soon Londoners were told that the King had categorically promised to legitimize his son. That night 'the City was in bells and bonfires', and aldermen supplied wine to drink the health of their saviour.[8] The mis-report was soon denied, but rumours of legitimization persisted throughout December, and early in January 1679 Charles was forced to swear before the Privy Council that he had not been married to Monmouth's mother.

Given the trust that Charles told Burnet he felt in his son on the matter of legitimacy, this remarkable declaration seems to have been directed less against the Duke himself than against his partisans, such as the Londoners who were so ready to celebrate Charles's misunderstood phrase in Parliament. The gesture did little good: those who wished to see York put out of the succession could easily 'explain' why Charles might wish to deny his marriage, and apart from verbal denials there was little else the King could do to *prove* that the marriage had not taken place. On the other hand documentary proof of it *might* some day be discovered. Thus Sir Thomas Armstrong busied himself in a very public search for Lucy Walter's 'Black Box' of marriage documents, and in his spare time tempted nobles such as the Earl of Oxford to contemplate Monmouth as heir to the throne. Because he owed everything to Monmouth's patronage and stood to be advanced with his master Armstrong's motives can be surmised, as can those of Ralph Montague, the fallen diplomat who had betrayed Danby to the opposition and who was now hoping to rise once more by advancing Monmouth's claim. Lord Gerard of Brandon, who canvassed support for naming Monmouth as heir in the first Exclusion Bill may also have been acting out of self-interest, but more probably he, like many other of the Duke's supporters, was propelled by genuine fear of a Popish successor. Monmouth's difficulty was not merely that he could not control such self- or public-interested 'champions' of his supposed cause; he could not even deny their assertions of his legitimacy without contradicting deep and emotionally held beliefs about his mother's virtue. He, therefore, tolerated their activities, and was thought ambitious for the succession; and in the same way his very personal feud with York could be misread as an attempt to replace the heir. Monmouth's actual intention was much simpler: to humiliate the man who had humiliated him. Indeed Monmouth's main purpose in 1679 was more limited and realistic than any claim to the throne. The key to it is found in a perceptive phrase used by one of Ormonde's correspondents. 'The Duke', he wrote in December 1678, 'appears of late to be more of a man of business than was expected he would prove'.[9]

The Popish Plot created a major political role for the Duke at precisely the time he was ready to adopt one. Gaining confidence and respect by his efficient use of troops in the first months of the crisis, enjoying the open favour of his father and the near-adulation of the London crowd, he found courtiers and politicians listening carefully to him and realized that he was, for the first time in his life, a force in the land. Sir John Reresby described him early in 1679 as 'the man in power'. He led discussion of reducing the army by sending 'excess' troops to Ireland; and threw himself into the parliamentary elections of January 1679 to obtain the return of his secretary as M.P. for Cambridge, Armstrong as Member for Stafford, and the army's Paymaster-General for Hull. After discussions with Shaftesbury and Essex his support for Danby ended in March 1679, though he still voted for lenient treatment of the fallen minister. By this time, according to Burnet, the King had decided to replace the brutal Lauderdale and quieten his northern kingdom by bringing 'all Scottish affairs into the Duke of Monmouth's hands', and matters were so far advanced that the latter 'was beginning to form the scheme of a ministry'. Meanwhile, the Duke polished his popular laurels by helping to contain a dangerous fire in London, blowing up houses in its path and by accident nearly killing Louis Duras, Earl of Feversham, his second in command in 1678, who tried to help.[10] Seven years later he had cause to reflect on the irony of this episode.

It was the Council-building experiment of April 1679 however which shows Monmouth most clearly in his new role of royal adviser. Sir William Temple claimed most credit for the reformed Privy Council announced by Charles II on 21 April 1679. Comprising thirty members, it would include office-holders and the more important Members of the Commons and the Lords, government supporters as well as leaders of the opposition. The intention was to create a council of national unity, to restore confidence in the King's government. It is clear, however, that several others were working towards this goal besides Temple. According to Burnet, Godolphin and Sunderland 'joined with the Duke of Monmouth to press the King to change his councils and turn to another method of government, and to take the men of the greatest credit into his confidence'. This was the account heard by York at Brussels, while a third report asserted that Sunderland and Monmouth alone had taken the initiative. Monmouth was active, too, when membership was being decided, joining Temple to overcome the King's reluctance to appoint Halifax, and then abandoning Temple to urge that Shaftesbury (unacceptable to Temple because of his support for the attack on the Netherlands in 1673) must also be included. An inner circle quickly developed among the thirty members, dignified with the title of 'Committee for Foreign Affairs', where Monmouth joined Shaftesbury, Essex, Sunderland, and Temple. Having played a large part in the Council's creation, the Duke then worked to make it effective. When Charles resolved at the end of May 1679 to prorogue Parliament his son 'did most earnestly entreat his Majesty to call his Council before he undertook so weighty a thing', and his remonstrance was 'mentioned by some much to the Duke of Monmouth's advantage'. During Monmouth's absence in Scotland Charles resolved to dissolve Parliament and so cut off the first Exclusion Bill, but was asked to delay the matter until Monmouth had returned, and it could be discussed at the Privy Council.[12]

Plainly no one politician planned or created the briefly-reformed Council of 1679, but Monmouth's part shows clearly that he was working energetically for a reconciliation between King and opposition, with himself as honest broker. But he remained more committed to the court than to the opposition, as the next episode showed. A fortnight after Charles had prorogued Parliament on 27 May 1679, following the second reading given to the Exclusion Bill, a rebellion broke out in Scotland. The Archbishop of St. Andrews was murdered, rebels then gathered until their number was estimated at twenty thousand, and local forces seemed powerless to check them. They attracted much sympathy in England. Lauderdale's regime was notoriously brutal, and his aristocratic opponents in England led by the Earl of Hamilton argued for negotiation. A petition was circulated in London urging the same course, and Shaftesbury and the Whigs saw in the crisis a means to force the King into concessions over Exclusion. Probably because of the Earl's pressure several notables refused to serve against the Scots, including Whigs such as Lords Grey, Russell, and Cavendish.[12]

Monmouth had different plans. Ordered north by his father to suppress the rebellion as quickly as possible, he accepted the charge on condition that he was given a free hand in Scotland when it was over, and Charles agreed that he could 'pardon, treat, and relax them of their burthens as he shall see cause'. His son then left London at three in the morning, was in Edinburgh three days later, and on the following day caught up with and defeated four thousand rebels at Bothwell Bridge over the River Clyde, near Hamilton. Less than three hundred rebels were killed and a thousand taken prisoner, mainly because the Duke prevented his troops from massacring the fleeing Scots. The prisoners were pardoned, the militia which had ravaged the countryside was disbanded, and the ban on holding conventicles relaxed. 'The very fanatical party confessed he treated them as gently as was possible', observed Burnet.[13]

The Duke stayed a month in Scotland, receiving petitions and dining with local nobles, before making his 'very triumphant' return to England. Charles was relieved at the revolt's speedy end (the parallel with 1639-40 was clear to all); the populace approved of his clemency after victory; and when some courtiers complained of his mercy, Monmouth tartly replied that 'he could not kill men in cold blood, that was work for butchers'. Lauderdale quietly limited most of the Duke's concessions, but in London Monmouth continued to bask in his fame as broadside and pamphlet spread details of the brief campaign, emphasizing both the completeness of his victory and the victor's complete devotion to the King. Monmouth was now at the peak of his career, 'in his greatest Height' as Sir William Temple observed. Shaftesbury tried to move closer to him, for legitimization of the Duke now seemed the best way to exclude York. An attempt to force Charles to divorce his Queen and remarry (and beget an heir in the direct line) had failed when Catherine's physician had been found not guilty in June 1679, of plotting to poison the King, with (it was hinted) the Queen's tacit permission. Monmouth kept his head, holding Shaftesbury at a distance, and writing to William of Orange that he had been 'ever against' inclusion of the Earl in the Privy Council—a lie but an indication how tenuous the link between Duke and Earl was.[14]

To some at court, Monmouth's stature was cause for growing concern. Halifax wanted a more balanced situation, Essex was frankly envious, and together with the Duchess of Portsmouth they were afraid for their future should Monmouth and Shaftesbury conclude an alliance. The Duke's flattering advisers and hangers-on worsened the position. Sir Thomas Armstrong roundly abused the Duke of York in public and was stripped of his army command, and a pamphlet giving some very dangerous *Advice to the Duke of Monmouth concerning the Present Times* identified him with England's greatest warrior-king, Henry V, 'Harry of Monmouth'.[15] A wholly fortuitous event resolved this increasingly unstable position, when on 21 August 1679 the King fell ill of a fever. For three days it was thought he might die and scenes of panic ensued.

During these days Monmouth divided his time between Windsor where the King lay, and London where his Guards were quartered. Halifax, Essex, and Sunderland watched his moves with deep alarm and, fearing a *coup*, wrote to the Duke of York at Brussels to return at once. The King then improved, York arrived and stayed beside his brother, and almost all the court, thinking Charles had summoned his brother back, hurried to bow before the heir. Even Armstrong tried to make his peace (and was publicly spurned), Monmouth and Shaftesbury were furious with the three conspirators whose action had so elevated York, and Halifax and Essex in turn found themselves cast off by the heir, who had no trust in them. As Charles recovered, he had to decide on his next move. York's pride was swollen by the court's acceptance of him as heir; Monmouth's anger was no less great, and after sending a man to Holland to look for evidence of his mother's marriage he spent much time with Shaftesbury; and Parliament was due to meet again in a month.[16]

Essex and Halifax then put forward a solution which neatly solved their problem as well as the King's. Both Dukes should go into exile. When Monmouth received his orders he found them unbelievable. For a year he had been the King's devoted servant and adviser, commanding his forces abroad, investigating the Catholic Plot, helping to create a new Privy Council, and suppressing a potentially dangerous rebellion: and exile was his reward. Though permitted to retain his offices he would inevitably lose influence whilst abroad, while York could simply rest on his laurels. Sir William Temple, no friend to either Duke, wondered how York had won 'so great a Victory', and Monmouth was left to draw what comfort he could from a crop of broad-sheets and ballads publicly expressing *England's Lamentations for the Duke of Monmouth*. His father was adamant and he sailed for Utrecht on 12 September, having paid his debts and assured his friends that his absence would be short. A day later York left for Brussels, 'with a very cheerful countenance' and thickly attended by nobility.[17]

At this point Monmouth had lost a battle, but not yet the war. Had he waited quietly he could well have regained most of his position. For a time he was patient, assuring the Prince of Orange, on the subject of the succession, that he was not *'assez fou pour avoir de pareilles visions'*, and telling Sidney that his future now 'depended upon the life of the King'. But he was taken up and 'feasted by the phanaticks', political and religious malcontents living in Dutch exile, and news of the 'Presbyterian plot' and Shaftesbury's dismissal from the Council increased his sense of mission.[18] Mid-October saw publication of the violent and effective *Appeal from the Country to the City for the preservation of His Majesty's Person, Liberty, Property, and Religion*, with its graphic description of a St. Bartholomew massacre enacted in London. Then York was permitted a three-weeks' stay in London, as he travelled from Brussels to a (purely nominal) exile in Scotland.

This was the final straw. Monmouth had never accepted the need for his temporary exile, and such indulgent treatment of his enemy detonated the smouldering resentment he felt against his father. He slipped quietly into London on the evening of 27 November, and when news of his return spread the following day, received a tumultuous welcome. By evening there were sixty bonfires in the City alone, and they grew until their number was more than had been seen since the Restoration. Passers-by were stopped and asked for money to drink Monmouth's health, or to 'join in the rabbles' prayers for the Protestant Duke'. A rash of pamphlets and broadsides appeared (by obvious pre-arrangement) descanting on their hero's military prowess and unswervingly Protestant faith. These demonstrations alone proved that the Duke was dangerously 'at present the idol of the people'; and there were other worrying signs as well. Among the pamphlets were some referring openly to Monmouth's legitimacy, and 'proving the right of his succession to the Crown, and the solemnity of a marriage with his mother'; and among the bonfires there were some lit by the Guards—ominously it was felt—to welcome back their commander. In public the Duke struck an appropriately heroic pose: to clear his name he would go to any prison the King named, even the Tower, but he would not return to exile for 'banishment was the badge of the male-factor'.[19]

Such postures increased Charles's fury at his son's disobedience. He refused to see the Duke or to accept messages from him, repeatedly ordered him to leave England, convinced Monmouth's Duchess that her husband must depart at once, and sharply repulsed Nell Gwynn when she pleaded that the Duke was 'grown pale, wan and lean and long-visaged' over his disfavour. Army officers were instructed to take no orders from him, and when Monmouth still did not depart he was stripped of his pension and most offices—Christopher, Duke of Albemarle receiving command of the Guards. When some courtiers demurred at sharing in the spoils because Monmouth might soon be returned to favour, 'the King's answer was, "No, he shall never be restored more" '. In January 1680 Monmouth was once more formally ordered to leave, and when he refused the Duke of York was temporarily recalled from Scotland. Monmouth's very name was banned at court. Shaftesbury stood by him for a short time, but then told him that the King's re-marriage would be the best solution to the political crisis; and Monmouth was not among the sixteen peers who in January 1680 petitioned Charles to meet Parliament at the date appointed. At court friends and enemies alike were saying that 'the Duke of Monmouth seems desperate in his fortunes'.[20]

At this point it would be plausible to argue that Monmouth, stripped of influence and bereft of ideas, turned to Shaftesbury and the Whigs, becoming their catspaw in the struggle to exclude York from the succession. Some observers indeed dated his becoming captive to Shaftesbury earlier, to 1679. Sir John Reresby wrote that, although Monmouth 'was very handsome and accomplished as to his outside, his parts were not suitable' to be regarded as a serious candidate for the throne. From the Popish Plot onwards, Reresby continued, the Earl simply used Monmouth as a figure-head to attract support, promising the gullible young man that 'the Duke [of York] once disinherited he had the fairest claime to the Crown, either by the King's declaring he was married to his mother, or by his being made legitimate by Act of Parliament'.[21] Reresby wrote as a courtier and after the event, but his view was shared by many contemporaries; and it has subsequently prevailed almost completely with historians, who stress in equal parts Monmouth's beauty, ambition, and stupidity.

There can be no doubt that Shaftesbury intended to exploit the Duke thus, nor that Monmouth's alliance with the Whigs added considerably to their following. What requires further consideration is whether Monmouth, though far less experienced and clever than Shaftesbury, yet had his own purposes in view, and was in turn trying to use the Earl and his party to achieve them. Since ambition over the succession is considered the means by which Shaftesbury tempted and controlled the Duke, it must be shown that this was the latter's sole or primary motive. And it must further be demonstrated that Shaftesbury was able to control Monmouth's actions during the Plot and Exclusion Crises.

Neither proposition can be well sustained.

As to his motives, it has already been argued that in 1679 Monmouth completed the steady approach toward political involvement which he had hinted at earlier in the decade. During the Popish Plot he became 'a man of business', 'the man in power', a close and trusted adviser to and instrument of the King, wholly enjoying the novel experience of real political authority. In 1679 he was also concerned to pursue a recently-arisen feud with his uncle; and to vindicate the honour of his mother, a subject not raised by him but inevitably connected with the politics of the time. Ambition over the succession competed uncertainly in the Duke's soul with several other powerful obsessions. In 1680 and later, it can be argued, this mixture or confusion of motives continued and indeed intensified. A spell of exile, followed by loss of offices, sharpened the Duke's appetite for authority, while increasing his rage against York whom he naturally blamed for these misfortunes. For his part York's arrogant carriage and 'very coole' behaviour toward Monmouth indicated a new and deep dislike of the younger man.[22] York strongly believed that the King must be obeyed in all matters, particularly by members of his own family; and to the impression of dishonesty created by the affair of the Captain-General's warrant was added the darker sin of filial disobedience. Continuing public speculation over Monmouth's legitimacy maintained the young man's sensitivity over his mother's morals, and made it impossible, whatever his ambitions concerning the succession, to withdraw from his apparent position as pretender to the throne.

Above all, Monmouth believed that he had a legitimate grievance against the King, over the circumstances of his exile and disgrace. No son could have been more loyal to his father as he searched into the Popish Plot, helped to create a new Privy Council of reconciliation, and suppressed a potentially dangerous rebellion against the wishes of his Whig friends. But the reward for such loyalty had been unmerited exile followed by public disgrace. Given his neglected childhood and over-indulged adolescence it can reasonably be argued that one of the Duke's principal aims, between 1680 and 1685, was to force himself back into his father's good favour, and so make Charles recognize the injustice he had inflicted upon his son. Few are more dangerous, or more reckless, than he who considers himself unjustly wronged; and after October 1679 Monmouth undoubtedly saw himself as an injured innocent with little to apologize for. And nearly twenty years at court seemed to have taught him that, given sufficient pressure, Charles could be made to bend. When the Duchess of Portsmouth in Reresby's words, 'to show her power with the King (which was very great) . . . would often make the King break his engagement' to men promised office or honour, could a spoiled favourite son expect to achieve less?[23]

In this web of conflicting emotions and ambitions, recognition as heir apparent had to take its place as one purpose among many. As circumstances changed, first one aim and then another would be predominant in the Duke, but overall the succession was probably a long-term consideration, less immediate and urgent than Monmouth's feelings over his father, his uncle, and his mother, and his ambition to be once again a man of political consequence. By supporting Shaftesbury's design to exclude York from the succession Monmouth could gratify several emotions at once, but the variety of his purposes make it unlikely that the Earl ever mastered him; indeed in a sense the Duke never mastered himself, and his failure to perceive clearly, and to choose between, his various ambitions must stand as one of the reasons for Monmouth's final downfall.

Two further considerations make it unlikely that the succession was Monmouth's principal aim. He was poorly educated and knew it, as the attempt at self-instruction revealed by the 'political instances' in his pocket-book shows. Commentators and memoirists regularly commented upon the Duke's semi-literacy, noteworthy at a time of near-universal education among the upper classes; and this, together with his general lack of political experience, partly explains their reluctance to support him as heir. At a deeper level, however, Monmouth was reluctant to contemplate the succession, for it involved thinking about a world in which his father was dead. Affection apart, everything he had depended upon the thread of Charles's life, as he recognized during his 1679 exile. During the King's illness in that year, and again in 1680, Monmouth was completely at a loss: confident and capable as an instrument or adviser, he was not fitted for ultimate responsibility in the state. Nor did he really seek it; though sensitivity over his mother, anger at his uncle, and pique towards his father frequently gave the impression that he did. And when admirers flattered him with this ambition, he could not disabuse them.

That Shaftesbury ever exercised much direct control over the Duke, his supposed political puppet, seems unlikely when Monmouth's political behaviour is considered. The two were on bad terms before 1679, and Monmouth mocked the Earl's more extreme plans towards the end of the Exclusion Crisis. The Duke gave strong support to his allies, but he would also disappear from political life for months at a time; and as at least six attempts to reconcile him with his father show, he was generally willing to rejoin the court provided honourable terms could be arranged. Near the end of his life Shaftesbury reproached Monmouth as 'an unfortunate man' for having failed to follow the Earl's counsel on three crucial occasions.[24] Shaftesbury no doubt intended to use Monmouth as a catspaw, but the Duke had similar ambitions for the Whigs. It would be exaggerated to argue that Monmouth supported the opposition simply to stir up so much trouble that his father would be forced to restore him to favour — the Duke's belief in the Popish Plot and detestation of Catholicism alone were too strong for that — but alliance with the Exclusionists did increase his stature and give him a major political role to play, while increasing the King's need for a reconciliation with him. In 1679 Monmouth had grown accustomed to authority and popularity, and to expect him to give them up, spurn the Whigs, and retire permanently to private life, was rather unrealistic.

Yet these were precisely the terms for reconciliation his father would have to insist upon. Charles saw in Exclusion such a threat to the very principle of monarchy that his steadfast opposition to the measure astonished friends and opponents alike. And once he resolved that in no circumstances would the succession be altered, the King's attitude towards his rebel son became a crucial test of his determination to defeat Exclusion. If Monmouth was readmitted to favour on any terms short of a total break with the Whigs, submission to York, and return to a wholly private life, all would believe that the King could also be made to give way over Exclusion. Years of easy-going compliance with mistresses and ministers had produced a mistaken belief that Charles was not a man of strong will, and only by severity toward his son could the King convince Whig and Tory alike that he was resolute in his veto of Exclusion. In this deeper and unintended sense Monmouth was, therefore, a stalking-horse for the Whigs. And just as Charles failed to comprehend his son's depth of resentment over the treatment he had received, so Monmouth failed to realize how essential it was for his father to separate him completely from the Whigs. When Charles spoke to Monmouth's Duchess after learning of his son's apparent complicity in the Rye House Plot he was weeping openly, and the tears he shed arose from a conflict between love and duty classic in its simplicity, necessity, and ultimate tragedy.

The difficulties facing Charles in convincing the public that he would insist upon his son's absolute submission were revealed almost as soon as Monmouth was disgraced. Late in 1679 and during the New Year several courtiers, noting that Monmouth had not been stripped of all his offices (he retained the Mastership of Horse and Chancellorship of

Cambridge), were careful to keep open their lines of communication with him. Towards the end of 1679 the Duchess of Portsmouth had written offering her friendship if Monmouth would 'live towards me as I desire', and over Christmas Nell Gwynn worked to arrange a chance meeting between father and son. Lord Huntingdon was still more open, offering to drink the Duke's health in public. Respectable and semi-respectable society in London also ignored his disgrace: when he entered the church of St. Martins-in-the-Fields the congregation spontaneously stood up for the Duke; and in January 1680 during a disturbance at a theatre Sunderland was called a traitor, and the audience cried out 'God bless his Highness, the Duke of Monmouth. We will be for him against the whole world'.[25]

Monmouth himself gave no indication of being cast down by his circumstances. He saw the old year out hunting energetically in Sussex, and returned to the capital so full of spirit that in less than a month he was the cause of two ladies being hastened to the provinces. His Whig associate Ford Lord Grey suddenly suspected his wife of being more than sociable toward the handsome Duke, and gave her only a few hours to gather her belongings and retire to the countryside. A fortnight later Lady Wentworth packed off her twenty-year-old daughter Henrietta 'in such haste that it makes a stir': Monmouth was once again responsible. The liaison (if such it was) with Lady Grey was brief and the two men were soon on terms again; but the relationship with Henrietta Wentworth developed into the deepest emotional attachment of the Duke's life, despite its casual beginning. Thomas Bruce, Earl of Ailesbury, once in love with Henrietta himself, recorded the affection that grew between the pair, and their belief that in the eyes of God they were truly man and wife. After the Rye House Plot Monmouth hid with Henrietta at her country home for several months while there was a price on his head, and she accompanied him into exile in 1684. His domestic happiness was an important reason why the Duke at first refused to lead a rebellion upon Charles II's death in 1685; and when it was over he insisted from the scaffold that Henrietta was a most virtuous woman and no casual mistress. She died less than a year after her lover, from a broken heart some said, others more vindictive, of mercury poisoning from over-painting her face.[26]

So confident was Monmouth in January 1680 that he could out-face his father, that he returned a defiant reply to a further strict order from Charles to leave the realm: he would do so provided certain evil advisers of the King such as Sunderland and Lauderdale went too. For a time it seemed that this intransigence would defeat the King. Worried by the impact of Shaftesbury's campaign of petitioning for Parliament to meet, Charles resolved to weaken the opposition by seeking to detach his son from it, and offered a return to favour on certain terms — an example of Monmouth profiting from his loose association with Shaftesbury, even though the latter had just moved away from him as being of less political consequence now that he was out of favour. But Charles could not bring himself to offer unconditional return to favour, for Monmouth would have to make 'certain disclosures'; and the Duke refused to become an informer, as he put it, 'on the point of honour'.[27] This same point of honour would wreck all successive attempts at reconciliation, for Charles could not allow Monmouth an unconditional return to favour, and the Duke would accept nothing less. A similar point of honour would oblige Monmouth in 1685, on learning that Argyle was organizing a rebellion, to be seen to do nothing less and launch his own venture; and honour once more made him go on when, half-way through the uprising, he recognized that barring a miracle it could not possibly succeed. More than stupidity or ambition, devotion to a high sense of honour was the ruin of this son of Charles II.

His father, however, saw in Monmouth's rejection of terms not honour but wilfullness, and for some time courtiers noted in alarm that 'the King has scarce been in a worse humour'. Proceedings began to have the Duke stripped of his Cambridge Chancellorship, and subsequently there was even talk of committing him to the Tower.[28] Charles's temper was made worse by a steady increase in talk about his son's possible legitimacy. Heard during the 1660s and early 1670s, tales of a marriage between Charles and Lucy Walters had subsided until invigorated by the early stages of the Popish Plot, and in the autumn of 1679 Sir Thomas Armstrong had tried without success to find documentary evidence to substantiate them. Monmouth's meteoric rise to prominence, and equally sudden fall that year, gave further life to speculations over his birth, and by April 1680 these had gained such force and circumstantial detail in taverns and coffeeshops that the Privy Council began an investigation of their origin and spread.[29]

After working for a fortnight the Council emerged with no evidence that the Whigs had invented the rumours, nor that they were particularly active in spreading them, although the members cautiously suggested that one opposition agent may have 'in some measure solicited' them. Three sources for the rumours were identified, all free from any political involvement. The first was Lucy Walters's death-bed confession to John Cosin, which by the time of the latter's death in 1672 had been elaborated into a tale of marriage documents put into Cosins's care. Following his death, a box of documents was supposed to have passed into the possession of his son-in-law Sir Gilbert Gerrard. A prominent Whig in 1680, the latter had not troubled to deny the story, but when questioned by the Council he repudiated all knowledge of the box.

A second source was Mrs. Gosfright (remarried as Mrs. Sambourne by 1680), the aunt with whom Lucy Walters had lodged when she arrived in The Hague from England in 1648. Gosfright spent her old age recollecting stories told her by Lucy's mother, her sister, among them that the girl was no mere mistress but was married to a King. From Lucy's brief spell in the Tower in 1656 came a recollection that 'a paper relating to a marriage or a dowry or a portion or a maintenance from the King to Mrs. Barlow' (a name taken by Lucy) had then been found in her possession. The document was none of these, but the £1500 per annum grant made by Charles in 1655 to silence his ex-mistress, transformed by the embroidery of oral transmission. Similarly Lucy's public threats to publish Charles's letters to her became 'letters from the King to the Duke of Monmouth's mother . . . [showing] that the King was married to her', or more simply 'a declaration under the King's hand' of marriage. Memories of the 1658 kidnappings also lent credibility to talk of the boy's legitimate status: why else should the King have bothered?

A miscellaneous collection of other people who had met, or known of, Lucy Walters during the 1650s comprised the third source of rumour. John Pierson, in 1680 secretary to the Lord Privy Seal, had thirty years earlier kept a register of persons entering England. Incautiously telling a friend that the celebrated Lucy Walters was known to him, the friend, a former colonel in the parliamentary army, had passed the information on to one of his military acquaintances, the Duke of Monmouth's unlikely genealogist and client, Sir Thomas Armstrong. Innocently or with intent to deceive, Armstrong quoted Pierson as one who knew the truth of Monmouth's birth. George Gosfright, brother-in-law to the sometime Mrs. Gosfright, Lucy Walters' garrulous aunt, and in 1680 also resident in England, entertained neighbours with talk that he had once met a 'Mr. Geleot of Liege' who owned the inn where the marriage was performed. Other gossips cited Dr. Clare (later Bishop of Lincoln and by 1680 safely dead) as the officiating priest, and a royalist soldier and exile, Sir Henry Pomeroy, as a witness. Pomeroy was still alive, and indignantly denied the story to the Privy Council.

There appears to have been no political calculation behind the initiators of these rumours. Like the man who claimed that his boatswain father had helped mother and child to escape from England in

1656, they were mostly humble people trying to impress their friends by claiming acquaintance with the great. Two men found systematically investigating these tales were less innocent: Colonel Mansell, a Whig, whom Dangerfield had tried to implicate in the so-called 'Presbyterian Plot' against the King of 1679; and William Disney, a London attorney and Whig agitator, who would be executed in 1685 for publishing the rebel manifesto. The purpose of these two, however, was not to invent or propagate the stories, but to investigate what truth they contained. No evidence was found to connect the pair with Monmouth, and though they may have been working for him it is equally possible that they were freelances, lured by the fortune that undoubtedly awaited the man who could establish Monmouth's legitimacy. As a pamphleteer observed at the time, if the Duke did not exert himself in the matter of his birth, others would gladly do it for him.[30]

Following their labours the Privy Council published just Gerard's refutation of the Black Box story, believing that public denial would only spread the other tales. This was probably a mistake, for it left these other stories apparently unchallenged. The results were soon evident. In a tavern on the Strand a joiner told his audience 'the story of the Black Box', concluding by saying that after Charles deserted her Lucy died of grief 'which would not have happened had she not been married to him'. In coffee houses circumstantial details confounded sceptics: Dr. Fuller was named as the officiating priest, and a bed on public display at Liège cited as 'evidence' of the ceremony's consummation. A bookseller of Great Queen Street, on being questioned over a pamphlet in his possession entitled *The Popish Massacre* which flatly asserted Monmouth's legitimacy, replied that the contents of 'Dr. Cosins's Black Box' would prove the claim. A London sculptor brought before the Privy Council for selling portraits of the Duke labelled 'His Royal Highness' pleaded ignorance of what the title implied, and escaped punishment. Less fortunate was the young Francis Storr of Lyme Regis, who told his partners on the town's bowling green that proof of the marriage would be found 'under a certain Bishop's hand'. After the game he found it advisable to disappear.[31]

Speculation over Monmouth's legitimacy thus continued, and for two principal reasons. Little was known for certain of his birth and childhood, and in this uncertainty rumour flourished. Though Charles had publicly sworn that no marriage had taken place, it was easy to reply — as pamphleteers did — that Kings often had to make such denials for reasons of state.[32] Moreover, many saw the hand of the heir apparent in Charles's declaration, York being thought a stronger character than his easy-going brother. To arguments that Lucy's morals and 'mere gentry' origin made her an unlikely choice for Queen, it could be replied that at the time Charles was only nineteen, separated from his family and most of his advisers, and almost at the nadir of his fortunes. Perhaps an irrational and emotional decision had been made: the more recent case of the Duke of York and Ann Hyde showed that princes sometimes married commoners whom they had made pregnant, even when it was against their interest to do so. The great favour shown by Charles to Monmouth, considerably more than to any other of his offspring, also suggested that this son was different.

The case for Monmouth's legitimacy, like the proposition that Charles should be persuaded to legitimize him, was also made essentially because people wanted to believe it. York, the heir to the throne, had been unpopular even as a Protestant in the 1660s, leading to speculation then about Monmouth's legitimacy: a decade later and a Catholic, the supposed beneficiary of a Catholic Plot, possibly even implicated in that conspiracy, the heir's manifest unsuitability increased the lustre of alternative candidates. And though William of Orange had the best strictly legitimate claim and was an experienced if authoritarian politician, there was general agreement that he lacked the popular appeal of Monmouth, whose weaknesses were unknown to the many who knew of him only through pamphlets or by common fame. Soundly Protestant, relatively young, married and with heirs, recently enjoying a military career which could be made to sound more impressive than it really was, the Duke's public accomplishments by 1679 appeared to mark him as a reliable and judicious man. Illegitimacy apart, his disadvantages as a prospective heir were known to a far smaller audience: his (now rather distant) career as a rake, his lack of education and political experience, his undoubted vanity and sensitive pride, the dubious friends he kept about him such as Sir Thomas Armstrong. As to his intelligence, the low rating given him by such enemies as York (not the most discerning critic) should be balanced against the 'wit' his father saw in him, praise Charles did not accord his other offspring. His wild behaviour in youth is no proof of lack of intelligence, and though happiest as a man of action, his application to politics in 1679 drew surprised notice from a variety of observers. His disastrous ending had causes other than stupidity, and death in disgrace was a fate shared by many intelligent Exclusionists, including the highly gifted Shaftesbury.

Until the Tory reaction began, treatment of Monmouth in the press made little reference to his weaknesses. Whig writers generally followed the line laid down by Shaftesbury in the Exclusion Bills, and rarely argued specifically in favour of Monmouth's legitimacy: indeed most implicitly conceded his bastardy with numerous references to illegitimates succeeding to the Crown, or to the legitimization of bastard contenders. The weight of their argument, as Dr. Furley has shown, lay upon the horrors to be expected from a Catholic succession, and responses to this peril could best be left for the reader to consider — specifics were rather too dangerous to set down in print.[33]

The mass of ballads, broadsides and pamphlets written about the Duke, usually prompted by some further crisis in his career, also avoided direct reference to his legitimacy, but the intention in this case was to deceive the reader by spiriting him over this awkward gap in their hero's merits. Popular writers emphasized Monmouth's royal paternity and the long-suffering virtues of his mother, and glided as rapidly as possible into his childhood and adolescence. Here his firmly Protestant upbringing was emphasized, to be followed by a catalogue of his martial accomplishments. The Duke's activities during the Popish Plot, and the Scottish uprising, were held to exemplify the deep love and loyalty he felt for his father, and the present embarrassing rift between the two was explained by the machinations of a wicked Catholic uncle, a man of course already under suspicion for different reasons. Few writers ventured to criticize the Duke before 1681, and even Dryden's 'Absolem and Achitophel' treated him with some care; and the Biblical tale of filial disobedience was countered by parallels drawn with such exemplars of classical piety and obedience in sons as Aeneas and Scipio.[34] The year of Monmouth's final disgrace, 1683, also saw publication of the most fulsome of his biographies the *Heroick Life . . . of the most Illustrious Protestant Prince, James, Duke of Monmouth*, the contents of which fully matched the panegyric of the title.

There is no evidence to connect Monmouth with these writers, although his entourage did distribute pamphlets during his two 'progresses' of 1680 and 1682; and in the latter year tickets enabling one to buy a copy of *The Second Part of the Growth of Popery, from 1672* could be obtained from the Duke's London house. Specifically Whig works apart, many broadsides, ballads, and pamphlets on Monmouth were written simply for commercial reasons: the subject was topical and popular. Indeed it was the Duke's lack of control over pamphleteers which frustrated his second opportunity for reconciliation with his father. In the middle of May 1680 Charles suddenly caught a fever and was ill for several days. Monmouth was reminded again how much he depended upon the King's life, and sent a very humble message to his father. Though falling short of an absolute recantation it was an excellent beginning, but its effect was lost when on 15 May, in the middle of the King's illness, the *Letter to a Person of Honour Concerning the Black Box* appeared. Possibly written by the Scottish Nonconformist and plotter Robert Ferguson (whose duplicity in 1685 influenced Monmouth into opting for rebellion), this stylish work dismissed talk of a 'Black Box' as a blind devised to divert attention from other and more convincing evidence of the Duke's legitimacy. The pamphlet culminated in a savage recital of York's 'manifold treasons' and Charles found it unforgivable. On 2 and 8 June he issued ever-fuller denials of having married Monmouth's mother, and startled the court by his uncharacteristically savage remarks about Lucy's 'being a whore to other people' before meeting him.[35]

The absolute rupture with his son which these statements betokened was re-emphasized when, on 10 June, a further pamphlet appeared commenting pungently on the King's denials. Laying most of the blame on York, it also reflected uncharitably upon Charles' incapacity in the past to keep his sworn word, argued that Parliament was the best judge of Monmouth's claims, and concluded with a brutal twenty-one point indictment of York for treasons against the nation. In no way could Monmouth have been responsible for these two works. They left him with a stock so low at court that even the thick-skinned Sir Thomas Armstrong was worried; and some of the moderate Whigs decided that they had little to gain from further association with the Duke, filling the summer with a fruitless project to persuade the Prince of Orange to visit England.[36]

Following these pamphlets, it was probably Shaftesbury's sensational attack upon the Duke of York, attempting in June 1680 to indict the heir as a common recusant, which caused Monmouth to ally himself actively with the Earl instead of simply dropping out of politics for a while. The prospect of revenge upon the common enemy was too tempting. For his part Shaftesbury found the King's son useful in rallying opinion. In that month and the next Monmouth made repeated public appearances in London, dining with fifty to sixty Whig nobles and gentry at a time, and invariably proposing the first toast — 'The King, and Magna Charta'.[37] These were but the prelude to the Duke's principal activity that summer, a tour from Bath and Longleat through southern Somerset to Exeter, which became a veritable royal progress.

Undertaken in public defiance of the King's wishes, and intended to strengthen support for the Whigs, two aspects of the tour nevertheless suggest that Monmouth was not wholly under Shaftesbury's direction at the time. None of the Whig grandees or the party's London activists accompanied him, and the tour's itinerary owed more to the wishes of the courtier Duke than to the political Earl. Between Bath and Exeter Monmouth followed the eastern and southern border of Somerset, visiting a series of gentlemen's houses and small towns. He ignored both Bristol and Taunton; and while the former was barely part of the south-west it was close to Bath where the tour began, it was the second city of the realm, and it contained probably the greatest concentration of Whig supporters outside of the capital. Taunton, next to Exeter the largest town in the southwest, was, however, an essential part of the region. It was a notoriously factious town, its leading M.P., John Trenchard a close associate of Shaftesbury and the man who moved the first Exclusion Bill. A visit to it would scarcely have taken Monmouth out of his way, because from the house of Edmund Prideaux at Chard it was scarcely a morning's ride to Taunton. If the tour was planned by Shaftesbury the exclusion of Bristol and particularly Taunton is odd: if on the other hand Monmouth was responsible, then the comfort and rural hospitality of Thomas Thynne at Longleat, George Speke and Sir William Strode at Ilchester, Sir John Sydenham at Yeovil, Edmund Prideaux at Chard, and Sir Walter Yonge at Colyton, sufficiently explain the route. Monmouth, too, may have wished not to provoke his father too far, and mass demonstrations at such Whig centres as Bristol and Taunton would have been hard for the King to ignore. Exeter was the natural end to the journey, but its strong Church and King loyalties might make a visit here less provocative.

Any thoughts of comfort and caution at the beginning of the tour however were swept away by the reception Monmouth received. Outside each town a procession of gentry on horseback and commoners on foot set out, up to several hundred in number, to march with him to his host's residence. At Bath two hundred townsmen and countryfolk braved the Bishop's displeasure, escorting Monmouth into the town to the accompaniment of bells and bonfires; while at Exeter the Church was defied once again, several hundred youths dressed in white leading their guest to the city centre, crying out 'God Bless the Protestant Duke'. Public attendances at church on the Sabbath emphasized this Duke's religion. Pamphlets were distributed in town and village, as the procession swept by, claiming that the Duke's legitimacy would be proven by people 'yet alive'; and perhaps carried away by the moment's intoxication Monmouth touched once — at Crewkerne — for the King's Evil.[38]

Relaxing with Thomas Thynne at Longleat on his way home Monmouth could reflect upon a great personal success. He was now indelibly 'the Protestant Duke', in the provinces as well as in London, and the reception he had been accorded — particularly from the gentry — would strongly influence his hopes of support in this area five years later. And though his Protestant religion and Whig allies doubtless accounted for some of the cheering, Monmouth could be in no doubt that he was the principal centre of attention. His entrances into towns were impressive: at the age of thirty he was still youthful and handsome, a tall figure on horseback, the mounted escort proclaiming his military reputation, the deferential train of followers, his royal birth. A master of ceremonial dignity, he could yet easily set it aside and appear to treat villagers as his equal, speaking courteously to the crowd, bowing to Quakers, and competing vigorously in foot races with all comers. The irresistible combination of superior bearing and egalitarian manner was further demonstrated in a visit Monmouth paid to Chichester in February 1683. Wearing a 'scarlet sute and cloke' the Duke attended divine service in the cathedral, but also spoke quietly to a Quaker outside, taking off his hat (while permitting the Quaker to retain his), and enquiring whether Friends were disturbed at their meetings. Visiting Oxford *en route* to London after the southwestern tour in 1680, he made his customary ceremonial entry — a company of Thames bargemen escorting him and shouting in unison 'God Bless the Protestant Duke' — and spoke familiarly to his audience.[39] But Oxford revealed reasons for the Duke's popularity apart from his personality and Protestant cause.

The Oxford crowd which chanted 'the Protestant Duke' later took up another refrain, 'No York, no bishops, no university'; and at the toasts, 'The Duke and Magna Charta' was followed by 'confusion to the Bishop of Oxford'. As night fell townsmen attacked any students they caught in the streets, to cries of 'no bishops, no university'. It was not an isolated outbreak: in April 1683 another riot began in an Oxford alehouse, when townsmen shouted 'A Monmouth, a Monmouth!' at students opposite them drinking the Duke of York's health, and then took to the streets, attacking undergraduates to cries of 'A Monmouth, no York!' At Chichester divisions were more complex, one section of the cathedral clergy warring against the Bishop, and enjoying the support of townsmen. A frequent visitor to the town since Ford, Lord Grey lived nearby, Monmouth was drawn into the conflict, the anti-Episcopalian clergy and townsmen looking to him for patronage. Hence the Duke's visit to Chichester in February 1683 was resisted by the mayor (under government pressure), the Bishop, the High Sheriff and by some local gentry; but he was welcomed to the cathedral by dissident clergy, and greeted enthusiastically in the town by 'broken Shopkeepers, Butchers, Carpenters, Smiths and such like', who lit bonfires, rang bells, and stoned the Bishop's palace. Taunton's support for the Duke owed much to the town's long-standing feud with its neighbouring gentry, and at Chester in September 1682 during his north-western tour, further local antagonisms took pro- and anti-Monmouth forms. In short, the Duke was often popular because he was, or could be regarded as, the patron or friend of a group engaged in a struggle against some part of the local establishment — university, bishop, or gentry. As a member of the national establishment (by birth) he was influential; as a rebel (by choice) against that authority, he was considered a natural ally by several local oppositions. The process could reach extreme lengths: told of the 1685 rising and its suppression, a pirate band in the West Indies 'seemed to deplore' the Duke's fate; while another group of privateers, 'confessing that they were rebels too', swore that Sedgemoor would have had another outcome 'if the Duke of Monmouth had had one thousand of them'.[41]

It was in the West Indies and the American colonies — territories quite unvisited by Monmouth — that the most remarkable reactions to 1685 took place. In Jamaica, Barbados, Maryland, Virginia, New Hampshire, New York and Boston, colonists, on hearing of the rebellion, drank the Duke's health, acclaimed him as rightful King, hoped he would come to reign, and spread 'malicious and factious reports'. A New Hampshire man predicted the rebellion early in 1685, two months before it actually began; in Bermuda a ship's captain, on hearing of Monmouth's defeat, hoisted his colours reversed in mourning, in full view of the Governor's residence; and in the same island news of the English rising sparked off preparations for a local revolt, the colonists arguing that there would never be a better time, and that 'the Duke was rightful King and no Papist'. The settlers' grievances against their governors and the metropolitan government were all that was needed to make them adopt Monmouth as their ally and patron, in several New World colonies.[42]

Closely related to these allies were three other categories of supporter. One was represented by Ford, Lord Grey, and Sir Thomas Armstrong: men whose unacceptable behaviour made them outcasts of their society, Grey through an affair with his sister-in-law, Armstrong by an unpunished murder and miscellaneous violence and disorder. Others, like the Whigs Disney and Mansell whom the Privy Council found investigating the Black Box stories, assisted Monmouth in the hope of rapid advancement; while a third and more miscellaneous group consisted of men with a personal or group grievance. Such a one was George Speke, the Somerset Whig who had been a royalist in the 1650s but joined the opposition because he was prosecuted by fellow-gentlemen after marrying a Nonconformist wife. At another remove stood a palace servant, a principal groom, who in 1681 raged at the corruption he saw about him at court, and swore that Monmouth would clear out 'all the whores and the whole gang that led the King by the nose'. The Duke's popularity among Somerset weavers, Oxford bargees, and Chichester's 'broken Shopkeepers' — not to mention pirates and rebels — derived in large part from the otherwise unspoken resentment of oppressed men, unable to change their condition or even to find the true causes of that condition, who identified themselves with another, greater and more glamorous victim, a man who courted their support, and who appeared to indicate by his familiar behaviour concern over their situation. Some may have hoped for material assistance from him; but others like the West Indies pirates who 'confessed they were rebels too', saw him as one of their company, the natural chief of their tribe. Such an argument does not deny the appeal Monmouth exercised on broader political and religious grounds: that he was 'the best man in the kingdom', as an Oxford boatman put it, the best qualified for authority by religion, birth, and political beliefs.[43] But it does suggest a personal reason for deeper commitment by some, from among the many who generally upheld the Whig cause.

Support of this nature would prove more dangerous to Monmouth, in the long run, than he probably realized. Reports of the Western tour conceded the large crowds he drew, but stressed that they were merely 'shabby people . . . few of good rank among them'.[44] By presenting him as a patron of the lower orders, a Lord of Misrule, royal propagandists strengthened reservations over the Duke as heir to the throne, and even as a sound leader of the Whigs. If Orange gained over Monmouth in Whig thinking as a replacement for York, it was not entirely because of disparities in character and political experience: Monmouth's supporters also told against him. Gentlemen began to discern a class basis to the Duke's popularity, well before his followers or the Duke himself did.

In the short term, however, Monmouth's acclamation in the West only increased his standing amongst respectable Whigs. On returning to London in October 1680 he took a house in the City and was waited upon by forty coachloads of visitors. He resumed public banquets with

Whig grandees; had some private talks with the Duchess of Portsmouth, and was known to have Nell Gwynn, the other royal mistress, working in his favour; and may even have met his father. The King was in a mood for accommodation because the Parliament he had prorogued to 21 October was due to meet, public opinion had not been diverted by aggressive foreign policy gestures, Sunderland and Portsmouth had joined York's opponents, and to protect his brother from Parliament Charles would once again have to send him out of England. In the shadowy discussions between King and opposition before Parliament began, it was said that Monmouth was offered the return of his offices if he would go into temporary exile, as part of a broad agreement that the Whigs would cooperate with the King if he consented to Exclusion.[45] It is significant that office and not the succession was the bait held up to Monmouth, suggesting that court circles felt the former was his real ambition; but he could never accept the price of exile, and talks collapsed.

In any case the Duke was intoxicated with public applause — at the Lord Mayor's Feast he 'was received with wonderful acclamations by the rabble below and the gallants above in the windows' — and at this point may well have come to consider himself the legitimate heir. The bar sinister was removed from the arms on his coach, and his entrances into Parliament were quasi-royal, a train of gentlemen bare-headed preceding him. The Exclusion Bill introduced into this Parliament also marked a subtle shift in his status. Unlike the first Bill of 1679 which had implied that the succession would pass to York's children, it simply stated that James should be excluded and said nothing about the succession, leaving it unspecified whether any could inherit through York. In committee the advantage this wording gave Monmouth was slightly reduced, with the succession to follow as though York were dead. The claims of Monmouth, and of Mary and William, were thus left equal.[46] Monmouth seems to have accepted this wording equably; setting aside the question of how strongly he desired the succession, his first object — like Shaftesbury's — was to exclude James. That achieved, he would hope to make his peace with his father and emerge again as royal favourite, commander of the army, and the King's trusted adviser. Settling the succession could be postponed indefinitely into the future, once York was out of the way. But put out he must be for Monmouth, like Shaftesbury and other Whigs, had now gone so far in his quarrel with York that there was no ultimate safety for him short of the heir's exclusion.

The Bill was defeated in the Lords, and Parliament dissolved less than a month later. It had lasted long enough for Monmouth to show his independence of Shaftesbury, and to win increased respect even from those M.P.s who demurred at him as heir. He spoke capably in favour of the Bill and, as the French ambassador noted, was singled out by Halifax for particular criticism when the latter made his celebrated attack on the measure. When Parliament was dissolved on 10 January 1681 almost the Commons' last measure was to resolve that the Duke should be restored to his offices, from which York's malignity had displaced him. Upon the Exclusion Bill's defeat Monmouth showed that he was tied to no particular faction of the opposition, by first assisting the more extreme Whigs in an attack upon some of York's dependants (including Louis Duras, Earl of Feversham), and then joining a more moderate fringe which offered the King parliamentary supply in exchange for Exclusion, and their return to office.[47]

At the next Parliament, held two months later at Oxford, it was Shaftesbury who moved toward Monmouth, offering Charles a sheet of paper naming the King's son as heir. When the Tories in Parliament tried to delay an exclusion debate by proposing a regency, the scheme was rejected by the Commons as unworkable and also, in Professor J.R. Jones' words, because the measure 'would not favour Monmouth'. A third Exclusion Bill had just been introduced, following its predecessor in leaving the successor's name an open question, when Charles unexpectedly dissolved the Parliament.[48] Surprised and shaken some Whigs stayed on for a few days, but eventually retired to London to consult further.

To an increasing number of them, their position was now becoming all too exposed. There was no prospect of another Parliament in the near future, and the Tory reaction was beginning to take shape. The Earl of Macclesfield read the signs and made his submission to the King in April, Huntingdon following in October, and Delamere early in 1682. Even the indomitable Shaftesbury, held in the Tower between July and November 1681, offered to leave England for Carolina. For much of the year it seemed that Monmouth, too, would make his peace. He visited Shaftesbury when the latter was arrested, but otherwise spent most of the summer of 1681 in Tunbridge Wells, emerging only to attend race meetings. He was not present at an important Whig policy-making dinner held in London on 5 April, preferring to attend the Northampton races; and his absence was noted at the opening of the trial of Fitzharris, the Whig informer, in May. Charles observed and rewarded his son's discretion, giving him £4,000 to pay debts in April, and a further £500 in September. Rumours of reconciliation naturally followed, but as the days went by and nothing happened the Duke's friends stepped into the gap. In July Monmouth's secretary James Vernon urged his master to approach the King. But Monmouth, encouraged by the recent gift of cash, stood on his pride. If summoned he would go to Charles, but since he had been rebuffed before (he said) he would not make the first advance. Lord Mordaunt tried again in October, urging the Duke's case with Charles till well past midnight, but to no purpose. Later still in the year York received reports that Portsmouth was once more active in Monmouth's interest, but the alarm he felt proved groundless.[49]

Simple pride on Monmouth's part frustrated what was, in retrospect, the best opportunity he ever had to mend the breach with Charles. The King was approachable (as his gifts show), and he dismissed as nonsense reports that Monmouth was fomenting trouble in his visits to Chichester.[50] But in the summer of 1681 Monmouth was under no pressure to make his peace; even his financial difficulties were reduced, thanks to Charles's well-meant but ill-judged benefactions. And the pride which prevented him from bowing before his father — let alone his uncle — though foolish, had very powerful springs in his childhood and adolescence. From those formative years came not only the conviction that Charles still owed him and his dead mother a great deal, but also the fatal belief that in a contest of emotional blackmail his father would be the first to give way.

But in 1681 the King could not give way, for urgent political reasons if for no other. Monmouth's emotions led him to see the contest with his father as a personal or family affair: Charles could never ignore its public or political aspect. Supporters of the two Dukes were moving dangerously apart. As early as September 1680 a servant whom Monmouth had been obliged to dismiss fought a duel with one of York's retainers; and in the summer of 1681 adherents of each peer began wearing coloured ribbons in their hats, red for York and blue for Monmouth. Coffee-house talk dwelt exhaustively on the supposed schemes of Monmouth, Shaftesbury, and the Whigs to recover their position. The pamphlet war, too, took on a new edge as Tory writers ended Monmouth's immunity from attack. The *Seasonable Invitation for Monmouth to return to Court* was still polite, though pressing deeply the charge of filial ingratitude; but *Lady Grey's Ghost* explored more brutally the motives behind Monmouth's friendship with Grey. A series of pamphlets then questioned the Duke's royal blood line, reaching a climax with *Grimalkin: or the Rebel Cat*, which contrasted the Lion's purity with the imperfection of his spotted son the Leopard, whose marks were 'so many legible and lasting Stains of his Mother's Lust and Pollutions'.[51]

The King was, therefore, watchful and resolute when the Duke, in October 1681, responded to the obligations of friendship and returned to London to attend Shaftesbury, when the latter petitioned for release from prison on the beginning of the law term. Less than two months later Monmouth was once more forbidden the court and 'beyond all hope of ever being restored', a swift passage to damnation even by his standards. Attending Shaftesbury's courtroom was a poor beginning, but thereafter the Duke was to some extent a victim of circumstances. On 2 November he joined with Lords Grey and Herbert in publishing an imprudent reply to a provocative declaration by the renegade Whig Lord Huntingdon, following this up by destroying copies of the latter's broadsheet wherever these could be found. Charles had to intervene to prevent the disturbances from spreading. A fortnight later Monmouth was — naturally — foremost in the traditional Whig parade celebrating Elizabeth's accession day; and he was prominent, too, at the court session which returned a bill 'ignoramus' to the charges brought against Shaftesbury. The King's patience was sorely tried as crowds with swords drawn roamed London that night shouting 'No York, a Monmouth!', and it finally snapped when his son offered to stand bail for Shaftesbury when the Earl was released from prison. He was banned the court, lost his remaining two offices, and was thrust into total disgrace. By early 1682 Halifax thought him of no political significance whatever; he was so pressed for money that his fine set of coach horses was up for sale; and he seriously considered taking service under the Marquis of Grana to fight against France in the Spanish Netherlands. He quarrelled bitterly with his old rival Albemarle over command of the Guards, saw his detested uncle successfully petition to return to England in March 1682, and lost one of his best friends when Thomas Thynne of Longleat was shot in a London street only minutes after parting from the Duke. Monmouth was with him when he died; and the Duke hunted down the murderers only to see the man who had procured the attack — a Swedish count named Königsmarck, jealous over Thynne's new wife — go free after blatant court interference, though the men who fired the shots were hanged.[52]

Monmouth's pride, and his anger with the King, only partly explain the speed and completeness of this particular rupture with his father. By October 1681 the court was wholly on the offensive: Whig small fry such as Fitzharris, College, and Rouse had been put on trial for life, Quo Warranto proceedings were beginning against Whig corporations,

Commissions of the Peace were being purged, and the great assault upon London's liberties was about to commence. Merely by being in the capital while still at odds with his father Monmouth would run foul of the court, because his Whig friends and allies were now fighting for their existence, and the Duke was bound to be involved. Gone now were any thoughts of the succession, and probably of office too; like the Whigs Monmouth's aims in 1682 were limited to restoration of the *status quo ante* — an end to enmity and a partial return to favour. Even for this, however, the price was high as Monmouth found when in May 1682, despairing of any other course, he sent Major Holmes first to see Secretary Conway, and then the King. Holmes was to fight with some distinction under Monmouth in 1685, but on this occasion he bungled matters. When the subject of York came up in his interview with the King he said — truthfully but undiplomatically — that, although his master would kneel before his father, he would never do so to the heir. Charles at once expressed 'great indignation', declaring in public particular resentment against his son, and forbidding any who valued his love to traffic with the Duke. Monmouth blamed Halifax for the fiasco (with some justification for the Earl had strongly opposed the Protestant Duke's return to court in order to keep York, too, out of England), and picked a quarrel with him in St. Martin's Church. Even then rumours of a reconciliation did not end. In August 1682 they sprang up after the two Dukes met for the first time in two years, unexpectedly in Hyde Park, and parted amicably; and they continued after entreaties by Monmouth's Duchess to save her husband's position.[53] At the same time Shaftesbury and other Whig grandees were making a last offer to live in peace with the King before they were completely lost. All efforts failed.

By the autumn of 1682 the Whigs' position — and Monmouth's with them — was, therefore, most alarming. Exclusion was dead, and York was permanently back in England at his brother's side. The Tory reaction was picking off Whigs in local and central government, London was lost to them, and Tory Sheriffs would empanel hostile juries in any trials brought by the government. Unable to make peace, but with nothing left to fight with, the Exclusionists could only wait as the court closed in. For a time they tried to disguise their position by re-enacting a past triumph. A ducal progress through north-western England was proposed, to rally popular support as in 1680, and unable himself to think of anything else, Monmouth agreed to go. As a tour, it was a great success. He travelled to Coventry and on 8 September rode to Stone, thence to Nantwich, Chester, Wallasey and Liverpool. He stayed at the houses of the Earl of Macclesfield, Lord Delamere, and Sir Henry Booth, before returning via Congleton and Knutsford to Stafford. At the major towns over a hundred horsemen would wait to escort him in, and countryfolk thronged the roads for up to two miles into towns to catch a glimpse of the 'Protestant Duke'. Cheering crowds, bonfires, guns, and bells accompanied his progress, spectators throwing their hats into the air and chanting 'Let Monmouth reign'. When he entered Chester so many bonfires had been lit, that those outside it 'saw the city as it had been in a flame'. He was spoken of quite simply as 'the King's son', his audience claimed that he was still his father's favourite, and they swore that 'they would not have a Papist to inherit and would venture their lives for the Duke of Monmouth'. A government informer heard arguments that the Duke was Charles's legitimate heir, being 'the King's primogenitus and, if the marriage was not according to the law of the land, yet in *foro coeli*, it went far with them'.[54]

Once again some of the enthusiasm arose from the opportunity to settle local scores — at Chester Tories had their houses stoned; and there was ample evidence of planning behind the visit, stocks of beer and blue ribbons having been assembled, together with spare horses. But above all, the Duke's personality made the tour a success. As in the west two years before he perfectly combined the ceremonial and the familiar, taking off his hat to the crowds, and when they cheered him he 'caressed them . . . with kind expressions and courteous behaviour'. He touched for the King's Evil near Wallasey, and then threw dignity aside to race on foot with, and defeat, all comers. At Chester he stood godfather to the Mayor's daughter, making a gift of the plate he had just won. When a tailor drank his health Monmouth took the bottle and pledged the man in turn. At the houses of Delamere and Booth he dined in public state, 'the doors [being] set open and the rabble suffered to . . . come in and view the Duke, entering at one door and going out another'.[55]

Monmouth's remarkable talent for charming the common people was once again the important point emerging from his 1682 tour. He possessed an easy, open, equal manner, which appealed to spectators as individuals; and a more formal and dignified bearing which excited them *en masse*. No less evident was his appeal as the King's undoubted son: for many this fact established his claim to the succession, irrespective of his legitimacy. Equally perturbing to royalist observers locally was the popular rejection of York because of his Catholicism, even so loyal an Anglican as the aged Dr. Mathew Fowler warning that unless the heir returned to Protestantism the crown would sit very uneasily upon his head. As the 'Protestant Duke', such anti-Popish sentiment naturally strengthened Monmouth's appeal. In 1682 he aroused a complex blend of personal admiration, 'legitimist' sentiment (as the King's son), and Protestant defensiveness, a mixture which should be remembered when explaining why men rallied to him in 1685. In 1682 — and in 1680 — he displayed and developed a capacity for making impressive entrances into towns, to be of great practical value in the early days of the rebellion, when his handful of followers had to grow into an army within a few days.

Though a remarkable personal success, the manner of the tour's ending brought Monmouth and his friends abruptly back to reality. At Stafford the Duke found a sergeant-at-arms waiting for him with a warrant, and he was conveyed back to London under arrest. The government had panicked at reports of mounting disorder, and though it was embarrassed when Monmouth was quickly released again on a writ of habeas corpus, its strength had been demonstrated. And with this tour the opposition found they had played their last 'constitutional' card: all hopes of reconciliation now gone, they were forced to choose between waiting passively for the government's revenge to engulf them, or considering armed resistance — a *coup* of some kind against the King and his brother. The latter path had been momentarily glimpsed in the summer of 1682, when the Earl of Argyle had stayed briefly in London, *en route* from Scotland and a trumped-up charge of treason to refuge in the Netherlands. In Grey's words the Whigs' talks then had 'served only to discover what little preparation . . . had been made for relieving themselves by forcible means'. Soon afterwards, as the struggle for the City reached its climax, Shaftesbury, Monmouth, Russell, Grey, and others began to sound out other Whig grandees on the possibility of more forcible resistance; and then considered whether, in London and the west country, they had the numbers for such a course. According to some accounts, Shaftesbury saw in Monmouth's Staffordshire and Cheshire tour a means of mobilizing further support for a rising, and he criticized the Duke sharply for ending the progress so tamely.[56]

By the end of the tour, in late September 1682, Shaftesbury was a desperately alarmed man — he would shortly go into hiding in London and then flee to the Dutch exile, where he died in January 1683 — but his biographer finds it uncertain whether even this marked leader of Exclusion seriously plotted a *coup* or uprising. And as the ablest of the Whig politicians the Earl undoubtedly had the clearest perception of their danger, the most reason to fear that danger, and the best contacts (with the London lower classes) to act to avert that danger. His failure to take any decisive action — an irresolution shared by all the other Whig grandees — simply reflected the hopeless position of them all. By late 1682 armed resistance was the only course left, but the briefest comparison with 1642 showed how desperate that prospect was. Tories were extending their control in corporation and county; no Parliament was in existence; the navy and probably the army, would be loyal to the King; the Whigs' moderate supporters had been frightened back to the Crown. . . . No national rebellion on the lines of 1642 was possible; at best it would be a *coup*, a minority affair to seize the King and York, supported by local risings in a few areas. In practical terms even this effort would stand next to no chance of success; and the Whigs considered it only because they were utterly desperate; and they did nothing but consider it because they knew it to be helpless. When they were arrested in June 1683 no real plans at all had been produced in the space of over six months.[57] This lack of substance to their conspiracy amazed and baffled the government when it investigated the Rye House Plot: it could not conceive that intelligent men would play such a dangerous game as to talk of treason with no intention of carrying it out; and yet this is what Monmouth and his friends did after the Chester tour.

All perhaps save Shaftesbury. Though finally committed to no clear plan of resistance, the Earl harangued his intimates on the need for action. He found little response. Monmouth could not conceive himself in danger from the King, and was too loyal *au fond* to plot in earnest, while the remainder were too oppressed by the difficulties or the dangers of serious conspiracy. After Monmouth's tour it was pointed out to Shaftesbury that no real preparations had been made for resistance, not in London, in the west, or in the north-west, and that they lacked even the draft of a Declaration justifying a *coup*. Near despair, Shaftesbury left the Whigs, going into hiding in London to discuss an uprising with his lower class associates in the capital. Monmouth heard that these radicals, and possibly the Earl too, were considering 'the lopping point', assassination as an alternative to capturing the King. In late October or early November 1682 he took Russell, Grey, and Armstrong with him to meet Shaftesbury at the house of a London wine-merchant, Thomas Shepherd. When the Earl spoke of over-powering the King's Guards as a prelude to a rising, Monmouth replied with ironical enquiries as to where in London Shaftesbury was hiding his 'invisible army'. Making no progress with his last group of allies Shaftesbury gave up, and fled to the Netherlands.[58]

His departure was greeted with relief by the Whig grandees, who continued to ignore reality and nibble at the edges of treason. Monmouth took over the unspoken leadership and, with an apparently significant political role to play once more, enjoyed the bustle of non-serious conspiracy, defying his father, ignoring his uncle, and accepting the plaudits of the crowd when he travelled outside London to such Whig strongholds as Chichester. With Essex, Russell, Hampden, Howard and Sidney he formed a so-called 'Council of Six', the last organized expression of Shaftesbury's Whigs. Deeply suspicious of one another, divided over aims and methods, unable to agree even on the extent of their common danger, the meetings held by the six during the first half of 1683 were, nevertheless, to be important two years later, for their halting discussions prepared the strategy — such as it was — followed in 1685.

Armed resistance was envisaged in four areas.[59] The west of England figured first in the Council's discussions, for Bristol's political clubs had been a nursery of moderate and radical Whigs; Taunton had a long history of faction, and its M.P. John Trenchard undertook to supply fifteen hundred armed men; and rural Somerset and Wiltshire were considered strongly favourable areas. After Monmouth's tour of Cheshire the north-west also came under scrutiny, with Whig lords such as Delamere, Macclesfield, and Brandon expected to lead out gentry and tenants. Scotland's history of resistance to English rule (together with the stimulus of Argyle's recent visit to London) naturally turned heads further northwards, and a lawyer, Aaron Smith, was actually sent to initiate contacts. London, inevitably, was considered a principal base of support, although the Whig grandees proved totally incapable of tapping or even contacting the radicals here, who had done most of their business with Shaftesbury and distrusted the other aristocrats.

With only the loosest of arrangements sketched in for these areas they became *faute de mieux* the basis for Monmouth's planning two years later, when a rising had to be improvised in the briefest time possible. In 1685 the Duke hoped for diversionary risings in London and Cheshire to support his main effort toward Taunton and Bristol, but he hoped in vain; and although Argyle landed in Scotland to split royalist forces, the coordination of the two rebellions was poor and the north was suppressed before the western insurrection was well under way. Discussions during 1683 had also raised the role of the King's army,

Monmouth here encouraging his fellow-conspirators to believe that the troops would stay neutral rather than fight against their old commander, although the most he did was briefly to examine sentry positions in Whitehall. An assumption that the army would remain neutral was carried over from 1683 to 1685, though it was a very doubtful proposition at the earlier date and grew less, not more, plausible, after two years' further separation between Monmouth and 'his' officers. Finally, the months of conspiratorial talk dragged a number of lesser Whigs into the toils of treason, and when the government eventually uncovered their activities, many escaped capture and reached the Continent, to provide a nucleus of supporters in 1685 — accompanying Monmouth in rebellion were Grey and Ferguson, the lawyers Goodenough, Wade, Nelthorpe and Ayloffe, ex-Cromwellian officers such as Holmes, Burton, Bateman and Norton, and the fiery Scottish defender of liberty Andrew Fletcher of Saltoun. To Argyle's Scottish expedition went Hume to Polworth, Rumbold and Cochrane.[60]

Most of these refugees had had little or no contact with the Whigs of the Council of Six in 1682-83. They were part of a separate and shadowy London conspiracy or set of conspiracies which, early in 1683, may well have discussed murdering the King as he returned to London from the Newmarket races, and gave the Rye House Plot its name. These London radicals and republicans were the first group betrayed by Josiah Keeling, when he made his initial accusations to the government on 12 June 1683. To these original Rye House plotters, however, the names of the aristocratic Council of Six were soon added after Rumsey, who moved in both circles, was arrested and turned King's evidence. Howard was arrested and informed on the other grandees, leading to Essex's capture and suicide in the Tower, and to the trial and execution of Russell and Sidney. Grey was arrested but escaped, and Monmouth went to ground with a price on his head at Toddington in Hertfordshire, the house of his mistress Henrietta Wentworth. Here he spent most of the summer while his friends and associates were imprisoned, fined, or executed. He once more considered becoming a mercenary soldier for the Spanish, offered to come out of hiding to testify in favour of Russell at the latter's trial (the gesture was declined), and whiled away his time writing bad verse on the virtues of a private life, and watching the local hunt.[61]

Charles soon heard of this 'tall man in country habit' at Toddington, but after trying once to lure his son to London resolved to leave him where he was. The revelation of Monmouth's apparent treason and worse — informers swore to the Duke's full knowledge of the Plot — greatly affected Charles, and he was in tears when speaking to his son's wife after a Privy Council meeting at which charges had been laid against Monmouth. For a time the King seemed to encourage contemporary denunciations of 'the monstrousness of such a parracide', but the observant Halifax soon noted the King's toleration of Monmouth's stay at Toddington, and his habit of referring to the presumed traitor as 'James' with an affectionate inflection. Partly to balance York's predominant influence at court, partly to shore up his own position, the Trimmer undertook a reconciliation, and to general surprise and consternation appeared to bring it off. In October 1683 Monmouth paid Halifax a surreptitious night-time visit and wrote the King a generally-phrased letter of submission, but one specifically denying any knowledge of an assassination plot. Charles gave his son a brief interview and a further penitential letter followed, polished this time by Halifax. Charles was satisfied, Monmouth made a generally-worded confession to the Council on 25 November, and to the amazement of most observers the King then led his son about court 'with a fondness that confounded all', and made him a gift of £4,000.[62]

But sudden beginnings beget sudden endings. York was doubly angry at the reconciliation: with Halifax for venturing to interfere in what was a family as well as a political matter, and with the King for pardoning Monmouth before he had also submitted to the heir. If opportunity offered York would insist upon a *full* repentence from the prodigal. And opportunity would offer. Public reaction to the Rye House Plot had initially been horror and condemnation, but as the months passed and charges were brought against only a handful of those arrested (because there existed so little substantial evidence to base charges on), Whig whispers of doubt over the conspiracy became louder. Monmouth's reconciliation with his father increased the coffee-house talk — the government's credit 'goes untowardly with ye mobile, who doe so raise up spiritt by reason of ye Duke of Monmouth as is not fit for mee to expresse' wrote one of Viscount Hatton's correspondents. To counter such doubts the court spread word that Monmouth's confession — given to his father on condition that it would remain private and would not be used against his friends — fully confirmed Howard's evidence against Sidney, who at the end of November 1683 had been tried but not yet sentenced. Upon York's urging a notice was put into the *Gazette* to this effect.

Monmouth was now in a very painful situation. Sidney would die irrespective of the Duke's confession for he had already been found guilty, but it was appalling for Monmouth to hear that his confession supposedly justified this death. Worse still was the position of Hampden, still awaiting his trial, and afraid that Monmouth might become the second witness to his treason. The Duke angrily denied reports about his confession, and called Howard's evidence against Sidney a pack of lies. Charles could not allow the Crown's major witness to be thus traduced, and at once made his son sign a second and more detailed confession on pain of instant disgrace if he refused. Monmouth signed, and then heard that Hampden saw this as the signature to his death warrant. Desperately afraid that Charles would not honour his promise never to use the confession in court, Monmouth begged for its return. His father warned him of the consequences that would follow, but the Duke was distraught at the loss of friendship and honour which threatened, and he persisted. Charles damned him, returned the paper, and disgraced him once more.[63]

Monmouth's period of grace had lasted just twelve days. Some courtiers found his fate 'something hard'; and even Dr. Fell the unsentimental Bishop of Oxford was shocked into philosophical reflection, writing to a friend: 'There are not such tides in the sea wherewith you are encompassed as there is in Court interest, and favour'. The fallen man took his £4,000, and after staying variously at London and Toddington, left England for Brussels in April 1684. His mistress and his horses joined him, and he settled down for a long exile in not-too-difficult circumstances. True to its record the government put his flight to good use, naming the Duke as its first witness against Hampden, knowing he could not appear, and hoping the court would suspect that Monmouth's non-appearance betokened criminal knowledge of his friend's activities. But Howard remained the only witness to treason against Hampden, and the latter suffered only a crippling fine.[64]

In exile Monmouth observed the unspoken terms for any future reconciliation with his father, keeping well away from the Whig debris on the Continent, and not reacting to the kidnapping and subsequent execution of Armstrong in June 1684. Even a visit to England in November of that year to arrange the sale of a manor was accomplished without fuss or notice. Received courteously by the Governor of the Spanish Netherlands, and by the Prince of Orange (who instructed his troops to salute the Duke and took his advice on promotions within the English regiments in Dutch service), Monmouth could anticipate that his good behaviour would ultimately bring its reward.[65]

Then the blow fell. Quite unexpectedly Charles died; and in a copy made of some pages of the Duke's now-lost Personal Diary there appears the entry:

Feb.16 [sic]. The sad news of his Death
by L. *O cruel fate!*[66]

Fate, in the shape of his father's sudden death, no doubt played a major part in depriving Monmouth so abruptly of his prospects; but for years the Duke had been gambling — perhaps unknowingly — that father would outlive uncle, and the gamble had now failed. A combination of bad luck, sensitivity over honour, and lack of self-knowledge, however, had put him in a position where his hopes could die literally overnight. He was unlucky that his entry into politics had coincided with so deep a crisis as that precipitated by the Popish Plot; unlucky too that his personal quarrel with York was followed so quickly by the Exclusion crisis, with the former being swallowed up in the latter.

Lack of self-knowledge resulted in the Duke's pursuing a variety of aims between 1679 and 1685, and when he failed to choose between them their mutual contradictions destroyed hopes of achieving any. But most fundamentally, it was the Duke's sensitive concept of honour which led to his position in February 1685. At worst this was a pride which prevented him from taking the first step toward his father, or apologising to his uncle; at best it was a refusal to betray his friends during the Exclusion crisis and after the Rye House Plot, even at the price of losing his newly-regained position as favourite, to endure disgrace and exile. Monmouth fell not through his own stupidity, or following the withdrawal of external guidance, but because he could not subordinate honour to political calculation, or indeed to self-preservation.

Footnotes: Chapter Four

1. PRO, PC Register, 2/66, ff.398 ff; M.Ashley, *Charles II*, pp.240, 241, 245.

2. *Lords' Journal*, xiii, 298-300; *HMC* 11th Report, House of Lords, MSS., pp.17, 54; *CSPD 1678*, p.524; J.P.Kenyon, *The Popish Plot*, London 1972, p.84.

3. *CSPD 1678*, pp.63, 117, 193, 142; J.Kenyon, *Popish Plot*, p.93; *HMC* Fitzherbert MSS., pp.12, 127; *HMC* Ormonde MSS., IV, p.492; K.Haley, *Shaftesbury*, p.492; *CSPD 1679-80*, pp.51, 71.

4. *HMC* 11th Report, House of Lords MSS., pp.5-6; J.Kenyon, *Popish Plot*, p.86; *CSPD 1679-80*, p.250; *CSPD 1678*, pp.451, 511; *HMC* 7th Report, Verney MSS., p.471.

5. A.Browning, *Thomas Earl of Danby*, Glasgow 1951, 3 vols., iii, 129-33, 127-

8; J.R.Jones, 'Shaftesbury's "Worthy Men"', *Bulletin of the Institute of Historical Research*, 30 1957, pp.232-41; G.Burnet, *History*, ii, 179; *HMC* 7th Report, Verney MSS., p.471; K.Haley, *Shaftesbury*, p.517; *HMC* Ormonde V, p.102; T.Courteney ed., *Memoirs of Sir William Temple*, London 1740, 2 vols., i, 335.

6. J.R.Jones, *The First Whigs*, London 1970, pp.29, 53; K.Haley, *Shaftesbury*, p.481; *CSPD 1678*, p.210; *HMC* Ormonde MSS.IV, p.325; Dartmouth MSS.I, pp.33, 34, 36, 37.

7. *CSPD 1677-78*, pp.51, 174-5, 411-13, 590; *Lords' Journal*, xiii, 350-3; *HMC* Fitzherbert MSS., pp.118, 119, 123, 124, 132, 141, 145; J.Kenyon, *Popish Plot*, pp.138-41.

8. *HMC.*, Ormonde MSS.IV, p.473 (16 November 1678); *Commons Journal*, ix, 536; *HMC.*, Ormonde MSS.IV, pp.470, 473; J.S.Clarke, *Life of James II*, London 1816, 2 vols., i, 525-6.

9. H.C.Foxcroft, ed., *The Life and Letters of the first Marquis of Halifax*, London 1898, 2 vols., i, 139; J.Jones, *First Whigs*, p.82; *HMC.*, Ormonde MSS., IV, p.493.

10. A.Browning, ed., *The Memoirs of Sir John Reresby*, Glasgow 1936, p.176; *CSPD 1679-80*, pp.53-96; K.Haley, *Shaftesbury*, pp.501, 507; *HMC.*, Ormonde MSS.IV, pp.56, 277; G.Burnet, *History*, ii, 234, 235.

11. J.R.Jones, *First Whigs*, p.61; K.Haley, *Shaftesbury*, pp.512-3; G.Burnet, *History*, ii, 208; *HMC*, 15th Report App.V, Foljambe MSS., p.129; H.Foxcroft, *Halifax*, i, 145, 148-9, 150, 170; *HMC.*, Ormonde MSS.V, pp.504, 519; R.Blencoe ed., *Diary of the Times of Charles II by Henry Sidney*, London 1843, 2 vols., i, 24-5.

12. *HMC.*, Ormonde MSS.IV, pp.522-3; V, 127, 135, 136; K.Haley, *Shaftesbury*, pp.535-6.

13. *HMC.*, Ormonde MSS.V, pp.135, 153; 11th Report, Hamilton MSS.VI, p.162; 4th Report, Selkirk MSS., pp.517-18; G.Burnet, *History*, ii, 240-1.

14. *HMC.*, Ormonde MSS.IV, p.527; G.Burnet, *History*, ii, 240; W.Temple, *Works*, i, 342; H.Sidney, *Diary*, i, 27-8.

15. W.Temple, *Works*, i, 339, 342; H.Sidney, *Diary*, i, 10, 13, 15.

16. H.Foxcroft, *Halifax*, ii, 187-8; *HMC* 7th Report, p.474; H.Sidney, *Diary*, i, 138; Bodl.Lib.Carte MSS. Vol.39, f.68.

17. *HMC.*, Ormonde MSS.IV, pp.536-7; W.Temple, *Works*, i, 344; Carte MSS. 232, f.60.

18. H.Foxcroft, *Halifax*, i, 187n; Sidney, *Diary*, i, 154, 163, 167, 168, 185.

19. *HMC.*, Ormonde MSS.IV, p.562; V, p.245; 7th Report, p.477; J.Jones, *First Whigs*, p.114.

20. *HMC.*, Ormonde MSS.V, pp.244, 245, 247; IV, pp.562, 563; 7th Report, p.477; H.Sidney, *Diary*, i, 207-8, 237; K.Haley, *Shaftesbury*, pp.560n, 564; Carte MSS., 228 f.153, 210 f.164, 39 f.107, 59 f.137.

21. J.Reresby, *Memoirs*, p.182.

22. J.Reresby, *Memoirs*, p.193; E.M.Thompson ed., 'Correspondence of the Family of Hatton, Vol.I', *Camden Society*, 22 1878, p.193.

23. J.Reresby, *Memoirs*, p.248.

24. K.Haley, *Shaftesbury*, p.712.

25. H.Sidney, *Diary*, i, 203, 237; Add.MSS., 28938 f.24; *HMC* 7th Report. p.477.

26. H.Sidney, *Diary*, i, 240, 263; T.Bruce ed., *The Memoirs of Thomas Earl of Ailesbury*, London 1890, 2 vols., i, 76-7.

27. K.Haley, *Shaftesbury*, p.565; Carte MSS.243 f.444.

28. H.Foxcroft ed., 'Some Unpublished Letters of Gilbert Burnet', *Camden Society*, 53 1907, pp.10, 17, 21, 28.

29. For the investigation see *CSPD 1679-80*, pp.447-52, 454-5, 460, 462-3; and Add.MSS., 28094 ff.71-2; K.Haley, *Shaftesbury*, p.563.

30. 'A Letter to a Person of Honour concerning the Black Box', *Somers Tracts*, VIII, pp.207-8.

31. *CSPD 1674-80*, pp.455, 460, 466, 528; Bodl.Lib., Rawl. MSS.A175 f.176.

32. 'A Letter to a Person of Honour, concerning the King's disavowing the having been married to the Duke of Monmouth's mother', *Somers Tracts*, VIII, p.199.

33. O.W.Furley, 'The Whig Exclusionists: pamphlet literature in the Exclusion Campaign 1679-81', *Cambridge Historical Journal*, 13 1957, pp.19-36.

34. For example, 'The Duke of Monmouth's Case', *Somers Tracts*, VIII, pp.403-4.

35. *CSPD 1682*, p.537; G.Burnet, 'Letters', *Camden Society*, 53, pp.28, 31; 'Letter to a Person of Honour', *Somers Tracts*, VIII, pp.189-95.

36. 'Letter . . . concerning the King's disavowing . . . the Duke of Monmouth's mother', *Somers Tracts*, VIII, pp.195-208; H.Sidney, *Diary*, ii, 78.

37. G.Burnet, 'Letters', *Camden Society*, 53, pp.31, 39.

38. *A True Narrative of the Duke of Monmouth's late Journey into the West*, London 1680; *CSPD 1679-80*, pp.516, 570, 575, 594, 597, 600, 604; *CSPD*

1680-81, pp.4, 9, 11-12; *CSPD 1683-84*, p.2; *His Grace the Duke of Monmouth Honoured in his Progress*, London, 1680.

39. Bodl.Lib.Tanner MSS., 38 f.126 (misdated 1679).

40. *CSPD 1680*, p.31; *HMC* Ormonde V., p.449; *CSPD Jan.-June 1683*, p.186.

41. Tanner MSS., 38 f.126; for Chester see below p.136; H.Pitman, *A Relation of the great sufferings and strange adventures of Henry Pitman, Chirugeon to the late Duke of Monmouth*, London 1689, pp.355, 364.

42. *Calendar of Colonial State Papers 1685-88*, pp.97, 158, 606, 151, 243, 41-2, 95, 136-7.

43. *CSPD 1680-81*, p.531; *CSPD Jan.-June 1683*, pp.369-70.

44. 'Hatton Correspondence Vol.I', *Camden Society*, 22, pp.235-6.

45. N.Luttrell, *A Brief Historical Relation of State Affairs*, Oxford 1857, 6 vols., i, 56; *HMC* Ormonde V, pp.454, 445, 446; K.Haley, *Shaftesbury*, pp.590, 592.

46. K.Haley, *Shaftesbury*, pp.597, 598.

47. H.Foxcroft, *Halifax*, i, 247n, 245; Ford Lord Grey, *The Secret History of the Rye House Plot*, London 1754, pp.1-3; K.Haley, *Shaftesbury*, pp.612, 615; J.Jones, *First Whigs*, p.155.

48. K.Haley, *Shaftesbury*, p.634; J.Jones, *First Whigs*, p.179.

49. N.Luttrell, *Relation*, i, 118; *HMC* Ormonde VI, pp.27, 400; K.Haley, *Shaftesbury*, p.646; *Calendar of Treasury Books, 1681-85*, Part I, pp.103, 269; 'Journal of Edmund Warcup', *English Historical Review*, 40 1925, pp.256-7; *CSPD 1680-81*, p.496; J.Clarke, *Life*, i, 723; *HMC* Dartmouth I, p.44.

50. *CSPD 1680-81*, pp.467, 495.

51. 'Hatton Correspondence, I', *Camden Society* 22, p.235; N.Luttrell, *Relation*, i, 111; *Grimalkin*, p.4.

52. *HMC* Ormonde VI, p.244; 'Hatton Correspondence II', *Camden Society* 22, p.11; *CSPD 1680-81*, pp.545, 572, 583; K.Haley, *Shaftesbury*, p.676; N.Luttrell, *Relation*, i, 150; *CSPD 1682*, pp.154, 190; H.Foxcroft, *Halifax*, i, 340; J.Reresby, *Memoirs*, pp.240, 243, 249-50, 255.

53. Carte MSS., 232 ff.105, 109; 216 ff.47, 53, 141, 157; *HMC* 7th Report, Graham MSS., p.352; H.Foxcroft, *Halifax*, i, 356; K.Haley, *Shaftesbury*, p.701.

54. *CSPD 1682*, pp.423, 396, 409, 415.

55. *CSPD 1682*, pp.391, 393, 402, 423, 409, 388, 422.

56. *CSPD 1682*, pp.428-9, 419, 432; F.Grey, *Secret History*, pp.14-15, 18-23; Nathaniel Wade's 'Confession', Brit.Lib.Harleian MSS.6845, ff.266-7.

57. K.Haley, *Shaftesbury*, ch.30; the best treatment of the Rye House Plot is D.J.Milne, 'The Rye House Plot', London Ph.D.Thesis 1949.

58. N.Wade, Harl.MSS., 6845, ff.266-7; F.Grey, *Secret History*, pp.19-23, 27-32; J.Ferguson, *Ferguson the Plotter*, London 1887, pp.416-20, 423, 427-30; G.Burnet, *History*, ii, 350; T.Sprat, *A True Account of the Horrid Conspiracy*, London 1685, pp.17, 40, 70, 87; *State Trials*, IX, p.962.

59. F.Grey, *Secret History*, p.53; Harl.MSS., 6845 ff.266-8; T.Ailesbury, *Memoirs*, i, 81; G.Burnet, *History*, ii, 383; T.Sprat, *True Account*, p.15; *State Trials*, IX, p.692.

60. F.Grey, *History*, p.38; J.Milne, 'Rye House Plot' (Thesis), p.289.

61. *HMC* Ormonde VII, p.62; N.Luttrell, *Historical Relation*, i, 264; G.Burnet, *History*, ii, 405; T.Ailesbury, *Memoirs*, i, 80.

62. J.Reresby, *Memoirs*, pp.304, 319-20; *HMC* Ormonde VII, p.95; 'Hatton Correspondence II', *Camden Society*, 22, p.41; H.Foxcroft, *Halifax*, i, 402-3; J.Wellwood, *Memoirs of the Most Material Transactions*, London 1740, App.XIV, pp.319-23.

63. J.Reresby, *Memoirs*, pp.322, 324; 'Hatton Correspondence II', *Camden Society*, 22, pp.33, 40.

64. J.Reresby, *Memoirs*, p.322; 'Hatton Correspondence II', p.41; N.Luttrell, *Relation*, i, 295, 298; H.Foxcroft, *Halifax*, i, 410-11.

65. N.Luttrell, *Relation*, i, 306; Add.MSS.,41832, ff.23, 25, 31; 41810, ff.118, 189, 236; Barillon's Despatches, PRO 31/3/158, ff.58-9, 62; F.Grey, *Secret History*, p.86.

66. J.Welwood, *Memoirs*, App.XIV, p.323.

CHAPTER FIVE
Lyme Regis to Taunton

One of the stranger aspects of the 1685 rising is that it was ever attempted at all. Monmouth's reaction to news of his father's death was not defiance, but despair and resignation. He began a submissive letter to his uncle but saw no point in completing it and, without waiting to be asked, prepared to leave the Netherlands. Accepting that his exile was now permanent, the Duke saw his only future as a mercenary soldier in some distant corner of eastern Europe, and was encouraged in this thinking by William of Orange who wished to be quit of his embarrassing guest as quickly as possible. To suggestions from English and Scottish exiles that he should lead a rebellion against the new King he gave a firm refusal, speaking of 'the Fear in some and the Ambition in others' which would leave an uprising without supporters of consequence. Hopes that a rebellion could succeed before the government settled in he dismissed as 'a Vain Argument'; and he concluded his refusal with a reference to the newly-discovered pleasures of a private life, and his wish to 'run the hazard of being thought anything rather than a rash inconsiderate man'.[1]

This attitude was consistent with his conduct during his year of exile. He had socialized with the Prince of Orange and other notables, but avoided politics and eschewed any contact with the English and Scottish exiles, many of them fellow-conspirators from the Rye House Plot. He saw his friends Grey and Armstrong only once, and made no protest when the latter was kidnapped to England and executed. The exiles had complained bitterly over his failure to help them during the trials of 1683, and spoke with equal resentment of his 'ingratitude' and 'numbness' towards them a year later. In part this dissociation occurred because the Duke obviously had to prove his reformation before Charles II would permit him to return; but the exiles were also a sad collection, with nothing to offer their former leader. Divided first between the English and the Scots, each solely devoted to the salvation of their own country, both groups were further split into distrustful factions. Most active among the English were the republicans, now extremists with little to lose. Those whose quarrel had simply been with the Duke of York, and who believed in the monarchical principle, had nothing in common with them. Among the Scots Archibald Campbell, ninth Earl of Argyle, claimed the leadership, but his ambitions for a quasi-independent fiefdom in the Highlands were too transparent for him to be trusted by the Lowlanders, who aimed principally at restoring Presbyterianism. The Earl was, moreover, personally unattractive, reputedly a secretive, devious, and autocratic man.[2] Given Monmouth's low opinion both of the intention to rebel, and of the men with whom he would be invading, why did he abandon prudence and commit himself? The answer lies partly in the increasing pressure he came under from a variety of quarters, partly in the effectiveness of the arguments used on him, and partly in the lack of real alternatives available to the Duke.

The first and least important pressure group was the English exiles, joined early in 1685 by Ford, Lord Grey, who had been disappointed in his hopes of service with the Elector of Brandenburg because of pressure from the English government. Like most of the English refugees Grey was penniless, like them his only recourse was rebellion, like them he assumed without thought that a change of monarch would be a favourable time to begin one. Equally thoughtless and even more energetic was the Scottish preacher and plotter Robert Ferguson, who urged the English exiles to impress upon Monmouth his duty to 'preserve the liberties of three kingdoms, and the Protestant religion in them, and by consequence in all Europe'. Despite his pessimistic first thoughts Monmouth was persuaded early in March 1685 at least to meet Argyle, and the Scots proved more effective in shaking the Duke than the English exiles. This was partly because their plans were extensive and well laid. A gift of £7,000 from a Mrs. Smith, the widow of a London merchant whom Argyle had met in 1683 and who had followed him to the Netherlands, had provided a solid base of men, munitions, and ships. With over a year to prepare, Argyle could claim an extensive network of contacts in the Highlands, his chosen invasion area. His clan would back him for tribal reasons, and the clergy would support him to establish Presbyterianism. Argyle needed a diversion in southern England, and was more than usually forthcoming to the Duke on his preparations and plans. A Scottish source claims that Monmouth actually offered to join Argyle's force, though this probably exaggerates the favourable impression made on him: in any case Argyle would brook no rival.[3]

More potent than the quality of the Scots' preparations, however, was the simple fact that within a matter of weeks Argyle intended to begin a rebellion. Monmouth's honour was, by consequence, fatally involved. How could he, son of the (possibly) murdered King allow his uncle to seize his inheritance; how could he, former leader of the Whigs, stand aside while another, much less damaged by James II than himself, bore the heat of the day? Bishop Burnet was later told by a Scot who joined Monmouth that the Duke had been 'pushed on to it against his own sense and reason: but he could not refuse to hazard his own person when others were so forward'.[4]

Even so, Monmouth did not finally commit himself until he had been deliberately deceived over his probable reception in England. Just after the King's death Robert Cragg was sent by the London republicans (and in particular by John Wildman the former Leveller) to enquire of Monmouth what his intentions were. The Duke was absent, talking to the Scots in Rotterdam, and Robert Ferguson met the messenger. Seeing an opportunity to commit Monmouth, Ferguson lied over the Duke's plans, saying that an invasion was intended, that Scots and English were even then concerting their plans, and that all that was needed was money. While Cragg returned to England with this message, Ferguson then told Monmouth that Cragg had carried declarations of much support in England if both parties of exiles made common cause. Not long afterwards a government informer described Cragg as the man 'whom Ferguson had imployed to draw in Monmouth by many false promises'.[5]

This double lie made the Duke's honour even more the issue at stake, drawing in all those conceptions of reputation, obligation, pride in leadership, and personal hatred of James II, which had misdirected him since 1679. It was clear to many that the Duke was now at the crisis of his career. Would he tamely withdraw to eastern Europe, or would he fight for what had so long been proclaimed as his inheritance? Would he assist and lead those who might suffer under a Popish King and who looked to him for leadership, for in England soon after Charles' death it was being said that 'the Duke would never prove so ungrateful as to see those who have stood up for his interest sink for want of his support'.[6] And as though these arguments and pressures were not enough, there was finally for Monmouth no safe alternative to rebellion. For all his and Orange's talk of service with the King of Hungary, or in Sweden, this was simply talk: no approaches had been made, no interest in his employment had been expressed. The forests and snow of eastern and northern Europe held little attraction for a man who had spent his adult life in the courts of London, The Hague, and Paris; while Lord Grey's recent disappointment with the Elector of Brandenburg showed how long was the reach of the English government. No exiles could now look for security or safety. In short, rebellion was scarcely more desperate than the only available alternative.

Beset by self-appointed advisers and allies, Monmouth retired for nearly three weeks to Gouda after his meeting with Argyle, to make his decision. He wrote at least once to the Scottish leader expressing once again his misgivings, but he could not now overcome the pressures which had governed him for six years.[7] James II after all had little personal popularity, and was suspected because of his religion and mistrusted over his autocratic temperament. Would not the cry of Protestantism and English liberties rekindle the fires of the Popish Plot? In Monmouth's favour were the popular view of his character, his religion, his military reputation, and his former political allies. The common people and the Whig gentry would rally to him, it was argued; and the army which he had once led would not fight against him. The latter point was crucial and Monmouth's hopes depended upon it. The Guards had built bonfires on their commander's return to London in November 1679; in the Rye House talks Monmouth had assumed army support; and the influence permitted him by William of Orange in 1684 over the English regiments in Dutch service further encouraged the Duke's delusion.[8] Belief in the English army's support, or at least neutrality, was as essential to Monmouth in 1685 as it would be to William three years later. Confronted by an uprising of the common people, an erosion of gentry support, and the neutrality of his army, there was every chance that James II would give way — as he did in 1688.

With such calculations to support a decision fundamentally taken for the sake of honour, Monmouth returned to Amsterdam to collect his forces. Time at once became the enemy. Argyle had settled his plans, bought ships and supplies, and was assembling his invading force of three hundred men. The latter could not be supported for long, nor would they remain quiet for long. The Scots had to sail by the beginning of May, and Monmouth agreed to embark a week later so that the landings would be nearly simultaneous. There was one month to make all preparations.

A landing site was quickly chosen. It had to be distant from London, within reasonable reach of the Netherlands, offer the prospect of immediate support, and contain no ultra-loyalist nobility who might crush the venture at birth. The scene of Monmouth's last public parade, Lancashire and Cheshire, was ruled out by the second and fourth criteria, being too distant for small ships safely to sail to, and strongly influenced by the Earl of Derby, a conspicuous bystander in 1682. In the south Chichester was close by, and was a town devoted to Monmouth, but it was too near the capital. In north-western England Monmouth had no personal following, and the Whigs only modest support. But the south-west was not too far to sail, was reasonably distant from London, and had responded enthusiastically to the Protestant Duke in 1680. Lyme Regis offered a convenient port: small, 'factious', and close to Exeter, Taunton and Bristol, all cities with much to commend them as the rebels' first objective. Moreover, the south-west had been the preferred locale for a rising during the indeterminate Rye House discussions, and in 1685 Monmouth had neither the time nor the contacts to devise any other plan.[9] Lyme Regis it would be.

Equipment, men, and ships were the next consideration. By pawning his goods and plate Monmouth raised some £3,000, and the Bristol lawyer and Rye House conspirator Nathaniel Wade was employed to spend it. The Duke exercised some direction — as a former general he knew what was needed, and in 1679 he had prepared a financial estimate for equipping ten thousand troops for service in the Leeward Islands. By the end of April the rebels had a modest arsenal of 100 muskets, 1,500 pieces of breast armour, 200 barrels of gunpowder, four small cannon, and two small ships hired to transport men and gear. They had few pikes, no horses, no wagons, insufficient guns, little food, and scant cash: plainly all would hinge on their initial reception in England. Some professional soldiers had been engaged. A Dutchman named Buys would manage the four cannon, and from English regiments in the Netherlands came some cashiered officers — Colonel Venner, Captain Foulkes, Ensign Parsons and others — who might be able to train their raw recruits. Some English mercenaries serving abroad were also attracted into the venture, such as Captain Bruce, once in the Elector of Brandenburg's service, Captain John Tillier, and a Captain Thompson. Others were Rye House plotters with some military experience in their past — Major Holmes for example and Captain Matthews — or adventurers with a taste for violence, such as Robert Perrott who had been with Colonel Blood when the latter had audaciously tried to seize the Crown Jewels in 1670.[10]

Though some trained men were essential there was no question of the rebels invading in any strengh — only eighty-two men accompanied the Duke — and they would have to rely on English supporters for manpower, money, and much equipment. Supporters needed advance warning, and messages had to be sent to them without revealing however the exact time and place. Early in April Monmouth sent his

'Master of Horse', Captain Edward Matthews, to contact John
Wildman and the London sympathizers, and then go on to Lords
Delamere and Brandon and the Earl of Macclesfield in Cheshire. A few
days later Christopher Bettiscombe, a young Rye House plotter whose
family owned land in Dorset, was sent to reinforce the London contact,
and then to proceed to the south-west where he was to prepare Whig
gentry such as Sir Francis Drake and Sir Walter Younge, and warn
John Trenchard to mobilize Taunton.[11]

With arrangements thus far advanced, Monmouth was startled to
receive two successive discouraging responses from London. The first
was borne by Rogert Cragg, returning to the Netherlands after taking
Ferguson's lying reply to the Londoners' original query. Wildman and
his friends opposed a rebellion in England and advised the Duke either
to join Argyle, or to hide in London until the result in Scotland was
known. Meanwhile, they had no money at all for Monmouth. Then a
letter came from Matthews, that Wildman had 'only spoken to him in
Hieroglyptics'. Cragg was sent back with a peremptory demand for
£4,000, and when Henry Ireton (cousin of Lord Grey and son of
Cromwell's Commissary-General) arrived with a prevaricating message
from Wildman, he too was returned to ask for money. Finally, as May
approached, another messenger the cabinet-maker John Jones was
despatched to England with the place and approximate date of the
landing, so that some Londoners could meet the invaders with horses
and arms.[12]

Meanwhile nothing was heard from Bettiscombe, who spent three
weeks in London possibly seeing the plotters, and then travelled west to
await his leader's arrival without apparently contacting any western
gentry; though a letter sent from Taunton to the conspirators in
Holland may have derived from his work. Matthews's letter from
London had said that the Cheshire gentry were 'believed' to be
favourable, but then nothing more was heard from him. The
unfortunate Ireton was arrested as he landed at Harwich, and so by the
end of April Monmouth had received no news from the north-east or the
south-west, and only discouragement from London. This alarming
situation followed inevitably from the venture's tight time-table, but
the Duke was now too far involved to back out, being 'engag'd by his
promise to Argyle', as Wade expressed it.[13]

Argyle now decided that he could wait no longer and his three ships
slipped out of Amsterdam on 2 May, sailing due north for the
Highlands. Monmouth's intention to follow within a week was over-
optimistic, but it was two strokes of bad luck which delayed him for

over a month. English warships were reported in the Channel, and though the north-bound Argyle would escape them, they made an escort essential for Monmouth's two small ships. It took three weeks to raise the money to hire and equip the frigate 'Helderenburgh'. The Duke sold his remaining goods, pawned what he could of Henrietta Wentworth's, wrote begging letters to English exiles, and would still have been £1,000 short had not the widowed Mrs. Smith once more stepped in, and with the last of her husband's money endowed her second rebellion within a month. Bad weather then further delayed the expedition. The rebels boarded ship on 24 May but could not clear the Texel for another week, and were then so buffeted by a westerly gale that what should have been a three days' passage took them ten.[14] Not until 11 June did they make landfall near Lyme Regis, and by then there was no chance of coordinating their invasion with that of Argyle. By that time the Earl was on the brink of defeat.

Nothing better illustrates the importance to a revolt of effective leadership than the sorry tale of the Scottish expedition.[15] With twice the money and three times the men, a year to prepare, the blessing of exiled clergy and the loyalty of a Highland clan, Argyle still caused the government far less trouble than Monmouth. Scouts prematurely landed on the Orkneys were captured and gave away his plans. He then dallied in the Highlands, but gained barely a tenth of the five thousand recruits he expected (and many of those stole away with the weapons they had been given). He pursued private vendettas with his former neighbours, and made excuse after excuse to avoid marching into the Lowlands where alone a decisive result could be obtained. When his ships were captured and he was finally manoeuvred out of the Highlands, the government was completely ready for him. Amid bitter recriminations the rebels, only nine hundred strong, crossed Loch Long and by 12 June were on the road to Glasgow. Four days later royalist troops intercepted them. Argyle failed to put his men 'in orderly battalia', and they were dispersed. The Earl was captured, and survivors found difficulty in expressing their depth of anger over his incompetent leadership. When Monmouth landed, nearly six weeks late, one jaw of the pincer had been broken and James II had been thoroughly alerted. He had recalled three regiments of Scottish troops in the service of the Dutch (declining William of Orange's curious offer to accompany the force), and begun preparing a train of artillery.[16] Both precautions would be useful against the English rebels.

The other principal handicap resulting to the latter by their late arrival was that they were confronted by a sitting Parliament. Elected after Charles II's extensive purge of the boroughs in 1683-84, James II's first Parliament was, when it met on 21 May 1685, as extravagantly loyal as any King could wish. Its members at once voted James handsome revenues for life, and referring to Argyle and other rebels resolved to 'stand by him with their lives and fortunes against all enemies'.[17] When he landed Monmouth would be condemned by a legally elected Parliament as well as by the King, and would have to appeal to some future Parliament to vindicate his cause.

The delays forced on Monmouth therefore cost him dear, but matters could have been worse. With remarkable incompetence, the English government's agents in Amsterdam had watched the preparations of both rebel expeditions and failed to stop either (waiting until the last minute, and then applying to the wrong authority in the case of the English). At home, the government was nearly as foolish. No orders were given to arrest possible sympathizers until 19 May, when Monmouth was on the point of sailing and Argyle was a fortnight gone. At this point key figures such as John Trenchard had become wary, and escaped detection. Further arrests ordered on 8 and 9 June were far too late to be effective; by then a handful of active sympathizers had already ridden out of London for the west. Only when the rebels were actually ashore were mass arrests ordered, of 'such as had been engaged in the late wars, and many good old ministers, and such private gentlemen, as were obnoxious to the government', as one observer put it.[18] The first two categories – ageing radicals, and Nonconformists – reveal the government's preconceptions concerning who was likely to rebel, and the assumptions made at this point have coloured all subsequent accounts as to who the rebels were, down to the present day.

The government's preparations for the rebels were similarly indecisive, mainly because London entirely failed to anticipate the invasion point of either rebel band. Northern Ireland was long predicted for Argyle, even after he had been reported in the Highlands. Monmouth was expected to land in northern England, and repeated warnings and directions to arrest suspicious persons were sent thither, particularly to Lancashire, Cheshire and Northumberland. Though the south-west also received directions to be alert, the danger here was discounted. On 4 June, James II wrote to the western Deputy Lieutenants, leaving it to their discretion whether to raise the militia and search for arms (most Lords Lieutenant were then in London for Parliament.) When Monmouth made landfall on 11 June, James was predicting of Somersetshire that 'all things will continue quiet there'; and next day as the Duke was occupying Lyme Regis, the King wrote to

William of Orange that the rebels would land in Lancashire or Cheshire, or in Scotland.[19]

Poor appreciations by the government meant that its troops were less ready to repel the invasion than they might have been. On the rebel side, the weak performance of Monmouth's agents sent to prepare support may not have greatly harmed him, for in early 1685 there was in any case much talk of the Duke's imminent return. 'Factious spirits' at Chichester insisted that their hero had been proclaimed King in Scotland, and drinkers at a London tavern were told that Monmouth was rightfully Prince of Wales 'and shall sway'. In the north of England James II's accession produced a disturbing prophecy that two dukes would do battle on a Yorkshire moor, with York slain. Beggars, nailers, and colliers in the Midlands spoke of going 'north' to join Monmouth, settling accounts on the way with the rich who mistreated them; and a tenant farmer of the same region referred meaningfully to the Lord 'looking upon them'. Another Warwickshire farmer 'spoke some words little less than treasonable . . . in favour of the Duke of Monmouth'. February and March saw a spate of reports that the pretender had landed in Scotland, that the late King had been murdered, and that the new one was guilty of firing London in 1666 and of other crimes against the people. The reception given to Titus Oates when he was set in the stocks 'much surprised' James II, who wrote sharply to the London sheriffs. Even in Yorkshire the local Catholics' reaction to the accession – 'hectoring . . . abusing' – led Protestants to bewail the death of Charles II 'with many fears for the gloomy prospect of Popery'.[20] Monmouth might hope partially to resurrect the old anti-Popish coalition, and in some quarters his return was eagerly anticipated.

This was true above all in the south-west. After its flurry of activity in 1684 Taunton greeted the new reign quietly, and Bridgewater became the new centre of discontent. In March 1685 a number of inflammatory letters were received first by a merchant Roger Hoare (later to welcome Monmouth into the town), and then by the borough's Tory mayor, emphasizing the new King's 'too forward and ungovernable zeal for Catholicism' which allegedly alarmed even his co-religionists. The town's loyalists wrote to London of their difficulties in controlling 'these Grindallizing self-willed humourists', doubted the soundness of many aldermen, and admitted that at the proclamation of the new King 'some people hung their heads'. At the end of May two more letters were intercepted, one at Ilminster the other at Taunton, advising that 'a certain person' would shortly appear in the west, advertising Argyle's 'great success', and warning the recipients to avoid being arrested.

Strong watches were at once set throughout the county and five suspicious horsemen travelling together were arrested. Though it was not realized, these men were indeed rebel supporters, sent from London by the cabinet-maker John Jones to welcome their Duke. Held for too long in Taunton prison they were freed when Monmouth took the town, and became officers in his army. Following their arrest a woman deposed that she had seen 'about eighty horsemen' gallop at night past her house near Taunton, there was furtive talk of Argyle's progress in Somerset taverns, and a new confidence was remarked in the bearing of Dissenters. Stricter watches were ordered, the militia raised, and troops attended the big fair at Exeter. But when a week passed and nothing further happened 'little credit [was] given to that thought of a rising in the west', and though the militia remained in Taunton and other towns, Monmouth's landing at Lyme Regis on Thursday 11 June caught the authorities totally by surprise.

This was ironic for his long passage had convinced the Duke that surprise would be impossible, and he planned to put two men ashore a day ahead of his main landing to raise the countryside and help create an army as quickly as possible. Consequently when he made landfall off Chideock in Lyme Bay at dawn on the eleventh, Thomas Dare the Taunton goldsmith with another man were rowed ashore to gather news from local fishermen, before striking inland for the Speke house at Ilminster, and Taunton. Nothing was learned from the fishermen, but they were told that Argyle in Scotland would shortly be joined by risings in England and Ireland, and were treated to sweet wine and neats' tongues to ensure that the message would be remembered. Dare and his companion then made off, and a little later the encounter was related to a customs official who called at Chideock. The three ships were still plainly visible, motionless, and three or four miles out. In some alarm the official returned to Lyme Regis, but too late to warn the port's customs officer against going out to the ships. Midday passed and the officer did not return, missing first his dinner and then his invariable game of bowls in the afternoon. The Deputy Searcher Samuel Dassall and the town's mayor sent a warning to local JPs to arrest the two travellers but did nothing more, even when the occupants of a passing fisher-boat were taken onto the ships and did not return, even when the post arrived with a newspaper account of three ships (remarkably similar to those in the Bay) having recently left Amsterdam with suspected rebels on board. The 'gaiety of their entertainment', it was hoped, might explain the failure of Searcher and fishermen alike to leave the ships.[22]

Sunset brought the tide's turn and an end to waiting. The three ships began moving closer onshore, and then put out seven rowing boats full of men. From the clifftops Dassall and the mayor saw with horror that they were armed with guns, and a scene of chaos followed. Dassall tried to man the port's great cannon and found that there was no powder for it. He ran down to the Cob and tried to persuade the master of a ship tied up there to open fire. Being asked for proof that the boats were full of the King's enemies and unable to reply, he borrowed some gunpowder and ran back to the town to break out muskets. He was just in time to see the boats ground on the shingle west of the Cob. Files of armed men sprang out, and moved into and around the small town. The mayor seized a horse and fled, and Dassall prudently abandoned both weapons and thoughts of resistance to watch what happened next.

For some time the confusion continued. Dressed in purple with a silver star on his breast, and carrying only a sword, Monmouth tried to lead his men up the main street but was besieged by people trying to kiss his hand and shouting 'A Monmouth! A Monmouth! The Protestant Religion' about him. With some difficulty a standard was set up and the Duke's 'Declaration' read aloud.[23] Written by Ferguson and approved by the leading rebels it carefully avoided claiming the throne, leaving a Parliament to adjudicate on Monmouth's claim, but it was in every other respect a much too extreme document. Charges that York had burned down London, inspired the Popish Plot, and murdered the King all belonged to the closing, extreme, phase of the Exclusion Crisis and in 1685 would undoubtedly frighten gentlemen away from the rebels, rather than rekindle the fires of 'no-Popery'.

At Lyme Regis, however, the faults of this Declaration mattered little. When Dassall asked their purpose, the Duke's followers replied tersely 'we come to fight Papists' and that sufficed. Two-thirds of the invaders were posted about Lyme's streets and the crumbling Civil War defences, while the rest laboured until dawn bringing their supplies ashore. They were enthusiastically assisted by the town's population, who began volunteering for the Duke's service as soon as he landed. Nathaniel Wade noted that 'sixty young fellows' had arms given them straight away, and as the night wore on more and more men came in from the surrounding countryside to enlist, aroused from bed by news of the invasion. As leader Monmouth behaved with aplomb, swearing they had arms for twenty thousand men, and seizing the arm of one of the first volunteers to declare 'Sir, thou art an honest fellow, and I'll take care and provide for thee, thou deservest encouragement'.[24] When Dassall left just after midnight, to ride to Crewkerne and send warnings to Exeter and London, it was plain that the rebellion had got off to an enthusiastic start.

For three days the rebels remained at Lyme Regis while volunteers flocked in. Recruits had their names listed, were sent to the town hall for arms, and were then allotted to companies which began drilling in the town's streets. On ship the Duke had divided up his followers into the officers needed for four regiments (sixteen of the more experienced for his own regiment) and into this cadre the raw recruits were now distributed. The first five hundred made up the Duke's regiment and a start was made on the next, under Colonel Holmes. Two more were begun, and the hundred or so Lyme Regis volunteers were formed into one independent company – a small example of Monmouth's intelligent handling of his force. Even with the arms captured in Lyme itself there was soon a shortage of weapons, but more urgent was the lack of horses for cavalry and for transport. By scouring the nearby countryside some forty or fifty animals were obtained, and on Saturday Thomas Dare returned with the nucleus of a cavalry force, forty men 'pretty well mounted but few of them armed and all but ordinary fellows', in Wade's estimation. But the horses Dare brought were dearly purchased, for a quarrel developed over who should have the best one between Dare and Andrew Fletcher of Saltoun, a Scot who had opted for Monmouth's expedition. Fletcher was a man of character, birth and education, 'of great parts', as his ex-tutor Bishop Burnett noted, but also 'very hot and violent, a most passionate and indiscreet asserter of public liberty'. The Scot's character undid him, for in the heat of the quarrel he shot Dare through the head. Monmouth had to send Fletcher back to the ships and he took no further part in the rising.[25] At a stroke the Duke had lost two of his most important lieutenants. Dare had been his secretary and paymaster, a man who knew Somerset well, and of considerable influence in Taunton. Fletcher was, according to Wade, Monmouth's 'best horse officer', and as Lieutenant-Colonel to Ford, Lord Grey, had been intended to supply the expertise needed to train and command the rebel cavalry. Lack of money, and deficiencies in the cavalry, were to be two critical weaknesses of the insurgent force.

By staying three days at Lyme to recruit, Monmouth was taking a considerable risk. The town's defences were not in repair, and the low hills encircling and overlooking it on the landward side made the rebels conscious that they held but a toe-hold. Dare had found that Taunton was strongly held by the militia, and volunteers told the Duke of government forces close by to the east and west, in Dorset and Devon. Two messengers sent earlier from Holland, Captain Matthews and

Christopher Bettiscombe, also rejoined them at Lyme and reported that the militia were holding the main roads in strength and examining all travellers, so that risings elsewhere were unlikely. Some sympathetic gentlemen such as Sir Francis Rowles and Mr. Stroud had been arrested, others like Sir Walter Yonge were 'very cool', and John Trenchard had simply fled abroad.[26]

With the militia so close and apparently so active, the rebels maintained a high state of alert, ready to attack any force which ventured near. When he learned on Friday that a guard of constables was stopping volunteers from coming in at Bridport six miles away, Monmouth sent Major Manley with fifteen horse of the invading force to chase them away. Instead of a few constables Manley found a large body of militia, but outnumbered as they were the rebels charged anyway, killing two opponents and scattering the rest; a significant demonstration of the rebels' spirit. That night Monmouth took a thousand foot and horse and three cannon out of the town, and laid an ambush in the hedges and narrow roads for the Duke of Albemarle's Devonshire militia, following rumours that the latter were coming to attack. Nothing stirred, and following Dare's return and death the next day the Duke decided to lift his followers' spirits by mounting an attack to clear the militia out of Bridport. Lord Grey was put in command of three hundred foot and forty horse, with Thomas Venner to advise him, and Nathaniel Wade in charge of a company of foot. They were to march by night and attack at dawn, a plan which, taken with the ambush laid the preceding night, demonstrates Monmouth's confident handling of his force, and his appreciation of the supreme importance of surprise.

At dawn the single street of Bridport was covered with mist. Grey began the attack, even though he had learned on the march that the militia were far more numerous than thought, 1,200 strong, so outnumbering him by four to one. In view of his later behaviour it should be noted that he went ahead nevertheless. Things started well, with the militia sentries surprised and dispersed and the town apparently falling into Grey's hands. But then most of the militia foot was discovered in a meadow just outside the town, while the cavalry officers who had been billetted in houses emerged and began firing. Venner was wounded and the rebels halted in confusion. Grey thought all was lost and fled taking some rebels with him, but Wade's men killed and wounded the officers in the town, and the militia foot were reluctant to advance into it. Shots and abuse were exchanged while Venner and Wade decided to abandon the attack and withdrew in good

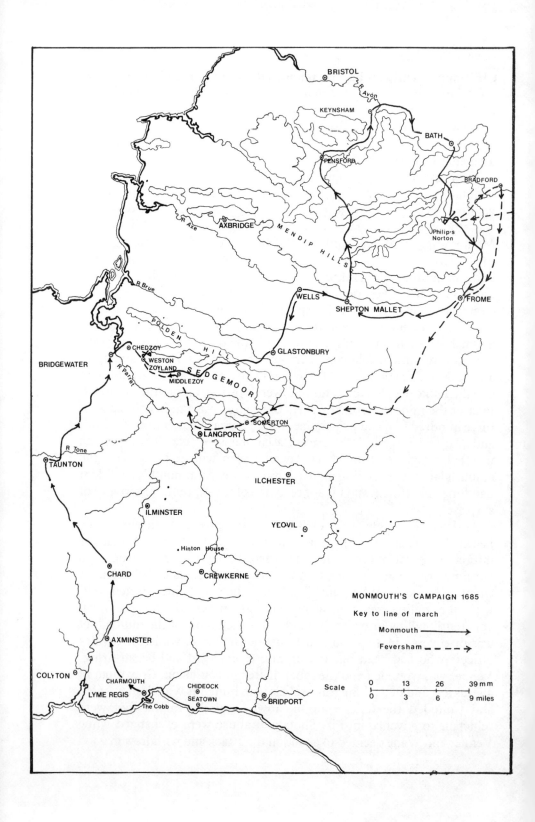

BRISTOL

KEYNSHAM

R. Avon

BATH

PENSFORD

BRADFORD

Philip's Norton

R. Axe

AXBRIDGE

MENDIP HILLS

FROME

R. Brue

WELLS

SHEPTON MALLET

POLDEN HILL

GLASTONBURY

CHEDZOY

WESTON ZOYLAND

BRIDGEWATER

SEDGEMOOR

MIDDLEZOY

R. Parret

SOMERTON

LANGPORT

R. Tone

ILCHESTER

TAUNTON

ILMINSTER

YEOVIL

Hinton House

CHARD

CREWKERNE

AXMINSTER

COLYTON

CHARMOUTH

LYME REGIS

The Cobb

CHIDEOCK

SEATOWN

BRIDPORT

MONMOUTH'S CAMPAIGN 1685

Key to line of march

Monmouth ⟶

Feversham ⟶

Scale	0	13	26	39 mm
	0	3	6	9 miles

order, having taken several horses and some prisoners. They set rearguards to ambush any pursuit and were in good spirits when they were met by Monmouth, two miles outside Lyme, heading a column hastening to their rescue. The Duke listened quietly as Grey's report of a disaster was contradicted, and was quiet, too, when Wade confirmed that Grey had indeed 'run away'.[27] There was nothing he could do, for Grey was the only other man of title in the rebellion and had to occupy a post of command. It was, besides, his first experience of combat and a skirmish even more confused than most. But Monmouth was also reluctant to believe the worst of this old friend.

It was now clearly time to move on, and on Monday morning 15 June they marched out. How late he had left it soon became evident to the Duke, for within hours they saw militia forces to the west and north also making for Axminster. Doubling their pace they reached the town just before the opposition, and actually had to drive out some militia scouts. Once again using natural cover to help his inexperienced force, Monmouth dispersed them behind thick hedges bordering the roads leading into the town. Albemarle's Devonshire men approached to within a few hundred yards but then withdrew. Wade and others began to follow them but were firmly checked by their leader: 'his business was not to fight but to march on'. An opportunity was perhaps lost, for while the Devonshire troops retired in good order the Somerset men's withdrawal north of the town was, as the rebels learned later, 'little better than a flight'. Militia coats and guns thrown onto hedges and subsequently brought to the rebels were evidence of a rout hidden from Monmouth by the same deep lanes he had used to shelter his force.[28] Though none in the rebel camp knew it, the government's first attempt to crush them had already collapsed.

This failure was no fault of the King's. Roused at dawn on Saturday the fifteenth when Dassall and Thorold arrived from Lyme with their news, James heard their tale, rewarded them with £20 apiece, and began giving orders. The Duke of Somerset, Lord Lieutenant of that county, was instructed to raise the rest of his militia and put them in readiness, and a similar message was sent to the Lords Lieutenant of Cheshire and six other counties in the Midlands. Sir William Portman and Colonel Strangeways, in London to attend Parliament, received special powers to command the Dorset militia and were despatched home, arriving at Dorchester on Sunday. The Duke of Albemarle, commanding the Devonshire militia, was ordered to shadow Monmouth and attack if opportunity offered, and if the rebels left Lyme Regis. All measures were to be taken to prevent people from joining the insurgents, and he was also instructed that the latter were far fewer in number than reports beginning to reach London later on Saturday had indicated. The House of Commons was told of the invasion by Dassall, and promptly resolved that it would stand by the King against all traitors. On Monday Parliament ordered a copy of Monmouth's Declaration to be burnt by the common hangman, and a Bill attainting Monmouth for treason was rushed through its readings. The London *Gazette* published a proclamation offering £5,000 for capturing the Duke alive or dead, and the Commons voted the King extra levies, on wine, vinegar, tobacco, and sugar for eight years, worth £400,000 altogether. Some regular troops were also ordered to march at once for Salisbury – Colonel Percy Kirk with a foot regiment and 350 cavalry and dragoons, and Colonel John Churchill with some cavalry. Churchill was placed in command of all regulars sent to the west, and was instructed to confer upon strategy with militia commanders. The arrest began of Whigs in the south and west who might support the rising, a trickle which within a month swelled to several hundred detentions.[29]

Only a few regular troops were ordered to the west because the King was confident, at this point, that the militia could deal with the small band of invaders. Though he considered Lancashire or Cheshire the most likely landing places, James had ordered some precautions in the west. The Duke of Albemarle was in Exeter with part of the Devonshire militia, and Colonels Luttrell and Phelips were in Taunton with two regiments of Somerset men. Portman and Strangeways would soon have the Dorset force in motion, and the rebels could then be pinned to the coastline by numerically superior forces attacking on three sides. Somerset's Lord Lieutenant was confident that in barely a week he would 'put a stop to this rebellion'.[30]

The only problem with the King's plan was that the militia was incapable of carrying it out. At Exeter the sheriff at first tried to call out the *posse comitatus*, a ludicrously inappropriate force, and when the mistake was corrected the Devonshire militia were found far from ready for action: a gift of £1,000 was needed (from the Bishop) to complete their equipment. The Dorset militia were threatening to desert because they had received no pay, and half their number were paralysed by the raid on Bridport; while the Somerset troops were uneasy because of reports reaching Taunton that their opponents were ten thousand strong. They obeyed Albemarle's order to leave Taunton and rendezvous with him at Axminster, but there panic set in as they met the rebels: 'upon a sudden, some persons were supposed to be seen of the enemy and an old soldier said we were all betrayed, and made some of our foot to run'. Reporting to the King, Colonel John Churchill was blunter. Within a few hundred yards of Axminster a captain had cried out that they were betrayed 'so the soldiers immediately look one upon another, and threw down their arms and fled . . . half, if not the greatest part are gone to the rebels . . . I never saw people so much daunted in my life'. So great was the disaster, he wrote, that unless regulars were sent at once 'we are like to lose this county to the rebels'.[31]

The rot quickly spread. At Taunton Lord Stawell's militia regiment had taken over the town when the other two forces marched south. Two days later on Tuesday the sixteenth they received the 'frightful news' from Axminster and, as the rebels marched steadily on the town, officers lost control of their men. By midnight on Tuesday they had panicked and fled, leaving behind their valuable stores and ammunition. At Wells the Duke of Somerset had to abandon his plan to march south with the county's fourth militia regiment, saying that it would 'hardly stand because the others have show'd them the way to run'. He withdrew to Bath, pleading for more regulars to be sent 'or else the whole county is lost', and ignoring Churchill's advice to send all the troops he could to check the rebels in the south of the county at Chard. Colonel Helyar with the Dorset troops suggested a general muster of militia at Crewkerne otherwise, he warned the Duke of Somerset, the whole country would be lost for 'Monmouth may march and fight us all severally'. In the south-east of the county Lord FitzHarding, too, found that there was 'little trust' to be placed in the militia, and 'beseeched' his commander for orders. None were given; and as the Somerset Deputy Lieutenants gained control over some men in the days that followed they found no instructions coming from their superior, and were led first to ask for Albemarle in Devonshire to be put over them; and then to 'pray that we may have a commander-in-chief appointed us, so that we may know whom to obey'. In the hour of trial the command, communications, and morale of the Somerset militia had broken down; the Dorset troops were indecisive and semi-mutinous; and Albemarle preserved his Devonshire force only by keeping so clear of the rebels that Churchill wrote for him to be pressed to bring them closer to the action.[32] Fairness requires the historian to add that this was the militia's first taste of action, and that some of the regiments later improved; but their master James II was a professional soldier with neither the time nor the inclination to be fair. He observed the militia's failure, and turned to his next line of defence.

The militia's dismal performance was, in part, simply the obverse of Monmouth's remarkable popularity. A record of the rebellion kept by the Independent church at Axminster saw the peoples' response in simple Old Testament terms:

> Now were the hearts of the people of God gladded, and their
> hopes and expectations raised . . . that the day was come in
> which the good old cause of God and religion that had lain as
> dead for a long time would rise again. And now was the
> sounding of trumpets and alarm for war heard . . . [as] they
> began their march . . . with much dread and terror to the
> amazement and wonder at what the Lord had wrought. A great
> number of sober and pious men marched forth with the army.

More prosaically, a royalist officer noted how well 'the country people'
served the rebels with provisions and intelligence by comparison with
their poor reception for him, and blamed 'the busie Phanatiques' who
said that the King's men were fighting against their religion, for the
invaders' popularity and the militias' 'heartless' condition.[33] As the
army marched by easy stages from Axminster to Chard, Ilminster, and
Taunton recruits poured in. At Chard, a large town, 156 volunteered;
smaller centres such as Axminster and Ilminster sent fifty to eighty,
heavily populated villages such as Colyton, Pitminster, and
Thorncombe, sent two to three score, and half a dozen other rural
parishes sent two dozen or more. Not surprisingly however the most
notable demonstration of support came from that centre of discontent,
Taunton.

When Lord Stawell's militia fled the town around midnight on
Tuesday the sixteenth the townsmen took over almost at once. They
broke into St. Mary's church to seize the arms left behind, and released
from prison men arrested by militia roadblocks. Loyalists' houses were
ransacked for weapons, and when one tried to remonstrate 'a sour saucy
fellow, with a musket on his shoulder . . . [said] "by God ye towne is
ours now, & you shall know it we are uppermost"'.[34] Flushed with
victory they would not wait for the Duke, but marched toward
Ilminster to find him. Monmouth was equal to the occasion, greeting
the column of townsmen warmly and sending them back with two
troops of his cavalry, under the command of John Hucker, the
prominent Taunton merchant Whig and rebel, to prepare for his entry
into the town.

The main rebel force marched into Taunton on Thursday 18 June,
attended by a large crowd which had walked out into the countryside to
welcome them. A camp was laid out in a meadow on the town's western
edge, cannon were placed to command the major roads, and the rebels
gave themselves up to their welcome. Officers slept on beds for the first
time since Lyme Regis, Monmouth moved into John Hucker's house,

and food was not only provided in abundance but was cooked by the townswomen for the army. Over three hundred Taunton men volunteered to join the Duke, and his three-day pause at Taunton gave time for men to come in from the surrounding parishes, particularly from over-populated weaving districts such as Wellington (59 volunteers), and Milverton (54). A fourth regiment under Colonel Bassett was created, composed largely of Taunton men, Monmouth once again exploiting local sentiment to strengthen his force. At Taunton, too, the shortages of arms and equipment began to be eased. On their arrival in the town the rebels had only 'about half a score wagons', but less than a fortnight later thirty-eight were counted in their supply train, most of the new ones appearing in Taunton. Here, too, the arms left behind by the militia, together with those taken at Lyme Regis and outside Axminster, together with some county supplies delivered by the constable of Ilminster, substantially increased their fighting capacity. Pikes remained in short supply, and Monmouth issued a proclamation for scythes to be brought in. With their blades somewhat straightened these were fearsome weapons, though lacking the reach of a true pike: a member of the Wiltshire militia referred to the rebels' 'cruell and New invented murdering Weapons'. A few Whigs living near Taunton sent money for the rebel treasury – £300 from Henry Henley, an unspecified sum from Edmund Stroud living near Street, and small amounts from Mary Jennings a married daughter of George Speke, and from two sympathizers of Honiton, all adding to the £100 Monmouth had seized from the Lyme Regis Customs.[35]

The tide of optimism running strongly in both town and army was strengthened by a ceremony held on Friday the nineteenth, the day after the rebels arrived. All the aldermen remaining in Taunton were rounded up at gunpoint and forced to stand at the head of a crowd which gathered in the market square to hear Monmouth's Declaration read. The Duke was then waited on at his lodgings by twenty-seven girls from the town school, each bearing a flag with motifs sewn on – one was described as 'the Golden Flagg JR a Crowne & Fringes of lace around'. When Monmouth appeared the colours were presented to him, and 'the captaine of the maids' stepped forward to place a Bible in his hands. Monmouth gravely accepted the gifts, and in turn presented the girl with his sword. He and Grey then mounted and slowly led a procession from town to camp, each girl carrying a flag and attended by an armed trooper. Throughout his stay at Taunton Monmouth acted with the same grace and dignity he had displayed on his western and Cheshire tours of 1680 and 1682. When a Quaker in Taunton apologized to the

Duke for his pacifism Monmouth replied, in his public vein of unfailing courtesy, that he would never force a man to fight against his conscience.[36]

To the rebel rank and file, therefore, all seemed set for success, their leader popular and their support increasing: as they left Taunton the insurgents would boast how soon London would fall. At Taunton, however, their leader had to solve two fundamental problems. The first concerned his total failure to attract gentry backing. If Monmouth was to topple James II without fighting, as he planned, he needed a wave of support from the landed class, and after a week there was no sign of it. His lieutenants argued that this was because their Declaration had appeared too republican: by honouring his promise to Argyle and the English republicans not to claim the throne but to allow a Parliament to determine his title, Monmouth appeared to be leading a commonwealth's revolt. Very few gentry would support this, and none would risk life and land without at least the assurance that he was fighting for a future King of England. These arguments were aired briefly at Chard and then put aside, but by Taunton they had become more persuasive. On the very day of the army's arrival a rumour swept Taunton that James II had died, and thus their pretender was indeed now King. Its timing makes the rumour unlikely to have had an innocent origin, particularly when it was followed next day by the ceremony of the colours – 'the Golden Flagge JR a Crown' could be understood by all. At a council of war summoned by Monmouth the republicans, Holmes, Hays and Nathaniel Wade, were overborne. Some officers, such as Samuel Storey, were genuinely convinced of Monmouth's title; others such as Lord Grey thought England needed a King whatever Monmouth's title; but the majority probably agreed with Robert Ferguson (who had drafted the first Declaration) that the gentry had to be brought in, and an open claim to the crown was the only way to attract them.[37]

The decision taken, Monmouth spoke individually to the republicans persuading them to accept it. A new Declaration was drafted, and on Saturday the corporation members were once more assembled at gunpoint in their robes before the market cross, and with their fellow townsmen heard a short statement of Monmouth's legitimate title to the throne and his proclamation as King of England. This was followed by a declaration guaranteeing Englishmen their rights and liberties, a sop to the republicans. Four 'royal proclamations' were then issued, to emphasize Monmouth's regal style. One denounced 'James, Duke of York', as a traitor, and offered a rather paltry £500 for his capture. A second gave Members of the present Parliament until the end of the month to submit to their new King; a third forbade payment of taxes to the present so-called King; and a fourth sentenced the Duke of Albemarle to a traitor's fate unless he too submitted to Monmouth. A private letter in much milder terms sent to Albemarle, however, offering pardon for his 'inadvertent' misbehaviour, showed Monmouth's deep anxiety to succeed without having to fight a major battle. Albemarle delivered a public, and scornful, reply to both addresses.[38]

The second problem facing Monmouth was no less critical, and was discussed at the same council of war. Put briefly it was, where do we go now? Since there was no point in staying in Taunton, three possible courses presented themselves. One was to withdraw to Exeter, and fortify themselves there. The town was large and wealthy, and there was little doubt that they could defeat the Devonshire militia to take it. But while its capture would increase their strength considerably, seizing Exeter would be a strategic retreat, leading inevitably to siege and defeat. London was the key to the rebellion's success and so the second course considered was to strike directly for it, for the capture of his capital would end James's rule, it was argued. But this course was as over-bold as the first was excessively cautious. Was the army ready for a long hard march? More importantly, could it be risked against professional cavalry on the open reaches of Salisbury Plain? In Somerset the rebels were protected by enclosed fields, thick hedgerows, and deep narrow lanes; but in open country their inexperienced cavalry would be brushed aside and the untrained infantry scattered by any horsemen who knew their business. London was, therefore, too risky. The third course was a compromise. By capturing Bristol the rebels could add immensely to their strength, preserve their onward momentum, and stay within the relative safety of Somerset. Occupying the country's second largest city might provoke a crisis at court, a rising in London, or a movement of the gentry toward the rebels. Marching north-eastward would also keep the rebels ahead of the regular cavalry coming up in the south of the county. An advance party had already skirmished with some rebel scouts in Neroche Forest ten miles from Taunton, and although the regulars had lost Lord Manoux the rebels had been scattered, with four dead and others wounded.[39] It was a warning to Monmouth, which he could not ignore, of the regulars' superiority to his own troops. Throughout his planning Monmouth had hoped and assumed that the affection of his former comrades in the army for their ex-commander would prevent them from fighting him, and he expressed this belief repeatedly until his army collided with the King's troops at Norton St. Philip. But it would not do to tempt the regulars: he should always try to keep his army ahead of them and just out of reach.

While the rebels reviewed their strategy, a similar exercise was taking place in London. James II's original intentions had been to leave the invaders – less than a hundred strong – for the local militia, sending only a few regular horse and foot as insurance. Within days the plan had collapsed. A useful role still remained for the militia of southern England: troops from Herefordshire, Gloucestershire and Monmouthshire were ordered into Bristol; some Cornish militia were put into Exeter, and Albemarle was ordered to keep up his guard on the Devonshire border; the militia of Berkshire, Surrey, Oxfordshire, and Kent were disposed in a screen about London; the so far untried men of Wiltshire and Hampshire were concentrated at Marlborough as an immediate reserve for the west; and all were ordered to watch the roads and arrest suspicious individuals. Professional officers were sent to 'advise' the south-western Lords Lieutenant, and John Churchill received a commission to raise a new regiment of Dorset militia, but was warned to use it only if he thought it necessary, and in the meantime to conceal it from the militia officers. Letters of encouragement were sent to the Devon and Dorset militia; but not to those of Somerset who seem to have been written off when their own commander admitted to the King that 'almost any report will startel them'.[40]

None of these secondary tasks could disguise the militia's failure in its basic function. To suppress the rebellion James now turned to his regulars. Three battalions of Foot Guards and six troops of dragoons and cavalry were got ready, and on 20 June they began marching from London to Bath. A train of eight guns accompanied them, and a further battery of sixteen heavier pieces was prepared. On 17 June James wrote to the Prince of Orange asking him to return the three regiments of English troops in Dutch service. This was in addition to the three Scottish regiments requested when the news of Argyle's landing was received: the latter were now diverted to England and landed at Gravesend on the thirtieth, with the English regiments only a few days behind them. There would thus soon be a reserve of professional troops behind those sent to the west, but to be quite certain the King began issuing commissions to dozens of unemployed officers to raise companies of foot and troops of horse: in one day alone forty-five were recalled.[41] These orders would create a new and greatly expanded army, officered in some measure by Catholics, but at the time they drew no criticism.

Lastly, there was the problem of command. It had originally been intended that the Lords Lieutenant should concert their militias' actions, seniority resting with the man in whose county an action was fought. The few hundred regulars sent to the west would be an independent command under John Churchill, and Percy Kirke with the foot troops early made it clear that he would accept no directions from civilian commanders. The decision to send three more battalions of regulars, making a total of over two thousand men together with cavalry and artillery, created a new situation. A supreme commander in the west was needed, leading not only the regulars but also the militia with whom they might have to cooperate. James's choice fell not on John Churchill, but on a man of French and Huguenot extraction, Louis Duras, Earl of Feversham.[42] Long a protégée of the King despite having been Monmouth's deputy in Flanders in 1678, Duras's limited military experience and (as the event showed) competence, was offset by his complete loyalty to and dependence upon the King. His English was passable, but he wrote French in his despatches to James II. Churchill had to be content with promotion to Brigadier.

A week after the rebels' landing both sides had grounds for a qualified optimism. Monmouth's swift capture of Taunton and scattering of the militia had shaken the government, and though James II had confidence in his professionals, unpleasant possibilities remained: that the rebels might capture Bristol; that the gentry might yet support them; that regular officers and men might desert to their ex-commander – and only a few defections could seriously affect the King's small army. At Taunton, too, there was confidence, as the rebels prepared on Sunday morning to march out for Bridgewater. The weather was fine; their number had increased; they had been well rested and drilled; three dozen wagons full of equipment rolled behind them; a crowd of friends and relatives cheered them on their way. Robert Ferguson had stolen the vicar of Taunton's surplice and preached a fiery sermon to the troops, and then pranced in front of the battalions as they wheeled out of the town, waving a sword and boasting of the reward set on his head. The rebel leader was more pensive, a Quaker witness describing him as 'very thoughtful and dejected in his Countenance'.[43] Would the gentry rally now that he had claimed the throne? Could they capture Bristol? Would the professional soldiers fight him? The last question would soon be answered, because Churchill's cavalry were now in Chard and his scouts had already scattered one of Monmouth's patrols. For the rebels the first, easy, phase of the rebellion was over; and a second, grimmer, one was about to commence.

Footnotes: Chapter Five

1. J.Welwood, *Memoirs of the Most Material Transactions*, App.XV, pp.323-5.

2. F.Grey, *Secret History*, pp.73, 75, 80, 85; on Argyle see 'Sir Patrick Hume's Narrative of the Earl of Argyle's Expedition' in G.H.Rose ed., *A Selection from the Papers of the Earl of Marchmont*, London 1831, 3 vols., ii, 8-30.

3. F.Grey, *Secret History*, pp.90, 85-6; 'Hume's Narrative', pp.6-14.

4. G.Burnet, *History of My Own Time*, Oxford 1823, 6 vols., iii, 25.

5. Harl.MSS.6845, f.370; Add.MSS.41818, f.181.

6. *CSPD 1685*, p.6.

7. J.Welwood, *Memoirs*, p.325.

8. Brit.Lib.Lansdowne MSS.1152, ff.243, 303.

9. Harl.MSS.6845, f.271. F.Grey, *Secret History*, p.99.

10. Lansd.MSS., 1152, ff.273-5, 278v, 304v.

11. Harl.MSS.6845, f.271.

12. Harl.MSS.6845; f.270; F.Grey, *Secret History*, pp.100-105; Lansd. MSS.1152, f.308.

13. Harl.MSS.6845, ff.301, 309, 271; *CSPD 1678*, pp.262-3; Lansd. MSS.1152, ff.243, 308.

14. F.Grey, *Secret History*, pp.120-1; Harl.MSS.6845, f.272; Lansd. MSS.1152, f.237; T.McCrie ed., *Memoirs of William Veitch and George Bryssom*, Edinburgh 1825, pp.314-23.

15. 'Hume's Narrative', pp.35-65.

16. H.Foxcroft ed., *A Supplement to Burnet's History of My Own Time*, Oxford 1902, p.156; *CSPD 1685*, pp.161, 175, 180.

17. *CSPD 1685*, pp.158, 163.

18. *CSPD 1685*, pp.157, 166, 176, 186-7; J.Hunter ed., *Diary of Ralph Thoresby*, London 1830, 2 vols., i, 180.

19. *CSPD 1685*, pp.149, 152, 184, 177, 188, 192.

20. *CSPD 1685*, pp.20, 37, 30, 23-4, 33, 6, 126, 2, 11, 137, 61, 156; *Diary of Ralph Thoresby*, i, 180.

21. *CSPD 1685*, pp.33, 37, 41, 54, 60; Harl.MSS.6845, ff.283-4v, 272; F.Grey, *Secret History*, p.120.

22. F.Grey, *Secret History*, p.121; Harl.MSS.6845, f.274 ff; Samuel Dassall's account is in Harl.MSS.6845, and is printed in *Somerset and Dorset Notes and Queries*, 27 1961, pp.45-51; it is the principal source for the Duke's landing.

23. 'Dassall's Narrative', *Somerset and Dorset N. and Q.*, p.49; Lansd. MSS.1152, ff.258-61.

24. 'Dassall's Narrative', pp.49-50; Harl.MSS.6845, ff.274v-275.

25. Harl.MSS.6845, f.275v; Burnett, *Supplement*, p.161.

26. F.Grey, *Secret History*, pp.121-2.

27. Harl.MSS.6845, ff.275v-277.

28. Harl.MSS.6845, f.277.

29. *CSPD 1685*, pp.193-6.

30. *HMC* 9th Report, Stopford-Sackville MSS., p.2.

31. Harl.MSS.6845, f.285v; *HMC* 9th Report, p.2; *HMC* 3rd Report, Duke of Northumberland MSS., pp.98-9.

32. Harl.MSS.6845, f.287; *HMC* 9th Report, p.3; *HMC* 3rd Report, pp.97-9.

33. 'Ecclesiastica, or a Book of Remembrancer of the Axminster Independent Church', copy in the Lyme Regis Record Office; see also W.MacDonald Wigfield, 'Ecclesiastica', *Somerset Archaeology and Natural History Society*, 119 1974-75, pp.51-5; Harl.MSS.6845, f.285v.

34. Harl.MSS.6845, f.287.

35. Harl.MSS.6845, f.287; Lansd.MSS.1152, ff.269, 240v; H.E.Malden ed., 'Iter Bellicosum, Adam Wheeler's Account of 1685', *Camden Society*, 18 1910, p.160; *Calendar of Treasury Papers 1556-1696*, p.265.

36. Harl.MSS.7006, f.195v; Harl.MSS.6845, f.287v; J.Whiting, *Persecution Exposed in some Memoirs*, London 1715, pp.141-2.

37. Lansd.MSS.1152, ff.237v, 243, 310; Harl.MSS.6845, ff.277-8.

38. Harl.MSS.6845, f.287v; Harl.MSS.7006, ff.184-95; *HMC* 9th Report, pp.25-6.

39. Harl.MSS.6845, ff.278, 287v.

40. *CSPD 1685*, pp.204, 219, 210, 207, 209; *HMC* 9th Report, p.2.

41. *CSPD 1685*, pp.210, 219, 206, 237, 197ff.

42. *HMC* 3rd Report, p.97.

43. J.Whiting, *Persecution Exposed*, p.142.

CHAPTER SIX

Honour and Trust

After leaving Taunton, the rebels marched for three days directly
eastwards through Bridgewater and Glastonbury, and on to Shepton
Mallett. They were on the road to London and Monmouth allowed the
rank and file to think that the capital was their destination, so good was
the belief for morale. Country-folk heard the troops 'declaring with
great assurance, taken from their sudden growth . . . that God was with
them, and that by Saturday following they would be in London to place
their new King in his Throne'. The rebels' reception at all three towns
also kept spirits high. At Bridgewater the mayor and corporation were
forced to attend another public proclamation of Monmouth as King,
and a merchant named Roger Hoare spoke passionately and at length
for the Duke. The former King, he said, had been murdered by his
brother 'for what will not a man do to come to a crowne'; there were
further reinforcements for the rebels coming from Amsterdam;
warships seen recently in Lyme Bay were Monmouth's and not the
government's; the Duke would probably succeed without any fighting
at all; and lastly, he would undoubtedly produce new evidence
concerning his birth which Parliament would accept and proclaim him
King. With such energetic assistance from a prominent inhabitant it is
not surprising that Wade remembered Bridgewater for 'very good
quarters . . . for the most part free'.[1]

Their reception at Glastonbury on Monday the twenty-second was
just as friendly, fortunately for the rebels because on that day the fine
weather ended, and after a march in pouring rain they needed 'great
fires to dry and refresh the men', laid in the abbey and churches.[2] News
that the militia were withdrawing from Wells to Bath lifted morale, and
next day lodgings for the army in houses at Shepton Mallet kept it high.
Despite the brevity of the army's overnight stays recruiting at
Bridgewater and Glastonbury had been satisfactory, forty-nine men or
perhaps one tenth of the town's adult males from the former, and half
that number at Glastonbury. Only five appear to have joined at Shepton
Mallett, perhaps because Churchill's cavalry were by then close by,
perhaps because the Duke was preoccupied by plans to attack Bristol

and gave no attention to recruiting.

Verbal and financial support was as strong in Shepton as it had been in the previous two towns. As the army marched in a tailor took off his hat and cried 'God bless your Majesty'. Another toasted 'the King, the late Duke of Monmouth' and, praying for his safe accession claimed 'the land is all Popery and Popery is at ye Dore'. The rebels were given free food and fodder, and received gifts of money, sometimes in small amounts – fifteen shillings from a Shepton man – sometimes much larger, such as the gifts of Roger Hoare and Mr. Whitbread of Bridgewater. Throughout the army's march horses were sold at purely token prices – 'a horse worth £7 or £8 for a shilling' noted Lord Weymouth's scandalized steward at Longleat House – so that the vendors could then truthfully claim not to have given help to rebels, but to have sold the animals 'to a stranger'.[3] At such prices Monmouth's small treasury could go a long way.

Money and supplies also came from less willing sources. At a village near Taunton a musket was simply taken out of a house window, and a well-to-do farmer near Frome found that 'his horses and wagons were prest by Monmouth'. Wheeled ploughs were also requisitioned by the rebels for use as transport wagons, while bread and cheese was the food most commonly seized, the insurgents seeking out their normal fare. Not infrequently they were given local advice on whom it would be profitable to loot, a Mr. Worthington Price of Shepton Mallett losing 'several parcels of goods' in this way. Neighbourly feuds were plainly prosecuted with the army's help, a Croscombe man trying (apparently in self-defence) to persuade the rebels to loot and set fire to the house of a 'murderous whore' in the village who 'went to seek his life'. Some targets of course required no prompting. From the house of Sir William Portman near Taunton the rebels took weapons and horses, and Lord Stawell's residence, too, was quickly plundered. The rebels' technique in both cases was simple but effective: servants left behind in the house were told that it would be burnt down unless they brought forth what the raiders wanted. A rebel with local knowledge, one Weely of Frome, led the party who visited Longleat, but they had only begun sampling the house's claret when a sudden move by their army called them away. They had no time to find and seize Lord Weymouth's useful little armoury – 9 muskets, 13 pistols, and six dozen pikes and halberds. A few descents on such well-armed landowners would have substantially improved the rebels' weaponry, supplementing equipment abandoned by the militia. Considerable sums of money may have been obtained in this way too, not all of it paid into the rebel exchequer. When he was captured the rebel paymaster Richard Goodenough held £300, but one of the Duke's servants carried a hundred guineas, and a trooper who had to flee suddenly from his quarters left 22 guineas behind with his equipment.[4] Opportunities for personal enrichment were considerable during the rebellion.

Very frequently this or the need for equipment was the only motive behind looting, but sometimes the reasons were more complex. Stawell and Portman suffered partly because they led the Tory reaction in Somerset since 1682, and the rebellion provided a chance to level old scores; while upon the capture of Taunton local Tories, including corporation members, were roughly handled and publicly humiliated – new men, they heard, ruled the town now. At Chard and Warminster ministers were attacked in the streets by rebels, not for personal reasons but because of their cloth; and in the latter town rebel sympathizers paraded up and down 'in Ranck and file', beating any who spoke for the King in London. Here, as in Lyme Regis and Taunton and no doubt in other centres, the rebellion was welcome to some because it briefly upset the local power structure, giving them a chance to order about their social superiors. In central Somerset respectable society noted uneasily that 'some of our meanest people met together, talked incessantly and in a menacing way' as the rebel army approached.[5]

In at least one case attention focused on a landowner because of his oppressive behaviour toward tenants and employees. Before he left Longleat for London in May 1685, Lord Weymouth had dismissed forty servants, and failed to pay the wages of many others: at the time of the rebellion over £100 was owed, some men had not been paid for two months, and all were becoming 'very clamorous'. Tenant farmers, too, were discontented over the rents they paid, and were talking of abandoning their leases if they were not reduced. Not surprisingly Weymouth's steward, left behind to guard the House, feared for the consequences 'if the Rabble hereabouts should take armes' with the rebels. He doubted the loyalty even of the domestic servants; and several employees did in fact join the rebels – a former game-keeper, a warrener, a baker, a labourer and a tenant farmer.[6] Through their influence a raiding party visited the house.

To a growing number of rebels, however, questions of a landowner's local behaviour or past politics were irrelevant. As time passed, and as no gentry joined them, they grew increasingly angry at men 'so cautious and wise, as to stand behind the Curtain to watch and see what the Rabble could do before they would venture to appear openly'. By the time Bridgewater was occupied many had given up hope of the upper classes, and were saying 'the Gentlemen come not in. . . . Well! we will do the work without them; and then we will have their Estates'.[7] Although 1685 was a rebellion over the succession rather than economic or social oppression class antagonisms were, for a number of reasons, developing when the affair came to its sudden end.

Just as the rebels did not depend wholly upon gifts but foraged actively for money and supplies, so recruits were searched for and not merely awaited passively in camp. Between Lyme Regis and Taunton, Monmouth had travelled slowly enough for a natural process of recruiting to work, country folk hearing of the army and walking in to see it and perhaps to volunteer. A small-scale foray had been made at Bridport to free possible volunteers, and Dare's excursion inland as the landing took place brought in at least one organized group, the forty horsemen under Charles Speke who joined at Chard. But until Taunton only a few volunteers were sought out. After Taunton however the army marched more quickly and never spent more than one night in any place, leaving little time for recruiting. Two attempts were, therefore, made to raise men in areas where the rebels made only a brief passage. Both expeditions were led by men with local knowledge, and both enjoyed some success.

The first was by a Quaker named Thomas Plaice, who observed that two events had created turmoil among the villages of the central Somerset levels. One was the march of Monmouth's army toward and through the area, en route from Bridgewater to Glastonbury; the other was a rumour prompted by a pair of navy ships seen patrolling the Bristol Channel, that thousands of French and Irish had landed on Somerset's northern coastline, and were heading inland. To the inhabitants of the central levels it appeared that two plundering armies were about to over-run them, and they reacted in a way which showed the strength of Civil War memories. This area had been a centre of Clubmen activity in 1643-44, and forty years later its population again took to arms in self defence. 'The Countrymen were disposed to meet together in order to the making of a Club Army that so . . . they might stand together for their mutual defence', was the report of a marsh-land vicar. Meetings of armed men were held on convenient hilltops, and messengers sent to learn the truth of the foreign invasion rumours.[8]

Hearing of these gatherings, Plaice approached Monmouth at his camp in Glastonbury on Monday 22 June, and asked for a commission to call for volunteers at the meetings – as a local man (from Bridgewater) he would be listened to. Some advisers demurred, but a Declaration was drawn up and Plaice returned to the marshes, calling a meeting for the next day. It was well attended – eighty armed men came from one village alone – and a friend of Plaice's read the Declaration, perhaps to satisfy the latter's Quaker conscience. The document had been drafted with some skill. It rehearsed the danger to the audience of having their throats cut and offered to lead them against their enemies, the French and Irish invaders, and the Duke of Albemarle with his Devonshire militia, then lying in Taunton. All were instruments, it was explained, of 'Popery and Tyranny'.

Though cleverly phrased, the audience on Polden Hill was not swayed by the offer and 'openly declared against it', but those present resolved to carry on with their meetings and to watch events. Plaice remained in the marshes, repeating the danger that all stood in from external and Popish invaders, and evading attempts by the militia (now in Bridgewater) to arrest him, although his companion who had read the Declaration was taken. The Clubmen meetings continued despite orders from the militia to end them, and Plaice had his reward when Monmouth returned through the area a week later, *en route* for Bridgewater and Sedgemoor. The Clubmen were waiting for him and according to a rebel officer about 160 joined up, less than Plaice had promised and Monmouth hoped for, but a useful addition so late in the rebellion. In a typically morale-building gesture the Duke placed the Clubmen at the head of his army and personally led them into Bridgewater, as the rebels occupied it for a second time. By joining when they did, these Clubmen were rebels for barely three days before Sedgemoor scattered them. If so many volunteers joined the army and stayed, so late in the rebellion, its morale must have been remarkably high.

The second foray for recruits was also made into a Club area of the 1640s, in eastern Somerset about Frome, although in this case there is no evidence of preliminary Club meetings in 1685. The two who led this appeal were again local men. One was John Kid, a former game-keeper at Longleat, dismissed probably because of his Whig politics, who was promoted to Captain and then knighted by Monmouth for his services. The other was a cloth-worker of Frome named Weely, who had been arrested at Bruton as he made his way to the rebels and sent to Ilchester prison, whence he had been released by Monmouth's advance. These two led a party of horse from Shepton Mallett to Frome, while the rebel army turned northward for Bristol. They sent advance word of their coming to Frome, Warminster, and Westbury, telling the people who then flocked to see them that 'the French were landed at Bridgewater, had fired the town and put man, woman and child to the sword', and of 'ye French landing near Mynehead and that Wells was on fire,' and other tales. These references to foreign, Catholic, invaders assisting James II were more successful here than in the marshes – a visitor reported the 'Warminster faction to be very busy in Rubbing up their weapons and I saw severall of them booted and very peremptory of all'; while at Frome Monmouth's Declaration was proclaimed and posted in the market place, remaining there for several days before Pembroke entered the still-rebellious town with some Wiltshire militia, and tore it down. Before then, however, Kid and Weely had led off to Monmouth an estimated five hundred men, colours fluttering in their hats, and armed with 'Hatchets, Clubs, Hayforks and Scythes revetted into Poles about 8 foot long'.[9] The instant success enjoyed about Frome, by contrast with the lesser and delayed achievements of Plaice in the marshes, perhaps echoes the Civil War Clubman activity of the two areas, in which the marshlanders were neutral (or if anything Royalists), whereas the rest of Somerset a little more favoured Parliament.

While he was at Shepton Mallett sending Kid and Weeley off on their mission, Monmouth had an unexpected visitor. The son of Major Manley arrived, sent by John Wildman in London, to know Monmouth's intentions. Furious at Wildman who had blown hot and cold throughout, the Duke sent 'young Manley' back with orders to create at least a diversion in the capital forthwith. In this way the critical regular troops might be tied down defending the government's base; and to reinforce the order the Duke later sent Hookes, his personal chaplain, to animate plotters in the city. Even when the rebellion was at its last gasp a week later Monmouth sent yet another emissary to the capital, Major Manley himself, to create this vitally needed 'second front'.[10]

The Duke's last item of business at Shepton Mallet was to decide how to go about capturing Bristol. His army was too small and poorly equipped to take this large city if it was defended with any purpose, but if only militia manned its long and crumbling perimeter defences a surprise attack, pressed home with vigour, might have a chance. Time being of the essence Monmouth was inclined to attack at the city's nearest point, in the south, but his two Bristol commanders disagreed. Wade and Tiley described the strength of the southern defences lying beyond the River Avon, and suggested crossing the river at Keynsham four miles east of Bristol, to attack the city unexpectedly on its eastern side.[11]

Seeing the opportunity to achieve tactical surprise Monmouth agreed, and next day made a long march to Pensford just six miles south of the city. Camping here would enable an early attack to be made next day; and if he was discovered the garrison would expect the attack to fall on the obvious, southern, approach. To reinforce this deception Monmouth intended next day to leave cavalry on the southern road to make a feint, while he led the main force, unobserved, around to the east. The deception was doubly necessary, to surprise the defenders, and also to throw off Churchill's cavalry who had now closed on the rebels. By marching diagonally from Chard to Langport Churchill had caught up with his opponents, as the latter travelled three sides of a quadrilateral from Chard to Taunton to Glastonbury. Outside Glastonbury a party of twenty regular horse caught and cut to pieces a rebel cavalry troop twice their number. Then for a day there were no cavalry attacks, as Churchill obeyed the King's instruction to get on the northern or Bristol side of the rebels, James becoming convinced by now that the city and port was Monmouth's immediate objective. The attacks resumed the following day, cavalry and dragoons harrying the rebel rear on the way to Pensford, taking several prisoners. One of these, 'Jarvice, a Feltmaker . . . a notorious fellow' was hanged by Churchill three days later, dying 'obstinately and impertinently'. His brother had been killed in the same skirmish.[12]

That night at Pensford, the rebels saw the glow of a great fire in Bristol. The sight depressed them, for it seemed to show that the defenders were alert and clearing fire zones outside the town; but in Bristol the fire also caused alarm, the city's defenders regarding it as a signal to the rebels from sympathizers within the walls. It was in fact accidental, the cargo of a ship in the docks catching fire, but to the royalist commander in chief, Louis Duras, Earl of Feversham, it was yet one more misleading event in a day crowded with them. He had arrived in Bristol the day before, Tuesday the twenty-third, with a few Wiltshire militia. Colonel Oglethorpe and some regular cavalry had been sent out to find the enemy, but until he reported Feversham accepted local estimates that the rebels were certainly no nearer than Glastonbury (two days' march away), and probably more distant. (At the time Monmouth was considerably closer, at Shepton Mallett). Believing the enemy at a safe distance, Feversham paraded Bristol's militia garrison and relaxed. On Wednesday he rode over to Bath, intending to speak to the Duke of Somerset, and collect some more of Pembroke's militia for the Bristol garrison. He also wanted to find out where his regular infantry was, having received reports that the rebels spoke of marching straight for London, which would bring them into unexpected and possibly disastrous collision with his unaccompanied foot. In a letter to the King that day Feversham paid due regard to his master's conviction that Monmouth would attack Bristol, but his actions reveal a belief that the Duke would bypass the city and strike for London.[13] Certainly he took no steps to order the destruction of the bridge at Keynsham, still standing despite the King's order to demolish it for Bristol's security, even though he rode past it on his way to Bath. Thus, while Monmouth was marching northwards on Wednesday and closing on Pensford, a few miles from Bristol and the base for his next day's assault, the royalist commander was ten miles away at Bath, looking for his troops and believing the Duke to be two day's march away, and probably heading eastwards for London. It was only by lucky chance that Feversham learned of the true situation, and even then his response was a mistaken one.

Colonel Oglethorpe had made a wide sweep through eastern Somerset looking for the rebels, and early on Wednesday he came upon them at Shepton Mallett. Following orders he drew off to Bristol to report, but because some of his men had mistakenly gone to Bath he went there to collect them, and so fortuitously met Feversham earlier than he would have done. Alarmed at Oglethorpe's news that the rebels were closer than he had thought, Feversham sent him out once more to find and trail them, but he still believed that their destination was the capital. Instead of returning at once to Bristol, the royalist commander rode in the opposite direction south-eastwards from Bath to Norton St. Philip where, astride the road to Devizes and London, he looked for news of the rebels, before returning to Bath for the night. Meanwhile Oglethorpe had also failed to find his quarry on the road leading eastwards out of Shepton Mallett to London, and as night fell he took his tired men back to Bristol. On the way he stumbled upon the rebels, encamped at Pensford, much closer to Bristol than any had suspected. At once word was sent to Feversham, who roused some of his Wiltshire militia, and by a forced march got back to Bristol as dawn was breaking. Knowing that Monmouth was camped to the south, and deceived further by the early morning cavalry moves the Duke had ordered about the city's southern approaches, Feversham then drew up his forces in the southern suburbs and cleared fields of fire. With the royalist forces still wrongly positioned, despite Oglethorpe's labours, Monmouth broke camp on Thursday morning and led his men, through heavy rain, north-eastwards to Keynsham and across the bridge, which his cavalry had secured and strengthened the previous night.[14]

At this point Monmouth could possibly have attacked and taken

Bristol with the city's defences so off balance, but he was betrayed by the weather. Rain was still falling heavily, casting down his troops' spirits and – even more important – soaking the smouldering ropes of match his musketeers carried to fire their guns. The attack was, therefore, postponed until evening, and the men ordered back to quarters in Keynsham village; with a number of Bristol men in his army to act as guides, an assault under cover of darkness could well succeed, even if the Duke's presence was detected in Keynsham during the day. But the plan miscarried, once again because of the energetic Colonel Oglethorpe. Realizing as the morning wore on that the screen of rebels south of Bristol was not their main force, he took his cavalry on a sweep about the city, and late in the afternoon found them at Keynsham. This time instead of merely reporting their presence he attacked, sending half his troops under a Captain Parker into the village, while he waited to attack any rebels who ran out. Monmouth heard the disturbance and, collecting some of his cavalry from a field outside the village, came up to investigate. He was seen by Oglethorpe who sent half his remaining force to attack the Duke. They lost their way and, with Parker still cut off and heavily engaged in the village, Oglethorpe charged with the last of his men and brought them out. Having suffered only half a dozen casualties and inflicted nearly a score on his opponents, Oglethorpe then drew off to Bristol to report.[15] Meanwhile three prisoners taken by the rebels were giving Monmouth a shock.

Under questioning they said that 'the King's army of 4,000 was at hand'. Monmouth was horrified: he had not guessed that the regulars were so close. How could he now go on to attack Bristol? Even if he captured it, there would be no time to organize its defences before another army fought their way in. There was no reason to suspect the prisoners' honesty, and though they slightly exaggerated the number of regulars (but not the army's total size including militia) the force was very clearly 'at hand'. Monmouth had no option but to call off the attack and get away before the regulars arrived. But where? A hastily-convened council of war could see only two possibilities. One was to continue northward into Gloucester and the Midlands, hoping to stir Whigs such as Macclesfield, Brandon, and Delamere into rising. Against this it was argued that the troops could not endure a fast four days' march, their footwear in particular needing attention. Furthermore, the royalists' energetic cavalry would harass and delay them until the infantry caught up and forced a battle. And would the Midlands Whigs rise?

The alternative was a short, one day's march, to the Wiltshire border.

Here, a Mr. Adlam assured them, 'a considerable body of horse' waited to join up. This may have been a reference to Kid's and Weeley's recruiting activities (although they raised no horse); but it is more probably an echo from the only sympathetic rebellion which did occur during the uprising, when the mayor of 'Limington' (probably Lymington in Hampshire) with nearly a hundred horse and foot terrorized the New Forest area for some time, before being suppressed. Marching to Wiltshire was an easier short-term option than the Midlands, and appeared to offer more certain reinforcements. Monmouth, therefore, decided on it, but an argument thrown in to support this course reveals how desperate the rebels' position had suddenly become. With this reinforcement of horse, it was said, they could stand and fight the King's army before it grew any stronger: if they survived, they were on the road to London.[16] Some of Monmouth's officers had, therefore, tacitly dropped the pre-condition which the Duke always regarded as essential to success, that the regular army would not fight them, and by flying from Bristol and the regulars their leader showed that he too doubted it. In military terms there was now little point in continuing the rebellion.

Turning away from Bristol meant that this was true politically as well. Besides neutrality from the army, Monmouth had hoped the rebellion would receive massive gentry support. This had not been forthcoming, and would now only appear – if at all – should the rebels seem likely to succeed. The capture of Bristol might just have made government and bystanders alike hesitate, and the King's behaviour in 1688 showed that unexpected reverses could shake him. Abandoning Bristol meant that Monmouth was abandoning his last strategy offering even a chance of success. At Keynsham he lost any purpose other than keeping ahead of his pursuers. Until that skirmish he had held the initiative; now he was simply responding to his opponent's moves. The delay between Lyme Regis and Taunton to recruit and half-train an army had proved fatal; yet that time had to be spent to create a credible threat. Monmouth was defeated at Keynsham not by his own mistakes, but by a modern standing army's speed of deployment which, just as much as its superior fighting skills, was making military victory impossible for popular revolts by the later seventeenth century. The Duke was defeated, too, by the strategic grasp of James II who saw, more clearly than his commander in the field, that Bristol was the key and rushed troops up to defend it.

The decision made, Monmouth allowed his troops to get what rest they could overnight in Keynsham, and next morning took the road past Bath. The city was strongly held by militia and was of no use to Monmouth, but to raise his troops' spirits he paraded them before it and formally invited the defenders to surrender. Even this piece of theatre went astray, for a lucky shot from the garrison killed the rebels' herald. In a mood of deepening depression the Duke led his force on to the little village of Norton St. Philip, to camp for the night. No horsemen from Wiltshire appeared, and Monmouth went to bed saying that all men had deserted him, in a melancholy so deep that his officers could scarcely get any orders from him.

In two days Monmouth's prospects had changed dramatically. Yet had he reflected on the matter, the royalist commander too would have been anxious, if not downcast. Feversham had misread his enemy's intentions, even though the King had repeatedly advised him that Monmouth would strike for Bristol; he had been caught ten miles away when the Duke appeared unexpectedly before Bristol; and he had defended the wrong side of the city when told of the rebels' position. Three major mistakes in two days is a poor beginning for any commander; and when Feversham heard on Friday that the enemy had marched safely away from Bristol, past Bath towards Wiltshire, his reaction (to judge from the consequences) was not one of thankfulness that good fortune and Oglethorpe's aggressive patrolling had saved him from the consequences of his actions; but rather that the time had come to end the affair once and for all. He was extremely conscious that the court expected a 'very good account' once he had arrived in the west with the regulars, and was aware too of the disappointment of such officers as Churchill that a foreigner had received the command which they coveted.[17] As he rode from Bristol to Bath to concentrate his scattered forces Feversham wanted a result without delay, and this attitude explains the fiasco which followed at Norton St. Philip.

Churchill was instructed to cease his patrols south of Bristol and proceed to Bath 'by the nearest way', bringing with him Colonel Kirk and his fast-moving five companies of foot which had joined Churchill's cavalry a few days before. Some Wiltshire militia were also ordered to the Bath rendezvous, and on Friday evening they were joined by the force Feversham most wanted to see, the two thousand foot under the Duke of Grafton, together with a train of light artillery. The army was still not complete for Dumbarton's Scottish regiment was still three days' march away, convoying the train of heavy artillery from Portsmouth. But Feversham now had a balanced force of two and a half thousand foot and horse, plus field artillery, with another three thousand militia in support if he chose to use them. Many of the regulars had seen active service in Tangier as recently as the previous year. Kirk's and Dumbarton's infantry had comprised much of the Tangier garrison, and had been hardened by vicious skirmishing against North African Arabs. Even on their approach march to the west in 1685 their brutality shocked Henry Sheres, the heavy artillery's commander, who wrote to Lord Dartmouth that he had 'seen too much violence and wickedness practised to be fond of this trade . . . for what we every day practise amongst this poor people cannot be supported by any man of the least morality'. The Quaker John Whiting, no supporter of the rebellion, wrote vividly of the fear which ran before the King's army as it marched into Somerset, and John Churchill had no compunction about hanging prisoners.[18] And the violence of 'Kirk's Lambs' as they hunted out survivors of the rebellion was long printed on Somerset folk memory.

The troops who paraded before their commander on Saturday morning appeared, therefore, sufficiently numerous, tough, and experienced to put an instant end to the rebellion; and to seek an instant end was Feversham's purpose. His determination, however, was not matched by his knowledge of the enemy's intentions, for the cavalry he had sent out during the night had come in the morning with only vague reports, that country folk said the rebels 'were marching or preparing to march', and with no indication of direction if they were moving. Feversham was barely six miles away from his opponents, and he needed to know whether his army was marching in pursuit or going into a battle. The erring cavalry were sent out once more, with orders not to return until they had been seen and fired at. But Feversham could not stand idly at Bath while the enemy was perhaps slipping away. He despatched five hundred dragoons and musketeers under the Duke of Grafton and Percy Kirk to march quickly to Norton St. Philip and if the enemy was still there to engage and hold him, while the rest of the army marched out at its usual pace. Feversham subsequently described this force as a 'vanguard', ordered to 'march at the head' of the army to prevent ambushes.[19] This was a lie. Such an over-large unit containing so many foot, and commanded by two very senior officers, was quite ill-suited to accomplish what the normal thin screen of cavalry could do far better. As a light striking force to delay the enemy, however, it was ideal, and its two commanders well-suited to their task: Kirk a hard experienced professional; and Grafton, Monmouth's illegitimate half-brother, only twenty-three years old and jealous of his brother's political and military successes, and of the love their father had given the older son. Feversham's lie was necessary however, because to throw a large force at an enemy without knowledge of his position is to risk a disastrous ambush, and that is what happened.

Approaching Norton St. Philip from Bath there was, beside the main road, a lane some four hundred yards long, leading into the village from a ploughed field alongside the main road. Lined by thick hedges on both sides the lane was so obviously suitable for a surprise attack that Monmouth had blocked it off with a barricade, and put fifty men to guard where it entered the village. From the barricade another lane ran through a courtyard into the back part of the village to a field, where the bulk of the foot were encamped. Reinforcements could be passed along this second lane to the barricade if necessary. Normal prudence dictated these arrangements; but Feversham's cavalry had also several times disturbed the rebel camp during the night, and the Duke's men were on the alert.

Grafton's and Kirk's force reached the ploughed field just as the second scouting party was pulling back down the road, having drawn fire and found that the rebels were in the process of leaving the village. Kirk wanted to examine the position but Grafton would tolerate no delay. He saw his chance of glory, and rushed down the lane with Captain Hawley's company of dragoons. They at once came under fire and, bunched together in the lane, suffered heavily. Grafton's horse was shot from under him, and with the other survivors he took cover in the hedges. From the head of the lane Kirk and the rest of the vanguard gave what supporting fire they could, while Feversham left the main force and hurried up to investigate the gunfire. He found Grafton's men pinned down and unable to move, and the rebels beginning to exploit the situation.[20]

Hearing the attack, Monmouth began moving a regiment along the second lane to the barricade. Here they spread out into the fields on either side of the lane to encircle Grafton's men. Two things saved the royalists. One was Monmouth's difficulty in moving five hundred men through the narrow lane, and deploying them properly beyond the barricade. The other was the covering fire organized by Feversham. Captain Vaughan was sent down the lane with some horse grenadiers, while musketeers under Captain Parker moved around to attack the barricade on its right flank. These men harassed the rebels severely, and Lieutenant-Colonel Holmes was ordered to clear them out. He did so, but only after an hour's shooting and confusion, during which Grafton's survivors had cut their way through the hedges and escaped across the fields. Grafton himself came back up the lane on a wounded horse and much out of breath, to be told dryly by his commander that such a dash down the lane could be tried only once in a life time.

With the survivors extricated, Feversham deployed the rest of the vanguard back in the ploughed field along some rising ground, and hoped that the main force would arrive before the rebels, advancing cautiously, reached the head of the lane. At this point defeat was still possible for the royalists: the vanguard's dragoons and cavalry 'had pressed so much upon each other that I do not know what would have happened if the rebels had come out' he wrote, and so he 'made them retreat one after the other without showing too much that things were not going well, for fear of alarming them if the enemy appeared'.[21] Gradually the rest of the army arrived and took position, and finally came the guns, much delayed by the poor condition of the roads. While his cannon opened fire Feversham considered the chances of a general engagement.

Monmouth continued to find difficulty in bringing his forces up through the lanes, and deploying them along the edge of the ploughed field behind a line of hedges. At first only two of his two-pounders replied to the royalist cannon, and then an hour later two more. The rest of the day was taken up with desultory cannon fire (lasting six hours according to Wade) at a range of a quarter of a mile or more. The guns were few and small, the range long, and the troops well protected, the rebels by a hedge the royalists by rising ground. Casualties were few. Neither side was willing to start a general battle, partly because the troops were shaken and tired from the first skirmish, but principally because rain had started to fall heavily. Musketeers saw their fuses hiss and smoulder out; cavalry watched the ploughed field get softer and heavier; and all were chilled, wet, and hungry.

Feversham seemed content to let the enemy make the first move – 'I thought at one stage that we would have to stay there in front of them for the whole night', he wrote to James II – but debate in the other camp was vigorous. All afternoon Monmouth hesitated over attack or retreat, hoping that the weather would relent. Towards evening Colonel Venner seemed to have persuaded him to retreat, but Wade and others vigorously opposed the decision. An attack was resolved upon, and troops began cutting passages through the hedges. Then the rain began to fall still more heavily, and Feversham gave his men orders to retire to dry billets for the night at Bradford-on-Avon. Monmouth made no response as the enemy withdrew, his cavalry being too weak to pursue. So anxious was he over the royalist cavalry on the other hand, that he kept his troops in the field until eleven o'clock at night, hours after Feversham's departure, to make sure that no horsemen would fall on his men as they left their defensive positions and took up marching order. Leaving fires in the fields to deceive any watching scouts, his army wearily completed their withdrawal from Norton St. Philip, begun fifteen hours earlier. They marched all night in miserably cold and rainy weather, labouring in places up to their knees in mud, to reach the relative safety of Frome at eight o'clock on Sunday morning. The march had tested his men 'almost to destruction', and Monmouth let them rest all that day and the next.[22]

As their troops rested only a dozen miles apart each commander cast up accounts of the action, and each saw little to be proud of. Feversham was deeply embarrassed, although 'vexed' (*fâché*) was the word he used in his report to James. The bald facts were not impressive. Having caught up with the rebels, the King's professionals had not only failed to crush them but had been ambushed, suffered casualties, and been compelled to leave the battlefield to the enemy – in strictly technical terms a defeat. Feversham took this last point seriously, admitting at the beginning of his report that 'rumour of a great battle and even a defeat' may have already reached London. He then minimized his losses, exaggerated those of the enemy, and blamed 'the very great valour' of the Duke of Grafton for plunging his men into a trap. The vanguard, he stressed, was merely an 'advance guard', and he said nothing of his instructions to it. His part in the affair had consisted wholly of extricating the ambushed force, and coolly preventing the rebels from exploiting their temporary success.[23]

It is unlikely that James was deceived. A professional soldier himself, he could see that Feversham had bungled matters a second time by acting without sound information concerning the enemy. And against Feversham's estimate of only seven or eight royalist dead and thirty wounded (with no officers), there is the testimony of a royalist artilleryman's journal that 'the rebels having been posted so expeditiously we lost about fifty men *besides* wounded' (my italics).[24] The rebels believed that Feversham had lost about eighty men; perhaps a hundred killed or wounded is a fair estimate, or most of the company which Grafton had led down the lane. Rebel losses were barely one-fifth of this number.

The most striking aspect of Feversham's report, however, was its conclusion. He now had no intention of forcing another battle quickly. He would wait to see whether Monmouth moved toward London, Bristol, or Taunton from his present camp at Frome; and until tents arrived to enable the royalists to camp out in the fields and so pursue the enemy closely Feversham would merely shadow the rebels by day and billet his men in the nearest village by night. There would be no more haste: even when tents arrived he promised only to bring Monmouth to bay 'within a week'. Conceding that such caution in crushing 'a company of vagabond' must 'appear to the world a little extraordinary', he asked rhetorically why he should risk lives by taking chances.[25] Risks to reputations – amongst them his own – were no doubt also in his mind.

News of Feversham's embarrassment would have been welcome at the rebel camp in Frome, where the mood was one of despair. The rebellion was going badly. Neither their first Declaration, nor the proclamation of Monmouth as King, had drawn any gentry in; and no risings had taken place in Cheshire or in London. A reply had been received to an earlier appeal to Colonel Danvers to begin a rising in the capital: the Colonel affected indignation that Monmouth had claimed the Crown, and felt 'not obliged to keep faith with one who had broken it with him'. More immediately, the five hundred Wiltshire horse promised by Mr. Adlam had not appeared; and at Frome, too, the rebels had heard of Argyle's total defeat, and knew that the King's entire army would now be concentrated on them. Above all, Norton St. Philip had shown that the King's army would fight them; and the skirmish had confirmed what Monmouth had always known about his men, that professionals would invariably beat them. The royalists caught in the lane should have been wiped out but were saved by the rebels' military failings – their slowness to deploy, and their inaccurate gunfire. Rebel casualties had been slight, but they included four of the slender stock of officers. Two captains of foot had been killed in the lane, and two more officers, Blake and Chaddock (the latter a captain of horse), had been accidentally shot by their own men, a clear sign of wild firing.

Monmouth's isolation increased the effect upon him of these reverses. His officers were a mixture of minor conspirators with no military experience, and junior-ranking professionals of little social standing: alone among them Lord Grey had the rank to be his friend and confidante, but Grey's ability and courage were in question after Bridport and Keynsham. A royalist noted how the Duke 'was heard often to express his despair of ever doing anything with such men as those . . . about him'. Small wonder then that Monmouth, when he convened a council of war on the Sunday after Norton St. Philip, was 'very depressed' and complaining that all had deserted him. He bluntly proposed that they accept the situation and wind up their enterprise, the officers fleeing to some seaport, and individual soldiers returning home to claim the benefit of James II's proclamation of pardon, which had just been published. There was much support for the suggestion. Captain Matthews echoed his master, saying that there was no trust to be placed in men. Colonel Venner and Major Parsons – two more with military experience – agreed that there was no prospect of success; and for different reasons they were supported by the republicans Wade and Tyley, joined now by Ferguson, the chaplain, who considered that 'since Monmouth was no longer in being', they should try to 'set up a free state' in some other manner. It took a remarkable speech by Grey to stem the tide, arguing that for Monmouth to leave the army now would be an act 'so base that it could never be forgiven by the people', and that if he fled the Duke 'must expect never more to be trusted'.[26]

Honour and trust: precisely the arguments which had kept Monmouth locked into opposition since 1679, and had driven him into conspiracy, exile, and rebellion. How could he deny their strength now? And objectively Grey's words contained some truth, for what life could the Duke lead abroad, as the failed leader of a failed rebellion? He, at least, had to persevere unto the defeat which military wisdom pronounced inevitable. Others, however, might shift for themselves; and some did, Venner and Parsons leaving the following day to escape to Amsterdam, with promises to begin a rising in northern Ireland. Their fantasies of seizing arms, blocking harbours, and blowing up arsenals show the unreal world many of these minor plotters lived in, and the desperately impractical advice Monmouth had to endure and ignore. Among the rank and file, experience of real fighting together with news of the King's proclamation also led to some earnest discussion, and although the Earl of Pembroke's later comment that thousands of rebels deserted at Frome was greatly exaggerated, a few common soldiers did leave. Prominent amongst the deserters were the Axminster Nonconformists, who had joined Monmouth *en bloc* as he had marched out of Lyme Regis. The Old Testament rhetoric of their narrative swung from messianic optimism – 'the Lord eminently appeared, filling this New Army with wonderful courage' – to an equally deep nadir after Norton St. Philip, where the saints were 'slain in the High Places of the field'. Their zeal evaporated and the congregation departed, Towgood, the pastor, and Lane, an elder, managing to return to their homes, though others were captured and suffered in the Assizes.[27] One band of a dozen or more cannot stand for the whole of the army, and many Dissenters served loyally as individuals or in small groups; but the Axminster men are the only Dissenters known to have enlisted as a congregation under their minister and elders, and following a collective decision, and the Biblical rhetoric of their account attests the strength of their self-conscious

Puritanism. That they were also among the first to desert the cause is a useful caution against presuming that religion was the prime motive and common denominator of the rebels, as well as the sole source of their remarkable morale.

After the stock-taking of Sunday, Monday found both commanders in a cautious mood. From his quarters at Bradford, Feversham was well-placed to intercept the rebels, should they move from Frome toward either Bristol or London; and having no wish to be out-manoeuvred again he sent scouts to cover both roads, while he ordered his heavy artillery up from Marlborough to Devizes, where it would be on hand should a battle develop. When the indefatigable Colonel Oglethorpe saw rebel supply wagons moving out of Frome on Monday afternoon, toward Warminster only six miles to the west, it seemed to Feversham that he had his answer. The royalist army was marched south to camp at Westbury. Here, only four miles from Warminster, they could intercept the rebels on Tuesday morning and bring them to battle, as Feversham jubilantly reported to the King.[28]

But once again the royalist general was disappointed. The movement of the royalist cavalry was observed, and Monmouth reasoned correctly what Feversham would then do. The supply wagons were recalled to Frome and the trap avoided. On Tuesday the rebels marched out of Frome, not toward London but in the opposite direction, for Shepton Mallett and central Somerset once more; the Duke encouraged in his decision by the return to the army of the Quaker Thomas Plaice, with the promise that a Club army of many thousands was waiting for them in the marshes. Once again, however, promise did not match performance, and Wade recorded that only 160 men joined them. Local enthusiasm for the rebellion was beginning to decline, and at Shepton the army had for the first time to take food and shelter by force instead of its being freely offered. Supplies were running low too, and when he heard of some royalist supply wagons left at Wells with only a small guard of dragoons, Monmouth marched from Shepton to Wells to take them. Here some rebels expressed their frustration by attacking monuments in the cathedral and, more practically, stripping lead off its roof to make into bullets. On Thursday the Duke marched from Wells into the Somerset levels, where he camped and received Plaice's 'club army'. Next day he re-entered Bridgewater, the three militia companies of the town's garrison fleeing at the rebels' approach.[29]

These three hundred men were from the Devonshire militia, pushed on into Bridgewater by the Duke of Albemarle, as he cautiously advanced from Wellington to Taunton several days after the rebels had vacated the latter. The militia in Bridgewater could not be blamed for their reluctance to face a rebel army ten times their number – though sieges have been conducted at odds no worse, and resistance for only a day or two would have enabled Feversham's regulars to catch up. More at fault was their commander, for not sending a stronger force into a potentially key town if the rebels turned back into central Somerset. Albemarle squandered his strength by sending three more companies to occupy Lyme Regis, under the impression that it was the rebels' base. He refused Churchill's suggestion to join their forces to attack the rebels at Taunton (whereas the Earl of Pembroke with the Wiltshire militia saw no problem in attaching his force to Feversham's regulars). Albemarle then capped his misjudgements by leaving the bulk of his troops in Taunton after the rebels had left, and rushing back to Exeter under the impression that the port was about to be attacked by the French. Royal navy ships patrolling off Lyme Regis were the source of this error. All in all, this unmilitary son of General Monck had a most disastrous campaign. He complained over the financial expenses of command, resented the prominence given to Churchill and Feversham, and was put out of temper by reports that his militia included many Catholics. Perhaps his worst moment came when his wife innocently wrote to him on 23 June, half-way through the campaign, that she expected to see him safely home soon, 'being the King has no service for you'. Shortly after Sedgemoor he resigned his commission as Lord Lieutenant.[30] The same age as Monmouth, and for many years his companion and rival, Albemarle had been outshone by the King's son as courtier, in the pursuit of women, and now in war.

Other militia commanders displayed incompetence of nearly equal proportions. While the rebels occupied Taunton and then marched on to Bridgewater and Bristol, Colonel Berkeley's Somerset men together with some Dorset militia occupied Crewkerne in the south of Somerset, believing that they were thus interrupting Monmouth's links with his 'base' at Lyme Regis. The Duke of Somerset refused to hand over a suspect to the Duke of Beaufort, in order to force the latter to concede that the Lord Lieutenant of Somerset could over-ride the Lord Lieutenant of Gloucestershire on any issue connected with Somersetshire. When Lord FitzHarding, in command of some Somerset militia, occupied Bath he gave Feversham valuable transport and supplies: Feversham was grateful, but not FitzHarding's superior, who wrote sharply that he was not to accept orders directly from regulars but only via the established chain of command, i.e. from the Duke of Somerset. In replying FitzHarding commented no less pointedly on Somerset's failure to exercise command over the county militia; a criticism confirmed when several other militia commanders requested their Lord Lieutenant either to join them and give orders, or to give the command to someone else who could. At present they were 'tied by the leg' by his absence. Somerset, for his part, complained that he had no troops: left with only one regiment after the Axminster debacle he stayed at Wells, fortifying the city as the rebels advanced on Taunton, appealing for men in turn to the Duke of Beaufort in Bristol, the Duke of Albemarle on the Devonshire border, and Colonel Churchill in the south of Somerset. None responded, and when Monmouth left Taunton Somerset retired upon Bath; prompting a strained letter from the King who pointed out the unimportance of Bath compared with Bristol, and suggesting that Somerset leave a few troops in Bath and put most of his men to defend the greater prize. James II, and then Feversham, also pointed out to Somerset the importance of destroying the bridge at Keynsham, to prevent the rebels from crossing the Avon to attack the city from the east or north, or from escaping out of Somerset altogether. But only a little damage was done, and no guard of consequence was mounted on the bridge, so that Monmouth was able to seize and use it when he wished to. When Sedgemoor was fought, a fortnight after the first order to Somerset concerning the bridge, he was still deliberating how to destroy it.[31]

With their commanders displaying incompetence of this quality, the low morale of militia rank and file is not surprising. The Somerset and Devon men had run when confronted by the rebels, and at Bridport the Dorset troops performed with little distinction. In Wiltshire matters were just as bad. At Devizes troopers 'cried like children' when mustered by their officers, and a town constable contemptuously observed that 'three valiant rebels may beat three score of them'. The officers were themselves discouraged by the condition of equipment they found in store: guns eaten to pieces by rust, no bullet moulds to be had, gunpowder supplies uncertain. At Warminster, with no rebels within fifty miles, one troop of horse mutinied and fled, while others drank the insurgents' health openly in the street. There were even reports from Salisbury that the Earl of Pembroke had threatened his men with castration if they broke discipline. All were discouraged by rumours sweeping south-western towns as the rebellion continued: that the slaughter of men in battle would be so great that women would bring in the harvest; that little corn would be harvested and that the government would import none, leaving the people to perish; that England would be ruled by three Kings in succession this year.[32]

In his first letter to the King from Somerset, John Churchill had warned that reliance on the militia would lead to the loss of the county; and the observant vicar of Chedzoy in central Somerset had trenchant comments to make on the levies' failures – 'the Militia first in Dorset might easily have crushed that Serpent in the Egg. . . . Next in Devon which . . . should have done more than run. . . . Lastly in Somerset where the Militia men did . . . leave the County open'. Now Feversham reached the same conclusion. He was 'so weary', he wrote to James, of their 'great disorder' that he was sending his three regiments of Hampshire militia out of the way to Devizes and Salisbury. This would leave him with only six battalions of foot, and he pleaded for the regiments from Holland to be sent along as soon as they arrived; but he preferred reduced numbers to the risk of a mutiny when he faced the enemy. The small number of Dorset militia in his ranks would also be dismissed because they were exhausted, but he would retain Pembroke's Wiltshire men – though these were kept safely in the rear as a reserve.[33]

Cutting down on the militia would also improve his army's speed of movement, and as Feversham marched from Westbury to Frome on Tuesday 30 June mobility was strongly in his mind. The light field artillery had already arrived; on that day Dumbarton's battalion also joined up giving him his six battalions; and with them came the tents he needed to pursue the rebels closely. His force was now balanced and complete, and rather than be slowed down in Somerset's narrow lanes he sent the heavy artillery back to Reading, using one of his redundant militia regiments as escort. FitzHarding had provided ample supplies at Bath, the army had local guides to lead it into central Somerset, and morale in the enemy camp was reported to be low. The end of the rebellion was not far off, he wrote to the King. Buried in these agreeably confident tidings was the admission that royalist losses at Norton St. Philip had been heavier than thought, especially among Captain Hawley's company trapped in the lane.[34]

While the King's army marched briskly from Frome to Shepton Mallett and then on to Somerton, reaching the county's ancient capital on Friday 3 July, the rebels entered Bridgewater on the same Friday and paused to take stock. Monmouth's intention was now to march past Bristol using the Keynsham bridge once more, and then to strike along the Severn past Gloucester into Shropshire and finally into Cheshire, where his former Whig friends might be persuaded to rise. To deceive the enemy, he issued orders for carpenters and two hundred labourers with wheelbarrows and spades to be brought into Bridgewater together with corn and cattle, as though he planned to fortify the town to withstand a siege.[35] If the royalists were misled into preparing for a siege, bringing up heavy artillery and provisions and finding their troops dry quarters in a nearby town, he might escape from their close pursuit and slip away with a considerable lead.

With a long and hard march in prospect, not to mention a highly uncertain future, Monmouth also did what he could for his troops' morale. The early part of Saturday was spent on drill and refurbishing equipment, but in the afternoon leave was given to all who wished to visit friends and relatives in Taunton. They were to return on Sunday morning; and according to Wade 'for the most part' they did. Considering the distance they had marched, their harassment by royalist cavalry, and the recent frightening skirmish, the number who returned when given ample opportunity to desert – copies of the King's proclamation of pardon were numerous in Taunton – shows that the Duke still retained his troops' confidence to a remarkable degree. Deeply pessimistic of success by now, Monmouth, nevertheless, concealed his thoughts from the men, and on Sunday began preparations for departure.

Then a Bridgewater man with some interesting news was brought before him. Earlier that morning the royalist army had left its quarters in Somerton, and marched down to the moor outside Bridgewater. It was now pitching camp on the edge of Weston Zoyland village, just three miles away.[36] With only the open moor between them and the rebels, Feversham had apparently left his troops open to a surprise attack.

Footnotes: Chapter Six

1. 'The Narrative of the Rev.Andrew Paschall of Chedzoy, Somerset', Brit.Lib.Add.MSS.4162, f.119v; Lansd.MSS.1152, ff.288v-289; Harl. MSS.6845, f.278.

2. Harl.MSS.6845, f.278.

3. SRO, Q/SR 162/16, 161/10; Longleat House Thynne MSS.Vol.22, f.185.

4. SRO, Q/S R 161/1, 162/16, 161/9; Thynne MSS.22, ff.193, 172v, 177v, 188; SRO, DD/PH 211, pp.242-7.

5. *HMC*, 9th Report, pp.25-6; Thynne MSS.22, ff.172, 181; Add.MSS.4162, f.120v.

6. Thynne MSS.22, ff.168, 171.

7. Add.MSS.4162, f.130v.

8. Add.MSS.4162, ff.120-122, 133 for the Plaice episode.

9. Thynne MSS.22, ff.176, 177, 181.

10. Add.MSS.1152, ff.242v, 273, 306, 310.

11. Harl.MSS.6845, f.278v.

12. Harl.MSS.6845, f.278; 'A Brief Journall of ye Western Rebellion by Edward Dummer', Brit.Lib.Add.MSS.31956, ff.2-4.

13. Harl.MSS.6845, f.278v; *HMC*, 9th Report, pp.4-5.

14. *HMC*, 9th Report, pp.13-14; Harl.MSS.6845, f.287v.

15. *HMC*, 9th Report, pp.13-14; Harl.MSS.6845, f.287v.

16. Harl.MSS.6845, f.279; *CSPD 1685*, pp.213-14.

17. Bodl.Lib.Clarendon MSS.Vol.128, f.26.

18. Add.MSS.31956, ff.3v-4; *HMC*, Dartmouth MSS.I, p.126; J.Whiting, *Persecution Exposed*, p.143.

19. *HMC*, 9th Report, pp.10, 14.

20. *HMC*, 9th Report, pp.6-8; Harl.MSS.6845, f.279.

21. *HMC*, 9th Report, p.7.

22. Harl.MSS.6845, ff.279v-280.

23. *HMC*, 9th Report, p.6.

24. Add.MSS.31956, f.4; Harl.MSS.6845, f.280.

25. *HMC*, 9th Report, pp.8-10.

26. Add.MSS.4162, ff.131, 123v; Harl.MSS.6845, f.280; Lansd.MSS.1152, f.277.

27. Harl.MSS.6845, f.280; Lansd.MSS.1152, f.277; 'Ecclesiastica', n.p., Lyme Regis Record Office.

28. *HMC*, 9th Report, pp.8-10.

29. Harl.MSS.6845, f.280v; Add.MSS.31925, f.123.

30. *HMC*, 9th Report, pp.5-6; 3rd Report, pp.98-9.

31. *HMC*, 3rd Report, pp.99, 98.

32. Thynne MSS.22, f.127v; *HMC*, 9th Report, p.11; G.Davies, 'The Militia in 1685', *English Historical Review*, clxix 1928, pp.604-5.

33. *HMC*, 3rd Report, p.99; 9th Report, p.11; Add.MSS.4162, f.119.

34. *HMC*, 9th Report, p.11.

35. Harl.MSS.6845, f.280v; Add.MSS.31956, ff.4-5; *HMC*, 9th Report, p.12.

36. Harl.MSS.6845, f.280v.

CHAPTER SEVEN
Sedgemoor

Pitching camp on open ground within a few miles of an undefeated enemy is not a particularly safe practice, but by Sunday 5 July Feversham was in his reckless mood again, having forgotten the caution learnt at Norton St. Philip. More accurately perhaps, he felt he was running out of time. Six days had passed since his promise to James II that the rebellion would be ended within a week of his acquiring a supply of tents. Even after the heavy artillery had been sent away, close pursuit of the rebels had proved unexpectedly difficult. On Tuesday 30 June, when he made his promise to the King, Feversham had been only a few hours behind his quarry, entering Frome on the same day that the rebels left. Next day this advantage was dissipated. The royalist commander wished to make public James's proclamation of pardon for all rebels who surrendered within eight days, but the inhabitants of Frome were sullen and uncooperative. Little more than a week earlier Kid and Weely had roused them on their recruiting venture; next the Earl of Pembroke had ridden in with his militia to pacify them, tear down Monmouth's Declaration, and arrest the town constable for collaboration; and the rebel army had then occupied the town for two days; before the royalists' arrival. After these disturbances there were such delays in getting a crowd together for the proclamation, that Feversham abandoned hope of marching that day and, to put a good face on matters, declared the remainder of the day a rest period for the army.[1]

This left the royalists once more nearly two days' march behind their opponents; Monmouth camping on the moor outside Bridgewater to receive his Clubmen on Thursday 2 July when Feversham had only just reached Shepton Mallett, left by the rebels two days before. The delay at Frome also infuriated Feversham's field artillery who, though they struggled to keep up with the army, had for several days reached the night's camp up to three hours after everyone else, and consequently got the worst billets. Sheres, the artillery commander, had already been angered by the Tangier troops' behaviour towards civilians, and his humour was not improved when Feversham reproved him for missing an officers' council because of a leg injury. At Frome the gunners had limbered up for an early start, been kept waiting for hours, and then told that the march was cancelled. Next day Sheres's temper snapped, when news came that Monmouth had captured some supply wagons left at Wells. Kirk blandly put the blame on the artillery, saying that he had been obliged to lend them the wagons' horse teams for the guns to keep up. Sheres sought out Feversham, threatened to resign, and wrote a full and bitter account to his superior (and crony of the King) Lord Dartmouth, the Master of Ordnance. 'Surprised and troubled' at the outburst, Feversham no doubt saw it as another good reason to bring the expedition to a quick end. At Somerton on Saturday 4 July it appeared that he would be given the chance.[2]

Royalist patrols brought back to their commander news of Monmouth's order for food and entrenching materials to be brought into Bridgewater. If the town was being fortified then a siege would follow, and to Sheres's sardonic amusement Feversham sent for the heavy artillery to turn about and rejoin the army.[3] But Bridgewater was not a strong town to defend (it had lasted only one day against the New Model Army in 1645); and Monmouth was not a commander to give up so tamely. Beginning at last to understand his opponent, Feversham perceived that talk of fortification might simply be a ploy to induce him to stand off and prepare for a siege, while the rebels stole away once more with a good lead over their pursuers. If this was the case, then Feversham's best move was to camp as close as possible to Bridgewater, so that he could intercept the enemy as they withdrew. And even if Monmouth was preparing for a siege, it should be possible for the King's army, from a base so close to the rebels, to strike a quick blow and seize both town and rebels before the defences had been extended. In short, whatever Monmouth intended, a camp close by Bridgewater was needed and after sending out strong patrols to clear enemy scouts off Sedgemoor, Feversham set out to find a site. Middlezoy some five miles east of Bridgewater was first considered, but then a position just as good and only half the distance from the town was found, at Weston Zoyland.

The artillery was characteristically disapproving – 'we are quartered where there is neither bread, water, nor anything to support man or beast', a gunner wrote – but from a tactical viewpoint Feversham had chosen well.[4] Situated on slightly rising ground, and straddling a good road into Bridgewater only three miles distant, the village had a commanding view over the moor. It was also protected by a deep drain, the Bussex rhine, running right in front of it on the Bridgewater side.

Infantry camping in tents in the fifty yards' wide strip between drain and village would thus have both their front and their rear secured. About six feet deep and mostly steep-sided, the drain extended from the Black Ditch north of Weston village, down to the River Parrett south of it. Containing more mire than water in the summer it was nevertheless a considerable obstacle for foot soldiers, and could only be passed by horse at two crossings or plungeons, at the northern and the southern ends of the village. While the infantry camped out in safety, most of the cavalry could be quartered in the village, behind the centre of the line; and the artillery could conveniently be left in a field on the camp's far left, close to the road and ready for an early start. Because his supporting militia had no tents they would be quartered in Middlezoy and Othery, villages a few miles further away. As his army wound down from Somerton on to Sedgemoor level on Sunday morning, Feversham could feel confident that whichever option Monmouth chose – siege or flight – the rebels' defeat was imminent. That by moving in so close he had given his enemy a third course, a surprise attack, seems not to have occurred to him.

Feversham made camp at Weston already half-convinced that Monmouth's intention was to steal away early the following day, and news brought to him that Sunday afternoon hardened his suspicion into firm belief. The rebel leader he heard, had paraded his army through Bridgewater and assembled it on a meadow just north of the town; roads nearby led to Bristol, or, via Glastonbury, to Wells and London. Wagons were being filled, farewells made, arms and equipment checked. The royalists even heard talk among the country folk that Monmouth was preparing for a battle.[5] All this activity was interpreted by Feversham as pointing to a stealthy rebel withdrawal, possibly on Sunday night, but more probably early on Monday morning. Hence, although his infantry was given the protection of Bussex rhine for the night, the cavalry and artillery were disposed where they could make an early start, and not where they might best repel a sudden attack. Above all, in his placing of patrols for the night, Feversham's preoccupation with detecting a withdrawal rather than preventing an attack can be seen.

Roads leading out of Bridgewater to Bristol, Glastonbury, or Taunton, were well covered by royalist patrols; but on the moor in front of the army there was only the sketchiest guard. Captain Upcott with forty horse was on the royalist left flank, patrolling the Weston to Bridgewater road, and the exit from Bridgewater to Taunton. Halfway along the Weston-Bridgewater road was a support group of fifty musketeers, placed there to help deal with any strong rebel patrols, rather than to stop a surprise attack. Far out on the royalist right flank was Sir Francis Compton and 140 dragoons, beside the Bridgewater-Glastonbury road, with a few individual sentries south of him spaced out on the moor. Also on the right, but even further forward, was the redoubtable Colonel Oglethorpe with one hundred horse, poised near Knowle Hill a little to the north of Bridgewater, watching the fork where the road north out of the town diverged to Bristol or to Glastonbury. On the royalist right and left flanks the exits from Bridgewater were thus covered with nearly three hundred horsemen, placed to discover any movement by the rebels down a main road. But on the moor itself in front of the army there were only half a dozen men outside Chedzoy village, and a few sentries to the south of Sir Francis Compton[6]. A night attack coming from this direction across the moor would stand little risk of discovery.

Only one officer in the royalist camp thought such an attack possible. Captain Mackintosh of the Scots Regiment offered to take wagers on it, paced out the distance from his company's tents to the ditch, and told his men where they should form up if called out that night. Because he was in the right flank battalion which received the first shock of the rebel assault, Mackintosh's foresight was shortly to be of some importance. The remaining officers, however, and Feversham himself, were unimpressed by his example, even though country folk were saying that Monmouth had the King's army penned up 'in a pinfold under Weston' and would fight them that night. Each day of the campaign the rebels had fled away from the regulars, and they would continue to do so, it was thought. 'Supiness and a preposterous confidence in Our Selves, with an Undervaluing of the Rebels . . . put Us unto the Worst circumstances of Surprize', wrote a royalist trooper, with the understandable vehemence of a soldier let down by his officers. More mildly worded but no less damning was the Reverend Andrew Paschell's allegation that many royalist sentries had been permitted to retire to bed before the attack, and that by the surprise they consequently achieved the rebels came 'as near to an intire Victory as they could well be [sic] and miss it'[7].

The casualness of Feversham's guard in front of the centre of his line resulted partly, of course, from awareness of the strength of his position. Any attacking force would have to negotiate the Bussex rhine, a difficult manoeuvre at any time, and at night with half-trained troops perhaps impossible. Fortunately for Feversham, however, his opponents did not know of the ditch's existence. When first told of the royalists' making camp outside Weston village, Monmouth asked his informer 'if they began to entrench', and on being told the royalists did not he sent the man back to confirm the point.[8] It was unfortunate for Monmouth that he did not ask a broader question about any defences or obstacles in front of the royalist position, for his informant answered only the specific point put to him, and assumed that the Duke knew of the ditch. This mischance considerably affected the course of the battle; though contrary to some accounts it was not the deciding factor, the battle turning on several other more or less fortuitous events. Apparently reassured that there were no obstacles in front of Feversham's army, Monmouth went up Bridgewater church steeple to examine the enemy position.

With the late afternoon sun behind him his spyglass showed the tents of Feversham's six small battalions laid out in a straight line at right angles to him. First came the men from his own old regiment the Scots' Guards on the northernmost end of the royalist line, forming their right flank marker, and then in turn two battalions of the First Guards under his half-brother Grafton, a battalion of the Coldstream in the centre, with Churchill's battalion of the Tangier regiment, and finally Percy Kirk's battalion of the Queen's regiment on the extreme left. The royalist artillery Monmouth could see was out of the way near Kirk's battalion, and the cavalry at quarters in Weston village. All told there were barely two thousand foot and about eight hundred horse, one or two hundred fewer than the rebels. Of the Bussex rhine Monmouth naturally could see no sign, and he descended the steeple convinced that an attack was feasible.

Despite its name the Sedgemoor that Monmouth surveyed was no featureless expanse of water, reed, and bog. Though not yet transformed into today's rich cattle pastures, it was sufficiently well-drained for its thirteen thousand acres to dry out in summer and support grass and, in places, corn. Most of it was rough pasture crossed by many narrow cattle tracks, and a few broad drains. From where Monmouth stood to the royalist camp, the distance in a straight line across the moor was just under three miles, but the army could not follow that straight line. Between Bridgewater and Weston lay the small village of Chedzoy and its extensive cornfields. To avoid this obstacle the rebels would have to follow a semi-circular route, taking the main road north out of Bridgewater before turning off to the right along a lane that led on to the moor, then curving southwards past Chedzoy to gain the enemy camp. In all his troops would have to cover at least five miles.

It would be a difficult march. To avoid detection Monmouth could not leave Bridgewater until dusk, and the moor would be crossed in midnight darkness, made worse that night by ground mist. The paths were narrow and faintly marked, and even with the local guide Monmouth proposed to take with him they would be hard to follow. The troops would have to proceed in single or at best in double file, and assuming a yard between each man the column would wind back for a mile from its van. Complete silence was essential, but in the darkness and the uneven going, it would be difficult to achieve. For nearly three hours the army would have to march in this manner, each soldier straining to follow the back of the man in front, trying not to stumble, trying not to make any noise. As they drew level with the enemy line the column's front would then have to march on for over half a mile more, to ensure that the rear was at least nearly opposite the royalist camp. Finally, still in darkness and still in complete silence, the long thin one or two rank columns of battalions would have to thicken up to four or five columns, before advancing to engage.

Once drawn up in front of the royalists, Monmouth's plan of attack was simple and direct. The light cannon would open fire from the centre, while Grey's horse fell on the enemy's right flank and then worked their way southwards down the line of tents. Roused suddenly from sleep by cannon-fire and cavalry attack, the royalist foot would pile pell-mell out of their tents, to encounter the advancing ranks of rebel foot. With no time to form a line, prepare their weapons, or obtain support from their horse or artillery, Feversham's infantry would be broken and swallowed up in hand-to-hand fighting, where their superior formation-training would count for nothing. Wade, and probably other rebel commanders, assured the men that their attack would be made when 'the King's Army was running'.[9] Once the foot had been shattered the artillery could be taken, and the royalist cavalry would be left powerless.

In the circumstances it was a well-considered plan, and Monmouth certainly behaved as though victory would be his. Two troops of cavalry were sent off to Minehead to capture six cannon reported to have been left there. On Sunday evening he also sent his supply wagons out of Bridgewater along the Bristol road. If successful, his army could readily catch up with them, and by despatching the baggage before the attack began he could keep Feversham thinking that retreat was his only intention. It would not do, however, to allow the royalists to realize too soon that Bridgewater had been vacated, and so guards were left at the southern entrance to the town to mislead royalist patrols[10].

Preparations for the night's work began on Sunday afternoon. The rebels were formed up by battalions in a meadow just outside Bridgewater, and their weapons and equipment checked. Musketeers received supplies of powder and ball, and examined their match to ensure that it would smoulder properly. Cavalry cleaned pistols, whetted swords, and muffled the metal parts of their harness: on a still night even small noises from several hundred horsemen would travel far. Each battalion of musketeers was strengthened by an extra company of pikemen, or more accurately scythemen, scythes mounted on long poles having been issued to those who were still without weapons, possibly five hundred in all. A church service was held for officers and men, at which Ferguson acted the New Model Army preacher and wrestled with God for a blessing on their enterprise. To calm nerves during the period of waiting cups of liquor, plundered from gentlemen's houses, were passed around so that a hostile commentator thought the army came 'half drunk' to battle.[11] But a three-hour march would provide more than enough time to sober up.

Not until it was growing perceptibly darker, at around ten o'clock, did Monmouth lead his army out. With Wade in the lead, commanding the Duke's own battalion of Taunton men, the five battalions filed out of the meadow one after another and on to the road north. They went past the first lane on their right leading to Chedzoy, and half a mile on to the second, Bradney Lane, where they stopped. Here the battalion commanders first gave the men details of their march, and issued the strictest orders for total silence. The night was very still, and anyone making a noise was to be hit over the head by the man behind him. Grey then took his eight squadrons of horse down the lane first, followed by the rebels' three light cannon under their Dutch gunner. In turn Wade followed, and then the battalions of Matthews, Holmes, Bovett and Foulkes. Near the end of the lane they turned off it to the left, to bypass the isolated Bradney Hamlet, following Marsh Lane down to a major drain, the North Ditch, which ran roughly parallel to their intended line of march. A contemporary map notes this area as 'marsh lands', and in the heavy going the rebel infantry began to string out. After about two furlongs the column turned right once more into the North Moor, marching parallel now to the Black Ditch, into the narrowing neck of land bordered by it on one side and Bradney Hamlet on the other. Safely past this defile they formed up into two columns, one of foot the other of horse, and began curving to their right and southwards, away from the Ditch towards the stepping stones crossing Langmoor rhine.[12] This drain, running from Chedzoy's corn lands into the Black Ditch, would be their last obstacle before they filed out across the moor to find the

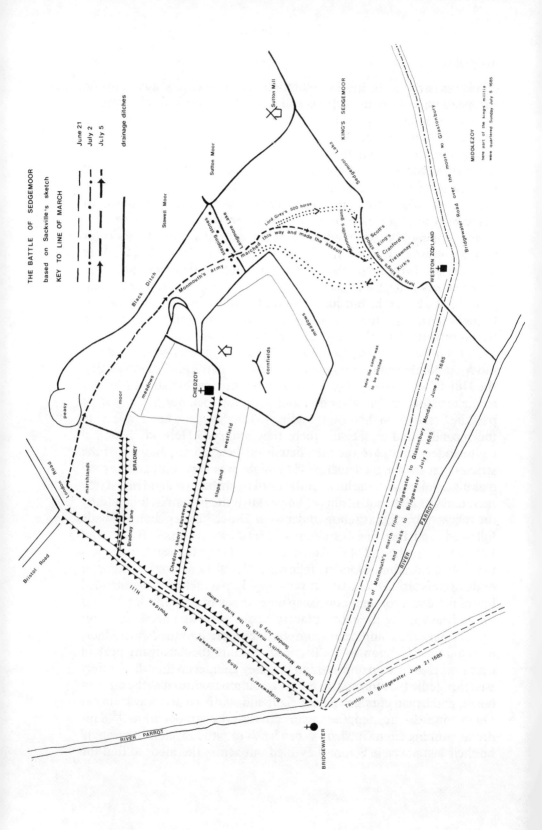

THE BATTLE OF SEDGEMOOR
based on Sackville's sketch
KEY TO LINE OF MARCH

June 21
July 2
July 5

drainage ditches

Sutton Mill

Sutton Moor

Stawell Moor

KING'S SEDGEMOOR

Sedgemoor Lake

Langmoor Lane

Bussex stores

Black Ditch

marched this way and made the assault

Monmouth's army

Lord Grey's 500 horse

Monmouth's guns

here the king's guns

Scott's
King's
Cranford's
Kirk's
Trelawney's

peasy

moor

meadows

marshlands

BRADNEY

Bradney Lane

Chedzoy short Causeway

CHEDZOY

westfield

slape land

cornfields

meadows

here the camp was to be pitched

WESTON ZOYLAND

MIDDLEZOY

here part of the kings militia were quartered Sunday July 5 1685

Bridgewater Road over the moors to Glastonbury

London Road

Poulden Hill

long Causeway to the king's camp

Duke of Monmouth's march Sunday July 5

Bridgewater's

Bristol Road

Duke of Monmouth's march from Bridgewater to Glastonbury Monday June 22 1685
and back to Bridgewater July 2 1685

RIVER PARROT

Taunton to Bridgewater June 21 1685

RIVER PARROT

BRIDGEWATER

northernmost or right hand flank of Feversham's camp. Thus far they had been undiscovered and, though they did not know it, luck was running their way.

The energetic Colonel Oglethorpe had been sent earlier in the evening, with a hundred cavalry, northwards across the moor to Knowle Hill, where he could watch the northern exits from Bridgewater to Bristol and towards London. By midnight Oglethorpe had seen and heard nothing and, tired of inactivity, he sent an officer to Feversham to report that he was going on to Bridgewater to confirm that the enemy were still there. Feversham did not receive this message until after one o'clock on Monday morning, not long before the battle commenced. Leading his men off Knowle Hill Oglethorpe took them on to the moor between Chedzoy and Bridgewater, directly across the rebels' line of march, but just a little too late to encounter them. He missed too the rebels' slow-moving baggage wagons, creaking up the Bristol road from Bridgewater. Continuing around the edge of the silent town he came finally to the southern gate, and the road to Weston Zoyland. There was no movement and he sent four horsemen up to the entrance. They found it barricaded and manned by rebel sentries, awake though scarcely alert. By pretending that they were a party of rebel horsemen who had lost their way, Oglethorpe's men learned that the rebel army had left the town some hours before. When they reported back to Oglethorpe the latter suddenly realized why the rebels appeared to be neither in the town, nor on the road: they were on the moor, moving in to attack the slumbering royalist army. Appalled, he galloped 'in haste' straight down the Bridgewater-Weston road to give the alarm, collecting Upcott's men on the way.[13] He arrived too late to alert Feversham, but in time to play a major role in the battle.

Ignorant of their good fortune in escaping Oglethorpe's patrol, the rebels were meanwhile struggling through the North Moor toward their next major obstacle, passage of Langmoor rhine. The path they were following had become still more narrow, slowing the pace of the column, and stringing it out still further. At the same time ground mist made it increasingly difficult to see where they were going, to see indeed beyond the next man in line. Orders had to be relayed in endless whispers; the long march and the uneven footing made troops tired; mist and darkness turned trees and hedges into royalist horsemen poised to cut them down. Tension was greatest among the cavalry at the head of the column, who would be the first to encounter any enemy patrol, and who would have to deal with it. So far they had always been worsted by royalist horse, and a dark moor with uncertain footing was not a good place to begin redressing the record. They reached Langmoor rhine, and tension grew while their guide searched for the stepping stones across it. For one trooper the strain grew too great, and seeing a shadow which seemed to move, he fired his pistol at it. The noise shattered the night and startled the one royalist dragoon left near Langmoor rhine. He wheeled and rode as hard as he dared back to camp, and standing at the ditch in front of Weston Zoyland shouted across to the men of the Scots regiment that, 'the enemy had come . . . beat your drums, to arms!'[14]

At his trial afterwards, one of the rebels, Captain Hucker, claimed that he had deliberately fired the shot to give the alarm. The claim was almost certainly untrue and made only to curry favour; and the pistol shot and subsequent alarm did not in itself ruin Monmouth's plan. Langmoor rhine was nearly three-quarters of a mile from the nearest royalist battalion at Weston Zoyland. In darkness and over broken grassland and scattered mire a horse could achieve little more than a trot, and would take at least ten minutes to cover the distance. Once at the ditch the sentry would get no instant response from the men he was shouting at, men sleeping heavily after a long day's march and not anticipating any alarm. Andrew Paschall's account has the sentry shouting 'with all possible earnestness . . . twenty times at least'.[15] The time it then took the royalist foot to turn out can only be guessed at: suddenly awakened at two in the morning, two thousand men had to throw on some clothes, seize guns and ammunition, and form lines in front of their tents, all in thick darkness amid shouting voices, the beating of drums, and imminent expectation of being shot at. Even for experienced troops fifteen minutes would seem fast work, and this together with the time needed by the sentry to reach the camp still gave the rebels nearly half an hour, and a fighting chance.

At Langmoor rhine, therefore, Monmouth faced, not ruin, but a rapid change in plan. He did not have the time to strike the royalists with a perfectly co-ordinated blow from all of his army – horse, cannon, and foot. What mattered now was to hit the enemy quickly with something. Grey was ordered forward with his horse as quickly as possible, to strike the top end or right flank of the royalist camp, while their foot was emerging from the tents. The three cannon were sent after him as rapidly as possible to rake the enemy line. The royalists would thus be under attack while Monmouth struggled with the longer business of bringing up his foot battalions.[16] This change was the best that could be improvised, but Monmouth thus put an intolerable strain on the training of his army, and things began to go wrong.

Grey had no time to draw his eight hundred horse together into a coherent body. They crossed the rhine and pushed pell-mell to where they supposed Feversham's right flank to be – and ran straight into a royalist force of 150 cavalry under Sir Francis Compton. This squadron had been placed in the moor on the royalists' right flank to watch the Bridgewater-Glastonbury road, and give support to the few individual sentries placed on the moor. Alerted by the noise from the Langmoor sentry Compton's men had advanced toward the rhine, to encounter Gray's larger but disorganized mass of horse. There was a confused exchange of pistol fire amongst the scattered groups of horsemen, and Compton was wounded in the chest. Captain Sands took over and, after a false start in which he mistook a party of rebel horse for his supporting troops and was himself wounded in the resulting fracas, he was able to lead his horsemen back to the royalists' right flank, to defend the vital top crossing of the Weston Zoyland rhine, which had to be held if the entire position was not to be outflanked.[17]

It was well that he did so, because a group of rebel horse a hundred or more strong under a Captain Jones, had regrouped and continued their course toward the royalist camp, perhaps following the retreating Sands. Another, but more hard-fought, skirmish then followed beside the Weston rhine as Jones and his men, finding the ditch and the crossing, fought desperately to clear the cavalry before them and pass behind to the royalist tents. The royalists were 'hard beset', and Jones led his force with such dash that some royalist officers afterwards thought him worthy of a pardon.[18] But he was unable to deploy all of the horse he had with him. Many of those who had followed him milled about near the ditch, unable to distinguish friend from foe and possibly even unaware that a vital crossing was being fought for. Without joining in the fight, they rode off to their left following the ditch, leaving the crucial royalist right flank further and further behind them until they reached Sutton Mill, where the Weston Zoyland and the North Ditches join, a mile away from the battlefield. Here they waited to see what happened, and when it eventually appeared that Monmouth had lost, they took flight. Deprived of their assistance Jones was beaten back, and Feversham's vital right flank was held until it could be reinforced. Thus it was not the sudden appearance of Bussex rhine which frustrated Monmouth's plan; for even after an accidental pistol shot had given the alarm some at least of the rebel cavalry had found the ditch and a crossing point, and were only denied by the leadership of a subordinate royalist officer. Even a hundred cavalry among their tents might have seriously disconcerted the royalist foot.

Jones' commander Lord Grey had meanwhile been even less fortunate. While his subordinate hotly pursued the enemy and so found both the Bussex rhine and its ford, Grey's main concern was to regroup the mass of his shaken horse and lead them on to the enemy camp. In the time this took him he inevitably lost touch with Sands' force and consequently, when he led the five hundred or so he had collected back toward their objective, he totally missed the crossing point and discovered to his dismay the deep and miry ditch, with the right-hand royalist battalion forming up behind it. His horse could never struggle across it and attack the tents, and a crossing had to be found. He gambled and struck off not to his left and Jones' skirmish, but to his right, riding with bated breath across the front of the stirring enemy lines towards their centre. A second crossing did in fact exist in this direction, but it was half a mile in front of Grey on Feversham's extreme left flank: to reach it the horse would have had to ride past all six enemy battalions in succession. In the circumstances they did quite well. On being challenged by the extreme right-flank battalion under Lieutenant-Colonel Douglas they answered that they were Albemarle's militia. Challenged by the next force in the line, the Guard's battalion, the rebels answered that they were for the King. Captain Berkeley commanding the right wing of the royalist musketeers then shouted back 'which King?', to which an unthinking rebel replied with their battle cry 'Monmouth and God with us'.

And with this reply Grey and his force then passed beyond all aid, human or divine. The royalist foot at once fired on them, and though individual targets could not easily be seen, a volley from a full battalion at little more than fifty yards panicked the recipients, horse and man alike. Leaving their dead and wounded on the ground they fled back into the moor, bringing confusion to some of their advancing foot on the way. Once well away from the ditch their panic flight slowed down, and as the rest of the battle proceeded and the light improved, the royalists could see the rebel horse in the distance 'in great confusion endeavouring to forme, but could not'.[19] Grey's troopers had done their best and fought three skirmishes, but cavalry fighting at night contains a large element of luck, and once this began to run against them the training of horse and men was too slight for them to retrieve the situation. After the battle Monmouth bitterly blamed Grey for what he termed the latter's 'cowardice', but this was less than just. Grey displayed resolution in regrouping his men after the encounter with Compton; he was unlucky in not finding Jones' skirmish, and unlucky, too, in turning right not left to look for a crossing; and he showed some courage in leading his men across the front of the royalist foot battalions. Once they were scattered into the darkness by the Scotch regiment's volley, it was probably beyond the power of any commander of horse to reassemble them.

After despatching Grey's cavalry to attack the royalist lines, Monmouth turned to his foot. Here again, speed was all that mattered. He allowed no time for the rear two battalions to catch up with those of Wade, Matthews, and Holmes in the van; he allowed no time for the leading battalions to reform from their extended marching order, into a more concentrated battle formation. Strung out as they were, he ordered them on the double to the royalist camp. At the head of the leading battalion Wade had a very difficult task. When the fighting began his battalion would hold the extreme right of the rebel line: it was, therefore, his responsibility to see that his troops faced and engaged the royalists' extreme left-wing battalion. Otherwise the whole of the rebel army would not be disposed against the royalist line, and the rearmost rebel battalions would find themselves too far to the left and facing no enemy at all. Wade's battalion was in fact the marker for the entire rebel line, and it was imperative that he position himself correctly. But with the alarm now given Monmouth simply told him to attack with all possible speed: the further down the royalist line he marched the longer the enemy would have to prepare, and in the darkness he had no clear idea how far the royalist line extended in any case.

And so Wade compromised. He directed his march towards the fires of the matchlocks in the royalists' right flank battalion, and then went on for a few hundred yards, hoping that this would be enough. In fact he brought his men about half way down the royalist line and quite close to the enemy troops. In his account he claims to have been within 'thirty or forty paces' of the Sedgemoor ditch, and a royalist account says they came up 'within halfe a musquet shot of our camp'.[20] But here Wade had to order a halt 'on pain of Death'. His troops were still in marching order and had to be drawn up into some battle line before attacking. Furthermore, at this close distance from the enemy he may have discovered the ditch protecting them, and such an unexpected obstacle had to be investigated and crossed, if possible, in good order. And finally, the activity on the other side of the ditch showed that the royalists were up and alert: an orderly attack, and no indiscriminate charge, was now necessary. The resulting pause in front of the enemy, however necessary, probably confused the troops who had been told earlier that all they had to do was rush upon a broken royalist camp.[21]

While Wade was trying to re-form his men, another battalion under Colonel Matthews came up on his left, and a third smaller battalion under Holmes took position to the left again. These three battalions, together barely two thousand men, were all that fought the actual battle on the rebel side. Two more battalions with perhaps up to eight hundred men (including many of the scythe-men), milled about in the rear as far back as Langmoor rhine, disorganized by their long march, frightened by the outbreak of firing, and uncertain whether the riders from Grey's broken cavalry whom they glimpsed in the darkness were their own or the enemy's. But quite apart from this disorder, the officers of the two forces were hamstrung by the darkness and their own inexperience. Monmouth had gone forward with the leading troops, and there was no-one to tell them what had happened (that Wade had not gone far enough down the enemy line); and what they should do — abandon their attempts to form up in front of the enemy where there was simply no room for them, and instead march to their left to form up on the royalists' right flank and rear. This is clear with hindsight, but in the darkness and confusion of the time the two commanders Foulkes and Bovett could not understand why their men had no room to form up, and were unable to think what to do.

Until this point the rebel foot had behaved with considerable discipline, marching in silence and deploying two-thirds of their number to face the enemy. But now their restraint snapped. For the men in Colonel Matthews's battalion in the middle of the rebel line, the shadowy line of enemy tents and soldiers only fifty yards away was too much. Without orders, and before forming up properly, a few fired their guns, the rest of the battalion followed, and Wade's and Holmes's forces joined in. After this it was impossible for their officers to control them, and any chance of making them cross the ditch and charge the enemy was lost. Transported by long-suppressed excitement and fear they stood, rooted to the spot, firing again and again at where they supposed the enemy to be. Their volume of fire was heavy, but it was mostly wild. Like all newly-trained musketeers they fired too high, and most of them shot at no individual target. Moreover, discipline within the royalist foot was good and there was very little return fire at this point, and consequently few muzzle-flashes for the rebels to aim at.[22] Royalist officers paid tribute to their opponents' courage and steadiness, standing and firing for two hours, and after a time absorbing some heavy return fire from royalist cannon. But it was their determination to stand, shout, and shoot, and not to press on to the enemy camp, which lost them the battle. The Bussex rhine played no part in their check because they did not come within fifty yards of it. It was their inexperience, in the end, which undid them.

But if Monmouth's musketeers did little harm to the enemy, this was not the case with his cannon. After ordering Grey with his horse and Wade with his foot to attack as quickly as possible, Monmouth saw his three small iron guns across the Langmoor rhine, and hurried them forward to the enemy line. Safely picking a way through his own troops Monmouth positioned the guns between Matthews's and Holmes's battalions, less than a hundred yards from the royalist tents. Here his Dutch gunner took over and worked his three gun crews with a coolness and accuracy that drew grudging compliment from the royalists. The account prepared for James II after the battle describes the guns as 'very well plyed', and when the royalist infantry was finally commanded to advance at the end of the battle they made a particular point of seizing the rebel cannon as quickly as they could. Feversham's two right flank battalions under Dumbarton and the Duke of Grafton suffered most of the royalist casualties during this part of the battle, the majority of them from cannon fire, and James II's account of the battle speaks of them suffering 'great execution' from the guns.[23] But the rebels had only three weapons of small calibre, and however well handled they could not alone have turned the battle, now that Grey's horse had been scattered and the foot immobilized in front of the Sedgemoor ditch. Monmouth stood by his cannon and watched the wild shooting of the infantry with mounting impatience, which turned to despair. As his troops grew less and less orderly, it became clear that the royalists were behaving with increasing confidence.

The royalists, however, had experienced a rude awakening, commander and troops alike. Feversham had not long gone to bed at Weston Zoyland when the alarm was given. A trumpet sounded from Dumbarton's right-flank battalion, and for the next ten to fifteen minutes confusion reigned as the royalist foot, horse, and gunners turned out. Feversham's first concern was to secure his infantry, for without them his line was lost. The foot battalions were ordered on pain of death to stay where they were, and not to try to cross the ditch. When Grafton's battalion shot at Grey's horse they were quickly ordered to cease fire, and the occasional return fire from this and Dumbarton's battalion was also stifled. The role of the foot was to stand ready in front of their tents until their commander could comprehend what was going on. In the meantime they had to endure the rebel cannon and musket shot, which crashed over and through their lines.[24]

It was undoubtedly the discipline and steadiness of their foot, tumbled out of sleep by a sudden alarm and forming up in darkness and under gunfire, which saved the royalist position. Their commander's reaction was prompt and energetic, but at least initially, quite mistaken. Feversham was quartered with the cavalry in the village of Weston Zoyland. When the alarm was given he and several hundred other men struggled into the streets to find and saddle their horses. As soon as four or five officers had their troops of cavalry or dragoons more or less in order Feversham rushed with them to where he assumed the attack to be coming from, along the Bridgewater-Weston Zoyland road on his left flank. That the rebels might have come across the roadless moor to attack his right flank seems not to have occurred to him. As he led his two hundred or so men past the lower plungeon or crossing of the Sedgemoor rhine and on to the road, he saw some horsemen riding fast down the Bridgewater road to the camp. They were Oglethorpe with his horse, rushing to give warning that the rebels were on the march. By now this news was too late to help Feversham, but equally important was the scouting party's information that the attack must be from the north, across the moor and falling on the royalists' right flank. During this conversation Feversham apparently regained some composure and began to think clearly. He left the cavalry he had taken with him where they were, on the road by the moor, in a position to protect his left flank. So long as they did not move without orders they would be useful there, however the battle developed. With Oglethorpe and his force he hurried back to Weston Zoyland, only to find the village now empty of cavalry. After he had rushed off, the rest of the horse had formed up and by listening carefully had realized the true direction of the attack. Without waiting for orders from their absent commander, they moved out of the village to cover their right flank. Feversham and Oglethorpe then rode up to join the bulk of the cavalry, just behind Dumbarton's battalion of foot, at the right hand end of the royalist line.[25]

A troop of the dragoons had already been in action. Their officer Lieutenant Ward had led them right up to the ditch on the right of the last of Dumbarton's companies. Holding their fire, they tried to find exactly where the enemy was, and soon realized that one of the rebel battalions was directly opposite them. It was in fact the smallest of the three actually engaged, that of Colonel Holmes, on the rebel left flank. Ordered not to open fire, Ward tried to confuse the enemy by calling out to them to stop shooting, that they were friends. The ruse succeeded, possibly because the rebels were hoping that some of their horse had got behind the enemy lines. The musket fire from Holmes's battalion ceased, and Holmes himself rode forward to the edge of the ditch to ask for news. Uncertain who the dim figure was, Ward asked him who he was for. In some surprise Holmes replied 'who but Monmouth', and was then fired on by a sergeant of Ward's troop. The shot missed Holmes but killed his horse, and the rider broke an arm in his fall. His men made no move to rescue him and for the rest of the battle Holmes lay semi-conscious beside the ditch. As the royalist horse passed over it to attack his leaderless men he was seen to lift his head to watch them, and a trooper asked him who he was. Holmes replied that he was in no condition to tell, and lay still until they had gone. He afterwards tried to escape but lost his way and was captured, wandering among the royalist tents.[26] The loss of their commander was of some importance to his battalion, because they held the rebel left flank and the royalist counter-attack, when it fell, would be a cavalry charge against them.

And that counter-attack would not now be long in coming. When Feversham joined his right-flank cavalry, the battle had reached a turning point. Lord Grey's horse had failed to attack the royalist tents, and were now scattered in confusion. The rebel foot had only been able to bring to bear half their force, and these men were rooted to the ground in front of Sedgemoor rhine, mostly firing wildly and quite incapable of any movement forward. The cannon were in place but their fire, though well aimed, was too weak to do significant damage. In short, Monmouth's attack had been delivered and its force was spent. But it took some time for the royalist officers to realize this. According to Andrew Paschall 'Victory seemed to be inclined to the rebels' for a considerable period yet.[27] Feversham's first positive response had been a mistaken one, and his next move was very cautious. He pushed Oglethorpe and some cavalry across the upper ditch, to reconnoitre the moor in front of his right flank. The intrepid colonel led the way and quickly met with a small band of rebel cavalry, possibly survivors of Jones's brave band. But they now had no stomach for another fight and after a brief clash retreated into the darkness. Feversham refused to let any of his men pursue them and drew up all his horse in a defensive posture, not knowing yet what had become of Monmouth's cavalry, and unwilling to commit his against the rebel foot while there remained a chance that they in turn might be counter-attacked.[28] Such inactivity, however, was too much for Colonel Oglethorpe who, apparently without orders from Feversham, led his strong troop to attack the nearest rebel battalion. Almost certainly this was Colonel Holmes' and his men fought well.

Shielded by darkness, Oglethorpe's force was able to break into their ranks and some desperate hand-to-hand fighting followed. Although Oglethorpe's force was of course greatly outnumbered by the whole of Holmes' battalion of some four hundred, in the area they attacked the cavalry would have enjoyed something like parity of numbers, the darkness preventing any support coming from the rebel companies not under attack. It says much for the rebel amateurs, therefore, that Oglethorpe's troop — so successful up to this point in the campaign — were beaten back with some losses. Oglethorpe's second in command, Captain Sarsfield, was knocked down by the butt of a musket and 'left for dead upon the place', and several other men were wounded or dislodged from their horses.[29] Feversham was confirmed in his belief that the time was not yet ripe for his cavalry to attack. And since the darkness was still too deep for his infantry to fire without wasting their shot, it was left to the cannon to hold the rebels and weaken them, before the horse and foot attacked.

The royalist gunners were perhaps the worst positioned of all their army, to counter Monmouth's attack. The train of artillery was not drawn up in the centre of the line where it could easily assist any part of the army, but on the extreme left, in the fields between Weston village and the Bridgewater road. Completely on the wrong side of the army, the guns had to be shifted the entire length of the royalist line to fire on the rebels. Drivers had to find and harness up their horses, draw guns and carts through the village and out onto the rough grass of the moor, and then unlimber and position their guns, all in near-total darkness. Yet the manoeuvre was performed with speed and precision: the gunner Edward Dummer recorded that such was the 'cheerfulness' of the artillerymen 'that they were allmost as readily drawn up to Receive them [the rebels], as a Preinformed expectation could have posted them'.[30] This exaggerates a little because only six guns — and those the lightest — were moved against the rebels. Three were placed half way along the royalist line between the battalions and very close to the ditch, and three were taken to the extreme right flank beyond even Dumbarton's battalion. These three obviously had a very wide field of fire, but they had no protecting foot in front of them, and only a rather uncertain screen of cavalry out of the moor somewhere to their right. Being so close to the enemy the six guns, even when simply firing into the darkness, caused considerable losses to Monmouth's infantry: Paschall says they 'made lanes among the Rebells', and another account observes that they 'plyed with Reb. very hard and did good execution'.[31] The three battalions under Wade, Matthews, and Holmes absorbed this heavy return fire for nearly an hour without breaking, but as the darkness slowly lessened they began to guess at the holes torn in their lines, and dimly perceived the royalist foot moving into position to crush them. Companies were moving from the non-engaged section of the royalist line to reinforce Dumbarton and Douglas, who were receiving all of the rebels' fire.

But this manoeuvre by the King's infantry was not accomplished without difficulties. It was becoming plain to Feversham and all his officers that less than half of their line was actually being fired on, and that three battalions on the left of their line were not engaged because the rebels had not deployed far enough down. These three battalions, therefore, constituted a reserve which, if thrown vigorously at the rebels, could destroy them. Feversham apparently rejected what would have been the most crushing move: if the middle battalion of the line had held its position and acted as a pivot the two battalions on its left could have moved forward in an arc, swinging towards the right and enveloping the whole right flank of the rebels. The muskets and pikes of three battalions hitting Monmouth's army on its exposed right flank would have quickly unhinged the entire rebel line. But the manoeuvre was difficult to time properly, would have involved the foot crossing the ditch, and could have been brought to confusion by the darkness. Moreover, Feversham was still uncertain whether all the rebel horse had been dealt with — he was holding in a strong force of his own cavalry on the other flank because of this uncertainty. The other alternative, less bold but more safe, was to detach the last two battalions on the royalist left flank and move them up behind the army, to reinforce the right flank. Once in position, they would make the battle safe for the royalists: the battered right flank would not now give way, and when the light permitted these two, and Dumbarton's and Grafton's battalions, could cross the ditch and advance to scatter the rebels at the push of the pike.

Very oddly, Feversham rejected this obvious and safe option too. Instead, he gave orders for one of the two Guards battalions in the centre of the line to pull out and march to the right flank, while Kirk and Trelawney each moved sideways a space to the right to fill up the vacant position in the line.[32] This curious order had perhaps the merit of reducing the distance any of the royalist battalions had to move, and was probably, therefore, quicker to execute than the alternatives, but it could have proved disastrous. During a battle, and particularly at night, it is essential for each unit to know exactly where its neighbour is, and to be in sight of or in touch with it. Otherwise the confusion may be irremediable. Feversham was proposing, in a darkness that was still deep, to withdraw the centre battalion of his line hoping that the two halves of his command, thus separated, would be able to find each other again and safely rejoin, without any shooting. And by this risk he was achieving only one battalion's reinforcement of his right.

Fortunately for him Churchill (now in command of the foot) was on the spot. Finding Colonel Sackville about to move the Guards battalion, Churchill simply countermanded Feversham's order and told Sackville to stay where he was. He then went down the line to Kirk and Trelawney and ordered them to march up the length of the royalist line, to take up a position on the right of Dumbarton. With two extra battalions and most of the cavalry the right flank would now deliver the royalist counter-attack, and Churchill rode with Kirk and Trelawney up the line, to be in a position to guide the counter-stroke. On the way they met with Feversham, who had come down the line to see his orders executed. What passed between Churchill and his commander is not known; the anonymous record of Feversham's western marches merely observes: 'But seeing my Lord Churchill marching with Colonel Kirk's and Trelawney's men towards him [Feversham] made Collonell Sackvil hault, and returned to the horse, leaving my Lord Churchill to march them to the right'.[33] Churchill had insisted upon control of the foot and with that, effectively, the battle. After two considerable miscalculations Feversham was probably in no mood to dispute this.

Even as Churchill reached Dumbarton's flank with his two battalions, however, the end was near. The rebel battalions of Wade, Matthews, and Holmes had stood their ground for some two hours, firing at where they guessed the enemy to be, and receiving in return shot from six cannons and (intermittently) the muskets of two battalions. They had failed to destroy the royalists by gunfire, and they had failed to engage them hand-to-hand. As the dawn light strengthened they saw the firm lines of the royalist foot, and dimly the mass of their horse. From his vantage point Feversham watched 'the Pikes of their Battalions begin to shake and at last to open out', as weariness grew into fear and despair. The light strengthened, and Feversham could see no sign of Monmouth's cavalry. Convinced at last that his horse ran no risk in attacking the rebel foot, he let Oglethorpe cross the ditch and once more attack Holmes' leaderless battalion. At the same time he ordered his battalions of foot forward to cross the ditch, and advance to push of the pike with the enemy. The rebels' discipline held briefly as the royalist battalions came towards them, but then Holmes's battalion was swept away by the cavalry. Their line broken, with horse on their left and pikes in front of them, the next rebel battalion in the line also collapsed and fled, before the royalist foot could reach them. Commanding the last rebel battalion on the front Wade was able to hold most of his men together as they faced about, but then they scattered in what he called 'a disorderly retreat', joining the men from the other two battalions in a desperate scramble across the moor.[34] They ran for the nearest cover, the cornfields about Chedzoy church. Their flight thus took them clear of the remaining two battalions, those of Bovett and Foulkes, which had been 'scowring away for some tyme in the rear in great disorder and confusion'.[35] The dispersal of the front three battalions now exposed these two unhappy battalions to the weight of the royalist cavalry and dragoons, and the first and only experience of battle their troops had was when horsemen suddenly appeared in the growing light to mow them down.

Up to this point the casualties suffered by the rebels had been relatively light, a royalist estimate suggesting that less than two hundred of Monmouth's army had died in front of the Weston rhine. But perhaps a thousand more were killed in flight, when they gave up the battle. Very many of these casualties came from the two rear battalions, caught unprepared and disorganized by several hundred royalist horse. With no cover on the moor, the running soldiers were easily visible in the dawn sun and were as easily ridden down, to be slashed across the back or head by a full arm blow from a sword. To pursue the retreating enemy and prevent him from regrouping was the cavalry's final responsibility in any battle, but there was never a chance of Monmouth's amateurs reorganizing themselves, and the last act on Sedgemoor was a merciless slaughter.

The destruction of Bovett's and Foulkes' rear battalions gave a brief respite for the other three, and many survivors from these managed to cover the half mile to the edge of the moor. Here, however, they were stopped by an obstacle, a 'deep and boggy ditch', separating the moor from Chedzoy cornfield.[36] And here the horsemen caught up with them as, covered in mud, and near exhaustion, the rebels clawed and scrambled up the muddy bank to get out of the ditch and into the cornfield. It was target practice for the royalists who pistolled them down without mercy, and probably several hundred died here, choking in the mire, their blood staining the water and mud at the bottom of the trench. Even for those who escaped from the horrors of that ditch there was no safety. They stumbled on into the cornfield, but the crop was too low to hide them as they ran. Dragoons and cavalry dismounted and fired muskets and pistols at them, and more rebels died, at once or slowly, amid the stalks of green wheat.

Only now, with their horses blown from the pursuit and themselves weary from killing, did the royalists began to give quarter and take prisoners. Several hundred rebels were captured and many of them brought into Western Zoyland churchyard, stripped of their coats and possessions, manacled together in tired and frightened groups. A drummer of the Earl of Pembroke's militia counted them as they went past: 55 men tied together; 32 more, also tied; 2 wounded, crawling into the churchyard; a single prisoner stripped to his trousers; another beaten by two horsemen as he ran in front of them; little groups of 8, 12 and 14 men, brought in as they had been captured. One prisoner even the drummer found 'very remarkable'. Shot through the shoulder and with a sword gash in his belly, this man was left lying naked in the hot sun all day, some ten or eleven hours, as the militia men (having taken no part in the battle) jeered at him, calling him 'Monmouth dog' and asking how long he had been with his 'King Monmouth'. He replied with spirit, saying that if he had breath he would answer them, and managed to shame his tormentors into pressing less closely about him, and putting a pair of trousers on him. He survived into the evening, and with a stick managed to stagger into the church to join his comrades. He died during the night, witness to the remarkable loyalty Monmouth won from his raw army.[37]

Within an hour of the royalist attack there was not a living rebel to be seen on the battlefield. Those not caught at once by the cavalry scattered, singly or in small groups, across the countryside. Pembroke's militia was now employed to pursue them, and survivors were captured up to ten or twenty miles distant, for several days afterwards. Some were ordinary soldiers; but others were men of more distinction, John Kid for example, the energetic and rebellious gamekeeper of Longleat House, or a dozen or so 'principal rebels' who had accompanied their leader from Holland, and who were sent under guard to London for special treatment.[38] One group of rebels managed to evade capture and keep together. After his battalion broke and ran, Wade had contrived to get 150 of them safely across the Chedzoy ditch and into the cornfield, before the cavalry arrived to disperse the remainder. With these 150 men Wade marched back to Bridgewater, where he found Ferguson the preacher and two full troops of Lord Grey's horse, under Captains Alexander and Tucker, who had been put to flight at the beginning of the battle. With two hundred men at their back Wade and the other officers for a while denied that they had been beaten, and discussed the possibilities of further resistance. Eventually they faced facts and decided to disperse, each man to shift for himself. Wade, Ferguson, the other officers, and some twenty men with fit horses rode westwards to the Bristol Channel. At Ilfordcombe they met up with two more troops of their horse under Captains Hewlings and Large, who had been sent to Minehead the day before to capture some cannon. They seized and victualled a ship and put out from Ilfordcombe, but were forced ashore again by two Navy ships sailing off the coast. The band now dispersed completely and Wade was captured and wounded in Devon, coming out of the house of one John Birch.[39]

Monmouth and Lord Grey covered a greater distance than this, and were at large for a rather longer period, before they too were taken. When first the horse and then the foot at Sedgemoor had failed in their attacks, the end was not difficult for an experienced soldier to predict. Monmouth, nevertheless, stayed beside his three cannon helping the Dutch gunner to train them, until Williams his servant told him that some of the royalist cavalry were beginning to move up on their flank. This was possibly Oglethorpe's first attempt to crush Holmes' left-flank battalion, which proved unsuccessful. But it was sufficient warning for Monmouth. He stripped off his armour, took one hundred guineas from Williams and, with Lord Grey, a German mercenary, and a handful of other men, slipped away from the field. They climbed Knowle Hill and looked down to see the gun-flashes marking where the army still fought. After reaching the Mendip Hills Grey and Monmouth left most of their party, changing course south-eastwards towards Ringwood in Hampshire, hoping to hide in the New Forest where Grey thought his connections might buy them temporary safety. From there it would be a short distance to a small Channel port, and a passage to the Continent.[40] Near Shaftesbury in Dorset the party obtained a local guide to take them off the roads, which were now watched, and through Cranbourne Chase. They stayed the night of the sixth at an inn where Monmouth disguised himself as a shepherd, but when they set out early next day the pursuit caught up with them. Grey and the guide were taken almost at once, at five in the morning, but although the surrounding countryside was closely searched Monmouth and his German mercenary evaded capture for the rest of the day. At dawn on the eighth the mercenary was captured, and revealed where he had separated from the Duke. With the search thus concentrated it took less than two hours to find Monmouth himself, hiding in a ditch covered with fern and brambles. He had green peas in his pocket which he had been trying to live off and was by now, three days after the battle, near the last stages of hunger and exhaustion. The prisoners were held for two days and sent to London. Monmouth entered the Tower on 13 July.

His ignominious capture in a ditch has, for some historians, seemed an appropriate end for a commander who fled the field to save himself, while his troops were still fighting. Most generals prefer flight to capture however, even when they do not — as Monmouth did — face the certainty of execution should they be taken. Monmouth made no bones about his flight and it is this lack of disguise, the absence of talk about rearguard actions or fighting withdrawals, which provokes censure. The battle was in its very last stage when he left, Feversham's cavalry beginning their final advance, and his departure could have made no difference. As he said of his own troops at the time, 'all the World cannot stop those fellows: they will run presently' — and they did.[41] At Sedgemoor Monmouth did all that lies in the power of a commander, devising a plan which gave his troops a good chance of success, without excessive casualties, and bringing them safely to the point where his intentions could be put into operation. After that, as Napoleon observed, no strategy survives contact with the enemy.

The plan itself was well conceived, because it gave his technically much inferior troops the possibility of success, which would have been totally lacking in any conventional battle between the two forces. By trying to employ surprise and darkness to offset the royalists' superior training and equipment, Monmouth confirmed the point made on several occasions in this narrative, that he was a commander of considerable tactical skill. Even when the alarm was given and surprise appeared lost he responded quickly, and by throwing his cavalry and foot forward at once might still have won. His ignorance of the Bussex rhine in front of the royalists' camp is usually cited as the major reason for the rebels' defeat — contemporary accounts were explicit on this point — but it is an over-simplification. The accidental discharge of a pistol at Langmoor crossing deprived his troops of total surprise, and forced Monmouth to rush his army forward in considerable disorder. The bulk of the cavalry were then held up by the ditch, but it was bad luck which led Grey to turn right and not left in search of a crossing, and it was the desperate resistance of Captain Sands' cavalry which prevented an equally small force of rebel horse from using the upper crossing to get around the rear of Feversham's camp. Most fundamentally, however, it was the failure of rebel officers to get their foot battalions moving forward again, once the firing had started, which cost them the battle. Excitement, fear, and lack of training, kept Monmouth's infantry rooted to the spot and shooting into the darkness, and not the sudden appearance of an unexpected obstacle in the shape of the ditch. And when they failed to close on Feversham's infantry the issue was decided, because it was then only a matter of time before the royalists regained their composure and sent their foot forward across the ditch. It was not the difficulty of negotiating this obstacle which made Feversham delay sending the infantry forward, (though it was easier to cross in the growing light), but fear that rebel cavalry might be lurking in the darkness to descend upon his musketeers. Better training and superior experience decided Sedgemoor, although the rebel troops did well in executing a difficult night advance, and fought very bravely when the action began; while as commander Monmouth did all that could be asked of him to create a situation in which, for an hour or two, 'Victory seemed inclined to the Rebels, and . . . the King's army was almost in despaire'.[42]

By contrast, little can be said for Feversham's conduct of the engagement. The attack had taken him completely by surprise, and only the good fortune of an accidental pistol shot had given the alarm, so neglectful was his positioning of sentries. Initially mistaking the direction of the attack and so riding off out of contact with his army for much of the battle's vital early stages, he then proposed a dangerous manoeuvre to bring more of his foot into the action. Saved from this miscalculation by Churchill he then regained control, forbidding his men to move or to shoot until the position clarified and he could order a general advance. James II made no public comment on his generalship, but Churchill's subsequent rise and Feversham's decline to obscurity demonstrate his judgement on the battle, and indeed on the entire campaign.

For a while, however, Feversham savoured the pleasures of victory. A party under Colonel Kirk was quickly sent to Bridgewater to ensure that the success was complete, with no organized opposition left to dispute it; and when Bridgewater was reported empty of rebels and occupied the redoubtable Colonel Oglethorpe was given his just reward, posted off to London to bring news of a complete victory to an expectant (and duly grateful) court. Various other officers received gracious mention and praise in Feversham's fulsome report to the King, and the volunteers and the remaining militia were dismissed. In a letter to Sunderland four days after the battle Feversham was still praising the conduct of his officers and men; heightening his story by stressing the gross disparity in casualties between the two sides, the rebels allegedly losing over a thousand dead and three hundred prisoners, the royalists suffering only fifty dead and two hundred wounded, with less than a score of officers among them. This minimized Feversham's own losses, but he underestimated those of the rebels too. The churchwardens at

Weston Zoyland in charge of clearing the battlefield received lists of corpses totalling 1,384, with more unrecovered in the Chedzoy cornfield. Great pits were being prepared for mass burials: one for the remains of 174 men was dug on the site of the rebel army's much-suffering left flank.[43]

And the summary executions were beginning. On Weston Moor the Dutch gunner was hanged, together with a royalist soldier who had deserted to Monmouth and then been captured and recognized. On the day after the battle six rebels were hanged outside the White Hart Inn at Glastonbury, their bodies left to infect the air. Kirk's troops marched from Bridgewater to Taunton spreading fear before them, while the militia reorganized itself to begin a great manhunt over the whole county.[44] The fighting was over; the terror was yet to come.

Footnotes: Chapter Seven

1. 'Iter Bellicosum: or a Perfect Relation of the . . . march . . . by Adam Wheeler', *Camden Society*, 18 1910, pp.160, 161.

2. *HMC*, Dartmouth MSS.I, pp.126-7.

3. *HMC*, Dartmouth MSS.I, p.217; Add.MSS.31956, f.5.

4. *HMC*, Dartmouth MSS.I, p.217.

5. Add.MSS.31956, f.5; Add.MSS.4162, ff.126, 127v.

6. *HMC*, 9th Report, p.16; Add.MSS.4162, f.127.

7. Add.MSS.4162, ff.127, 126, 128; Add.MSS.31956, f.4.

8. Harl.MSS.6845, ff.289-296, 'The King's Account of the Battle of Sedgemoor', f.289; Harl.MSS.6845, f.281.

9. Harl.MSS.6845, f.281; Add.MSS.4162, f.132.

10. Add.MSS.4162, ff.127v, 128.

11. Harl.MSS.6845, f.291; Add.MSS.4162, f.131v.

12. Harl.MSS.6845, f.291.

13. Harl.MSS.6845, f.290v; *HMC*, 9th Report, p.17.

14. Add.MSS.6845, f.128v.

15. Add.MSS.4162, f.128v.

16. Add.MSS.4162, f.128v; Harl.MSS.6845, f.291v.

17. Add.MSS.4162, f.128; Harl.MSS.6845, f.291v; *HMC*, 9th Report, p.17.

18. Add.MSS.4162, f.129.

19. *HMC*, 9th Report, p.17; Harl.MSS.6845, f.292v.

20. Harl.MSS.6845, 281; *HMC*, 9th Report, p.17.

21. Add.MSS.4162, f.131v.

22. Harl.MSS.6845, f.293.

23. Harl.MSS.6845, f.293; *HMC*, 9th Report, p.18.

24. *HMC*, 9th Report, p.18.

25. Harl.MSS.6845, ff.283-94; *HMC*, 9th Report, pp.17, 18.

26. Harl.MSS., 6845, f.294.

27. Add.MSS.4162, f.129v.

28. Harl.MSS., 6845, f.294.

29. Harl.MSS.6845, f.294.

30. Add.MSS.31956, f.5v.

31. Add.MSS.4162, f.132v; Harl.MSS.6845, f.292.

32. *HMC*, 9th Report, p.18.

33. *HMC*, 9th Report, p.18.

34. *HMC*, 9th Report, p.18; Harl.MSS.6845, ff.294v, 281.

35. *HMC*, 9th Report, p.18.

36. Harl.MSS.6845, f.295.

37. A.Wheeler, 'Iter Bellicosum', *Camden Society*, pp.163-4.

38. *HMC*, 9th Report, pp.18, 21.

39. Harl.MSS.6845, ff.281v, 295v.

40. Harl.MSS.6845, f.295.

41. Add.MSS.4162, f.132.

42. Add.MSS.4162, ff.132, 129v; Harl.MSS.6845, ff.290, 291v.

43. *HMC*, 9th Report, pp.19-21; A.Wheeler, 'Iter Bellicosum', p.164.

44. A.Wheeler, 'Iter Bellicosum', *Camden Society*, pp.164-5; Add.MSS.31956, f.6v.

CHAPTER EIGHT

Retribution

On 12 August 1685 James II granted a surprising honour to the child of a convicted traitor. Permission was given for 'the late Duchess of Monmouth to bury her daughter in such part of Westminster Abbey as she shall desire'. Unhappily, interment in this national shrine did not mean that the King was generously putting an end to the feud with his late nephew: rather, James II was trying to quieten a guilty conscience. At the time the girl was 'dead in the Tower', for with Monmouth's other children she had been lodged there as a hostage, and remained in that noisome place even after her father's capture and execution. On the scaffold Monmouth had been urged to recommend his widow and children to the King's favour. The Duke had innocently replied why, 'what harm have they done?'[1] His own experiences as James II's prisoner should perhaps have enlightened him. As an attainted traitor Monmouth could be put to death with no further formality, and James intended to allow none. An execution order was drawn up on 12 July as he entered the Tower; once lodged in it, he was told on the fourteenth that he would die next day. Even this schedule was not too tight to prevent the Duke from writing two letters to the King and one to the Queen, petitioning for mercy. Any begging letter may sound servile when the writer's life is at stake, and these three appeals do not show Monmouth to advantage. He 'longs to live to show you Sir how well and truly' he can serve the King; he hints at matters he can only reveal to James personally; and he refers to supporters in Cheshire (unnamed) to be denounced to the King.[2]

Taken with his earlier flight from Sedgemoor when defeat had become obvious, these letters appear to complete a picture of a vainglorious but empty courtier, a coward in adversity. But contemplation of one's certain death is a terrible thing, particularly for a favoured son who had always escaped hitherto; and doubly so for a man drained by exhaustion, and by the strain of solitary command, in a cause which he had realized for some time could only end in defeat. When captured, Monmouth had been on the run for three days and was starving and exhausted, filthy and friendless. Furthermore, there was a germ of truth in his plea to James that he had never considered rebellion, until tempted to it by 'some horrid people'. He saw his first, loyal, reaction to news of his father's death as some extenuation for his later actions. Self-pity completed the work of exhaustion, and in the Tower he broke down.

Surprisingly, James agreed to see his nephew; and though he adamantly refused to consider mercy, he permitted some concessions — the rebel might see his children one more time, the scaffold could be decorated in black, the axe substituted for the rope. The King also personally checked security arrangements for the execution, still anxious perhaps over his nephew's popularity. For his part, the Duke signed an acknowledgement that Charles II had told him that he had never married Lucy Walters but, his courage reviving, he would go no further. The Bishops of Ely, and Bath and Wells refused him communion ('he was in error and in sin'), and on the scaffold badgered him to confess the sins of his rebellion, and of his conduct with Henrietta Wentworth. To no avail. Monmouth refused to admit he had led a revolt; described his mistress as a 'religious, godly lady'; and declined to talk any more, saying that he had come there to die. Lord Russell's bungled execution was on his mind, and he asked the executioner not to repeat it. In vain: the first stroke was too light, and the Duke turned round to stare at the axeman. Two more blows fell, but Monmouth remained alive and the executioner threw down his axe saying he could not finish the work. Threatened by the Bishops he resumed, and after two more attempts severed head from body. Monmouth's courage was tested to the last. The remains were taken back to the Tower and buried in the Chapel of St. Peter ad Vincula.[3]

A day of national thanksgiving was ordered, with special services in churches in which the Bible, and particularly the Psalms, were plundered for apposite texts on ingratitude and treason. James II struck medals to commemorate his victory, there was a brisk business in packs of cards decorated with scenes from the rebellion, and in at least one parish a bell was cast specifically to commemorate England's deliverance. Monmouth's execution, however, produced an unexpected reaction among some. Despite the speedy and public beheading, a rash of rumours spread that the Duke had escaped, was alive, and would return. They began within weeks of the execution, and were heard in London and the north, as well as in the west. In Dorset two men claimed that Monmouth had not been taken, and 'would come againe'; and in Lyme Regis a man was arrested for saying that the Duke lived, because 'an old man with a beard' had taken his place on the scaffold. In March 1686 a carrier proclaimed that 'the right King of England is alive' from Bolton's market cross; adding a rider — 'I hate all Papists' — making it clear which 'right King' he meant. Charles Floyd was charged at the New Sarum Assize with 'Pretending himself to be the Duke of Monmouth', and in October 1686 John Smith was whipped from Newgate to Tyburn for impersonating the dead rebel. The most remarkable tale, however, was that five men had been chosen to impersonate the Duke, dressed alike, and each sworn to total secrecy. One had died on Tower Hill thus tricking the government, for 'the Duke of Monmouth is not really dead, but only withdrawn until the harvest is over, and then his friends shall see him again in a much better condition that ever they did yet'.[4] Monmouth had become a sleeping hero who would return to save his people, the apotheosis of his popularity with the masses.

In the weeks after Sedgemoor such rumours did not trouble the King. A procession of the Duke's lieutenants was brought to the Tower: Benjamin and William Hewling of Taunton, Sampson Lark the Anabaptist preacher, Josiah Askew, Robert Parrett who had helped steal the Crown jewels in 1670, William Williams the Duke's personal servant, and a dozen others. Nathaniel Wade was delayed by a wound, but would arrive in September to make his detailed and valuable confession. They were brought to London partly to satisfy the King's deep curiosity for particulars of the rebellion, and partly to be held and surveyed as trophies of battle, like the pikes made from scythes, collected on the battlefield. But there was a further purpose. Sedgemoor, and the victory in Scotland, had netted many of the small fry connected with the Rye House Plot — Richard Rumbold, Major Holmes, Nelthorpe and Ayloffe, Christopher Bettiscombe, and Richard Goodenough. These men would certainly now provide the evidence which had been lacking in 1683 to convict the last of the Whig grandees; and to participation in the Rye House Plot could surely be added charges of complicity in the late rebellion. Edmund Prideaux was charged with the latter offence, and had to buy his way out; and Henry Ireton was closely questioned over arms found in 1683. But most attention fastened on the Earl of Stamford, Lords Delamere and Gerard, the London alderman Henry Cornish, and John Hampden who had been tried for misdemeanour in 1684.

Lord Grey and Richard Goodenough quickly struck bargains with the authorities, and were provided with writing materials. Goodenough had been undersheriff to Cornish and his new evidence helped to send the latter to the gallows. Grey received a pardon in November 1685 for his *Narrative* of the Rye House Plot, published half a century later. By keeping him alive the government was also able to extract £7,000 from his heavily-entailed lands, more than all the other fines and forfeitures of 1685 put together. But although Grey was spared as an informer, to the world it appeared that the estate of Monmouth's second in command had purchased his life, an unfortunate circumstance when so many poorer rebels were losing theirs. The *Narrative* itself, detailed but unreliable, helped obtain no new convictions, for of the important Whigs only Stamford and Cornish were put in trial, and only the latter was found guilty.

But if examination of leaders in London was disappointing, the gentry in Somerset were quite literally having a field day with the rebellion's common soldiers. A third or more of the rebel army had escaped from Sedgemoor, and for months these men were hunted down. Colonel Kirk's regulars, retained in the west to garrison Taunton, left an evil reputation over their manhunts; but most active in this work were the local gentry and the militia, anxious to obliterate their incompetent record during the rebellion. An observer noted how the hunt was led by 'several of the County Gentlemen (who hardly dar'd appear before)'. They were not very particular in their methods, threatening to burn down houses, frightening villagers with guns, abusing them, and lying about evidence against individuals to coax further confessions and accusations. It was said that officers gave their troopers five shillings per rebel taken, or the victim's goods if he was propertied.[5] Thus encouraged and licensed, the militia hunted their quarry like game, and the more notable captures were reported to London.

Some rebels escaped. Returning home secretly they were hidden by friends, or harboured by strangers in isolated cottages. They were glimpsed in the woods outside Lyme Regis, and in hills near Chard where Somerset meets Devon. Not all were frightened solitaries: in late October 1685 there were three reports of rebel bands up to twenty strong, defeating the tithing men and militia sent to arrest them. Begging food or stealing it, such fugitives endured a hard winter before the long-awaited general pardon was published in March 1686. The delay in issuing it seemed to some observers a piece of calculated brutality, the forces of law and order being given a little more time to hunt down starving men, the fugitives being punished once more before they were safe.[6] By the time the pardon appeared, a surprising number of rebels had contrived to find a boat and return to the Netherlands. They included two of Monmouth's colonels, Matthews and Foulkes, both of whom later served in William III's army; two unrepentant plotters, Manley and Danvers; Robert Ferguson, would-be chaplain to the army; Joseph Tiley who had proclaimed Monmouth King at Taunton; and some clothiers or sergemakers of Somerset — Christopher Cooke, Hugh Crosse, Peter Parrys, and Joseph Hilliard. The latters' escape suggests what money and business contacts could do; as does the flight of John Trenchard, who had anticipated the gentry's poor response, and left England as the rebellion began.

But only a few score escaped overseas, and only a few hundred lay hidden in England. Some 1,300 rebels were captured on Sedgemoor or near to it. Most of them were crammed into half a dozen west country prisons — nearly four hundred at Ilchester alone. There the rebels were so crowded that there was scarcely room for all to lie down to sleep at night. The heat of summer, together with inadequate ventilation and no sanitation, produced appalling conditions. Prison authorities allowed one and a half pence per day per man for food and water, straw and covering. Fever and smallpox were endemic, robbing the scaffold of many victims. Twenty-two prisoners were buried in the churchyard of St. Mary's Taunton; and eighteen died at Dorchester, in the months after the Assize, thus relieving some over-crowding. Many rebels lay with appalling wounds — splintered jawbones and shattered skulls, deep gashes in chest and belly, bullets and pieces of shot still in their bodies. Some were patiently bandaged and nursed, so that they could stand trial to be hanged or transported. The doctors presented their bills to the magistrates, £2 and £3 per operation, because their patients were too poor to pay.[7] Demoralized by over-crowding, stench, and illness, the prisoners waited throughout July and August for the King to set up his engine of justice. When it came, most would not be in a condition to resist.

They had to wait so long partly because their principal designated judge, Lord Chief Justice George Jeffreys, was recovering from a painful attack of stone in the kidneys. Immediately after Sedgemoor a special commission of Oyer and Terminer had been issued to Jeffreys and four other judges, Sir William Montague, Sir Cresswell Levinz, Sir Francis Withens, and Sir Robert Wright. These five were to clear the gaols of Hampshire, Dorset, Somerset, and Devon of all prisoners, rebels and others. Their task was a large one, and they met in London on 20 August when Jeffreys had partially recovered to consider it. The problem was one of numbers. Their justice must be swift and salutory — but they had some 1,300 suspects to try. Some had been captured on the battlefield, or with weapons or wounds which proclaimed their guilt; but there were many hundred less certain cases, and the law of treason required two witnesses to the treasonable act for each suspect. Literal application of the law could result in over a thousand trials, lasting for up to two years. The case of Dame Alice Lisle illustrated the difficulty. Tried at Dorchester for sheltering two rebels, she was too old and infirm to offer any defence, but merely attempting to coax the appropriate lines from reluctant witnesses took Jeffreys six hours.

Such hiccups could not be risked in the main series of trials. The solution was for prisoners to plead guilty, and to have them make confessions accusing each other, before the judges arrived. In July and August Henry Pollexfen, the Crown prosecutor, set about the business.[8] He used a Deputy Clerk of Assize named Loder, the Somerset assize clerk David Trim, and other assize officers and prison gaolers, as his agents. Two witnesses in separate prisons agree in their account of the methods used. The prisoners were called out, individually, or in small groups. They were told that the King was very gracious and merciful, and intended to execute only the principal rebels. To deserve mercy, however, they had to show penitence, and this required a full confession of guilt, containing details of when and where they had joined, and who else had joined with them. Conversely, refusal to confess would bar the prisoner from mercy, for the King 'would certainly punish all such wilfull and obstinate offenders'. In some cases confessions were obtained by promises to help these confused and frightened men at their trial — 'pretending if they would confess, they would do them all the kindness they could at the Assizes'. According to Monmouth's surgeon Henry Pitman, Judge Jeffreys seconded these offers in court, urging that 'if we would acknowledge our crimes, by pleading Guilty to our Indictment, the King who was almost all mercy, would be as ready to forgive us as we would be to ask it of them'. Powerful hyperbole to offer men locked away from the world, exhausted, sick, and fearful.

The offer seemed reasonable. How could the many hundred prisoners all be hanged? Some must be reprieved. And did not the criminal law condemn most of those brought before it; but then respite many from death, combining justice and mercy? All knew of the pardon offered by James to rebels who surrendered during the campaign, and it seemed that these officers were now bringing them a second chance. And quite apart from their natural wish to go on living, some prisoners probably also felt that they deserved a pardon in any case, for they had not 'truly' rebelled against the King. Near the end of June a rumour had spread in the Duke's army that James II was dead; and a royalist could later 'remember myself to have heard many of the prisoners insisting upon this report of the King's death as the principal reason why they had joined Mon'.[9] But finally of course, they accepted the bait and confessed because they did not believe that the King would lie to them, or permit his officers to do so.

After these preparations, the Assizes commenced in some anti-climax. Following a ceremonial entry into Winchester and the reading of the royal commission, the court began work on 26 August. Hampshire had not been affected by the rebellion and all the trials here, except one, were not connected with it. But that one achieved a brief notoriety. Dame Alice Lisle, aged 70 and the widow of a Regicide, was accused of sheltering two fugitives after Sedgemoor: John Hickes, a Nonconformist minister, and Richard Nelthorpe, a London lawyer already attained for complicity in the Rye House Plot. The case showed Jeffreys' determination to make justice the servant of the King, for it had to be proved that Lisle sheltered the two men knowing them to be fugitive rebels. Although Nelthorpe was a proclaimed traitor, it could not be maintained that he should have been recognized by this aged widow living quietly in the countryside. But Lisle was a Nonconformist and she undoubtedly knew, or knew of, the minister Hickes. Did she however also know that he was a fugitive rebel? Jeffreys worked in vain to make the witness, who had guided the pair to Lisle, admit that he had told her who they were. The judge had then to contend that she must surely have guessed. The jury, however, could see that she was elderly, and of weakening faculties. They were disturbed, too, by the fact that Hickes was only a suspected and not a convicted rebel, for he had not yet been brought to trial. What did the law say on this? They needed (and received) a very plain ruling from Jeffreys on these two issues, before finding Lisle guilty of sheltering traitors. Sentenced to burning at the stake, she petitioned the King and was hanged instead six days later.[10] Her limited offence, her age, sex, and social status, and the dubious evidence accepted; all made this an unsatisfactory opening to the Assizes.

Anti-climax persisted during the second round of trials, held on 3 September at Salisbury. Here again no rebel was put on trial, though a number of cases concerning seditious words marked an increase in the rebels' popularity about this area. Whippings were prescribed, and the judges moved on to Dorchester where on Saturday 5 September their real work began. Thirty-five rebels had resisted official blandishment and pleaded not guilty, the work probably of a rebel named Matthew Bragg who, according to a royalist newsletter, 'pretended to the law'.

Bragg and the others were the first to be tried in Dorchester, because their not guilty pleas could upset the judges' whole strategy. Dorchester held three hundred more prisoners who could not be allowed to repudiate their confessions. All thirty-five were tried and sentenced in one day, suggesting barely fifteen minutes per prisoner. But evidence was considered since five men were found not guilty, and a sixth was pardoned. The remainder were sentenced to death, and because the next day was Sunday they were appointed to die on Monday 7 September. The speed of the executions was plainly intended to terrify other prisoners into submission, for the two London executioners Jack Ketch and Pascha Rose immediately protested that they could not manage twenty-nine in one day. Only thirteen died that Monday, but they were sufficient to leave Dorchester decorated with heads and human quarters, coated with tar and lined up on poles.[11]

Saturday had also seen sentence passed on sixty-eight other rebels who had pleaded guilty; but that night Jeffreys was tortured by the stone and depressed at his slow progress, and having written to the King wrote again to Sunderland, to beg pardon 'for the incoherence of what I have adventured to give his Majestie the trouble of'. But matters improved rapidly on Monday. With Ketch and Rose doing their work just outside the prison 'this sudden execution frightened all the rest, and they, except for three or four, pleaded guilty hoping to save their lives'.[12] 103 prisoners were arraigned and all pleaded guilty except two, both of whom were acquitted. Next day sixty-nine more were brought to the bar, and all pleaded guilty. A few more pleas of guilty were heard on Wednesday and Thursday, but by then the prison had been sufficiently cleared for the judges to examine those who claimed benefit of the King's pardon. On Wednesday only eight out of seventeen had their claims allowed; more were considered on Thursday and in all twenty-five men received pardons on this ground.

The last two days at Dorchester also saw a number of trials for 'misdemeanours' concerning the rebellion, usually over seditious words, and the charges here contain a little more detail than the stereotyped 'levying war against the King' of the rebels proper. One man was fined £1,000 for publishing Monmouth's Declaration, and another was fined and whipped for saying: 'I am a Monmouth, and a Monmouth I will love.' William Holman had boasted of a captain's place with the rebels; John Sanders had persuaded men to join the rebels; and Henry Allen told the already-discouraged militia that they were mad to carry arms 'for the Duke of Monmouth has the best of it and shall have the best of it'. Two women were fined and whipped for spreading false news — one of the few indications of female involvement, though gossipping about the rebels was probably common, and certainly important.[13]

Two men were tried for giving more elaborate assistance. Mark Warman was an 'Astrologer and Physician' who, according to a fellow prisoner, had been asked to predict the rebellion's outcome. Rashly abandoning equivocation in favour of what the enquirers plainly wanted to hear, he predicted that James would be undone and replaced by the Duke. Dorchester magistrates heard of it and imprisoned him; he escaped with a fine and whipping. No less fortunate to escape with his life was John Tutchin alias Pitts, a young writer of twenty-four, who spread two separate and quite false stories. In one he said that all Hampshire was in arms for Monmouth, and that he had seen rebel forces on a hill outside Christchurch. In the second he claimed that Argyle had been victorious in Scotland and now was marching southwards, so that his much-increased army was within sixty miles of London. Released from prison in 1686 Tutchin married the daughter of John Hickes (the Nonconformist minister in the Lisle case), using the contacts he thus acquired, and his memories from Dorchester prison, to produce a series of circumstantial and often fictitious dying speeches of the condemned rebels. When political conditions grew safer in 1689, he had a hand in a short anonymous pamphlet *The Protestant Martyrs, or, the Bloody Assizes*, which flowered later that year into a full-blown *Western Martyrology*. Reprinted with additions seven times before his death in 1707, this work's detailed but often unreliable biographies of those executed provided early historians of the rebellion with much of their raw material; and in its equally detailed and unreliable accounts of Judge Jeffreys' hectorings, established his reputation as one of the most violent, vindictive, and merciless, of England's hanging judges.[14]

That there was some truth in this picture of Jeffreys is unquestioned. In treason cases judges felt a responsibility toward finding for the King; and Jeffreys was also an ill man during the Assize, suffering recurring attacks of the stone. He was furthermore ambitious: the sixth son of a minor gentleman living near Wrexham, he had become Lord Chief Justice in his mid-thirties and was angling for the position of Lord Keeper when that should become vacant. But in 1685 he simply did not have time for the long abusive speeches 'reported' by Tutchin; his severe stare was part of a judge's professional manner; and he did find a few men not guilty, and allowed pardons to others. Treason, however, required exemplary treatment of the guilty, and in Dorchester having tried 317 men and released 32, he pronounced 61 more sentences of death to add to the 13 men already executed. Because that town was already decorated with the dead, these further sentences were to be carried out in Dorset's other principal towns: 12 at Lyme Regis, 10 at Bridport, 11 apiece at Sherbourne and Poole, 12 shared between Weymouth and Melcombe Regis, and so on. Nowhere were more than a dozen to be executed, evidently the maximum for a full day's work. The most noteworthy prisoners went to Lyme where the rebellion had begun — Sampson Lark the Anabaptist minister, John Kidd the energetic game-keeper of Longleat, John Manders the constable of Crewkerne, Benjamin Temple the Duke's personal physician, and Christopher Bettiscombe, younger son of a Dorset gentry family living near Lyme, and a fringe conspirator in the Rye House affair. Others were officers in the rebel army — Abraham Holmes, William Hewling, Josiah Askew; and Henry Watts who was wealthy enough for the Treasury to confiscate his estate. All were to die within a week or ten days of sentencing.

Jeffreys was the more resolute in ordering these exemplary punishments because two days before he had been informed of Lord Keeper Guildford's death, after a lingering illness. As Chief Justice Jeffreys was directly in line for the office, but he was deeply chagrined at being out of London at this critical time, and wrote to Sunderland begging the latter's patronage 'with more importunity than ordinary'. The Chief Justice thus arrived at Exeter on Saturday 12 September in a mood to display his entire service to the King; and was further encouraged by a letter from Sunderland waiting for him there, assuring him that the King entirely approved his proceedings at Dorchester. Jeffreys' restraint at Exeter on Monday, the Assizes' only day of court-business there, is, therefore, very interesting. Of twenty-six rebels three pleaded not guilty, and were tried, sentenced, and executed according to the familiar formula. The remainder pleaded guilty and received the death sentence, but no date was set for its implementation. Sixteen others were whipped and fined for various misdemeanours — assisting rebels to escape, proclaiming Monmouth King of England, and speaking seditious words.[15] When Jeffreys left for Taunton it was not only most of the prisoners who congratulated themselves on an apparently lucky escape; for the local Justices, constables, and militia had been able to produce only twenty-six rebels for trial, whereas parish by parish returns of those absent during the rebellion totalled over three hundred for Devonshire. Some Devonshire rebels were probably held in Somerset prisons, but two dozen was a paltry haul compared to the three hundred of Dorset.

Jeffreys' restraint continued in Taunton, where he dealt with over five hundred men in two days. With accused and accusers now well-versed in their roles, the judges tried and convicted 385 prisoners on their first day, Friday the eighteenth. Only four pleaded not guilty. They were promptly tried and convicted, one was pardoned, and the other three — a joiner, a tailor, and a yeoman all from near Taunton — were executed on the following Monday. Delayed by no more pleas of not guilty, Jeffreys convicted the remaining 120 prisoners held in Taunton on Saturday. He then sentenced all five hundred to death, but again without specifying any date for execution. When the judges left Taunton only three men were definitely set down to die, and the remainder might hope for their lives. From Taunton he went to Bristol where, in the absence of any rebels to try, the Chief Justice turned his attention to rumours that substantial citizens (including members of the corporation) were kidnapping local destitutes and selling them to West Indian planters. That these merchants were also notorious Whigs probably increased the judge's zeal, and in open court he accused the mayor of kidnapping, took securities from other suspects, and sent papers relating to the case to Sunderland.[16] But in the few hours at his disposal Jeffreys turned up no solid evidence, and though he frightened some guilty men, he punished none.

By this time Jeffreys was plainly in a hurry to return to London, to press his suit over the Lord Keepership. At Wells on Wednesday 23 September, the last day of the Assize, the judges broke all previous records by trying and sentencing 541 prisoners in one day. Only one was delivered for execution, William Mangell, a servant to the rebel Colonel Matthews, who had the temerity to plead not guilty and was duly punished for it. He died on the afternoon of his trial. Even on this day, however, some discrimination was preserved in the hearings. Most of the prisoners were charged with levying war against the King; but nine were accused of 'aiding and assisting the rebels against the King', one of these being Charles Speke, youngest son of the notorious George Speke, and another John Hickes, the cleric for whom Alice Lisle suffered. Others were charged with speaking seditious words, one with assisting a known rebel, and six produced certificates of pardon which the judges allowed.[17] Evidence was thus considered in some cases, and an effort was made to base some charges on the facts available. After this last effort the judges returned to London, Jeffreys arriving on 26 September. Two days later he received the Lord Keepership.

From the government's point of view it had been a very successful Assize. Nearly 1,300 rebels had been tried, eighty-one executed and most of the remainder sentenced to death; all in less than one month. A puzzling feature, however, is the change in the judges' attitude. At Dorchester they had ordered the death of seventy-four men; but at Exeter, Taunton, and Wells only half a dozen were executed, although hundreds were left under sentence of death. This change was not ordered by the King; on the contrary, Sunderland conveyed James's entire satisfaction with the sanguinary proceedings in Dorset. But it was indirectly caused by the King. On 14 September, just as the Assize was finishing at Exeter, Sunderland wrote to Jeffreys outlining the King's intention to sentence a number of rebels to transportation to the West Indies. Planters would pay £10 to £15 per head for white servants, and the King proposed to give between one and two hundred rebels each to a group of courtiers, and some to the Queen. The proposed total came to 1,000, and the judges realized that they could not continue at Taunton and Wells as they had begun at Dorchester. If the King desired so many for transportation, best to execute only those who pleaded not guilty. After receiving this letter Jeffreys's mind was plainly more fixed on transportation than executions. On 19 September he wrote to the King on precisely this subject, entrusting the letter to no less a person than Colonel John Churchill, now returning to the court from the west. The choice of bearer was significant, for in the letter Jeffreys remonstrated as strongly as he dared against the King's decision to give courtiers the money from the transportations, instead of saving it for men 'that served you in the soldiery, and . . . the many distressed families ruined by this late rebellion'. He begged James to listen to his proposals, upon his return to London.[18]

Transportation was thus the major issue, but the judges may also have felt that the Dorchester blood-letting had accomplished the exemplary purpose of the law, and that the relative mercy of transportation could now be allowed. Exemplary justice, followed by no less exemplary mercy, were the twin principles underlying the criminal law's operation. To the general public, and to the condemned men in prison, the execution of only the most obdurate who still pleaded not guilty at Exeter, Taunton, and Wells must have suggested that mercy was on its way, the mercy promised to prisoners who confessed. Public and prisoners were, therefore, the more shocked when Jeffreys returned to London, and almost at once, on 26 September, signed a warrant for the execution of 239 more prisoners, nearly four times as many as had died in Dorset. A few more executions of prominent rebels was regarded as inevitable, but this large number, so suddenly, was quite unexpected. One prisoner commented bitterly that they now saw the truth of the saying 'confess and be hanged'; while others were horrified at the use made of their confessions, feeling 'the guilt of poor men's blood . . . some hanged for a little hay, or letting them have a few victuals, which was not perhaps in their power to hinder', as a Quaker fellow-prisoner wrote.[19] And by waiting until Jeffreys had returned to London, James made it perfectly clear where the order had come from. To the public it appeared that the judges had begun a course of mercy, only to have it countermanded by the King.

The number executed in this second round was less than the 239 ordered. Comparison of Jeffreys's warrant with the number actually reported as executed in various towns by the newsletters suggests that only two-thirds to three-quarters of those named went to the scaffold: a total of around 170. The balance had died in prison. Overall, the figure of 251 given by Tutchin in his *Western Martyrology* seems a reasonably accurate grand total for the Bloody Assizes' victims. Wholly accurate figures cannot be obtained, because the executions dragged on into October and November 1685, and were by then only reported occasionally in the press.[20] These lingering executions, caused by the impossibility of dealing at once with the number of victims, were one feature of the Assize which produced revulsion. Another was the way the hangings covered all the major towns and villages of Somerset: apart from the nineteen men who were to die in Taunton, the victims were to hang in batches of three to twelve in thirty-seven different localities. Devon, too, was not forgotten, for the remains of ten rebels were to be divided — literally — between twelve towns and villages there which had sympathized with the rebellion. Executions were one thing to the hardened London crowd at Tyburn; quite different to small rural settlements, which had heard of such things only as the distant consequence of an Assize.

A bureaucratic horror, familiar to the twentieth century, informs the preparations made for these executions. The corporation of Bath was required to erect a gallows in the most public place of the town. Halters were needed, and 'sufficient firewood' to burn the bowels of four traitors — not easy to calculate. They would also need a 'furnace or cauldron' to boil the heads and quarters, half a peck of salt per man, and some tar. Spears and poles would be needed to set up the remains. Four oxen and a wagon were needed to carry the prisoners to their execution. Constables and other officers, together with a guard of forty men, should assemble at eight a.m. on the day specified to assist the sheriff. A macabre postscript shows that the writer nearly forgot that an axe and cleaver would be required . . . Such preparations were expensive. The total cost of executing twelve men at Weymouth was £16.4s.8d., or twenty-seven shillings per man. Even stakes for the quarters were itemized: the mayor of Lyme Regis submitted a bill of 1/6d. to replace a post bearing some remains, which had fallen down. Several Somerset towns economized by spreading quarters over 'gates, bridges, and crossways'.[21]

Where ten or twelve prisoners were to die, a long and bloody day was in prospect for the town. These were not the relatively neat hangings practised on criminals at Tyburn. Each rebel was first hanged (or probably choked half insensible); then disembowelled and the entrails thrown into a fire; the head cut off and the torso divided; the remains boiled in a brine solution, before being coated with hot tar; and finally set up for public viewing. Each man required at least half an hour's labour; and all the time the next victims were watching from their wagon. The fires, the blood, the stench of burning entrails, repeated again and again for each man, repeated in two score towns and hamlets, produced a mixture of horror and disgust. One witness found it revolting to force 'poor men to hale about Men's Quarters like Horse Flesh or Carrion'. At times revulsion was openly shown: the festering remains were sometimes taken down and buried, though the penalty was a whipping if caught. As the executions continued a series of escapes took place from Ilchester prison; first sixty men, and then when twenty-three of these were recaptured they got out again. Even the 'respectable' classes showed some dismay. The sheriff of Somerset allowed a decent burial in St. Mary's churchyard to eight of these executed at Taunton; and among the spectators was the courtier Sir Charles Lytletton, a prey to very mixed feelings. On the one hand the rebels 'shewd no shew of repentance, as if they died in an ill cause, but justified theyr treason and gloried in it'; on the other 'we shall heare more of [this] when ye Parliament meetes . . . of the execution of so many of ye traitors here . . . and all quarted, and more every day in other parts of ye country . . . near three hundred; and most of theyr quarters are, and will be, set up in ye towns and highways so that ye country looks already like a shambles'.[22] Even the King's most loyal supporters felt that the affair had got out of hand. Such mass executions had not been seen in England since the 1550s, not even during the Civil War; and though the parallel was much too dangerous openly to be drawn, the fires and stench may well have stirred memories drawn from the vivid pages of John Foxe's account of Protestant sufferings under an earlier Catholic monarch, for *Acts and Monuments of the Christian Reformation* was the second most popular book in England, after the

Bible. The 'second round' of executions in 1685 must rank as the earliest of James II's disastrous series of miscalculations.

Severity, and failures of judgement, also marked James's attitude to the transportees. They were given to nine courtiers to be sold, (some of them Catholics such as the Queen and the west-countryman Nipho), despite Jeffreys's pleas that those who had borne the heat of the day should have the profits. The King missed an opportunity to reward the deserving, and create even a small vested interest in the Assize, outside of the court. As a punishment for rebellion, transportation was well established in 1685; in Cromwell's time seventy of Penruddock's followers had received this sentence, and more recently so had 270 of the Scots defeated by Monmouth at Bothwell Brig. But the scale of James II's sentences was new to England, for 850 men received the ten year sentence to obligatory labour in the West Indies. Given the white death-rate it was to their family a death sentence, and only a slightly delayed one to the prisoners. Five years was the normal period of forced labour for convicts and rebels sent to the West Indies, but James considered it insufficient, and on his orders colonial legislatures doubled it.[23] The number transported also meant that the King pardoned very few of the convicted rebels. Out of 1,300 men held at the beginning of the Assize, around 350 were executed, died of illness, or had certificates of pardon allowed; leaving some 950. Of these at least 850 were marked for transportation. James set free very few of the convicted rebels.

Greed led to the transportation of so many, and greed coloured most aspects of the prisoners' treatment. Even children were not exempt. When he entered Taunton, Monmouth had been presented with a set of colours, by some girls from a local school. They were young and had plainly acted under adult direction, and Jeffreys did not bother with them at the Assize. But the parents of some were wealthy — a paper drawn up for the government described the parents of four as 'rich' or 'very rich', and noted that others had fathers who had been colonels or captains with Monmouth and were, therefore, perhaps propertied. A royal pardon was thus decreed necessary for their misdemeanors, and James gave to the Queen's Maids of Honour the right to set and collect that pardon's price. The figure was put at £7,000, and until it was paid the 'Maids of Taunton' remained in prison (where at least one died), threatened by a suit of outlawry. After months of brutal haggling the Maids of Honour accepted a price based on £50 to £100 per girl, less than half their original demand.[24]

Those shipping the convicts could also make extra money. Bribes to release the prisoners were too dangerous to risk making in England, but for a price a rebel's friends or family could be assured that he would step ashore in the West Indies a free man: though penniless, he would not be bought or sold. Thus for £65, Azariah Pinney's Nonconformist father gave his black sheep the freedom which eventually built up another Pinney fortune, on Nevis. But others were swindled: the family of the surgeon Henry Pitman paid £60, but he was sold into servitude like the rest. There were also hopes of money from the confiscated estates of rebels, and on their return to London the judges compiled for the Treasury a list of prisoners convicted. Although Exchequer records for the period are incomplete, it is clear that very little was collected. Rents from 'forfeited lands' in 1685-86 came to only £376 and 'forfeitures for treason' were nil, whereas income from 'Lord Grey's lands' amounted to £5,060. In 1687-88 nothing came from 'forfeited lands', and 'forfeitures for treason' rose to only £1,400, just £100 more than Grey's lands over the same period. The estate of a Taunton rebel John Sachell realized £320, but more typical was Mallachy Mallach's in Devon, merely £27. Eight Somerset rebels supplied only £400 together. This hardly paid the costs of finding and processing the properties.[25]

Between executions and transportations, deaths in prison and deaths on shipboard, fines, blackmail and forfeitures, Monmouth's rebels had been severely dealt with by James II; and the survivors had good reason to rejoice at his overthrow in 1688. Yet for many of those serving their ten years' exile in the West Indies, the Glorious Revolution was the prelude to further brutal treatment, this time at the hands of their 'allies'. William III's accession changed the transportees from traitors into martyrs for the Whig cause. In July 1689 the Lords of Trade and Plantations agreed that new instructions were needed from the King concerning these exiles, and on the following 9 January laws passed in Barbados, Jamaica, and the Leeward Islands concerning them were disallowed. A group of Somerset and Devon gentlemen now took up the rebels' cause, petitioning the King for a full pardon to enable the convicts to return to England as free men, and paying over £30 in fees. The pardon was granted in February 1690, but the West Indies governors protested as soon as they heard of it. The loss of these transportees would, it seemed, jeopardize English security in the Caribbean and inflict heavy costs on their masters. After careful consideration, William's government announced a compromise. The convicts were freed from servitude; but could not leave the islands without their Governor's permission.[26] They were free men . . . but not free to depart.

The more quick-witted of them had already left in 1688, working their way to North America or simply stealing boats and putting to sea. Some eventually reached England, like the surgeon Henry Pitman, after adventures worthy of a Robinson Crusoe involving desert islands, castaways and pirates.[27] But none of Pitman's companions survived their attempt to escape. Most of the 850 transportees lived and died in exile. The few who returned worried for a time over their uncertain legal status, before they found that no one was bothered with them. In the England of the 1690s, they were ghosts from a very distant past.

Footnotes: Chapter Eight

1. *CSPD 1685*, p.303; *An Account of what passed at the Execution of the late Duke of Monmouth*, Bodl.Lib.Rawlinson MSS.A139, f.284.

2. Rawl.MSS.A139, ff.1-4; Harl.MSS.7006, ff.197-8.

3. Bodl.Lib., Rawl.MSS.A139, ff.8, 284-5; Rawl.MSS.D 316, f.149; *CSPD 1685*, pp.261, 268.

4. F.Inderwick, *Side-lights on the Stuarts*, London 1891, pp.405-6, 427, (the Appendix pp.398-427 prints the Gaol Book for the Western Assize 1685); G.Roberts, *The Life of James Duke of Monmouth*, London 1844, 2 vols., ii, 166, 167; *HMC*, 14th Report App.V, Kenyon MSS., p.183.

5. J.Whiting, *Persecution Exposed in some Memoirs*, London 1715, p.144; SRO,DD/PH 211, pp.242-7; J.Coade, *A Memorandum of the Wonderful Providences of God*, London 1849, pp.6-10.

6. *CSPD 1685*, pp.372, 373; J.Whiting, *Persecution Exposed*, p.157.

7. SRO, DD/PH 211, p.87; DD/SF 40/560; J.Whiting, *Persecution Exposed*, p.145.

8. H.Pitman, *A Relation of the Great Sufferings . . . of Henry Pitman*, London 1689, pp.336-7; J.Whiting, *Persecution Exposed*, p.153; S.Schofield, *Jeffreys of the Bloody Assizes*, London 1937, p.183.

9. Harl.MSS.6845, f.288v.

10. The fullest guide to the Assize is J.Muddiman, *The Bloody Assizes*, London 1929, esp.pp.24-36. See also F.Inderwick, *Side-lights on the Stuarts*, and S.Schofield, *Jeffreys*.

11. J.Muddiman, *Bloody Assizes*, pp.29, 195-7; F.Inderwick, *Side-lights* pp.399-400.

12. *CSPD 1685*, p.320; H.Pitman, *A Relation*, p.337.

13. F.Inderwick, *Side-lights*, pp.405-6.

14. John Tutchin's narrative, in 'The Western Martyrology' printed in J.Muddiman *Bloody Assizes*, pp.142-3; F.Inderwick, *Side-lights*, p.405; J.Muddiman, *Bloody Assizes*, pp.5-10.

15. *CSPD 1685*, p.323; J.Muddiman, *Bloody Assizes*, p.187; F.Inderwick *Side-lights*, pp.406-7.

16. S.Schofield, *Jeffreys*, pp.191-2.

17. F.Inderwick, *Side-lights*, pp.415-24.

18. *CSPD 1685*, pp.329, 332-3.

19. Add.MSS.34516, ff.21-4; H.Pitman, *A Relation*, p.337; J.Whiting *Persecution Exposed*, p.153.

20. J.Muddiman, *Bloody Assizes*, p.41.

21. J.Muddiman, *Bloody Assizes*, pp.39-40; W.B.Barrett, 'The Rebels in the Duke of Monmouth's Rebellion', *Dorset Natural History and Antiquarian Society*, V, p.109.

22. J.Whiting, *Persecution Exposed*, p.153; F.Inderwick, *Side-lights*, p.427; J.Muddiman, *Bloody Assizes*, p.41; 'Correspondence of the Family of Hatton', ed. E.M.Thompson, *Camden Soc.* 22 1878, p.60.

23. A.Burns, *A History of the British West Indies*, London 1965, p.325 and n.

24. G.Roberts, *Life of Monmouth*, ii, 249; Harl.MSS.7006, f.195.

25. R.Pares, *A West Indian Fortune*, London 1950, p.10; H.Pitman, *A Relation*, p.338; *Calendar of Treasury Books 1685*, Vol.VII, pp.xxvi-xxx, Nos. 522, 1046, 1544-5, 1630.

26. *Calendar of Colonial Papers 1689-92*, Nos. 1, 193, 222, 698-700; SRO, DD/SF 243/3874.

27. J.Coad, *A Memorandum*, p.141; H.Pitman, *A Relation*, pp.350-67.

CHAPTER NINE

The Rebels

Two points are remarkable about the rebel army of 1685. The first is the speed of its creation. Monmouth landed with eighty-two men; ten days later he had nearly three thousand. The second is its composition. The rebels were almost entirely common people: gentry, and the upper classes generally, took no part in the rising. Royalist spectators made this latter point with pleasure and relief; Monmouth observed it with near-despair; his followers reacted to it with bitterness against the landowning class. Only three or four of the names in the Assize lists for death or transportation are described as gent. or esquire, and Treasury officials seeking estates of convicted rebels to confiscate could find only half a dozen worth £50 or more, and most were not worth the trouble to collect.[1] This absence of propertied rebels partly explains the decision to sentence so many prisoners to transportation, for the £10 per head they brought; and it helps account, too, for the survival of Ford Lord Grey, whose estate was so comprehensively entailed that it was easier to collect a fine from him than to attempt confiscation; and for the blackmail suffered by Edmund Prideaux of Ford Abbey, who, though free from complicity in the rebellion, chose to buy his accusers off rather than try to prove his innocence to Jeffreys.

The loyalty felt by these commoners for Monmouth was shown in other ways besides the speed with which they flocked to his banner. There were few desertions from the army, even though a royal pardon had been proclaimed for rebels who gave themselves up, and even though the weather turned desperately cold and wet, and the first skirmish at Norton St. Philip badly frightened this collection of civilians. On the day before Sedgemoor Monmouth gave his troops permission to visit families and friends in Bridgewater and Taunton; and virtually all returned when desertion would have been easy. At Sedgemoor itself his men fought bravely for several hours, well after the Duke had given up hope. But it was not a very big army. Immediately after the rebellion parish constables in Somerset, and the adjoining portions of Devon and Dorset, were ordered to report the names of all men absent from home during the period of the rebellion. The returns were consolidated into a single list containing 2,691 names, the 'Constables' List', now held in the British Library.[2] It is by far the longest list of participants in the rebellion, for the only other record is the Assize listings of those sentenced to death, transportation or given a pardon, totalling just 1,300 names. It is also by far the more useful list, because it gives parish of residence for all those named and the occupations of 551, whereas the Assize lists contain name only, with no indication of residence or trade. The 'Constables' List' is thus the key document for analysis of the rebels, and its completeness and accuracy must be established.

Though they were ordered simply to record those absent from home, the parish constables knew perfectly well what the list was for, many of them heading their return 'Out in the Rebellion', or 'went to Monmouth'. It is thus unlikely that they would have recorded villagers known to have been away on legitimate business. Moreover, the period of absence had to coincide closely with the duration of the rebellion, five weeks between 12 June and 6 July. On the other hand, it would have been very dangerous not to record villagers who had joined the rebels and not returned, for no one knew who had been captured and an incomplete return might thus be exposed. It would have been dangerous, too, to try to cover up for villagers who had returned from the rebellion, for one word from an informer to the Justice of the Peace, the militia, or the regular army officers watching the operation could lead to a charge of misprision of treason. The presence after Sedgemoor of an occupying army, the horrifying stories of the battle, and the appalling sight of the wounded, made constables well aware of the gravity of their situation. Fear or favour would undoubtedly have led to some concealments, but it is unlikely that there were very many. There may have been some confusion over the small number who had returned home before Sedgemoor to claim benefit of the King's pardon; and the even smaller number who, like nineteen men at Lyme Regis, joined the rebels but then failed to march out with them. No parishes in Wiltshire were ordered to list absentees, and this probably also saved a score or two of men. But overall the Constables' List can be accepted as a reasonably full and fair enumeration of the rebels, although to allow for the omissions which undoubtedly existed, the total should probably be raised to 3,000.

Absence from home during the rebellion is of course simply a presumption of participation, though a strong one; but it should be noted that a similar presumption of guilt must be made for many appearing in the Assize lists as 'convicted rebels'. For almost all of those convicted, no evidence was offered in court of their participation beyond a confession, extracted through the hope of a pardon held out to frightened men for the most part ignorant of their rights at law. Several of those transported protested their total innocence most vigorously. In real terms the 'Judges' List', the record of sentences meted out at the Assize, is based upon evidence no firmer than the Constables' List, besides being much less informative. The Constables' List is, therefore, the primary source for analysis of the rebels. It reveals not only their numbers and the districts they came from, but provides a sample of occupations, and can be used to determine the social standing of many of the insurgents. Inferences can be drawn concerning their motives in joining the rebellion, and suggestions made as to why they were prepared to fight when so many of their neighbours were evidently not inclined to.

The army the List discloses is considerably smaller than the five thousand usually given as its size. Early royalist estimates in fact put the figure at ten thousand, but reports from Feversham's camp halved this and most historians have accepted the revised royalist estimate. The true figure of barely three thousand is very close to the number of royalist troops engaged, suggesting that at Sedgemoor the Duke's raw volunteers performed very well. A figure of three thousand is also more consistent with other evidence about the army than anything larger. Monmouth did not have the equipment for a big force. He landed with very little money or supplies; and only partly made up the deficiency by material captured from the militia, given to him, or taken from the shops and houses of traders and gentlemen. Several hundred of his men were armed only with improvised pikes made from scythe blades attached to long poles and examples of these, captured at Sedgemoor, can be seen in the Tower of London. His supply train, too, was adequate only for a small army: a contemporary estimate required 1,200 wagons for an army of 15,000 men, or one wagon for every 12.5 soldiers.[3] Monmouth possessed just forty wagons: for three thousand men this meant a ratio of one wagon for every seventy-five men. Carrying only ammunition and spare equipment, and depending for food and shelter upon the towns they stayed in, this was still a perilously slight train even for an army of three thousand. The Duke could not afford the time to raise more troops, and the few days he spent collecting and training volunteers cost him his already slim chance of taking Bristol by surprise and acquiring the base he needed in the west. He did not have enough experienced officers to train a large army; and indeed he did not need a very large one, for James II could at first assemble little more than two thousand men. Monmouth's intention in any case was not to fight his way to London, but to seize the Crown by popular acclaim. His relatively small army, therefore, does not reflect upon the Duke's popularity but arises from limitations upon time and equipment, and from his intended strategy.

The army was drawn from a very clearly defined area of Somerset, Dorset and Devon, as the map based upon the Constables' List shows (page 250). The rebels came from two hundred parishes, almost all of them lying within a twenty mile belt extending northwards from Lyme Regis to Bridgewater, with a further and narrower extension eastwards from Bridgewater to Glastonbury and Frome. Three-quarters of the rebels came from Somerset, Devon and Dorset being affected only at their extremities where they border Somerset; and though almost the same number of parishes was affected in Devon as in Dorset (23 and 25 respectively), Devon contributed twice as many rebels as Dorset, 489 compared to 261. When the exceptionally large Lyme Regis contingent (ninety-five men) is removed from Dorset the small part played by that county is further emphasized; but with only 19 per cent and 9 per cent of the rebels respectively both Devon and Dorset were considerably less important than Somerset.

Even within Somerset, however, two-thirds of the county was unaffected by the rebellion; the west, the north, and most of the south-east contributing virtually no volunteers. Diverse reasons — economic and social, religious and political — explain why some areas strongly supported the rebellion whereas others failed to participate at all, but two important fortuitous factors should first be noted. The first was the route and timing of the Duke's march. Most support for Monmouth is found in a belt some ten miles wide, extending on either side of his line of march from Lyme Regis to Taunton, then fading out from Bridgewater onwards. This ten mile boundary is plainly the outer limit from which a man could hear of the rebellion, and walk in with time to catch up to the army. Monmouth took ten days to cover the twenty-eight miles between Lyme Regis and Taunton, to give time for volunteers to come in and be organized; but once past Bridgewater the pace quickened, initially to try to surprise Bristol, and then to stay ahead of Feversham's troops. Recruiting was also heaviest between Lyme Regis and Taunton because enthusiasm for the rebellion was at its height in the first few days, when the weather was fine, the King's regulars had not yet arrived, and the strength of the government's response was still unclear. But then professional troops replaced the militia, Bristol was reinforced and held, fighting began at Norton St.

Philip, and heavy rain began to fall. Recruiting slackened, and in the circumstances the 150 men who enlisted in and about Frome showed remarkable faith in the enterprise.

The second fortuitous factor affecting distribution of support, particularly in the rebellion's early stage, was the presence or absence in any area of royalist troops. A failure when confronting the rebel army, the militia of Somerset, Dorset and Devon nevertheless performed a valuable service by establishing road blocks, to stop travellers and would-be volunteers from approaching the rebels. Their activity partly explains Monmouth's very limited support in northern and eastern Somerset, while the Devonshire forces under the Duke of Albemarle were responsible for the sharpness of the line marking the edge of Monmouth's support here. And although some of the Dorset militia were surprised early in the rebellion and ousted by the rebels at Charmouth, their presence so close to Lyme Regis tended to check volunteers in Dorset. The case of Frome, however, shows that a large and determined pocket of support could for a time overcome the militia's influence.

Returning to the map, several factors explain the lack of support for the rebellion in the west, north, and south-east of Somerset. In part these areas were simply too distant from the Duke's line of march to participate. In the west and much of the north isolation, and a thin, scattered, population are also relevant points. South-eastern Somerset, however, was neither isolated nor thinly populated; and the total lack of supporters here is to be explained (apart from their distance from the action) by the influence of the energetic Tory Lord FitzHarding who was resident here; and by local issues, such as the town of Bruton's courting of royalist favour to win the grant of a Quarter Session. It is noteworthy, too, that the Clubmen of south-eastern Somerset in the 1640s had shared the slightly pro-royalist sentiments of their neighbours in Wiltshire; whereas in the cloth and dairying area about Frome Clubmen had inclined toward Parliament during the Civil War, and been on the fringes of the anti-court Western forest riots of the 1630s.[4] Past allegiances also partly explain another area of limited support for Monmouth, the central levels of Somerset, where the Clubmen during the 1640s had been well organized and decidedly neutralist in their attitudes. Here, however, it may be doubted whether the map fully records the region's sympathy for the rebellion. Both Andrew Paschall (a local clergyman) and Nathaniel Wade (Monmouth's treasurer and one of his officers) believed that the rebels recruited quite strongly here on their second passage through the

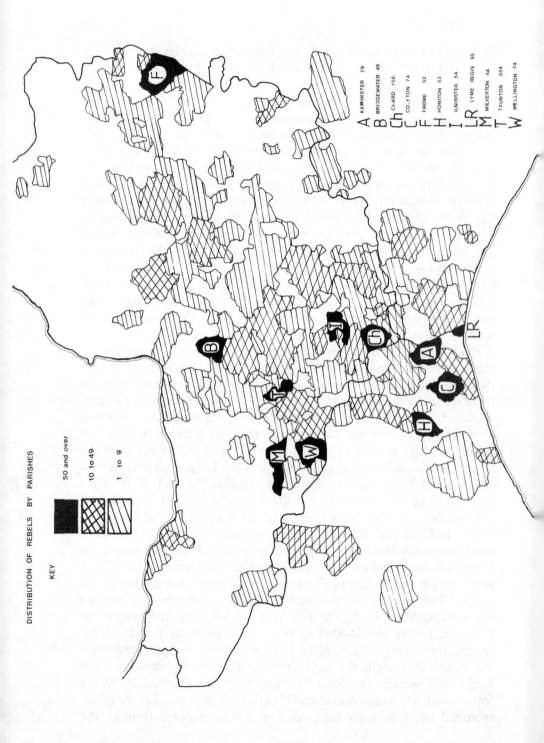

DISTRIBUTION OF REBELS BY PARISHES

KEY

■ 50 and over

▨ 10 to 49

▨ 1 to 9

A   AXMINSTER   79
B   BRIDGEWATER   49
Ch CHARD   156
C   COLYTON   74
F   FROME   52
H   HONITON   53
I   ILMINSTER   54
LR LYME REGIS   95
M   MILVERTON   54
T   TAUNTON   354
W   WELLINGTON   74

marshes; and the few rebels named in the Constables' List would have appeared rather ridiculous placed in the van of the rebel army to lead it into Bridgewater, as Paschall asserts they were. The moorland parishes were the one area of Somerset where some cover-up for one's neighbours might be expected, and rebel strength here was probably minimized in the returns.

Within the major belt of support, the map shows that recruiting was very uneven, with many parishes sending just two or three men, and some none at all. Although southern Somerset and the adjoining portions of Devon and Dorset were in general well populated, the area contained a number of isolated and thinly populated hill or moorland parishes, where news of the revolt would be tardy in reaching a small and dispersed population. Just south of Taunton, weakly rebellious parishes are found in the hidden slopes of the Neroche Forest and the Blackdown Hills. In Devon the well-populated and rebellious towns of Colyton, Honiton, and Axminster, lie in river valleys separated by short, steep, and thinly populated hills which gave scant support to Monmouth; while in Dorset the under-populated and unrebellious rise of the Downs divided the numerous rebels of Lyme Regis, Wootton Fitzpaine, and Marshwood, from their no less fervent comrades in Axminster, Chard and Thorncombe. Gaps in the map of rebel support became explicable when contour lines are drawn in over parish boundaries. Local politics could also sharply limit support. Sir William Portman's influence was strong in the small parish of Orchard Portman just south of Taunton and probably explains its weak response; while at Winsham a vicious local feud between Anglicans and Dissenters possibly tarnished the Protestant Duke's appeal.[5]

More significant than the small number of parishes in south Somerset which gave no support at all, is the much larger number who sent only a handful of men to the rebellion. Of the two hundred parishes from which men volunteered, 139 or 69 per cent contributed less than ten men apiece, the average for these parishes being 3.6 each. This surprisingly large penumbra of thin support may to some extent by explained by distance. About thirty of these parishes were many miles distant from the main area of support — Crediton in Devon; Dulverton and Minehead, Stogumber Whitchurch and Sherborne in Somerset; Marnhull and Powerstock in Dorset. Living up to forty miles from the rebels' line of march, only very determined men from these parishes would catch up with the army. Alternatively, a few men from these parishes may have been visiting a town closer to the rebels' route when the Duke came by and they volunteered, but in either case only a handful could be involved. This explanation may hold good for another forty or more 'thin-support' parishes on the edge of the 'ten mile boundary', where a considerable effort was needed to join up; but there remain some sixty parishes well within walking distance of the rebels' march, where only three or four men volunteered. Though some of these parishes were thinly populated — in the hills south of Taunton, in the Devon and Dorset uplands, or in the marshes between Taunton and Glastonbury — most were fertile, accessible, and well-populated, suggesting that the agricultural population as a whole took little part in the rebellion. With men joining in threes and fours from these parishes, very personal factors may have been most influential, village misfits seeing in the rebel army an answer to their problems, although some rebels may also have been farm labourers or younger sons with no prospects of future improvement.

The greater part by far of the rebels, however, came not from small rural parishes but from a handful of towns: 1685 was an urban, or more precisely, a small-town rebellion. Eleven towns account for 40 per cent of the Duke's army, and if twenty-two smaller centres are included, the proportion rises to over two-thirds. Half of the army came from seventeen towns and large villages: Taunton, Bridgewater, and Chard; Frome, Ilminster, and Lyme Regis; Axminster and Axmouth, Honiton and Colyton; Glastonbury, Milverton, and Wellington; Kingsbury and Pitminster, Thorncombe and Crewkerne. In some areas Monmouth recruited up to one-third of a town's adult males — 95 of Lyme Regis' 350 men, 354 of Taunton's 1,000; while the 156 recruits in Chard, 75 from Axminster, and 74 apiece from Wellington and Colyton, made up one-quarter of the men-folk of these modest towns. The Duke received volunteers from every town and village of note in a belt twenty miles wide and forty-five miles deep between Lyme Regis and Bridgewater, and that within a day or two of the rebels' arrival in the area.

The rebellion was based upon towns in part because these were the only large centres of population where Monmouth paused long enough to recruit; but the numbers he collected and the speed with which volunteers arrived, reveal the deep and spontaneous enthusiasm which existed in them, early in the rebellion. His poor recruiting in the towns visited after Bridgewater — 13 from Wells, 5 from Shepton Mallet, 3 from Bath — shows the caution created by the arrival of the King's army; although the exceptional numbers at Frome prove that a well-populated cloth-working centre, with a radical past, could give enthusiastic support well into the rebellion's latter stage. Most of the towns where Monmouth collected volunteers were distinguished — as

Chapter One showed — by considerable and growing poverty, and by a large and strained cloth industry; but these factors did not automatically lead to heavy support for the rebellion, as witness Wells and Shepton Mallet. The case of Lyme Regis further shows that the presence of a cloth industry was not always essential for a town to support the rebellion. Active for Parliament in the 1640s, containing many Exclusionists in the 1680s, and chosen by the Duke as the place for his landing and appeal to the nation to depose James II, Lyme shows the importance of an active political history. Broadly speaking, however, the concentration of support for Monmouth in southern Somerset reflects the number of towns and greater density of population in that area, and its concentration of cloth workers. It was also a region with many dissenting congregations; and with Taunton in the lead, it was deeply stirred by the Popish Plot and Exclusion Crisis. But external factors, such as the speed of the rebels' march and the presence of militia forces, to some extent exaggerate the relative rebelliousness of this region by limiting the opportunities for men in other districts — and counties — to join the Duke.

With so many rebels coming from towns, and such small groups of them coming forward from rural parishes, the proportion of farmers and farmworkers in the Duke's army might be expected to be low. Two samples of rebels' occupations confirm that it was. The Constables' List supplies callings for 551 men, coming from nineteen towns and villages. Of these only 10 per cent were yeomen, husbandmen, or labourers, the remainder being craftsmen and clothworkers. As it stands, however, this sample unduly minimizes the agricultural wing of the rebels, because four-fifths of the 557 came from the three towns — Taunton, Lyme Regis, and Frome — where the proportion of farmers and farmworkers was likely to be low. Out of the nineteen centres supplying the rebels in this sample however, twelve wholly rural parishes can be identified centred upon a village or a very small market town, where the proportion of inhabitants living by agriculture would be closer to the county average, and indeed somewhat above it. Scattered across south-eastern, central, and western Somerset, these twelve parishes provide the occupations of sixty-two rebels. Agriculturalists prove numerous but scarcely predominant, with 37 per cent of the Duke's volunteers; and clothworkers (34 per cent) and craftsmen (24 per cent) make up most of the balance.

A second occupational sample suggests a rather lower figure for farmers and their labourers. One ship load of convicted rebels sent to the West Indies had their trades recorded.[6] These sixty-seven men were a truly random sample of the insurgents, because the ship-loads were made up arbitrarily from the hundreds of prisoners held in west country prisons, by any one of the half dozen agents responsible for them. Thoroughly mixed up in their flight from the battlefield, mixed up once again in the prisons where they were held for Jeffreys to judge them, taken out quickly and in large numbers to be sent to the ports where ships were waiting, there can be no systematic bias in this sample. On board the *Jamaica Rose*, one of the agents Mr. John Rose collected a group of exiles of which just 24 per cent were described as 'plowmen' (one of them in fact a 'husbandman'). The remainder were clothmakers and craftsmen.

These two samples set an upper limit of one-quarter to one-third for the proportion of farmers and farm labourers in the rebel army, and even this is very probably too high. The sample from the twelve wholly rural parishes over-weights the rural element in the rebel army, since two-thirds of the insurgents came from the region's middling and smaller towns. The very small numbers coming from each rural parish must also be borne in mind: an average of just over five apiece from the twelve rural parishes. Overall, the rural parishes supplied scarcely one-third of the total rebel force; and according to our rural occupational sample only one-third of these in turn were agriculturalists, the remainder being craftsmen or clothworkers. Some of the men from the towns could of course have been farmers or farm workers, but not enough to offset their heavy under-representation in the villages. The conclusion must be that agriculturalists made up scarcely 20 per cent of the rebel army.

Such a low proportion implies of course that they were most disproportionately under-represented in the rebel army. One half of the Somerset inventories for 1681 to 1685 were of farmers or farm labourers, and it would be difficult to conclude that they and their families constituted less than one half of the county's total population. This poor showing by the agricultural community in 1685 had several causes. Distance from the rebellion, isolation, and a thin population have already been mentioned as factors affecting some areas. But even very well-populated parishes close to Monmouth's line of march contributed few men, and in these cases their social structure is relevant. The county had a high proportion of middling and smaller farmers working their own land, and as their inventories show, enjoying a modest prosperity. But their standard of living depended upon constant labour: in contrast to craft and cloth work which were afflicted with frequent spells of idleness and semi-employment, there was always work to be done on the family-sized farm. And here a fortuitous element in the rebellion is once again important: its timing. The accidents which led to Monmouth's appearance at Lyme Regis as late as 12 June were considered in Chapter Five. The consequent duration of the rebellion, from mid-June to early July, coincided with the hay harvest when few farmers could take any time off. Livestock were essential to Somerset's predominantly mixed farming, more valuable on most holdings than the grain; and so although small farmers may have sympathized with the cause, it was simply the case that most could not afford to join the rebellion when it occurred.

This was the case, too, for many agricultural labourers, who depended upon the long hours of work and good wages of harvest time — hay as well as corn — to see them through the rest of the year. In any case, the strength of yeoman and husbandman farming in Somerset, and the importance of mixed farming, probably meant that the proportion of agricultural labourers in the population here was lower than in more arable counties, and that the pool of rural discontent consequently was less extensive for the rebels to draw on. The number of 'plowmen' on the *Jamaica Merchant* (all but one of the agricultural contingent) perhaps implies that most agricultural rebels were wage-earners rather than independent farmers; and the pattern of four or five men coming from each rural parish is consistent with a handful of discontented day labourers in each village seeing better prospects in a rebellion — or at least a change in employment.

For both farmers and labourers, however, it is clear that in the Somerset of the 1680s none of the triad of forces which might radicalize a rural community was particularly strong. There had been a decade of good harvest since the partial failures of 1673-74. At Exeter wheat prices averaged 32 shillings per Winchester quarter between 1675 and 1695, compared to the 54/- and 52/- of 1673-74. Only twice in these twenty years did prices reach 40/- (in 1677 and 1681), and in the period 1682-84 they varied between 36/- and 38/-. On the other side of Somerset at Bristol, prices set at the Assize of Bread suggest only a little more hardship. Between 1677 and 1685, prices set every two to three months averaged 4/8d per bushel, though they reached 5/-, 5/1d, and 5/3d in the years 1682-84.[7] Even so, the good harvest reflected in these prices meant comfort to the small family farmer, and although the rebellion in 1685 took place before the corn harvest, a fine summer was so obviously leading to a bumper crop that few farmers were feeling dissatisfied.

Enclosure too was not a relevant issue. Somerset was an 'early enclosed' county with a relatively small amount of common land. Three areas had experienced anti-enclosure riots in the seventeenth century — the eastern woodlands, the central levels, and the southern Forest of Neroche — but most disturbances had occurred at the beginning or in the middle of the century, and in Somerset during the 1680s enclosure was of no importance except in the central marshes. Rent levels too caused no serious dissatisfaction, though there is less certainty here. Landlords nationally complained in the 1660s and 1670s of static or falling rents, and there is no evidence in Somerset that the good harvests and agricultural prosperity of the 1670s and 1680s led to any increases in rent except in the case of Lord Weymouth, newly possessed of the Longleat estate. This case apart, family papers and Quarter Sessions records reveal no evidence of, or reaction to, a drive to increase rents. Surveys of manors in Wellington and West Buckland between 1649 and 1676 show no appreciable increase, and nor do surveys of the parish of Culmstock between 1663 and 1666. The same is true for manors in South Brent, Coombe Pyne, Colyton and Axminster, to judge from surveys made in the years after 1660. In 1667 an agent of the Earl of Rochester remarked on 'how much fines could have been raised' on Somerset land owned by his master, but no action followed.[8] The samples are limited, and rents per acre not easy to relate from one estate to another, but there is no clear evidence that Somerset landowners were trying to reverse the general post-Restoration trend of steady rent levels, and likewise no widespread evidence of discontent over rent in the rural community.

Craftsmen participated in the rebellion in numbers more proportionate to their county-wide strength, and although they may have been slightly under-represented the imbalance was far less than for agriculturalists. Of the 551 men whose occupations were given on the Constables' List, 30 per cent were craftsmen, with another 8 per cent in the retail trades, or professions. The sample is best broken down into its component elements, however, because one town (Lyme Regis) supplied almost nothing but craftsmen, having no cloth industry nor rural hinterland to speak of. Taunton provided the largest single total of occupations, 272 of the 354 rebels here having their callings listed. Of that 272, 61 or 22 per cent were craftsmen. In Frome and its adjoining four parishes, one-sixth of the 129 trades listed were craftsmen; and in the twelve rural parishes referred to earlier the figure was 19 per cent. Of the random sample on the *Jamaica Merchant*, 23 per cent were craftsmen. In rural areas, therefore, craftsmen amounted to one-fifth of the rebels; in towns with a substantial cloth industry they might rise to nearly one quarter; and only in towns containing no cloth industry would they rise over these proportions; and in the area of Somerset, Dorset, and Devon, whence the rebels drew their strength, there were few such towns of any size. The percentage on the *Jamaica Merchant* is probably close to the craftsmen's overall strength in the rebellion.

As a group craftsmen were not, in the mid-1680s, subject to any particularly strong economic pressures disposing them to rebellion. The decade of good harvests before 1685 had given them low food prices, and put money in the pockets of farmers and gentry who bought their products. In the later seventeenth century the wages rated for craftsmen by JPs were 50 per cent to 100 per cent higher than those for weavers and combers.[9] Their inventories show craftsmen to have been generally more prosperous than weavers, and in some cases they approached the standard of living of small farmers. Against this must be set the political uncertainty of the Popish Plot and Exclusion, which led to economic recession; and with consequent heavy unemployment among clothworkers it is difficult to believe that craftsmen were not also affected. Since so many of the craftsmen joining the rebellion lived in towns they were exposed to the flow of talk and rumour spread by travellers, pamphlets, and (in some cases) by habitués of coffee shops, and political and religious motives for supporting Monmouth may consequently have been stronger than feelings of economic dissatisfaction.

The case that individual conviction, rather than the economic experience of the social group, was crucial in leading urban craftsmen to volunteer, is possibly supported by a curious feature of the craftsmen's occupations. Some notoriously poor trades were strongly represented among the craftsmen rebels, but these apart a very wide diversity of occupations is exhibited. Once tailors, shoemakers, carpenters, and (in Lyme Regis) sailors, are removed, we find just one or two representatives from almost all the crafts of a town or village. In Taunton the 61 craftsmen rebels were spread among 23 different trades, and when the 28 tailors, cordwainers, and carpenters are taken out we are left with 33 men in 20 trades. At Lyme Regis 88 men followed 32 different crafts, and subtracting 39 tailors, cordwainers, carpenters, and sailors, the remaining 49 men cover 28 callings. Even in the twelve rural parishes 15 craftsmen followed 12 different trades, while on the *Jamaica Merchant* 16 craftsmen had 10 different occupations. For large samples and small the pattern is the same: most crafts were represented in the rebellion, but only by one or two men, with a few obvious exceptions. This suggests that craftsmen perhaps joined the rebellion not for reasons (for example poverty or unemployment) common to their type of trade, but for reasons more personal to themselves. These possibly varied from dislike of their employer, or their work, to strong political convictions, or religious beliefs. Given the impact of the Plot and Exclusion (not to mention the Duke's western progress of 1680) upon the towns where they lived, politics or religion may have been uppermost for many. As malcontents or as men of principle however, they volunteered regardless of their trade, and the result was a wide and random spread of urban occupations.

If agriculturalists and craftsmen comprised only one-fifth and one-quarter respectively of the rebel army, the only other large occupational group left, the cloth workers, must have been heavily represented. Sample figures support this conclusion. Of the 551 occupations in the Constables' List, 52 per cent were clothworkers of different kinds. In the much smaller sample on the *Jamaica Merchant*, 51 per cent worked in the industry. Individual centres could produce even higher figures. Of the 272 Taunton men whose occupation is known, 174 or 63 per cent were clothworkers; and here combers outnumbered the better-known weavers by 79 to 52. The strength of this heavy and dirty trade in Taunton is explained by the town's concentration upon serge-weaving, which required the long fleeces to be combed out of the wool before spinning. On the *Jamaica Merchant* the proportion of weavers to combers was more normal, 15 to 13 respectively. In Taunton, as on the ship, these two trades accounted for the great majority of clothworkers, but in Taunton fullers were surprisingly well represented with twenty-six rebels, and while there was only one dyer, the eleven 'sergemakers' of the town showed the involvement of some small entrepreneurs.

The percentage of clothworkers was high, too, at Frome with two-thirds of the rebels, craftsmen and agriculture dividing the remainder between them. Here weavers were the largest single sub-group within the industry (serges not being made here, with consequently few combers), but wire-drawers and card-makers accounted for one-fifth of the cloth-working total. Only in Lyme Regis was clothworking relatively insignificant, with only thirteen representatives among the rebels, none of them weavers. No occupational figures are available for the 156 rebels who joined at Chard, or the 74 from Wellington or the 59 from Milverton, but these were all cloth-working centres, and a high proportion of weavers and combers is to be expected.

Economic reasons for the clothworkers' massive response to the Duke's call are obvious. Their low wages, the numbers of poor people entering the trade, and the prevalence of abuses such as payment in truck, suggest their poverty and inventories confirm it. Half of the sample of weavers examined in Chapter One owned two or more looms yet their median of total moveable goods was little more than that of an agricultural labourer. Their household possessions — an index of material comfort — did not reach double figures. Poor as they were, however, they had to live off their trade alone, since just over one half of them owned neither land nor animals, and for those who had these supplements their size was scant enough. And these were the men who, mostly owning two or more looms, employed other weavers and were therefore doing relatively well. The number of weaving parishes in Somerset which, in the 1670s and 1680s, appealed for assistance with their poor to the Quarter Sessions, shows the growing size of the problem.

For most weavers underemployment was probably a greater scourge than low wages. There was an over-supply of labour for the industry, particularly in such large 'open' Somerset towns as Taunton, Chard, and Frome. Demand for the finer cloths produced in Wiltshire and eastern Somerset was declining; while uncertain overseas markets, the strains of changing over to serge production, and political uncertainty and economic recession in the 1680s, all made conditions very difficult in the south of the county. Weavers and combers might wait for days or weeks for the market to pick up and a clothier send them fresh wool or yarn. When Monmouth landed he found a class of workers not only poor and discontented, but idle for long periods and, therefore, immediately available for his service. They had no land to tie them down, and often no work either; and in his army they would eat well and regularly, and be treated with respect. Living from hand to mouth on their wages, they knew they had no prospect of improving their lot; and a gamble on a military venture led by such an eminent general could well appear worth taking, since a successful pretender would certainly reward his friends.

Poverty and idleness were not the only spurs to action. Clothworkers in England and on the Continent had a reputation for, and a tradition of, disorder. In Germany they were prominent among Luther's early followers, and weavers were active in France's civil strife during the sixteenth and seventeenth centuries. In 1564 Lord Burghley observed that 'people who depend upon the making of cloth are of a worse condition to be governed than the husbandmen'; while a century later John Aubrey speculated that their poor diet produced in clothworkers a tendency to theft and sedition; and in the eighteenth century weaving in Wiltshire was said to provide 'employment for the lowest sort of people,

[with] idleness and debauchery rooted in them by . . . alehouses'. There were good grounds for these views. Weavers in the west were 'on the verge of revolt' in 1586; they rioted at Warminster in 1595; in 1613 they swore they would die rather than see their families starve; and their miseries in the 1620s produced widespread disturbances in the west and south-west. More riots occurred around Melksham and Warminster during the dearth of 1647, and a generation later a strike to force up wages was organized at Trowbridge. In the 1690s Devonshire clothiers had to combine to resist their employees' wage demands, and here and in Somerset weavers' clubs had come into existence just after the turn of the century. In Somerset, Wiltshire, and Gloucestershire weavers' riots occurred in 1726, 1738, and 1756.[10] By Monmouth's time western clothworkers were well practised in mutual and violent association to protect their interests.

In part this was the result of exploitation; but other low-paid workers were also exploited without achieving the weavers' notoriety. Clothworkers were different because of their numbers, their concentration in particular areas, and the very social character of their work, all of which made joint action in large numbers more possible for them than for other trades. Since their work was so labour-intensive and co-operative combers and spinners worked in small groups, as did the weavers, with two men operating the loom and a third 'tidying up' about it. The constant passage of material from comber to spinner to weaver, and on to shearman, fuller, and dyer, further encouraged contact: and in the clothier most clothworkers had a figure to discuss and blame for their troubles. The work of combers, weavers, and spinners, was easily learnt and soon became repetitive and boring. Hours were long and breaks few, once the yarn was on the loom. Talking or reading within the group were natural ways of passing the time. The poet Dyer noted the conversations, though he probably idealized their subject:[11]

> Or, if the broader mantle be the task,
> He chooses some companion of his toil.
> From side to side, with amicable aim,
> Each to the other side darts the nimble bolt
> While friendly converse, prompted by the work,
> Kindles improvement in the opening mind.

In mid-seventeenth century Kidderminster Richard Baxter observed the weavers' practice of reading to one another at work:

It was a great advantage to me that my neighbours were of such a trade as allowed them time enough to read or talk of holy things; for the town liveth upon the weaving of Kidderminster stuffs, and as they stand in their loom they can set a book before them, and edify one another.[12]

For such men it was an easy passage from controversial works on religion to 'factious' books on politics; and the deluge of pamphlets on the Popish Plot, Exclusion, and the Duke of Monmouth's claims supplied an obvious topic for discussion in the 1680s. Dr. Cressy's work suggests that combers and weavers in Stuart England were more literate than virtually all other craftsmen, with illiteracy rates of 45 per cent to 49 per cent in the samples used, compared to rates of over 60 per cent for glovers, masons, carpenters, and coopers etc.[13] It was noted in Chapter One that one-fifth of the sample of Somerset weavers owned books valuable enough to be mentioned in a probate inventory. Converted by Whig pamphlet literature, very many clothworkers would have joined the rebellion because they were convinced that Monmouth was the legitimate King of England, and that only under him would religion and liberty be safe. Literate and politicized, poverty-stricken and frequently idle, numerous, concentrated, and with a tradition of riot, western clothworkers were a volatile group and likely to take to the rebellion in considerable numbers.

A rebel army is only partly described by the occupational and geographical pattern of its membership. To broaden the picture we should seek to establish the social status of the insurgents, the degree of respect accorded them locally, and village and town offices they may have held. This can be attempted by comparing the Constables' List with parish and county administrative records. Were many rebels to be found among the respectable (though not necessarily very wealthy) men who supplied the churchwardens and overseers of the poor, filled up juries, and took apprentices, held land, paid local rates, and appraised their neighbours' goods for probate? For answers of any significance, parishes which sent at least a dozen men to the rebellion are needed, with records going back five to ten years immediately before 1685. Eleven centres were found in Somerset and a twelfth in Dorset. They include larger towns such as Taunton and Lyme Regis, as well as rural parishes such as North Curry and Combe St. Nicholas. In almost every case the conclusion was the same — few or no rebels are found amongst the 'respectable' men of the parish.

Ilminster is typical. Set in the far south of Somerset and containing little over one thousand inhabitants, it provided fifty-four rebels. Between 1682 and 1685 seventy local men were named here for juries of presentment. Of these only three can be identified as rebels in 1685, although four more with the right surname but the wrong forename, may have been from the same family as a rebel. The rebel list and the jury list together account for nearly one half of the town's adult males, and yet there is an almost total lack of correlation between them. On the reasonable assumption that the jury lists contained the town's men of worth, the insurgents plainly came from the lower half of Ilminster's population. West Buckland, a well-populated rural parish between Taunton and Wellington, provided fourteen rebels. A special poor rate levied here in 1682 had thirty-five payers, none of whom was a rebel, although five had the same surname as a rebel and may have been related. A manorial rent roll of the 1670s for part of this parish contains the names of twenty land-holders, of whom none were rebels, though three may have been relatives. Another rent roll for West Buckland of 1687 names over fifty tenants, again with no rebels but three possible relatives. Wellington itself strongly supported the rebellion with seventy-four volunteers, but a rental of the early 1680s identifying twenty-six landholders provides only two identifications with rebels, each of them paying a rent of only a few shillings per year. Two rural parishes on the edge of the central moors, North Curry and Stoke St. Gregory, and a third in south Somerset, Combe St. Nicholas, contributed from twenty-three to twenty-six men apiece to the rebellion. Full churchwardens' accounts surviving from 1676 to 1685 for all three parishes provide the names of most parish notables. For two parishes there are virtually no correlations, none of the twenty-two churchwardens at Combe St. Nicholas being rebels, and only one out of twenty churchwardens at North Curry. But at Stoke St. Gregory there were four presumed rebels out of only twelve churchwardens, an exceptional case which gives point to the otherwise general absence of correlation.

Apprenticeship indentures provide the names of ten craftsmen and twenty churchwardens and overseers of the poor for Wilton, a small and thickly-populated cloth-working parish on the western edge of Taunton. Out of these thirty names only one man (a worsted weaver) joined Monmouth, although twenty-four rebels enlisted here. On the eastern side of Taunton lies Creech St. Michael, for which a manorial survey of 1675 contains forty-five names. Just two of these tenants, holding only two and three acres apiece, can be identified among the eighteen rebels here. Surveys of two manors in the strongly rebellious parish of Chard (156 volunteers) list two dozen landholders, of whom only one was a rebel. At Crewkerne near Chard twenty-eight men enlisted, and here jury rolls, presentments, and fines for non-attendance at the manorial court, name fifty tenants: of these only two were rebels. In the moorland parish of Curry Rivell ninety men and twenty-four women were assessed to pay the poor rate in 1677. Three men, all paying at the lowest rate of 2d. were subsequently among the parish's eighteen rebels, and four more paying from 4d. to 3/- may have been related to rebels. No rebels, however, were among the dozen or so here who received regular Poor Law doles, though two were among the larger number who received occasional assistance.[14] Virtually all of the parish's insurgents neither paid nor received poor relief.

So far, therefore, very few rebels have been found among the villagers who became churchwardens, took apprentices, held land, or paid poor rates, though a few more may have been related to a rebel. The pattern is the same at the rebellion's major focus of support, Taunton. Although virtually all of the town's records have been lost, some of its more important citizens can be identified. A drinking-club for the better-off which flourished in the early 1680s with a score of regular attenders contained no rebels — not surprisingly, for much drinking at 'The Society' was in response to loyal toasts. None of six churchwardens who can be identified in the 1670s was a rebel, and only one of the seven men to whom they leased church land. None of the thirty inhabitants who were trustees for the town's major charities joined Monmouth, though three shared their surname with a rebel. Presentments at the manorial court of Taunton Deane, comprising land in the town and the adjacent parish of Wilton, produce the names of only two rebels, although up to twenty-four men were cited each lawday for various minor offences. Pauper apprenticeship indentures for the town between 1672 and 1685 supply the names of ninety-six masters in different trades.[15] Only nine of these can be identified as rebels, but a further twenty each share the surname of a rebel, suggesting perhaps that master craftsmen were generally respectable, but their relatives less so. Only when a very wide net is spread are many Taunton rebels found. The men who appraised their neighbours' possessions for listing in a probate inventory were required to be men of good standing and with some knowledge of the deceased's affairs, but they were not necessarily wealthy, or even literate — 15 per cent of appraisers in the town made their mark rather than signed. Between 1681 and 1685 120 different Taunton men performed this last service for a neighbour, and of these 21 were subsequently rebels, and a further 26 may have been related.

When a wider test is applied than the respectability implied by parish office proportionately more rebels are found.

Lyme Regis, however, provides evidence that at earlier stages of the rebellion slightly more town 'worthies' may have been involved, though the term must be used with caution in a town only one-third the size of Taunton, and comprising little over three hundred families in all. Five of the town's twenty-four freemen were disfranchised for taking part in the rebellion, and of thirty-one constables, churchwardens, way- and Cob-wardens identifiable between 1681 and 1685, thirteen were rebels. Two jury lists of 1681 and (early) 1685 contain 4 out of 15, and 7 out of 23 respectively. But few rebels were wealthy. Out of 129 contributors to the poor rate in 1683 (in a total population of some 1,400) only seventeen were among the town's ninety-five rebels, and almost all of these paid at the bottom rate of one penny or less (the town's M.P. paid at five shillings). But few rebels received from the poor rate either: men and women in regular receipt of alms numbered 141, with a further eighty being given occasional aid. No rebels received regular alms, and only three were given occasional payments, repeating the pattern found at Curry Rivell. Rebels it seems were mostly too poor to pay, but too fit to be assisted.

They might also be law-breakers. Twelve Lyme Regis men were charged with smuggling in 1680 after a night-time chase over cliff-tops, but no contraband was recovered and they were discharged at their trial. Half of them went on to join the Duke. Two years earlier an all-female riot had taken place at the port to destroy imported linen and canvas, which was putting local people out of work. Twelve women were tried as ringleaders and fined, of whom two were married to later rebels, and four were spinsters each sharing a male rebel's surname.[16]

Outside Lyme Regis, many rebels had a history of criminal or disorderly behaviour. Somerset Quarter Sessions depositions between 1681 and 1685 contain thirty-four cases of theft or assault in which one of the parties had the same forename and surname and place of residence as a rebel, and can, therefore, be probably identified as a participant. This is just over one-tenth of all Somerset men involved in cases of theft and assault during this period, a much higher proportion than any random sample would produce, since the 2,700 rebels in the Constables' List were but 4 per cent of the county's total of some sixty thousand adult males. Furthermore, the rebels were almost always the party accused. They were charged with theft in 13 cases out of 14, and with assault 17 times out of 20. Probable rebels appeared only twice in illegitimacy cases, but were charged six times for vagrancy. In South

Petherton where twenty men joined the rebellion, three out of the eleven alehouses suppressed in 1681 following complaints from the better sort were run by men who later joined Monmouth. At Bishop's Hull near Taunton, another later rebel was forbidden to run an alehouse after complaints of disorderly behaviour.[17]

All crime figures require cautious handling, and none more than those for the seventeenth century. It will only be claimed here that these statistics are consonant with an emerging picture of the rebels being drawn from the less propertied, less respectable, section of parish society. This need not, however, simply mean that they were very poor. The sixty-seven men transported on the *Jamaica Merchant* provided one more — and vital — item of information. Besides name and occupation, their ages were listed. Most of them were young, their median age being just 22 years. The youngest aboard were a fifteen- and a sixteen-year old, the oldest a man of forty and another of thirty-eight. There were only nine aged thirty or more, and the largest single year group was the thirteen twenty-year olds. The average age of marriage for men at this time was twenty-seven; and only thirteen of the sixty-eight on the *Jamaica Merchant* were older than this.

Before the implications of this low median age can be explored, the trustworthiness of the sample must be considered. Prisoners in 1685 were assigned from their gaols to different agents who were responsible for seeing them on board ship. They were all valued at £10 per head, and nowhere in the official correspondence is there any suggestion that men of a particular age or occupation were to be chosen. With 850 men to move any policy of selection would have slowed matters down; and in any case there was no need for choice, because the West Indies colonists were crying out for any kind of white servants, because of the high death rate among whites. Younger men were not especially sought after — indeed older men could be more valuable because they were more likely to be skilled, and capable of giving orders and helping to run a plantation. The sample is, therefore, random, and not biased towards younger men. But it is small, and in no other case was the age of the transportees noted. Attempts to establish the ages of rebels by seeking their names in parish birth registers proved inconclusive for Taunton, Lyme Regis, and Colyton, because so few men — one-third or less — born in a parish proved still to be there twenty to forty years later. As Mr. Laslett has established, the turnover particularly among young servants in a village could be total within a period of ten years or less: unmarried, without property, and usually unskilled, they were easily the most mobile section of the population.[18] The small stock of

Christian names in use in a village, the influx of immigrants, and the practice of giving a newly-born child the name of one recently dead (but not necessarily recorded in the parish register of burials), complicates the matter still further. Attempts to find subsequent rebels in parish birth registers simply showed that most had not been born in the parish where they were living at the time of the rebellion: a point noteworthy but not surprising, and of no help concerning their age.

One contemporary account of the rebellion lends support to the possibility that the rebels recruited most heavily among young men. Sir John Reresby, a professional soldier, established courtier, and follower of the Duke of York, noted that Monmouth had recruited 'about five thousand men and boys'. Teenage drinkers in taverns were among those who supported the Duke's title to the throne before 1685; and the troop of 'several hundred young men dressed in white' who led Monmouth into Exeter on his western progress of 1680 indicates a strong and organized youth following. Recent works on the 'youth culture' in the early modern period lends weight to the possibility that many of the rebels were youths or in their early twenties. Professor N.Z. Davies has explored the well-structured youth groups of sixteenth-century France which organized a wide variety of public and semi-violent activities; and less developed, more ephemeral associations of young men have been found in England, associated about skimmingtons, football, and other violent sports, and behind intermittent riots at fairs and during holidays; although Dr. B.S.Capp has found a chapbook relating the imaginary deeds of a more formally organized group. Young men might act together to defy their elders and betters in quite small communities; thus Myddle in Shropshire was, in 1657-58, racked by a dispute over the occupancy of church pews by village youths — 'it was held a thing unseemly and indecent that a company of boys, and of persons that paid noe leavans should sitt . . . above the best of the parish'. The collective actions of youths could have more directly political significance. Their leading role in London's 'Evil May-Day' riot of 1517 was repeatedly stressed in Hall's 'Chronicle' account of the event; and in 1586 five young men, all under twenty-one, were caught planning a similar attack on Dutch and French in the capital. During the 1640s the same age group rioted first in favour of Parliament just before the Civil War, and then in favour of the King immediately after it. Sectarian groups attracted young people to such an extent that a Fifth Monarchist preacher in 1656 was heard 'also [to] much encourage youth, that they should be firm in the faith'. Besides their well-known exploits in pulling down London brothels in the reign of Charles II, the capital's apprentices could play an active role in politics, as they showed during the Exclusion Crisis when they formed an association to organize signatures to petitions.[19]

Historians have not, so far, considered the age of participants a very significant aspect of rebellions, but there exists some evidence that rebels (and sometimes soldiers more generally) may have been quite young. Fifteenth-century armies normally included a good proportion of mercenaries, mostly older men on long-term contracts, but a sample of 112 French men-at-arms and archers between 1454 and 1494 revealed that 40 per cent were aged between 20 and 25, and a further 38 per cent aged 26 to 30. Dr. R.L. Storey has recently observed of England's Wars of the Roses that 'a large proportion of all combatants . . . were probably teenagers'; while skeletal evidence of rebels massacred in 1525 at the close of the German Peasants' War shows that two-thirds had barely reached their late twenties, and that a quarter were aged twenty or less. There is evidence that some rebels in the 1536 Pilgrimage of Grace were young men who joined up 'as in sport'; while in 1596 the Privy Council was scandalized to find that those planning a revolt in Oxfordshire during that year of famine were 'young men, not poor', bachelors genuinely angered at the suffering they saw about them of older men with families.[20]

A strong contingent of young men among the rebels would explain a number of points made earlier about the Duke's army. The general absence of the propertied and respectable was the consequence not so much of poverty, as of youth. Too young to be property-owners as yet, these youths were also too junior to hold parish offices — even the radical Gerrard Winstanley would have restricted public office to mature men of forty and more.[21] The number of parish worthies who shared their surname with a rebel may denote older and propertied men, with a more impetuous son, nephew, or cousin. As young men the latter would also not contribute towards, nor receive from, parish poor rates: and a young age group was probably the more likely to be charged with assault or theft, explaining the rather high crime rate Quarter Sessions records reveal for rebels. The curious pattern of one or two rebels from almost all of a town's trades is also explained: the common factor was their youth, a random sample of young men in a town being likely to include a wide variety of occupations. The handfuls of three or four men apiece from rural parishes may have been a few of the younger men, dissatisfied and landless labourers, many perhaps younger brothers. Of the sixteen 'plowmen' on the *Jamaica Merchant*, all but one was in his teens or early twenties.

Young men may have been attracted into the rebellion for two further reasons. One has already been mentioned: the Duke was a celebrated military figure who, in 1685, offered travel, adventure and companionship; a gun, some fighting, and (explicitly at Lyme Regis) advancement if the venture was successful. Recruiting sergeants commonly do well with younger, unmarried men, dissatisfied with their trade, or simply unemployed; and by 1685 Monmouth had considerable experience in making impressive entries into country towns. Private dissatisfaction may in some cases, however, have been an equally strong motive for volunteering. Reliable biographical evidence concerning individual rebels is difficult to find, for most were obscure men, and such an obvious source as *The Western Martyrology* cannot generally be trusted because of its hagiographical purpose. But six 'brief lives' can be established for men who were not leaders among the rebels, and a common pattern is visible. They were young men, not from the lowest ranks of society, and all had been involved in some form of conflict with family or employer.[22]

Azariah Pinney is the best-documented example. The letters of his pious father reveal him as the black sheep of the family, the youngest child, and 'a great affliction' to his parents before he was out of his youth. Joining Monmouth at the age of twenty-four was simply the last of a series of acts of rebellion by this talented but wilful young man, one of the very few transported rebels who made a position for himself in the West Indies. Another who came from some estate was one Livesay of Bury in Derbyshire, whose nephew subsequently wrote of him that he 'was very loose in his youth and sold the estate his father left him', entered the royal army but deserted in 1685, and to the best of his family's knowledge 'fell in the Duke of Monmouth's army in that rash invasion'. Of somewhat propertied origin, too, was Christopher Bettiscombe, eldest son of a minor Dorset gentry family. Born around 1660, the boy became so unpopular with his father that when the latter died in 1670 Christopher had been cut out of his will. The youth left home, subsisted on payments of up to £100 p.a. from his family, and when barely out of his teens had became involved in Exclusion and then the Rye House Plot, as a minor Whig supporter. He was only in his mid-twenties when he joined the rebellion and was subsequently executed. Another lesser Whig involved in the rising as a young man was John Tutchin. Born in 1661 Tutchin had a stormy youth, being expelled from his school at Stepney for theft, before becoming associated with the London Whigs. At the age of twenty-four he took part in the rebellion, and escaped severe punishment by taking the false name of

Thomas Pitts. Out of his memories of Dorchester prison in 1685 he constructed the first draft of what would become, with the assistance of Titus Oates, the Whig publisher John Dunton, and the informer William Fuller, the *Western Martyrology*. Less prominent than Bettiscombe or Tutchin was the young Lyme Regis apprentice Richard Davey, sent by his parents to Morlaix to improve his trade prospects. There he misbehaved and failed to return home, 'to the grief of his parents', though he was back in Lyme Regis in time to join the Duke and then suffer as a traitor. Another discontented young man was Thomas Pocket, born in 1664. The son of a joiner, he was first apprenticed to a printer, but left him to work as an attorney's clerk. Dissatisfied with this master he again quitted service, and in 1685 at the age of twenty-one joined the Duke, escaping after the rebellion to die in 1724 a man 'of a Considerable Estate' and living under a false name. It may be argued that all these young men saw the revolt, in some measure, as a solution to or escape from personal difficulties, relating to parents or employers.

Not all the young rebels were, of course, malcontents. Some may have been 'conscripted' into the army by agreement between the rebels and their master, like Daniel Manning, an apprentice farrier from Taunton taken into the insurrection, he claimed, because of his useful trade. Nor were all malcontents in the army necessarily young: Monmouth's appeal to various groups of the discontented during the Exclusion Crisis has already been noted; while to those living in poverty-stricken exile following the Rye House Plot he represented, literally, their last hope of recovery.[23] Their own actions had made outcasts of many of the men who stepped ashore with Monmouth at Lyme Regis.

Among the army as a whole, malcontents were probably a minority (though an influential one); and young men may not have been much more than a majority — there were men in their thirties on board the *Jamaica Merchant*. But even if males in their teens and twenties constituted not three-quarters of the rebels, but one half or even less, two important general points can be made. Firstly, historians normally emphasize the positive motives behind revolts — religious or political beliefs, or economic hardship. But granted a certain level of such discontent, the minority who actually join a rebellion — as opposed to the majority who cheer from the side-line — may be selected by the negative factor of who was free to act at the time. Family responsibilities, the demands of farm or workshop, or even advancing age or declining health, may be crucial in differentiating active from passive supporters: and the minority who act may well comprise the young, fit, unpropertied, and unmarried. Secondly, the active minority may also be determined at least in part by very personal motives — dissatisfaction with a master, boredom with work or unemployment, the wish to cut a figure before neighbours or peer group, or hope of sudden and quick advancement. On this argument, the poverty of the cloth industry and some other trades, and the political and religious tension following the Plot, Exclusion, and the Tory reaction, left very many people in the west willing to support a rebellion; but a small range of social and personal factors decided who would actually participate. While economic motives were important, this was not a rising of desperation. In the cloth industry, combers and weavers were not markedly worse off in 1685 than in any previous year: the difference was that in 1685 they were offered a chance to escape from poverty, semi-employment and boredom, and so on the economic side the rebellion may be termed one of improvement and hope, rather than reaction to intolerable conditions.

It was certainly not inspired by class antagonism, though even here some caution is needed. Monmouth's programme was purely political and very simple — to remove James II and, with Parliament's blessing, to take his place — and if his followers thought of economic benefits they did so purely as members of a victorious army. There would be no general levelling of society to make room for them. But as the revolt progressed, and the gentry failed to support it, some grumbling against the upper classes began. If landowners lacked the will to act, then supplies could be taken from them by force — and were. The simple and brutal way provisions were obtained at Longleat — by threatening to burn the house down — was probably used at other places; and the Longleat episode certainly suggests that the rebel commoners were beginning to enjoy having the whip hand. And because the rebel force was so purely lower-class, references to the rebellion among the upper classes — including former Whigs as well as Tories — contain more than a trace of social outrage and fear. England's rulers were quick to see in the rising hints of a class revolt; and by the time it ended many rebels were beginning to see the supine gentry as their enemy, as well as James II. In the course of even a short revolt motives and attitudes may change sharply under the pressure of violence, fear, and revenge; and beginnings should be noted which had no time to develop further, cut short by the arbitrary timing of a final battle.

Upper class abstention in 1685 was almost total. A few sons of gentry can be found such as Charles Speke or Christopher Bettiscombe, a handful of merchants such as John Hucker of Taunton, and a few clothiers and sergemakers; but apart from Ford Lord Grey, Monmouth was accompanied by no men of title. This alone was sufficient reason for gentlemen to treat the rebellion with caution. Many had also been successfully intimidated by the government ever since the failure of Exclusion, and after three years of Tory reaction they had learned to keep their heads down. Even when William III arrived in 1688 with a fleet and ten thousand men, the western gentry were very slow to make any move towards him. Furthermore, Monmouth had been declared a traitor not only by the King, but also by Parliament: by landing just after the 1685 Parliament had been elected he found both bodies of the constitution united against him, and his appeals to a 'free' Parliament were bound to be in vain. Fundamentally however Monmouth failed to gather gentry support because most of them had already judged him, and found him wanting. They decided upon his claim to the crown by their own rules regulating the descent of property, and the conclusion was clear — a bastard could not inherit. Granted there was some uncertainty concerning the Duke's birth, but after years of search no marriage document between his parents had been produced, and there must come a time for uncertainty to end. The Duke of York's title was clear and unambiguous; he had been endorsed in the strongest terms by Charles II; and though a severe man he had during his residence in Scotland given proof that he could rule. Having made its decision when Charles II had died, the political nation was not going to unmake it four months later in favour of an illegitimate adventurer.

These considerations weighed less with the lower classes. Not so exposed as individuals to the Tory reaction, only a few of them had learnt the virtues of caution by 1685. Less convinced than the ruling class of the necessity of primogeniture and legitimacy (some because they had no property to bequeath, others because they bequeathed it to all their sons), the lower classes were less disturbed by Monmouth's dubious birth: he was undisputably Charles's son, and that sufficed. The 'Black Box' rumours were believed by them long after the gentry became sceptical, partly because they wanted to believe them, partly because they were not educated to discriminate in such a debate. The dispossessed among the general population, the younger brothers and the sons of poor men, may have sympathized with the Duke's struggle to save his inheritance from a wicked uncle, but much of the common support for Monmouth had less to do with the merits of his case than with his appeal as a personality and as a leader. Handsome and still young-looking, a very public Protestant and reputedly a notable military leader, Monmouth looked as though he might be another Henry V, with whom he was frequently compared. His tours of the west and Cheshire had taught him how to make an impressive entry into a town and this effective display, together with his reputation and his affable and courteous public personality, must account for a good deal of the instant response to his call for a Protestant army to save England.

Attractive as the Duke was, however, his cause was as important as his personality: and no group has been thought more willing to serve that cause than the Dissenters. For a recent historian indeed the Duke's army was 'made up almost entirely of Nonconformists', and was 'the last godly army in English history'. It was shown in Chapter II how strongly Nonconformity was entrenched in Somerset, and how forcibly it reacted to attempts to suppress it, so that a ready Puritan response to Monmouth's proclamation might have been expected in 1685. There is considerable evidence of Nonconformist participation in the revolt. Three or four ministers joined the army, including the celebrated John Hickes. Such leaders probably took some of their flock with them, and it is known that an entire Independent congregation from Axminster (numbering a dozen men) marched in behind their pastor, one Stephen Twogood.[24] Individual Dissenters to the number of nearly two score can be identified in the trials and from the pages of the *Western Martyrology*, and the south of Somerset whence Monmouth drew most of his support was notoriously a centre of Nonconformity, as the 1669 and 1672 religious surveys reveal.

But such evidence does not prove that Dissenters comprised the entire army, or even a large part of it. Most Nonconformist ministers watched cautiously from the sideline in 1685, and there is no evidence that those who joined brought many supporters with them; and even the dozen Independents who enlisted with Stephen Twogood were only a small part of the seventy-nine who volunteered from Axminister. Where Somerset Dissenters can be identified, in the early 1680s, by name and place of residence, very few are found subsequently to have become rebels. Fifty-three men were charged with attending conventicles in Somerset between 1682 and 1684, and the four parishes they lived in provided eighty-nine rebels: but only two of these rebels are to be found in Quarter Sessions lists of Dissenters.[25] If they were not particularly numerous it may nevertheless be argued that the Nonconformists' zeal gave them an impact much greater than their numbers would suggest. But it must be noted that Stephen Twogood and his congregation were among the very few rebels known to have deserted in mid-rebellion: unnerved by the limited bloodshed of

Norton St. Philip they dropped their Old Testament rhetoric and returned home. And while the two thousand men who volunteered in south Somerset probably included Dissenters from the area's many congregations, this part of the county also contained most of its cloth industry, its larger towns, and its poverty. Contemporary accounts of the rebellion from both camps make no reference at all to prayer-meetings, sermons, or psalm-singing among the Duke's followers; and an observant rebel captain such as Nathaniel Wade would have no reason to conceal this behaviour in his general confession to James II, which contains no hint of Puritan commitment among the insurgents.

There is, therefore, unequivocal evidence for only a limited Nonconformist presence in Monmouth's army, and the view that the godly comprised most of the force comes from two sources, one late seventeenth-century, and one modern. The first source originated with the problem faced by the gentry of the south-west just after the rebellion, when they had to explain why it had occurred (and their failure to suppress it) to an angry and suspicious King. Some Dissenters found among the rebels, and the Nonconformist reputation of the area where the rebellion had occurred, gave them the answer. It was all the work of the Dissenters, they chorussed, in addresses of loyalty which flooded into Whitehall. The mass of the population were quite innocent and perfectly loyal, but had been overborne (like the gentry) by the fanaticism of that disloyal crew. Since James believed Nonconformists had played a major role in the Exclusion Crisis, he was willing to be convinced. And when Nonconformity was suitably chastened, and the activists lanced, he found no difficulty in offering toleration to the remainder in 1686. Events two years later consolidated the dissenting myth of 1685. The Glorious Revolution transformed Monmouth's army from a collection of traitors, into a gathering of Protestant martyrs who had struck bravely but too soon. Heroes by posthumous accolade, they were seized upon by Nonconformists who after 1689 wished to justify full religious toleration for themselves. Dissenters' arguments were seconded by Whigs wishing to make respectable their Nonconformist allies. The result of this alliance can be read in *The Western Martyrology*, a hagiography of those who suffered under Jeffreys, which ran through five editions between 1689 and 1705. Compiled by Titus Oates (who was attempting to resume the public stage), John Dunton a Whig propagandist, and John Tutchin, a rebel who had fought for Monmouth at the age of twenty-four, the account carefully avoided points of denominational detail in its biographies of the martyrs, to stress instead their deep Protestant piety, and their spiritual kinship with Mary Tudor's victims.[26] Dissenters the rebels were, but of the broadest and most acceptable kind.

Established by Whigs, Nonconformists, and the western gentry, accepted by James II, and with the evidence laid out in the selective examples of the *Western Martyrology*, later historians simply embroidered the myth. In the eighteenth-century White Kennett, Archdeacon Echard, and John Oldmixon, saw 1685 as a revolt inspired by politics and religion and fought largely by Dissenters. Daniel Defoe joined the chorus: hinting broadly that he spoke as a former rebel, he commended Taunton in his *Tour Through England* of 1724-26 as 'noted for the Number of Dissenters . . . it was always counted as a Seminary of such: They suffered deeply in the Duke of Monmouth's rebellion'.[27] The careful ambiguity of his last phrase (suffered as rebels, or suffered after the rebellion?) suggests that Defoe had reservations over their role; but Macaulay's superb prose then set the Nonconformists' role in marble.

Any lingering doubts faded as modern historians discovered the strength of anti-Catholicism in Tudor and Stuart England, for here an important misconception can creep in. Because Puritans may be defined as 'the hottest sort of Protestants', it is easy to conclude that Puritans were, therefore, the hottest Protestants against Popery. Reference to Laudianism and Latitudinarianism would then suggest that the established church was by comparison tolerant towards Catholicism, and anti-Popery emerges as a largely Puritan phenomenon. Dissenters may then be seen as the principal opponents of James II in 1685. The reasoning rests on a false assumption, for anti-Catholicism embraced the entire Protestant community in England. It was central to English nationalism, and was presented as the key to English history in John Foxe's enormously influential *Acts and Monuments of the Christian Reformation*. A deep vein of anti-Catholicism is found in the established church's literature, in sermons, controversial works, and that stand-by of the rural parson *The Book of Homilies*. Anglicans believed in the Popish Plot, for long supported Exclusion, eventually drove James II from the throne, and in 1689 helped conclude a toleration which still excluded Papists. Members of the Church of England could believe as deeply in their principles as Nonconformists, and were no less determined and bigoted in defence of their position against Rome.

To emphasize that the rebellion was not primarily an uprising by Dissenters is not, of course, to reduce the role of religion as a motive. Indeed, by stressing the importance of anti-Catholicism in the beliefs of the loosely Protestant mass of the population, the religious causes of 1685 are set even more firmly in the centre of the stage. Poverty, unemployment, and the hope of economic improvement, were undoubtedly considerations which affected many who became rebels; although it has been my argument that these factors did not so much drive people to rebellion, as create the conditions in which they would feel free to join Monmouth if for other reasons they wished to do so. Economic need was an important condition for the rebellion, but not a direct cause. The major direct cause, for many rebels, was the political and religious issue, the fear that now James II was King, he would behave as the Exclusionists had long proclaimed he would, and introduce Popery and tyranny into England. How could a Catholic King not wish to make his subjects Papists; how could such a severe authoritarian not wish to choke off opposition?

But the fears Monmouth harnessed in 1685 did not derive only from the arguments of the past seven or eight years, despite the force and frequency of their reiteration. The Duke drew directly upon England's long anti-Catholic tradition. For over a century sermons and religious tracts, broadsides, chapbooks, and almanacs, plays, poems, and the puppet theatre, had driven certain 'facts' about Catholicism into the English Protestant mind.[28] Rome was sworn to destroy their political freedom and independence. It would strive unceasingly to re-establish Catholicism and extinguish heresy. And it would stoop to any cruelty, devilish plot, or immorality, to achieve these ends. It was a system too politically dangerous, and too carnally appealing to corrupt man, to be tolerated. History was ransacked to show its cruelty, its endless appetite for power, its particular malice towards England — Mary Tudor's persecution, the Armada, Guy Fawkes' and other Catholic plots; the French Religious Wars, the Revolt of the Netherlands, and the Thirty Years' War; the Fire of London, Louis XIV's wars, and the Popish Plot in more recent times.[29]

These examples, and the arguments they illustrated, had been made even more familiar by five years of crisis after 1678; and outside London no area had been more affected than the south-west and Somerset in particular, a county with its own tradition of dissent and political faction, maintained through the Restoration years. Local Whigs drew upon this tradition as they first mobilized the county to support Exclusion, and then tried to fight against the local Tory reaction. Somerset was politicized not just by the Popish Plot and Exclusion Crisis, but also by the bitter struggle of 1682-84 when the anti-York faction here had to struggle for survival. Monmouth landed to resume

Exclusion, but many of his supporters rallied to continue an even more recent struggle than that. The county was still divided in 1685, and though the rebels' watchword was political and religious liberty, the number of private scores settled on the margins of the revolt shows that revenge for years of humiliation and bullying was in the hearts of some.[30]

For his part the Duke carefully appealed to religious and political sentiments, presenting his landing as the last Act of the Exclusion drama. The manifesto published at Lyme Regis rehearsed the oldest and most scurrilous Whig charges against James II as the preamble to a call for a free Parliament; and in the same spirit Monmouth refrained from directly claiming the Crown, leaving his title for Parliament to judge. The same emphasis upon politics and religion is seen in the Taunton ceremony, at which a number of virgins presented the Duke with a Bible and a sword, obvious symbols of his mission. Only desperation over the gentry's non-appearance led him to claim the Crown, and this expedient made no difference to his followers, for whom he was 'the Protestant Duke' to the bitter end. Though not the 'last godly army' of recent hyperbole, it would be cynical to deny that many, perhaps most, of the army were clear about the political and religious ends for which they fought. The rebels held no prayer meetings, sang no psalms, but their leader attended the Anglican service where he could, and was always careful to stress the Protestant nature of his cause and his deep respect for Parliament.

The memory of these ends persisted. Two years after the rebellion, at a fair in the north Somerset village of Burnham, a riot took place. Nearly a hundred local men, with some ex-rebels among them, declared that they were 'for the Duke of Monmouth', and challenged all comers to battle. Having beaten up their opponents and won the day, they 'did in great triumph hold up a bloody handkerchief declaring it to be Monmouth's colours'. After singing 'songs concerning the Duke of Monmouth', the episode closed with the leader crying aloud 'now Holland (meaning ye said Riotters whereof he was one) had conquered France'.[31] Monmouth was identified with Holland (and Protestantism and freedom); France with Popery and absolutism; and in the replay right had won. The mock-battle shows how well villagers had understood the essence of 1685; and the extensive depositions concerning it collected by the authorities suggest that they too perceived the episode's significance.

Footnotes: Chapter Nine

1. See above, p.242, fn. 25.

2. British Library, Add.MSS.30077.

3. J.Turner, *Pallas Armata: Military Essays*, London 1683, p.281; D. Chandler, *The Art of Warfare in the Age of Marlborough*, London 1976, pp.13-20.

4. D.Underdown, 'The Chalk and the Cheese: contrasts among the English Clubmen', *Past and Present*, 85 1979, pp.31, 37-47.

5. SRO, Q/S R 164/18.

6. PRO, State Papers Colonial vol. lxiv, 152.

7. W.Stephens, *Exeter*, p.181; Bristol Record Office, Assize of Bread 1677-1825.

8. SRO, Somerset Archaeological Society, C 795, SE 121, 124; DD/SF 110/2404, 2281, 2476, 2293; DD/HP C39; DD/SF 52/1028.

9. T.Rogers, *A History of Agriculture and Prices in England*, Oxford, 7 vols., 1887, v, 668-71.

10. R.H.Tawney and E.Power, *Tudor Economic Documents*, London 3 vols. 1965, ii, 45; J.Aubrey, *National History of Wiltshire*, London 1714, p.110; G.Ramsay, *Wiltshire Woollen Industry*, pp.72, 112, 129; J.Mann, *Cloth Industry in the West of England*, pp.108-9; K.Ponting, *West of England Cloth Industry*, p.110.

11. Quoted K.Ponting, *West of England Cloth Industry*, pp.99-100.

12. N.H.Keeble ed., *The Autobiography of Richard Baxter*, London 1974, p.80.

13. D.Cressy, *Literacy and the Social Order*, Cambridge 1980, pp.132-3.

14. SRO, DD/Ppb, Ilm; SAS, C795, PR35, PR 35/4, SR12, PR175, PR90, PR89, PR46/12, PR 442; SAS, C1193 No.3, C2072, ff.2-3.

15. SRO, SAS, TN11 Minutes 1681-84, C795 TN105, TN15; DD/MT box 44; Apprenticeship Indentures Taunton St.Mary and St.James.

16. Lyme Regis Records, M1, M2, M5, F1; Q/S Rolls A 4/3, 28 January 1681, 17 January 1685, October 1680, 11 September 1678, n.d.1678.

17. SRO, Q/S Rolls 147-166; Q/S Minute Book 1676-82, ff.256v, 184v.

18. P.Laslett, 'Clayworth and Cogenhoe', *Essays to David Ogg*, ed. H.Bell and R.Ollard, London 1963, pp.157-82.

19. J.Reresby, *Memoirs*, p.380; N.Z.Davies, 'The Reasons of Misrule: Youth Groups and Charivaris in sixteenth-century France', *Past and Present*, 50

1971, pp.41-75; E.P.Thompson, 'Rough Music' – le charivari anglais', *Annales E.S.C.*, 27 1972, pp.295-298; R.W.Malcolmson, *Popular Recreations in English Society, 1700-1850*, Cambridge 1973, Ch.1; B.S.Capp, 'English Youth Groups and "The Pinder of Wakefield"', *Past and Present*, 76 1977, pp.127-33; R.Gough, *The History of Myddle*, ed. D.Hey, London 1981, p.117; J.Thurloe, *State Papers*, iv, 650; *The Life and Errors of John Dunton*, London 1705, p.50; R.H.Tawney and E.Power, *Tudor Economic Documents*, London 1965, 3 vols., iii, 83, 85, 86, 89; H.Ellis, *Original Letters Illustrative of English History*, London 1874, 3 vols., ii, 306-8. For the teenage drinkers see Chapter Two, p.72, fn.52; and for the Exeter youths Chapter Four, p.127, fn.38.

20. P.Contamine, *Geurre Etat et Société à la fin du Moyen Age*, Paris 1972, p.456; review by R.L.Storey in *Times Literary Supplement*, No.4180 13 May 1983, p.484, col.2; D.Fevre et.al., 'Anthropologie des paysans massacrés en 1525 près d'Epfig', in M.Steinmetz ed., *Der deutsche Bauernkrieg und Thomas Müntzer*, Leipzig 1976, pp.28-9 (I am indebted to my colleague Dr. Henry Cohn for this reference); *CSPD 1595-97*, pp.316, 344; *Letters and Papers of Henry VIII*, vol.11, no. 1230 (I owe this reference to Mr. Richard Parnell of Warwick University).

21. C.Hill ed., *The Works of Gerrard Winstanley*, London 1973, p.361 ('The Law of Freedom', Ch.V).

22. G.Nuttall, *Pinney Letters*, pp.xv, 13-14, 21-3; R.Pares, *A West Indian Fortune*, Ch.I; 'The Diary of James Clegg of Chapel-en-le-Frith, Part III', ed. V.Doe, *Derbyshire Record Society*, 5 1981, p.906 (I owe this reference to the kindness of Dr.Joan Lane); Dorset County Record Office, Battiscombe Papers, D198/14, D17; J.Muddiman, *Bloody Assizes*, pp.5-7; Lyme Regis R.O., Q/S Rolls A4/3; Cambridge University Library, Cholmondeley (Houghton) MSS., Correspondence 1119, (I owe this reference to Mr. E.P.Thompson).

23. *Calendar of Colonial S.P.1685-88*, pp.148-9; and see above Chapter Three *passim*.

24. W.M.Wigfield, 'Ecclesiastica, The Book of Remembrance', *Somerset Archaeological and Natural History Society*, vol.119 1975, pp.51-5; for the 'godly army' see P.Earle, *Monmouth's Rebels*, London 1977, pp.6, 11.

25. SRO, Q/S R, 114/48; 150/1; 156/12, 13; 157/14.

26. See J.Muddiman, *The Bloody Assizes*, pp.1-21.

27. D.Defoe, *Tour*, i, 267; see also M.Ashley, 'King James and the Revolution of 1688 . . . Recent Historiography', in *Essays to Ogg*, ed. Bell and Ollard.

28. For puppet theatres see Ben Jonson, *Bartholomew Fair*, Act V, scene 1, lines 1-18.

29. See R.Clifton, 'The Popular Fear of Catholics during the English

Revolution', *Past and Present*, 52 1971; C.Weiner, 'The Beleaguered Isle', *Past and Present*, 51, 1971.

30. SRO, Q/S R 162/16, 161/9, 161/10.

31. SRO, Q/S R 169/1-12.

CHAPTER TEN

The Last Popular Rebellion

'The last popular rebellion' is both a title and an assertion, and requires clarification if not justification. 'In England' is understood, and 'so far' is unnecessary. More seriously, it can be argued that 1715 and 1745 were essentially Scottish affairs, that eighteenth-century England was profuse in riots but produced no larger disturbances, that the Swing riots amounted to a revolt but not a rebellion, and that the Chartists and other nineteenth-century groups talked of resistance but put no body of armed men into the field. In 1688 the Glorious Revolution was popular in that all save Catholics applauded it, but not in the sense that the masses played any part in planning or executing it. To the political nation indeed 1688 was glorious precisely because it was so far from being a popular rebellion, with all that term connoted of uncontrolled violence and lower-class radicalism.

1685, therefore, closes a long chapter in English history. Governments would still be questioned and resisted by the lower classes, but new organizational forms would be found, more controlled and less dangerous than outright warfare. The Monmouth rebellion was the last occasion when thousands of Englishmen gathered together in arms, seeking to impose by force drastic changes upon the government of the day. Seen in this light it is more than a mere 'episode',[1] a footnote to the Exclusion Crisis, or an unhappy preface to 1688; still less simply a fitting conclusion to the life of a confused Restoration courtier, politician, and rake. Previous rebellions in Tudor and Stuart England had also failed, but the outcome of 1685 was final in a way that other defeats were not. Sedgemoor demonstrated that the massed uprising had, in most imaginable circumstances, had its day.

One reason for this was immediate and military. 1685 signalled the appearance, for the first time, of the standing professional army in England. Ket's rebels in 1549 had been overwhelmed by an army which contained a thousand foreign mercenaries, but they were only a part of the Earl of Warwick's army, and they did not become a permanent presence. 1685 opened the period in England when any group of armed rebels would have to confront a well-disciplined and well-equipped army. Ways would be found for civilian protestors to cope with troops, but these did not include armed combat. Before the creation of a standing army English rulers had had to defeat rebels as much by guile as by force, for there was little difference between a royal and a rebel army in terms of arms, training, speed of movement, or capacity for manoeuvre. 1685 exposed the startling gap which had opened up during the seventeenth century in all these respects between regulars and armed civilians, even when the latter were commanded by an experienced and able ex-professional.

Upper-class caution was another reason why there were no more popular rebellions after 1685. Monmouth's speed in assembling several thousand armed men, together with lower-class involvement in the Exclusion Crisis and memories of the Civil War, persuaded England's rulers that henceforth the common people must be kept out of high politics if at all possible, and 1688 was tailored with almost as much care to exclude the lower orders as to remove James. While gentlemen were welcome at William's camp in 1688, the role of the masses was limited to a cheering crowd or two, and the rebellion's necessary measure of force was provided by ten thousand reliable Dutch troops. If 1649 and 1688 taught Kings that in the last resort they were disposable, 1685 was one of the experiences which reminded England's upper class that the cost of deposing a ruler might be unacceptably high, and that differences among the country's rulers had, therefore, to be contained.

A secure line of soundly Protestant rulers after 1685 was another reason why Monmouth's was the last popular rebellion. William III's Calvinism, the devout Anglicanism of Anne, followed by the stolidly Lutheran and Anglican Hanoverians, put religion out of contention between Crown and Parliament for over a century. Religion (in the sense of bigotry and intolerance) continued to be a vitriolic issue in the eighteenth century, but the riots were between different tribes among the King's subjects, not between King and subject. The Stuarts' long and disastrous flirtation with Catholicism had been ended, removing the one issue which could at the time unite Englishmen of all social conditions and political persuasions, to create a truly popular rebellion.

In its place came new and deep economic discontents, as population grew in the eighteenth century, and towns and manufactures expanded. An older paternalism which had tried to apply some moral criteria to prices and wages was displaced, and 'market forces' allowed full rein.[2] The protests resulting from this process were strong and violent, but also inevitably sectional and often local, with no national character until a working-class consciousness was created in the early nineteenth century. 1685 was the last occasion when a cause which was basically religious (but with political implications) created a popular movement; it would be over a century before economic issues could do the same.

For a variety of reasons, then, 1685 was the last of the Tudor and Stuart popular rebellions. But though it shares a number of common features with these disturbances, in one important respect it is different. It was the only popular rebellion in England between 1500 and 1700 to intend the deposition of the ruling monarch. Other revolts spoke simply of forcing the government to change its religious or political policies, or to implement its own legislation on economic matters; and though behind the programme of Wyatt in 1554 or the Northern earls in 1569 there may have lurked thoughts of displacing the Queen, they were never publicly avowed. In this respect 1685 belongs not to the Tudor and Stuart pattern of rebellions, but to an earlier series of revolts, the baronial wars of the mid-fifteenth century. With a platform consisting simply of the King's deposition, summoned by an illegitimate Pretender of royal birth, this leader prompted as much by personal honour and pride as by public motives, the resemblances of 1685 to the Wars of the Roses are at first sight striking.

There is, however, one very significant difference, a difference which 1685 also presents when compared to most Tudor and Stuart revolts. The commoners who comprised Monmouth's army made their own decision to join, without influence or example from landlords, patrons, or employers. Lordship was not a factor in creating mass support in 1685, because with the solitary exception of Ford, Lord Grey no aristocrats or substantial gentry supported the rebels. Indeed, the men who fought with Monmouth did so against the express command of their social superiors, many of whom were ranked in the militia against them. In some earlier revolts commoners had acted without influence from the gentry, but these disturbances had always been over economic issues which pitted them directly against the local landowners — Ket in 1549, the Midlands Revolt of 1607, and some of the forest and fen riots of the late 1620s and 1630s. With the possible exception of the Civil War, 1685 was the only politico-religious revolt in which the lower class made their own decision to volunteer. It is a rebellion which proves that the masses were capable of independent political thought and action; but perhaps only under special circumstances. Artisans and farmworkers in Somerset had been strongly politicized before 1685 by two factors. In common with the rest of the country they had been deeply stirred by the Popish Plot, Exclusion Crisis, and Tory reaction, experiencing the 'torrents of these talking times' as a local vicar expressed it.[3] Secondly, however, there existed in Somerset — and particularly in Taunton — a strong tradition of political and religious dissent dating from Civil War times. Such a tradition was most certainly not unique to this region, and there is no evidence to show that the tradition survived more aggressively in Somerset than in some other areas. The point is simply that in Somerset, the area chosen by Monmouth for the rebellion, national agitation was strongly reinforced by a local spirit of 'faction', helping to explain why commoners here joined a rebellion so quickly and in such numbers.

Religion, in the form of the heir apparent's Catholicism, was of course the central issue in the six years' preparation for the revolt. Among previous rebellions those most directly threatening the monarchy — 1536, 1554, 1569, and to some extent 1642 — had been essentially, or to a large extent, concerned with religion, and 1685 may be added to the list. Like these earlier rebellions, in 1685 'religion' meant a change in the country's religion, thought either to be contemplated or under way. But again, like the earlier revolts, 'religion' in 1685 comprised a package of issues. It included detestation of Catholicism and fear of persecution, but also concern for Parliament's and the subjects' rights and liberties. In the first 'Declaration' he issued at Lyme Regis Monmouth underlined his respect for Parliament by announcing that he would ask it to adjudicate on his title to the Crown; in the meantime he would depose his uncle but leave the throne vacant. Only when the gentry failed to turn out for him did he, at Taunton, actually claim the Crown.

Given the importance of religious and political issues in 1685, the rebellion would appear to have little in common with those among its predecessors which arose over economic issues — Ket's rebellion in 1549, the Midlands Revolt of 1607, the forest and fen disturbances of the 1620s and 1630s. In part this is the case, for in 1685 the harvests had been good for a decade, only a small part of Somerset had recently been disturbed by enclosure, and rents and entry fines appear to have been stable. But 1685 shows how indirectly economic factors may operate. The county contained a mass of poor and semi-employed artisans created by the cloth industry. Their condition in 1685 was poor because of market problems and political uncertainty, though certainly no worse than it had been in the 1620s, or in some years of the 1640s. The clothworkers did not rebel directly over their economic plight, but many among them were sufficiently poor and desperate to snatch at the chance Monmouth appeared to offer of sudden improvement, and unemployment amongst them left hundreds of weavers and combers free to join in the rebellion if they wished. 1685 provides an example of how the politico-religious causes of a rebellion may be combined with the socio-economic. Religious and political issues made most of the commoners sympathetic to the Duke's cause; but it was economic and social factors which determined precisely who among that majority would step forward to create the fighting minority. Poverty and unemployment were important among these economic and social factors; but so were others, including the youth of the rebels, and the consequent absence of family or property ties among them, their social standing locally (or lack of it), and the personality and appeal of their leader.

The analysis of Monmouth's supporters has considerable implications for the thesis recently advanced by Dr. Buchanan Sharp, that 'peasant revolts' between 1586 and 1600 were more the work of rural artisans than agriculturalists proper.[4] In some ways 1685 supports this claim. Farmers and agricultural workers were grossly under-represented in the rebel ranks, while artisans made up at least three-quarters of the Duke's army. But it should be noted that over three-quarters of these artisans in turn came from just one industry, cloth. Subtracting them from the artisans' total leaves the latter represented more or less proportionately to their total strength in the county.

More importantly, however, 1685 emphasizes the importance of contingent factors in determining the extent and nature of support for a rebellion, and hence is a warning against generalizations. By landing near and marching through one of England's major cloth-making areas, at a time when the trade was depressed, Monmouth almost guaranteed strong clothworker involvement. By landing in a county where the family farm was the norm, and large estates with many landless day labourers relatively few; at a time when farmers were generally enjoying some prosperity; and in a month when they were concerned with the hay-harvest, the Duke equally almost guaranteed a low agricultural turn-out. Because he had to recruit quickly Monmouth spent a day or two in several towns but very little time in the countryside, limiting once again the rural wing of his support. Furthermore, the militia held most of northern and eastern Somerset in some strength, together with Devon and Dorset, and though they retreated before his advance, their presence handicapped volunteers here from reaching the rebels.

Monmouth's character, or more precisely his public reputation, was another significant variable influencing support for the rebellion. Commander of England's army for many years, a war hero before that, his military reputation enhanced by a swift and merciful defeat of

Scottish rebels in 1679, the Duke cut an impressive figure on horseback, was relatively young at thirty-five, and possessed the casually informal manner of many 'soldiers' generals' who have commanded great loyalty from their troops. He was a very effective recruiting sergeant, and though the rebellion's purposes were political and religious, more immediately he offered volunteers a weapon, travel, and the prospect of some fighting, the hope of glory, local respect, and some loot, and the rough male cameraderie of the armed camp, all under a warm June sun. The combination could well prove irresistible to restless twenty-year-olds watching the rebels march into town.

In the face of this range of variables the perils of generalization are evident. More positively, however, 1685 does raise two points concerning support for rebellions. Firstly, historians might well study the age, marital status, and local standing, as well as the occupational and religious affiliations of their rebels. Secondly, besides the positive factors such as economic conditions and political or religious circumstances which 'pushed' man into a rebellion, they should consider the negative factors — lack of property, employment, family, or local roots — which 'allowed' him to join up. And though they are much harder to quantify, or indeed to recognize, personal factors such as a feeling of being a misfit or outcast in a community may also be relevant. Such individual causes may explain the many cases of only two or three men from a village joining the rebellion. Where biographies of rebels can be constructed, personal discontent or resentment is regularly to be found; and it can be traced, too, among many who supported Monmouth, the Whigs, or Exclusion before 1685.

The motives, and the abilities, of its leader are crucially important to a popular rebellion, as the examples of Aske and Ket show, and though this work has avoided treating 1685 as 'Monmouth's Rebellion', there can be no doubt of his importance in deciding its aims and raising popular support. The paradox is that when the *Helderenburgh* sailed from Amsterdam the Duke would have regarded himself as the least free of men, driven into a course he had at first rejected by the expectations of his followers and by his own sense of honour. This lack of freedom of choice derived from Monmouth's activities since 1678, when he had come to epitomize, for many, the Protestant cause against the Catholic York. The title all in Somerset knew him by in 1685 was 'the Protestant Duke', eloquent testimony in itself how cause and man had merged. Beyond being an effective recruiting sergeant Monmouth was, therefore, vital to the rebellion because, to some who distrusted James II, he appeared the logical and immediately available alternative.

But the Duke was more than a convenient rallying-point. Many joined the rebels, or supplied them with food and shelter, because they also positively supported Monmouth's title to the throne. They took him as King for two sets of reasons, reflecting it seems two distinct views of kingship. To some supporters it was enough that he was the King's eldest son. His illegitimacy was either denied, like the Portsmouth woman who only a month before the rebellion told neighbours 'that for aught she knew the Duke of Monmouth was no more a bastard than she was'; or simply ignored, like the Staffordshire townspeople who during the Duke's tour of 1682 said that whether his parents were married or not, Monmouth was the King's son, and nothing else mattered. Contrasting with such expressions of support consequent on the Duke's hereditary right, was a more conditional or even contractual view of the monarchy. It lay behind a statement made in a Portsmouth tavern during the rebellion, that the Duke 'had a great force (with him) . . . and he was a true Protestant'. Here emphasis fell upon the religious qualification, but Monmouth won support too because of his broader attributes. An Oxford boatman in 1683 called him 'the best man in the kingdom' in the context of talk concerning the Duke's right to the throne. This speaker may have heard contractual theories of government argued by abler theorists than himself, for a Fellow of Lincoln College, Oxford, was accused of helping to incite a pro-Monmouth riot in that town during April 1683 (to which the boatman quoted above also contributed), by making a remarkable statement in an Oxford tavern. The King and House of Lords, he said, could legally be abolished, 'but that the House of Commons could not be so laid aside because the King represented himself alone, and the Lords themselves, but the Commons were the people's representatives and could not give away the rights of the people, and that the dominion was in the people'.[5] Contract theory had been the very essence of Leveller propaganda in the 1640s, and had reappeared during the Exclusion debates. With statements such as the above, made in very public places, small wonder if some upheld Monmouth's claim during both Exclusion and the rebellion, on the ground that he was 'better qualified' to rule England than the Duke of York.

That he was better qualified is not a judgement with which many historians would concur, though the short order in which James II threw away his crown should warn of the need for realism when assessing the Stuarts. In dealing with Monmouth my purpose has been not to judge him, but to explain why and how he became a rebel. Character flaws dating from childhood are the starting point. He had been abandoned in infancy by a father who took no further interest in the child until he arranged for the nine-year-old to be kidnapped from his mother. Before then the boy had been raised solely by his mother, who was young and pretty, emotional and violent. The child was almost completely uneducated, lived in poverty, and watched his mother move from one lover to the next simply to survive until she died, probably of venereal disease.

In the 1660s the boy's environment changed totally, but probably not much for the better. Poverty was banished, and he became his father's outrageously indulged favourite. He learned to gamble and hunt, drink, dance and duel, to become by the age of twenty the uncrowned leader of the court rat-pack. He had idealized his mother, learnt (he thought) how to manage his father, accepted all favours given him as due compensation for his childhood, and acquired little further education, culture, or self-control. By 1670, with a mutilation and possibly a murder to his credit, he was the dangerous epitome of a Restoration courtier; and here summaries of his character usually stop. But service in the army, and then effectively its command, added a more responsible layer to the Duke's personality, so that in the 1670s he progressed from being considered as a figurehead Lord Lieutenant in Ireland to an effective replacement for Lauderdale in Scotland. Monmouth was beginning to look for an independent political role when the Popish Plot propelled him into the centre of the stage. It was his misfortune that the Plot developed into the far more dangerous issue of Exclusion; his misfortune too, that just before the Plot he had quarrelled violently with his uncle, the heir to the throne. Until August 1679, he kept a middle course between the Whigs and the King; but Charles' command sending him into exile, followed by York's return to England *en route* for Scotland, brought out understandable anger at his treatment, and possibly some long-suppressed antagonism toward his father. From that point on he was controlled, not by Shaftesbury, but by violent emotions concerning his father, mother and uncle; and by pride, honour, and resentment. It was fitting that the decision to invade was taken in 1685, against Monmouth's first and better judgement, not because timing and circumstances were thought propitious, but because the Duke could not sit by and watch another fight in his cause.

Once committed, however, he proved a very effective rebel leader. Recruits came in and were organized, he took his army first to Taunton and then on to Bristol, the two key points if the expedition was to prosper; and he resisted the temptation to waste time by pursuing the militia in search of a cheap victory. Tactically he showed considerable resource in handling the army. He deployed them behind natural cover outside Axminster when the militia seemed likely to attack; he employed deception to confuse the defenders of Bristol; and after Norton St. Philip he left decoy fires in the fields to discourage pursuit. Above all he showed the great captain's appreciation of surprise, from the dawn raid on Bridport at the beginning of the rebellion, to the night attack at Sedgemoor which concluded it. The importance of his generalship to the rebels can be seen when he is compared with other commanders in 1685. Only John Churchill displayed equal competence, his dash as a cavalry commander and coolness at Sedgemoor marking him out as a natural leader; and one of the lesser consequences of 1685 was the boost it gave to the career of the future Duke of Marlborough.

The same cannot be said for other leaders. Argyle conducted the Scottish uprising disastrously, his procrastination and obstinacy throwing away the expedition's many advantages. In England, Feversham enjoyed a moment of glory at Sedgemoor before sinking into obscurity as James assessed his conduct as the royalist commander; and the Duke of Somerset's failure to rally his broken militia, and to deal with the vital bridge at Keynsham, have been noted. Among the King's commanders, however, none had a worse campaign than Monmouth's peer and long-time rival, Christopher Monck, Duke of Albemarle. Criticized by Churchill during the rebellion, he resigned his Lord Lieutenancy soon after it, and then found his position so intolerable that in 1687 he quitted England to become Governor of Jamaica. Arriving soon after the transported rebels whom he had helped to send into exile, the Duke's residence on the island was even more brief and inglorious than theirs. In the words of Sir Alan Burns, he 'quickly gave evidence of his incapacity', and soon his orders had to be countermanded from England. He took to drinking heavily and died within a year, 'in the circumstances [an end] fortunate for Jamaica'.[6] Comparison with Albemarle's unhappy career suggests that Monmouth had some talent, and enjoyed some success.

Explanations of why he became a rebel return at a number of points to his father, and the relationship between Duke and King throws further light on this complex monarch. A man who loved few and trusted none, Charles II showed a capacity for remarkably deep affection toward his son, not simply for the attractive and energetic teenage boy, but for the mature rebellious adult too. He wept after the Privy Council meeting which heard details of his son's involvement in the Rye House Plot, and his complete happiness as he conducted Monmouth about the court after their reconciliation at the end of 1683 was so unguarded that courtiers were startled. Such love further emphasizes the King's political intelligence and strength of will, when he disgraced the Duke in 1679 and kept him in disgrace so long as he associated with the Whigs.

Yet this perceptive ruler made numerous and grave mistakes in dealing with his son. The impulsive gestures of affection made during the 1660s inevitably acquired political significance; and though the King was no doubt contemptuous of such entrails-reading, the memory persisted among politicians, courtiers, and not least with Monmouth himself, of how the bastard had been treated as a legitimate heir. And while no blame can attach to Charles for abandoning the child during the 1650s, the indulgence he allowed in the following decade is another matter. Although the Duke did grow out of his wild behaviour in time, fatal concepts of pride and honour had been permanently acquired.

At the end of the 1670s two misjudgements by the King were the immediate occasion of his son's defection from court. After encouraging Monmouth to play a leading role in the army for several years, Charles mishandled his son's renewed application, in 1678, to become titular commander. He over-rode the Duke of York's opposition to the request, but then acceded to the latter's insistence (well before the Popish Plot and Exclusion) that Monmouth's illegitimacy be specified in the warrant, thought it had not appeared in many previous patents made out for the Duke. This set the stage for Monmouth's disastrous personal quarrel with his uncle; though the latter had probably been suspicious and perhaps envious of this rising sun for some time.

The second misjudgement was still more serious. After allowing and encouraging Monmouth to play a major political role during 1679, and using him to clear up the potentially dangerous Scottish rising of that year, the King then sent him into exile so that he could also be rid of the Duke of York's politically inconvenient presence. Even a temporary exile spelled a reduction in Monmouth's political influence, and the order came just when he had begun to enjoy the exercise of authority. The exile might still have been borne, but York was recalled within weeks from Brussels to a purely nominal exile in Scotland, and allowed a long delay in England *en route*. Monmouth's sudden return was most rash, but scarcely unprovoked.

In the years of estrangement Charles's treatment of his son was dictated partly by political requirements, but also by his deep anger at the Duke's persistent and public defiance, which undermined the most basic rule of political and familial authority. Possibly for this personal reason the terms for reconciliation were set high, for Charles was determined not merely to separate Monmouth from the Whigs (which might have been done on less severe terms) but to break his son's disobedient spirit. On these terms no reconciliation was possible until the remaining Whigs had been virtually wiped out, and in 1683 Monmouth, having no political allies left to be loyal to (or to play the leader among), came to submission. That Halifax's mediation failed was partly through the Duke of York's malicious interference, partly the result of bad luck in timing, but mostly the consequence of a distrust between father and son too deeply rooted, after nearly four years, to be conjured away by a form of words. A spell of several years in exile was needed to let the wounds heal; and Monmouth was unfortunate once again when, within a year, the wrong royal brother died.

York's accession inevitably ended Monmouth's hopes of a comfortable exile. He did not even complete a letter of submission he commenced to the new King, and began preparations to move from the Low Countries even before James applied pressure on William to remove his guest. An offer of reconciliation would have been too much to ask of James II, who kept people in the pigeon-holes where his first judgement had put them, but the new King's hard attitude did not make rebellion inevitable. It was Monmouth's final misfortune that there was one other man among the exiles with the rank to lead a rebellion; and (because of a liaison with a merchant's wife who suddenly become a rich widow) the money to pay for one. Once Argyle began collecting men and equipment, Monmouth was trapped by his past and by people's expectations of him.

The rebellion was defeated and Monmouth executed; but for James II it was in many ways a costly success, for it led him into some of his serious and early miscalculations. The first of these concerned the Assizes. None doubted that examples had to be made, but the King contrived to make his justice appear both capricious and wantonly brutal. He spared the life of Ford, Lord Grey partly for financial reasons, while the seventy-year-old widow Dame Alice Lisle was beheaded. Yet Grey was second in guilt only to Monmouth himself, whereas Lisle because of her age may not even have realized that she was sheltering fugitive rebels. The transportations, too, were not well handled. Sentencing convicted rebels to forced labour in the colonies was accepted practice by 1685, but not in such numbers and for such a period of time; and trafficking in the business by the Queen and her Maids of Honour did the court's reputation little good. The attempt by

Somerset gentlemen five years later to redeem the surviving exiles shows they had not been forgotten, and implies how they were regarded. The King's delay in issuing a general pardon until nearly a year after the rebellion was also thought by some to be needlessly hard; but James's reputation was most damaged by the pause and then renewal of the executions.

Exemplary justice seemed to have had its fill when Jeffreys ordered sixty executions at Dorchester, followed by only two or three apiece at Exeter and Taunton, and there were reasons to hope for mercy when the judges returned to London. From his letters to the King, Jeffreys was by now more concerned with the money for transportees than with further deaths. But then over two hundred more executions were ordered, carried out in small batches, so that every considerable town in Somerset played host to a grim day-long ordeal of fire and stench, with blackened human quarters decorating roads in the west for a year afterwards. And because the order for the renewed executions had followed so closely upon Jeffreys' return to London, it seemed plain that its author was the King. For a Catholic ruler whose next task was to persuade his Protestant subjects that Catholics should be granted toleration, it was an ill-judged performance. It soon appeared to be a cynical one as well when, a year after massacring these reputed Nonconformist rebels, James II attempted to strike a deal with their national leaders over toleration for all Dissenters, Catholic as well as Protestant. The Assizes revived Protestant legends of blood-thirsty Papists and unprincipled Popish rulers, at precisely the time when James II most needed the trust of his subjects.

Even more damaging was the effect of the rebellion upon James himself. There is no evidence that it led him to question the loyalty of the bulk of his subjects. But he was well placed to draw what military lessons could be learned from the rising, having served with the French army in the 1650s, and led the Royal Navy against the Dutch a decade later. All his commanders in 1685 sent him detailed reports, John Churchill writing in particularly frank terms. To James three major points emerged from the rebellion. The first was that the militia had proved useless. Capable of manning road-blocks or holding friendly territory, they were simply a liability if called on to fight opponents possessed of any degree of resolution. The cause might be inferior training and leadership, or possibly simple cowardice; but it might also lie in lukewarm loyalty to the King. Whatever the reason, James II had no time for military incompetents. The militia was a broken reed and should be discarded.

The second lesson of the rebellion was that with no support from the militia, the King's authority rested on a very small force of regulars. Less than three thousand professionals had fought at Sedgemoor, probably no more than the rebels. Though the three remaining regiments in Dutch service had been recalled from Holland, and new companies were daily being made up from disbanded ex-regulars, Monmouth could have been in London before the reinforcements were ready. James commissioned a history of the rebellion, the 'King's Account', of which the manuscript is held in the British Library.[7] For the most part a pedestrian narrative, it closes with a revealing reflection undoubtedly dictated by the King himself. Drawing upon his personal experiences James observed that the God of Hosts 'has in our days saved from total ruine and destruction, with a handfull of men, not only these three Kingdoms, but France itself in 1652, when nothing but the immediate hand of God could have preserved that Monarchy from being entirely destroyed by Rebellious subjects and foraigne enemies'. Sedgemoor was fought by just such a 'handfull of men', and if a collection of civilians could cause such trouble what might a trained foreign army do? As an experienced soldier James was disinclined to depend too much upon the hand of God. The second lesson was plain — a larger army was needed.

But greater size would be of no use without greater loyalty. From the rebels' confessions James learned how much store Monmouth had set on the benevolent neutrality of the royal army he had once led. A few regular troops had mutinied during the rebellion, and disloyalty might explain the militia's performance. Could all the officers and men of a larger army be trusted? Unless special measures were taken would not virtually all of them be Protestants, like the men of the militia? Best to play safe and raise the ratio of Catholic officers and men in the army as much as possible, for they alone could be depended upon.

None of these conclusions could be implemented without political controversy. Ending any effective role for the militia would cross England's gentry, and the Parliaments they controlled, in a very sensitive area. Even under a Protestant such as William III Parliament would always prefer a militia to a standing army. Increasing the regular army's size would first provoke dispute over the taxes to pay for it, and then raise the very dangerous issue of military rule *à la* Oliver Cromwell, and the loss of subjects' rights. Finally, commissioning more Catholics into the army would strain the King's suspending and dispensing powers to the limit and test Protestant toleration to breaking point. The role of the rebellion in causing these developments should not be overstressed, for James would in any case almost certainly have wished to strengthen his army and increase its Catholic element. But 1685 showed how urgently these changes were needed, and made reasoned opposition utterly impossible — or so it seemed to the King.

Parliament did not agree. Ultra-loyal though it was (having been elected after three years of Tory reaction), in November 1685 it voted the King little more than half the supply he had asked for to support his 'good Force of well disciplin'd Troops in Constant Pay'. Some Members blandly asserted that the militia had been 'very useful in the late rebellion', argued that a larger Navy would be safer than a stronger army, and spoke of the dangers of arbitrary rule. It was not at all what James had expected, and he scolded them soundly in his reply.[8] This difference set the tone for the subsequent deterioration in relations between King and Parliament, and the rift grew worse as the King revealed his intention to ease the condition of Catholics.

Historians have recently revised Macaulay's celebrated picture of James II as a monarch intent upon establishing absolute rule and suppressing the liberties of Parliament and subject.[9] It is argued instead that he had no very clear aims beyond obtaining a permanent toleration for Catholics, and that while he naturally wished to see Catholicism spread, he had no intention of harming English Protestantism. But when he encountered opposition, particularly from Anglicans who had so recently sung the praises of non-resistance, his language and to some extent his actions were liable to become intemperate. Parliament and the nation unfortunately drew their conclusions from his rash words and deeds, and not from his more moderate but unexpressed intentions.

Though the revision may have proceeded a little too far, there is no doubt that Macaulay's tyrant-with-a-timetable must be abandoned. In the context of this reinterpretation of James, the immediate political significance of 1685 can be seen. The military lessons to be drawn from the rebellion were to the King so plain and urgent that he began work on the army at the same time as he commenced his other programme, securing toleration for Catholics. On this interpretation, there was for James no connection at all between the two policies, each having quite distinct origins and purposes. But it was much less evident to the nation that the two were unrelated. Parliament did not share James's view of the military lessons to be learned from 1685, it had no way of knowing how far the King proposed to ease the position of Catholics, and the Assizes had carried an unpleasant air of the legendary Popish cruelty towards Protestants. Suppose the King's two programmes were linked, as purpose and method? 'Popery and tyranny' would then change from an ancient war-cry into a frighteningly close possibility.

In one more way his victory in 1685 may have ultimately harmed James. He lost his throne in 1688 essentially because he panicked and made two mistakes: he failed to lead his army out against the invader; and he decided to flee the realm, presenting his opponents with an empty throne. James's panic was most uncharacteristic, and has never been fully explained. He was personally a brave man whose instinct in a crisis was to stand and fight, not to run away. A further passage in his 'Account' of 1685 may supply the key. Praising his 'old troops' at Sedgemoor, he remarked on the great 'difference there is between such, and new raised men'.[10] Monmouth's raw levies could not stand before the King's experienced soldiers. But three years later the positions were reversed, and it was James's army, recently increased in size, which was full of 'new raised men', whereas his opponent fielded 'old troops' well blooded in wars against France. Military logic had predicted the outcome in 1685 and — a man of military training who believed in military logic — James had drawn confidence from it. But the same military logic predicted victory for the more experienced troops in 1688; and faced with the 'certainty' of defeat the King panicked and fled, first from his army, and then from his kingdom. In 1685 Monmouth, too, had faced the military certainty of defeat, once it was clear that the King's regulars would not stay neutral. But the Duke, unlike the King, still looked for an opportunity to fight his superior enemy on equal terms, and when a desperate chance was offered, he seized it. Uncle and nephew both thought as soldiers, but it was the latter who could see somewhat beyond his training.

Sedgemoor was the last pitched battle to be fought on English soil. The men who composed the army of the 'Protestant Duke' may be analysed for their occupations, age, and status; dissected for their political and religious beliefs, and history of opposition to the government; and the results used to explain their presence opposite Feversham's army, in the hours before dawn on 6 July. No explanation would be complete, however, without one factor more, which a historian may point to, but is not equipped to discuss. Individually and collectively, the amateurs who gripped their weapons and filed out onto the moor to attack the King's army behaved with quite remarkable courage. And not just at Sedgemoor: in preceding encounters opponents had remarked on their bravery, and when the royalists hanged them as traitors, they saw the rebels die still convinced of their cause. The duration of the rebellion, and its fleeting chances of success, owed something to Feversham's incapacity, and something to

Monmouth's generalship; but most to the courage and loyalty of the individual rebels. Seven centuries before Sedgemoor another military leader had tried to drill his raw levy into battle order, before leading them against a more experienced enemy, the Vikings. Like Monmouth, the Anglo-Saxon commander Beorhtnoth 'taught the warriors how they were to stand and keep rank, and bade them hold their shields straight, firmly with their hands, and not be afraid'.[11] Like Monmouth's, his army was overwhelmed. Lines from the Anglo-Saxon poem on the Battle of Maldon describing the resolution of Beorhtnoth's men as the fighting turned against them, may stand as a fitting epitaph to the courage displayed by Monmouth's followers as they fought on in the pre-dawn darkness at Sedgemoor:

> Hyge sceal thȳ heardra, heorte thȳ cēnre,
> mōd sceal thȳ māre, thȳ ūre mægen lȳtlath.

> (Courage shall be the harder, heart shall be the braver,
> Spirit shall be the greater, as our strength grows less.)

Footnotes: Chapter Ten

1. B.Little, *The Monmouth Episode*, London 1956.

2. E.P.Thompson, 'The Moral Economy of the English Crowd', *Past and Present*, 50, 1971.

3. See above p.63, fn. 39.

4. B.Sharp, *In Contempt of All Authority*, University of California Press 1980.

5. A.J.Willis, ed., *Portsmouth Record Series: Borough Sessions Papers 1653-1688*, Portsmouth 1971, pp.123, 124; *CSPD Jan.-June 1683*, pp.369-70, 319; above p.136, fn. 54.

6. A.Burns, *History of the West Indies*, London 1965, p.336.

7. Harl.MSS.6845, ff.289-96; f.296 for the quotations.

8. Brit.Lib.Lansdowne MSS.253, ff.28, 52v, 36v.

9. See particularly J.Miller, *James II*, Wayland 1978; and J.R.Jones 'Main Trends in Restoration England' and J.Miller, 'The Later Stuart Monarchy', in J.R.Jones ed., *The Restored Monarchy 1660-1688*, London 1979.

10. Harl.MSS.6845, f.296.

11. Lines from 'The Battle of Maldon' are quoted from P.S.Ardern ed., *First Readings in Old English*, Wellington New Zealand 1951, pp.71, 172.

APPENDIX 1

Parish lists of those absent from their residences during the rebellion, and presumed to have been participants. From Brit.Lib.Add.MSS.30077.

SOMERSET

Aller 1
Ashcott 3
Ashill 11
Ash Priors 3

Babcary 2
Bathealton 1
Barrington 10
Bath Forum 3
Beckington 15
Beercrocombe 1
Berkley 4
Bishops Hull 28
Blackford 1
Bradford 8
Brewham 4
Bridgewater 49
Broomfield 8
Buckland St.Mary 7
Butleigh 1

Cannington 1
Carhampton 2
Catcott 1
Chaffcombe 4
Chard 156
Charlton Mackerell 1
Cheddon Fitzpaine 9
Chewton-s-Mendip 5
Chillington 2
Chilton 6
Chiselborough 4
Clapton 4

DEVON

Axminster 79
Axmouth 32

Bampton 19
Beere and Seaton 11

Churchstanton 3
Colyton 74
Combe Raleigh 6
Coombe Pyne 5
Crediton 3

DORSET

Allington 4

Beaminster 24
Bridport 23
Broadwindsor 7
Burstock 2

Chardstock 21
Charmouth 15
Chetnole 1
Clifton Maybank 1
Corscombe 3

SOMERSET   **DEVON**   **DORSET**

Combe Florey 2
Combe St.Nicholas 23
Corfe 6
Creech St.Michael 18
Crewkerne 28
Crickett Mallett 4
Croscombe 14
Cudworth 7
Curland 1
Curry Rivell 13

Dinnington 1   Dorchester 2
Ditchett 4
Donyatt 18
Dulverton 4
Dunster 11
Durleigh 8

East Brent 6
East Butleigh 1
East Dawlish 8
East Woodlands 18
Edington 1

Fivehead 5
Frome 52

Glastonbury 28   Gittisham 8
Goathurst 3

Hardington 3   Honiton 53
Haselbury Plucknett 5
Hemington 1
High Ham 1
Hillfarrance 6
Hinton St.George 6
Huish Episcopi 5
Huntspill 7

Ilchester 8
Ilminster 54
Isle Abbotts 4
Isle Brewers 1

Kilmersdon 7
Kingsbury Episcopi 31
Kingston St.Mary 5
Kittisford 3
Knowle St.Giles 10

SOMERSET	DEVON	DORSET
Langford Budvile 8	Luppitt 32	Lyme Regis 95
Langport 7		
Leigh-on-Mendip 6		
Ling 2		
Long Sutton 7		
Lopen 6		
Lovington 1		
Lydiard St.Lawrence 1		
Marston Bigott 3	Membury 17	Marnhull 2
Martock 19	Musberry 22	Marshwood 10
Meare 1		
Mells 7		
Merriott 20		
Milborne Port 2		
Milverton 59		
Minehead 5		
North Barrow 1		Nether Compton 6
North Curry 26		
North Petherton 14		
Northover 2		
Norton St.Philip 3		
Norton Fitzwarren 3		
Oake 3	Offwell 2	Over Compton 3
Orchardleigh 1	Ottery St.Mary 9	
Othery 6		
Pilton 1		Pilsdon 5
Pitminster 42		Powerstock 2
Queen Charlton 2		
Ruishton 11		
Rodden 2		
Road and		
Woolverton 28		
Sampford Arundell 2	Sidmouth 18	Sherborne 2
Seavington St.Mary 7	Sidbury 9	Stalbridge 1
Seavington St.Michael 2		Stanton St.Gabriels 3
Shepton Mallett 5		Stockland 20
Somerton 3		Symondsbury 2
South Petherton 20		
Spaxton 1		
Staplegrove 4		
Steeple Fitzpaine 3		
Stocklinch 1		

SOMERSET	DEVON	DORSET
Stogursey 2		
Stoke Lane 3		
Stoke St.Gregory 26		
Stoke St.Mary 5		
Stoke Trister 3		
Stoke-s-Hamdon 5		
Stowell 3		
Stratton-on-Fosse 2		
Street 12		
Sutton Mallett 1		
Swell 1		
Taunton St.James 81	Thorncombe 38	
Taunton St.Mary 273	Tiverton 10	
Thorn Falcon 5		
Thurloxton 13		
Trent 4		
Trull 21		
	Upottery 32	
Wanstrow 1		Wareham 2
Wayford 11		Wooton Fitzpaine 24
Wedmore 19		
Wellington 74		
Wellow 3		
Wells Forum 13		
West Buckland 19		
West Bradley 1		
West Chinnock 5		
West Dowlish 2		
West Hatch 5		
West Monckton 9		
West Pennard 5		
West Woodlands 16		
Weston Zoyland 8		
Whatley 3		
Whitchurch 2		
Whitelackington 5		
Whitestaunton 2		
Wincanton 18		
Winsham 7		
Witham Friary 2		
Wilton 24		
Woolavington 2		
	Yarcombe 7	Yetminster 1

Index